THE NEO-LIBERAL STA

The Neo-liberal State

RAYMOND PLANT

OXFORD
UNIVERSITY PRESS

OXFORD
UNIVERSITY PRESS
Great Clarendon Street, Oxford, OX2 6DP,
United Kingdom

Oxford University Press is a department of the University of Oxford.
It furthers the University's objective of excellence in research, scholarship,
and education by publishing worldwide. Oxford is a registered trade mark of
Oxford University Press in the UK and in certain other countries

First published 2010
First published in paperback 2012

Impression: 1

British Library Cataloguing in Publication Data
Data available

Library of Congress Cataloguing in Publication Data
Data available

ISBN 978–0–19–928175–6(Hbk.)
ISBN 978–0–19–965057–6(Pbk.)

Printed in Great Britain by
MPG Books Group, Bodmin and King's Lynn

To Isabel, Charlotte, Grace, and Lara

Contents

Preface

The themes and issues addressed in this book assumed their final shape when I delivered the Boutwood Lectures at Cambridge University in 2006 on the theme of Neo-Liberalism, Social Justice, and the Rule of Law and when I delivered another series of lectures on the same topic at Sciences Po in Paris as the Vincent Wright Professor. I am very grateful to Corpus Christi College, Cambridge for the invitation for the Boutwood Foundation Lectures and I particularly want to thank The Master of the College for the invitation, Nigel Simmonds, who chaired the lectures and Trevor Allan, Raymond Geuss, and Christoph Kletzer who acted as commentators. I learned a lot from these encounters and I am very grateful to them. It was a particular privilege to present the lectures since in the past they have been delivered by some people who have been among my intellectual heroes, including Isaiah Berlin, Martha Nussbaum, and Amartya Sen. The series was inaugurated just before the Second World War by T. S. Eliot whose poetry is almost always on my mind – although I am not a follower of his political philosophy!

At Sciences Po I owe a great debt to Patrick LeGalès who acted as my host, and to M. Descoings, the Director, who made me feel very welcome. My students also helped me to see many things more clearly than I would otherwise have done through their animated involvement in the course. I also became aware for the first time about the French background to neo-liberalism and in particular the work of Louis Rougier. There is now a very impressive corpus of work in French on neo-liberalism which is rather ironic since France is often seen to be the main bulwark against neo-liberal ideas. I would, however, like to pick out Serge Audier's book *Le Colloque Lippman: Origines Du Néo-Libéralisme*, which focuses on the coming together of neo-liberal thinkers in Paris in 1938 to discuss Walter Lippman's *The Great Society.* It was at this colloquium that the term 'neo-liberalism' – which seems to have been coined by Rougier – passed into public use. I found *Néo-Libéralisme: Version Française* by Francois Denord a mine of information and I also derived great benefit from reading Gilles Campagnolo's book on Carl Menger, *Carl Menger: Entre Aristote et Hayek, Aux sources de l'économie moderne.*

Some of the chapters in the book have also been presented at the Political Studies Graduate Institute at the Catholic University of Lisbon. The Head of the Institute, Professor Joao Espada, has also been a very valuable interlocutor on many of the topics covered in this book over the past decade. I am also grateful to him for the study of my ideas published as *Social Citizenship Rights: A Critique of F. A. Hayek and Raymond Plant* with a Foreword by Lord Dahrendorf (Macmillan, St Martins Press, 1996), which has acted as a stimulus to further work on my part of which this book is a result.

The theme of this book has been on my mind on and off for most of the forty-two years that I have taught in universities, and I would like to offer my grateful thanks to those who have been most helpful to me in developing my ideas about the nature and scope of the modern state. I am indebted to W. H. Greenleaf, R. N. Berki, and Bhikhu Parekh of Hull; Hillel Steiner, Geraint Parry, and Harry Lesser of Manchester; Peter Johnson, Liam O'Sullivan, and Arvind Sivaramakrishnan of Southampton; and John Gray, Sudhir Anand, Ralf Dahrendorf, and David Miller of Oxford. I have also benefited from attending Liberty Fund Conferences which over the years have enabled me to have intensive and interesting discussions with Friedrich von Hayek, James Buchanan, and Robert Nozick (a fellow of St Catherine's College where I was then Master, with whom I was also able to engage in memorable discussions when he delivered the Locke Lectures). I also benefited from many discussions with my great friend and collaborator, the late Professor Kenneth Hoover of Western Washington University. I have also had the opportunity to discuss some of the themes of this book with and in think tanks, including over the years, the IEA, the Social Market Foundation, the Institute of Fiscal Studies, the Centre for Policy Studies, the Fabian Society, and the IPPR. I have learned a great deal from the books on Hayek by Andrew Gamble, John Gray, Norman Barry, Chandran Kukathas, and Jeremy Shearmur. I was privileged to have been able to examine the doctorates of Chandran Kukathas and Jeremy Shearmur, and I learned a great deal more from them than they did from me.

In the Lords, my political science colleagues Lord Smith of Clifton (Trevor Smith) has kept up my spirits and has been a source of very sound advice and has pointed me towards work of which I would otherwise have been unaware, and my PhD supervisor Lord Parekh has played an important role in terms of looking over the manuscript and ensuring that it did in the end come to fruition. Their friendship and guidance for over forty years has been invaluable. I have also benefited enormously from the help and support of Dr Selina Chen who has been a constant source of advice, support, and encouragement as well as being a cool appraiser of some of my wilder philosophical ideas. A small part of this book at one time formed part of a manuscript which I wrote with Gordon Brown and Ed Balls. Because of changes in political fortunes (theirs not mine!) that book will now not be published. I did, however, learn a great deal from them both over a two-year period when we held frequent discussions about the draft of the book.

Jane Parker at Southampton and Lorraine Stylianou at King's College, London, provided invaluable and sustained help with the preparation of the manuscript. I would like to thank Mr Ohri, consultant cardiac surgeon at Southampton University Hospital who crucially kept me alive as the book went to press. As always, I owe a great debt to my wife Katherine and family, mainly for keeping me sane (or what passes for it). The dedication is to our four granddaughters who, at least over the weekends, take me well away from the preoccupations of this book.

London and Paris, 2008
Raymond Plant

Introduction

In this book I have two main aims. The first is to give a faithful account of the major aspects of the neo-liberal theory of the state and its relationship to the economy and the wider society. This will be the theme of Part I of the book. The second aim is to provide the basis for a critique of these doctrines. I attempt to do this mainly, but not exclusively in Part II, of the study. In the case of neo-liberal ideas about freedom, social justice, and rights which are central to the coherence of the neo-liberal position, I have provided three chapters in Part II devoted to a detailed critique of neo-liberal ideas on these matters. In the case of less important but still controversial aspects of the neo-liberal conception of the state I have indicated some of the main lines of criticism alongside the exposition of the ideas in Part I.

The book proceeds mainly by means of an immanent critique of the neo-liberal position. That is to say that I have tried to present the strongest case for the neo-liberal theory that I can, and then have tried to point out the serious defects which emerge within that theory. Trying to make the strongest case for neo-liberalism has led me to construct what I suppose is a composite position into which I have drawn what have seemed to me to be the most cogent arguments presented by a range of writers including: Friedrich von Hayek, Ludwig von Mises, James Buchanan, Robert Nozick, and other members of the neo-liberal persuasion. I have also drawn on others – notably Michael Oakeshott and Murray Rothbard who are not neo-liberals but who, it seems to me, present arguments which can often illuminate and, indeed, add considerable substance to the neo-liberal case.

No doubt there are many different ways in which neo-liberalism can be expounded and assessed. In this book I have presented it as a political, legal, and economic doctrine and I have particularly focused on the role of the state – its nature and its powers because I believe that this is what gives neo-liberalism its coherence and cogency. I have also focused on the issue of the rule of law because there has been a debate going on for the best part of a century around the neo-liberal claim that its main rival, namely social democracy, cannot in fact be made compatible with the rule of law. I think that this debate equally illuminates important aspects of neo-liberalism and, indeed, social democracy. This theme helps to give a degree of unity to the study. I have not attempted to present fully developed alternatives to neo-liberal views on all the topics discussed, but I have tried to indicate fairly precisely where the weaknesses are and the lines on which more cogent positions could be developed.

Part I

The Basis of the Neo-liberal State

1

The Nature of the Neo-liberal State and the Rule of Law

The idea of the rule of law lies at the heart of the neo-liberal view of the nature and role of the state. More than this, however, it is the deep fault line that divides neo-liberalism and social democracy and, for that matter, more radical forms of socialism. On the neo-liberal view social democracy and socialism are outside the rule of law. On the face of it, this might seem to be rather an arcane point. Nevertheless, I hope to show in this book that the issue of the rule of law and its ramifications goes to the heart of modern debates about the nature of the state, social justice, the nature of freedom, the scope of rights, the relationship between governments and markets, and civil society and the voluntary sector. This is not all. Deep issues about human motivation and the extent to which it can be understood in 'rational economic man' or utility maximizing terms, the scope of altruistic behaviour, and the relationship between altruism and institutions are all engaged by the nature and scope of the rule of law. So, I shall argue, it is a theme central to the coherence of neo-liberalism and to social democracy and in pursuing this topic in a systematic way we shall be involved in considering the deeper questions in political, legal, and constitutional thought and the relationship of those to the economic life of modern society.

In this chapter and the next I want to do two things. The first is to characterize the nature of the rule of law in neo-liberal thought; the second is to look at the various justifications within neo-liberal thought for this conception of the rule of law. In so far as the second point is concerned, as we shall see, there are rather different and not wholly compatible approaches to be found in neo-liberal thought.

So, first of all we need to look at the character of the rule of law from a neo-liberal perspective and why it is to be seen as *a*, if not *the* central virtue of institutions – to echo John Rawls' famous claim that justice is the first virtue of institutions.[1] On the neo-liberal view an understanding of the nature of justice has to take its place within the more comprehensive and governing idea of the rule of law.

I believe that the best way to begin to elucidate the nature of the rule of law as understood by neo-liberals is to start with the work of Michael Oakeshott who is *not* a neo-liberal. Nevertheless, his thought is, in many ways, close to that of neo-liberal thinkers – his distance from it lies in the fact that he distrusts all general theories of politics and at least in some forms (in the work of Hayek for example) the articulation and defence of neo-liberalism assumes the shape of a general theory.

In the second volume of *Law, Legislation and Liberty: The Mirage of Social Justice*[2] Hayek points out that in his lectures at the London School of Economics Michael Oakeshott drew a distinction between a *telocratic* order of society or a *telocracy* (an order devoted to the pursuit of some overall end, goal, or purpose) and a *nomocracy* (a rule governed order not devoted to the attainment of particular ends). Hayek regards this distinction as being of basic importance and corresponding to similar distinctions made in his own works. However, we shall look at Oakeshott first because the distinction between telocracy and nomocracy is very well drawn in his work and it is grounded in a good deal of historical detail so it appears to be less of an abstract philosophical distinction than otherwise might be the case. As we shall see the distinction is of fundamental importance to neo-liberal thinking about the rule of law.

In his writings Oakeshott draws a sharp and influential distinction between *nomocratic* and *telocratic* politics. He also draws the distinction in a very clear manner which makes the exploration of these ideas a good basis for considering neo-liberal ideas in the same topic. Nomocratic politics focuses on the idea of political institutions as providing a framework of general rules which facilitate the pursuit of private ends, however divergent such ends may be. It is not the function of political institutions to realize some common goal, good, or purpose and to galvanize society around the achievement of such a purpose. Rather, nomocratic politics is indifferent to common ends and has an interest in private ends only in so far as they may collide: when X's pursuit of his goal *A* may prevent Y from pursuing his goal *B*. Such collision may be avoided by adherence to rules and not by government preferring one private end over another. So, given nomocratic politics, the rule of law is about the essential features of the general rules which govern the terms of political association. The rule of law in this view is not therefore *subordinate* to another value. There can be no justification for avoiding or suspending the rule of law because of the claimed importance of some other common or collective values. Neither Oakeshott nor neo-liberals are much given to using terms like 'the common good', but if there is meaning to such a term then for Oakeshott and the neo-liberals it means the framework of rules facilitating the achievement of private ends; it does not lie in some substantive, collectively endorsed moral goal or purpose in society.

One can see why, on this nomocratic approach to policies which is endorsed by neo-liberals, the rule of law has such a central place as the overriding virtue of institutions. Other values such as freedom, justice, and rights have to be compatible with the rule of law, understood (for the moment) as a framework of general rules for the achievement of private ends. All of this will be subject to full exploration in later chapters but, for the moment, we might cite as illustrations of the general thesis outlined earlier the claim that freedom has to be understood as the absence of coercion and coercion has to be understood in relation to the rule of law; social justice is incompatible with the rule of law because its demands cannot be embodied in general and impartial rules; and rights have to be the rights to non-interference rather than understood in terms of claims to resources because rules against interference can be understood in general terms whereas rights to resources cannot. There is no such thing as a substantive common good for the state to pursue and for the law to embody and thus the political pursuit of something like social justice or a greater sense of solidarity and community lies outside the rule of law.

In a nomocratic state, then, the rule of law is central but, according to Oakeshott, this is not so in the telocratic state:

> [W]hile in a telocracy, rule of law is not forbidden, it is never something valued on its own account: the only thing valued on its own account is the pursuit and achievement of the chosen end which is a substantive condition of things.[3]

and

> [T]elocracy does not necessarily mean the absence of law. It means only that what may roughly be called 'the rule of law' is recognised to have no independent virtue, but to be valuable only in relation to the pursuit of the chosen end.[4]

A telocracy implies the organization of the state and its institutions in pursuit of a single overriding goal or a comprehensive goal within which other values will be given a subordinate place. A telocratic state may be and frequently has been a religious telocracy in which obedience to what is discerned to be the will of God is the dominant end – Oakeshott gives the example of Calvin's Geneva. It may, however, be a secular telocracy and for Oakeshott German National Socialism, Italian Fascism, and Soviet Communism would all be telocracies. However, there can be other much more seemingly benign forms of telocratic government, one of the main examples of which for Oakeshott and the neo-liberals would be post Second World War welfare and social democratic states. These states also embody an overriding goal and, as we shall see, for the neo-liberal are equally incompatible with the idea of the rule of law both in the sense that the rule of law will be seen as subordinate to the overriding end and thus not as a principle with independent value or, more subtlety but, for the neo-liberal, more insidiously, social democratic legislation cannot be reconciled to the demands of the rule of law even if social democrats profess respect for the principle.[5]

Oakeshott's argument about the rule of law in his *Lectures in the History of Political Thought* parallels the distinction he draws in *On Human Conduct* between enterprise and civil associations. A telocratic state is an enterprise association galvanizing and mobilizing resources in the pursuit of a dominant end; a nomocratic state is a civil association.

The telocratic state or enterprise state has laws which specify what is to be achieved by the state for its citizens; the state as a civil association (a nomocracy) has laws which do not define the 'what' of politics – the specific goals to be collectively attained – but rather the 'how' of politics – defining the terms and conditions of civil association and the rights and duties which will enable individuals to pursue their multifarious goals.[6]

The telocracy–nomocracy distinction implies for Oakeshott as it does for the neo-liberals a sharp distinction between *government* and *policy.* In a nomocracy, the government (*a*) is recognized as having sovereign authority to make and promulgate the law but the law is not to be seen as a means of attaining common or collective goods or outcomes; (*b*) is 'the guardian of a system of prescriptive conditions to be subscribed to in making choices'[7]; and (*c*) is concerned with the maintenance and improvement, where necessary, of the set of rules constituting civil relationships between individuals who entertain different views about their wants, goals, needs, and purposes. The law in a nomocracy is, in Oakeshott's view, both neutral and impartial in respect of those circumstances. Politics in a nomocracy is concerned with the business of 'considering authoritative prescriptions from the standpoint of their worth and of reconsidering subtractions, additions, or amendments' to such prescriptions. Politics is concerned with improving the framework within which we engage in 'self chosen actions'. In a nomocracy, government is more like a governor in a complex engine. It is not part of what directly makes the 'engine go', but rather regulates the speed at which the various parts move.[8] The ensemble of rules and prescriptions, independent of ends, goals, and purposes, authoritatively determined by government following political consideration of amendments and improvement to this framework of prescription constitutes the rule of law in society.

In a telocracy, in Oakeshott's view, issues of policy displace the concern with the rule of law. After all, a telocracy is based upon the idea of the achievement of a common or collective end or purpose and the rule of government and politics is to galvanize the members of society and their resources in the pursuit of this common goal – 'energising and directing a substantive purpose'.[9] The character and scope of law is made subordinate to the achievement of the common purpose as has been said and, as such, policy may be said to be more important than law and indeed, as we shall see when we look at Hayek's criticisms, such policies cannot be made subject to the rule of law. On this view of things, as Oakeshott says: '[N]othing but the chosen end is valuable in itself'. It is in the different view of the nature and scope of state, law, policies, and the rule of law that the major fault line between neo-liberalism on the one hand and social democracy on the other lies. The state, idealized as a nomocracy, is a *Rechtsstaat*, a law-based state. One based on telocratic principles – a set of goals or purposes may be seen as a welfare state in the very broad sense that secures goods to satisfy individuals' wants, whatever they may be. So a welfare state of the social democratic sort or fascist or national socialist state may all in their different ways be types of *Wohlfahrtsstaat*. The difference between nomocracy and telocracy in Oakeshott's view also leads to a fundamental difference in relation to the law in these different sorts of states: the fundamental differences between *adjudication* and *arbitration*.

Whether in a nomocracy or a telocracy laws and rules will always be general and they will need to be interpreted and specified in particular contingent circumstances. Nevertheless, Oakeshott wants to argue that this process of relating the generality of law to specific circumstances differs in quite a fundamental way between nomocracy and telocracy.[10] In a nomocracy the laws are rules and prescriptions providing a framework for self-chosen actions and because these rules may be broken or because their import may, in particular circumstances, be unclear then adjudication

> is to be recognised as a procedure in which the meaning of *lex* is significantly, justifiably, appropriately and durably amplified: significantly, because such a conclusion is not given in the *lex*; justifiably, because the authority of the amplification must be its relation to *lex*; appropriately, because the conclusion must resolve a specific contingent uncertainty or dispute about the meaning of *lex*; and durably because it must be capable of entering the system of *lex* and becoming available not only to 'judges' to be used in resolving future uncertainties or disputes, but also to *cives* to be used in choosing what they shall do.[11]

So adjudication in this nomocratic sense is central to the rule of law and its maintenance. All law is general – indeed that is one of its central virtues for the neo-liberal – but in relating the general to the particular through adjudication in all the aspects just distinguished, adjudication is central to the rule of law, its maintenance, and its durability. It has to be distinguished clearly from the exercise of discretion which is the other main alternative in linking the general and the particular.

This is the major contrast with a telocracy or the state being seen as an enterprise. As we have already seen from a nomocratic point of view this is a fundamental defect of the state as an enterprise because it subordinates the rule of law to the enterprise. In an enterprise state, however, alternatives to adjudication reinforce the distance between an enterprise state and the rule of law. This actually follows from the earlier claim that in an enterprise state questions of policy will dominate – the policy for achieving the aims of the enterprise. Because the enterprise cannot be captured in terms of law and rules but its pursuit involves responding to changing circumstances, there is a need for a decision about the direction of policy to be made. In an enterprise state this is going to be a *managerial* decision and is also going to involve a very high degree of discretion. Because the enterprise will be much more vulnerable to contingency compared with a set of rules governing the framework of individual choice, managerial decisions will be less durable than adjudicative ones within the rule of law.[12]

Unlike a *Rechtsstaat*, governed by the rule of law, a *Wohlfahrtsstaat* cannot build a durable body of decisions or conclusion because the governmental and rule governed management of the enterprise will be subject to constant change just because government is attempting to manage constantly changing circumstances, for example, in health or education.

Similar considerations apply in respect of reasoning and discretion. In a nomocracy adjudication is not to be seen as a discretionary or subjective exercise of will on the part of the judge. There is a *text* first of all – the law whose relation to the particular case is under judgement and there is a process of reasoning (although not deductive reasoning) which yields the conclusion. This reasoning is open and transparent. It is public and when emanating from a lower court can be subject to challenge and revision. This is not so with the decision-making of the manager of the enterprise state or an arbiter of a dispute about what is produced by the enterprise – the goods of the enterprise. There is no text or body of law for the process of decision-making to be based upon – only previous managerial decisions. In the absence of a text and precedents reasons will run out and the decision will embody a discretionary and subjective act of will. Nor is there a requirement or even an expectation that a similar decision would be taken in other similar circumstances. Managerial decisions of this sort do not create anything comparable to a corpus of law and a jurisprudence.

The same is true of *arbitration*. In a situation in which an arbitrator is needed there will be different interests at stake linked to the subjective goods secured, allocated, and distributed by the enterprise state. So disputes might be about, for example, whether X has got his fair share of health care, education, or whatever. Arbitrators making determinations in such cases are bound to act in subjective and discretionary ways partly because there will be no corpus of law to which appeal can be made in such cases for reasons already given and because the interests to be arbitrated will always be changing and shifting in a much more radical way than an interest in maintaining the nomocratic framework within which individuals make their own choices.

This is a point made by Oakeshott in his *Lectures in the History of Political Thought*. Arbitration is essentially a compromise between groups with different interests with varying weights and, as such, these will vary a good deal from case to case. He argues that this is quite different to adjudication in the law.

- The law as the current system of rights and duties provides the answer to disputes not the weight of the interests or the power of the parties.
- The law becomes a third party in a two-party dispute and provides independent grounds for resolution rather than a compromise between the interests of the two parties.
- Such a solution does not relate to one particular occasion but applies in a more general manner and becomes a more established determination than an arbitrated solution.
- The law applies across the whole of the society whereas arbitration is confined to two parties.
- The law is known in advance and parties guide, moderate, and constrain their actions according to the law.[13]

The managerialism and the central place for discretion in a telological state again put such a state outside the rule of law on this sort of analysis. Politics is essentially a matter of arbitration and bargaining and discretion is at its heart. These baneful features are central, so neo-liberals argue, to the socialist and social democratic state.

These distinctions are also to be found in Hayek's *Law, Legislation and Liberty, Vol. 1: Rules and Order*. He is absolutely clear that the role of a state in a nomocratic order is quite different from the role of the head or the manager of an organization with dominant goals and purposes. In this he follows Fuller who criticises the idea of law as a system of power and command rather than as a set of rules of conduct. Hayek emphasizes, as Oakeshott does, the importance of the judge in 'maintaining an ongoing order of action'.[14] In other respects however, his arguments are rather different from those of Oakeshott. He argues that people have legitimate expectations in respect of the law: that is 'expectations on which generally his actions in that society have been based'. The role of the law is to facilitate the framework to secure the satisfaction of legitimate expectations. Thus the role of the judge can become that of adjusting the law and expectations so that they match as far as possible. 'Legitimate expectations', however, seem quite close to what Oakeshott calls interests and which for the latter fall within the scope of arbitration rather than adjudication, legality, and judgement. At the same time, however, while they may differ somewhat about the boundaries between judgement and arbitration, they both agree that the judge's judgement is not arbitrary and discretionary but must be embedded within the existing corpus of law and jurisprudence whether this is statute law or common law. It is a matter of the judge discerning the law embedded in practices and expectations rather than inventing or creating law. The guiding thread of this discernment must be for Hayek that the law should work in such a way as to match and render mutually compatible peoples' divergent legitimate expectations. As we shall see throughout the book this leads him to the view that these divergent expectations can best be rendered mutually compatible by a legal framework which essentially protects negative freedom – freedom *from* rather than positive freedom *to*; negative rights – rights to non-interference rather than positive social and economic rights; and procedural rather than social justice. These become central to the fundamental jurisprudence of the nomocratic order.[15] This thought is quite fundamental to Hayek and has wide ramifications for his social, political, and legal theory.

But surely, it might be argued, a nomocratic state and its laws have to acknowledge some set of goals. It cannot be impartial or indifferent to all goals. Law cannot be pointless. It cannot be totally non-instrumental. It has to facilitate the achievement of some goals. If this is recognized, it might be argued, it will modify the sharpness of the distinction between a nomocratic and telocratic state, between a civil association and an enterprise association.

Oakeshott clearly recognizes in his *Lectures in the History of Political Thought* that there is a goal or set of goals central to a nomocratic account of the state. He refers to Aristotle in this context and argues following him that members of such a state will have in common a number of what Aristotle called 'admitted goods' and equally a number of admitted or agreed evils. He goes on to say (and this is all he does say):

> Among the most cherished of these 'admitted goods' is the freedom to make choices for themselves; and among their strongest antipathies is interference with this freedom.[16]

There are two points to be made here. The first has to do with a central issue in Oakeshott's argument about the non-instrumental nature of the rule of law but on which he has rather little to say. He accepts that it is central to his case for a distinctive mode of organization called a civil association or nomocracy that it does indeed embody the pursuit of certain aspects of social life and he mentions freedom, peace, and security in this context. So, on the face of it the critic might say that a nomocracy is not to be distinguished from a telocracy in the light of its purposelessness since there are nomocratic purposes namely freedom, security, and peace. However, in his essay on 'The Rule of Law' Oakeshott argues that these are not substantial or particular ends of the sort pursued in telocracy. Rather, freedom, peace, and security are not consequences of civil association, nomocracy, or goals to be realized. They are, he argues, inherent in its character.[17] The rules of laws of a nomocratic state do not prescribe ends to be pursued, rather freedom, peace, and security 'characterize this mode of association but not as consequences'. Thus, in his view, the adverbial character of the rule of law is preserved while at the same time endorsing certain human goals as inherent in the adverbial process. These goods – freedom, peace, and security – are part of the framework necessary within which individuals can then pursue their own chosen goods and goals. This is also very much Hayek's point in *Law, Legislation and Liberty, Vol. 1: Rules and Order*. The goal of nomocracy is not a particular kind of good like social justice, welfare, or greater social solidarity as might be the case in socialism or social democracy, or more sinister goods such as racial purity and national ethnic identity of the *Volksgemeinschaft*, but rather in Hayek's view consists of abstract goods – for example the good of negative freedom which is a condition for anyone to use his or her limited knowledge in highly specific circumstances to meet one's needs. It is not itself a substantive goal. It is a condition, as it is for Oakeshott of being able to pursue substantive and divergent goals in society. This is a point to which I shall return in the later critique.

The second point, Oakeshott's reference to Aristotle might be misleading here in that his view of goals in relation to ethics and politics did turn not just upon agreement, but was also rooted in an account of the human nature and the human *ergon* – its characteristic function. If freedom of choice and the conditions and rules for exercising it are understood in this context, then it might be thought that underlying the idea of a nomocratic state is a universalistic and almost certainly metaphysical theory of human nature. Whether acknowledged or not, there is no doubt that some defenders of a nomocratic and neo-liberal or libertarian state, as we shall see, do indeed develop ideas about such a state on the basis of a metaphysical theory.

In Oakeshott's case, however, his citation of Aristotle in this context is rather misleading because it is not his intention to provide a metaphysical case for a nomocratic order rooted in and deduced from some kind of philosophical anthropology with human freedom at its heart. Rather, as he makes clear in *On Human Conduct*, ideas about individual liberty and the broader individualism within which liberty is set have their basis in a complex set of historical circumstances which have developed in Europe since the thirteenth century and became more prevalent in the sixteenth century. Individualism and liberty are not just subjectively endorsed 'bright ideas', nor are they metaphysically grounded. Rather, they are complex ideas with equally complex historical roots and very different forms of expression: religious, philosophical, ethical, political, and aesthetic. Equally, ideas about the nomocratic political order to accommodate such a set of values are also a historical development rather than a philosophically grounded theory for Oakeshott. Part of *On Human Conduct* shows the concurrent development of ideas about individualism and political order in Western European history and in the political thought of Europe since the sixteenth century and the emergence of two types of political organization: nomocracy and telocracy.

The same points hold true for telocratic ideas too. The goals which telocratic governments seek to secure for people whether the welfare goals of health, education, and social security and goals of a darker hue such as racial, ethnic, national, cultural, or religious purity equally have their roots deep in European history. They are not arbitrary sorts of goals, nor does their appeal rest on metaphysical considerations.

What Oakeshott points out is that those historical circumstances make these different ideas of government and the goals which they can achieve *intelligible*. He argues that neither nomocracy nor telocracy are arbitrary and unaccountable 'dispositions of thought in modern Europe'. Each has a 'context of circumstances' which makes it intelligible.[18] It is important to have a very general grasp of those intelligibility factors for both 'dispositions of thought' about the modern state. Oakeshott has a clear preference for the nomocratic approach, but it is important to recognize that this preference (for him) arises out of an understanding of Western European history and is not predicated upon some general or metaphysical theory of the good and human nature. Others, who also from a more distinctively neo-liberal perspective, prefer the nomocratic order take a rather different view of the justification of the nomocratic state, or the *Rechtsstaat* – the state that embodies the rule of law. Typically they appeal to a rather idealized version of evolution as in Hayek, natural law as in Rothbard, or contractual theory as in Buchanan, or a rights-based theory such as that propounded by Nozick.

So let us consider briefly the conditions which in Oakeshott's view make the *Rechtsstaat* and the enterprise state opposing, but nevertheless wholly intelligible states or dispositions of thought about politics and law in the light of European history.

In Oakeshott's view, the following characteristic aspects of Western European history make a telocratic approach to government appear plausible:

- The fact that every emergent European state was 'born in diversity' – there was therefore a need to create a sense of solidarity as the basis of the state and the pursuit of the goods that would make for such solidarity is a telocratic/goal-directed enterprise.
- The civil rules of modern states inherited a lot of the power of medieval kings and much of the authority of the Church. This combination of power and moral activity often led in a telocratic direction.
- There is a relationship between telocracy and power. There is no point in positing an end to be pursued without the power to do it. A telocracy requires the mobilization of the capacity of government to meet its posited aims. In Oakeshott's view the modern European state has now amassed the power to pursue such goals and thus 'telocratic government seems more rational

now than it did in early modern times . . . because power has made it more possible'.[19]

- War has also given a major impulse to telocratic states. The resources of society are managed by the government to meet its overriding aim of victory in war. Total war in the twentieth century has no doubt enhanced this impetus. Indeed it is arguable that the case for planning post Second World War in Britain was greatly strengthened by the fact that the state had been able to mobilize resources in a national way to meet an overriding goal. What could be done in war time could also be done in peace time.
- The process of colonization also increased the emphasis on telocratic forms of governance. Colonies were to be managed rather than just ruled and managed in the interests of an overall end – namely the interests of the 'mother' country. Oakeshott also believed that the techniques of telocratic governance were also much developed by the process of colonization.
- The belief in telocracy is likely to be predominant in a society in which there appears to be some overriding problem to be solved. The obvious case is war but there are other examples too where it has been thought that there is an overriding problem which could undermine the stability of society. The obvious problem in peace time is poverty and unemployment. To overcome the problem has required a massive mobilization of resources and a very high level of bureaucratic organization by government.
- As he makes clear in the closing pages of *On Human Conduct* there has been an abiding human desire for a sense of community, of solidarity, with others. This desire is of great significance in accounting for the salience of telocracy. While freedom for Oakeshott has been one of the major motivating forces behind nomocratic politics, nevertheless for many freedom has been seen as a burden to be escaped not a condition to be embraced. This escape can be provided by telocratic forms of politics.

These conditions, which are set out rather skeletally in Oakeshott's *Lectures in the History of Political Thought* are explored in more detail and with more emphasis on political and legal thought about these things in *On Human Conduct*. As Oakeshott wryly observes in his essay on the rule of law in *On History* the Germans always had a word for it – *it* being the state as a kind of enterprise association.[20] Indeed they did, and the bewildering range of terms used over the centuries in Germany just shows the diversity of the understanding of the state as an enterprise and of the theoretical embodiment of such understanding: *Verbändestaat* (interest group state), *Gewerkschaftsstaat* (trade union state), *Beamtenstaat* (administrative state), *Bildungstaat* (the state with an educative and spiritual ideal), *Führerstaat* (state based on the will of its leader), *Machtstaat* (power state), *Fürstenstaat* (model state), *Hausstaat* (dynastic state), *Kulturstaat* (state as the embodiment of the cultural life of the nation), *Obrigkeitsstaat* (the authoritarian state standing above politics), S*ozialstaat* (social state), *Volkstaat* (the state of the racial people), and *Wohlfahrtsstaat* (welfare state). These terms denote complex and to a very large extent mutually exclusive conceptions of the state. Each of these conceptions has its own complex theoretical elaboration, but what they all have in common is the idea of the state as a telocracy, as an enterprise and with its fundamental aim the management of society in pursuit of overall goals and aims.[21]

Equally for Oakeshott there are complex historical circumstances which render the alternative political disposition – the pursuit of nomocracy – intelligible. These factors include the following:

- While as we have seen, one of the pressures for a nomocratic view of the sate was the diversity of the communities and groups of which it was composed. A telocracy provided a galvanizing goal to integrate such diversity. Equally, however, as Oakeshott points out the impact of diversity on the development of a state could underpin a nomocratic approach – that integration could come via law and via civil associations as much as by the pursuit of common ends.
- As a matter of fact modern states began and developed in the context of a legal order – a set of rights and duties defining relationships and obligations between subjects and their government.
- The early law making of modern states was a process of emancipating subjects from feudal and corporate subjections. Feudal lordship and the corporate nature of feudal life particularly in work and religion, had a very strongly telocratic approach, then emancipation from these features encourages the nomocratic disposition of both thought and practice.
- The emergence of a money economy also played its part in establishing nomocratic ideas in the sense that as money grew in importance the state was seen to be the custodian of the stability of the currency and not the director of how national income should be disposed. This is a parallel to the nomocratic role of the state outside the economic sphere – maintaining the stability of general laws, leaving individuals to pursue their own ends within those laws.
- The growth of nomocratic beliefs was also the result of a reaction against telocracy on the part of those subjects of modern states with a growing sense of individuality and personal freedom. For subjects such as these 'in so far as they were able to impress themselves upon governments, ruling was turned in a *nomocratic* direction'.
- Experience of contending telocratic beliefs within and between states – for example different religious denominations – what Oakeshott calls the 'civil war of telocracies', led to a positive view of nomocracy 'whose office was to maintain peace and the more elementary "admitted goods" by means of a substantially neutral legal order'.[22]
- In Oakeshott's view religion too, often seen as one of the most powerful telocratic motives, played a significant part in the growth of nomocracy. The reason for this is that while God might be thought to have some overall purpose for mankind he has also endorsed men with free will and thus man [*sic*] had the opportunity to conform to or diverge from this purpose. If God rules man nomocratically what is the justification for the state to rule telocratically?

Oakeshott regards nomocracy as having a number of defenders among political philosophers including, despite their many differences: Hobbes, Locke, Halifax, Hume, Burke, Kant, Adam Smith, Tom Paine, the authors of the Federalist papers, Benjamin Franklin, J. S. Mill, Proudhon, von Humboldt, Tocqueville, Acton, T. H. Green, Hegel, and Bodin. They provided a theoretical understanding of a disposition of thought and action which is much less varied than telocratic conceptions. The latter are now multifarious because the valued goals of the enterprise state have in history been more varied. A nomocratic form of government is more limited in scope and does not have overall purposes. There will be differences between theorists about the justification of this form of government and less about its essential character. So reverting back to the German examples, we might cite the *Rechtsstaat* (the state governed by law) as a fundamental form of nomocracy along with *Justizstaat* (the state as the defender of the rights of individuals) and the *Nachtwächterstaat* (the nightwatchman state).

Within the nomocratic context there could be important differences about the size and scope of a nomocratic state because it is important to recognize that for Oakeshott, at least, the contrast between nomocratic and telocratic government is about the character of each mode of government not its *size*. It is also about the contrasting scope of government and law: law as subordinate to governmental purpose in a telocratic state; law as non-instrumental and adverbial in a nomocratic state. It may, of course, be very likely that a nomocratic state will, in fact, be smaller than a telocratic state but it is not part of its essential nature that it should be.

So, there is a close relationship between a nomocratic state and the rule of law – indeed, the rule of law is constitutive of the nomocratic state but so far, apart from the insistence that law should be general and should not serve particular purposes. I have not focused upon the detailed characterization of the formal features of the rule of law. Oakeshott himself does this in his essay 'The Rule of Law' and in doing so, without citing him, specifically seems to follow the ideas of Lon Fuller in *The Morality of Law*.[23] Oakeshott argues that these formal characteristics of the rule of law would include the following features:

- Rules have to be public and non-secret.
- Rules should not be retrospective.
- No strict obligations save those imposed by law.
- All associates equally and without exception should be subject to the obligations imposed by law.
- No outlawry.
- *Audire alteram partem* (listen to both sides in a legal dispute).

For Fuller, these criteria, which Oakeshott cites, and his other criteria such as the need for the law to be clear, to be mutually non-contradictory, not to require the impossible, to be constant through time, and that official action be congruent with the law constitute the 'inner morality of law'. Oakeshott seems to be ambivalent on this point. On the one hand he seems to agree with critics of Fuller who have argued that his criteria are not in fact moral criteria at all but rather the conditions that law must satisfy if it is to be law at all. They are *efficiency* rather than *moral* criteria. Oakeshott agrees with the critique when he says that these 'considerations' as he calls them are 'inherent in the notion, not of just law, but law itself'.[24] However, immediately afterwards he seems to reinstate them if only minimally as moral criteria when he says that it is 'only in respect of these considerations and their like that it may perhaps be said that: *lex injusta non est lex*' (unjust law is not law).

There are two big issues raised by these ideas. The first is that if Fuller's characteristics are thought to be efficiency criteria, which any system of law must embody to some degree if it is to be effective as law, then they could be regarded as being capable of being embodied in any set of laws however immoral the purposes to which those laws were devoted or indeed whatever the content of the law – moral or immoral. If the law is just seen as a tool which can be used for good or bad purposes, then Fuller's criteria are about the efficiency of the tool rather than about the morality of the law even though he regards them as constituting the inner morality of law. On the efficiency view of Fuller the criteria which he adumbrates are not part of laws's moral ideal, they are rather part of the efficiency conditions for any legal system. This leads us quite close to the idea that any legal system and any state in fact is a *Rechtsstaat* just because to be effective that legal system will embody Fuller's criteria to a greater or lesser extent.

The second point is that there is quite a large question which we shall take up later in the chapter as to the extent to which Fuller's criteria for the rule of law are compatible with received views about the common law. Hayek, for example, wants to preserve a central role for the common law in a *Rechtsstaat*, but there must be a question as to how far common law can in fact embody to the extent that statute law can some of these criteria.

Both Oakeshott and, as we shall see, Hayek are critics of legal positivism. Positivism defines law by its sources and rejects the idea that moral considerations have to be invoked to identify law – such that, for example, unjust law is not law. The positivist insists that whatever is correctly authorized by the legal sovereign is law; the question of whether it is good or just law is a separate question. For a positivist what counts in respect of the rule of law is that it is duly authorized and a positivist might be able to accept Fuller's criteria for the rule of law as efficiency conditions without which it might be impossible for law to operate. Nevertheless, for law to be law it does not have to meet a moral standard. Oakeshott, however, wants to argue that there are genuine questions to be asked about the justice of law, or as he puts the point frequently the *jus* of *lex*. On the face of it this is a difficult question for Oakeshott to address because law in a nomocracy is not to be understood as serving particular goals; it is non-instrumental – even freedom, security, and peace, recall, were not to be regarded as part of laws's *telos* as opposed to conditions of a legal nomocratic order. So, given this, what can make for the justice of law or of individual laws? This latter distinction is perhaps the point. The rule of law overall is to be non-instrumental and constitutive of a nomocracy but individual laws can be regarded against that background as just or unjust.[25] So what would be the basis for that judgement for

Oakeshott? Individual laws in a nomocracy would be unjust if they sought substantial and particular benefits to individuals. Individual laws would be unjust if they were concerned with any of the following:

- the merits of different interests
- satisfying substantive wants
- the promotion of prosperity
- the elimination of want
- the equal or differential distribution of reputed benefits or opportunities
- with arbitrating competing claims to advantages or satisfactions
- the promotion of a condition of things recognized as the common good.

The law can prescribe the rules under which these goods are sought but must not be concerned with securing them to individuals or groups through legal rules or rights. So, while welfare conferring laws may satisfy the positivist's account of legitimacy as law duly authorized, they are not *just* laws in a nomocratic understanding of the nature and purpose of law.

Beyond this Oakeshott argues the justice of law is not to be determined by its accordance or discordance with some conception of natural law or universal values however naturalistic. Rather what will be determined as just or unjust particular laws is an 'appropriately argumentative discourse to deliberate the matter'.[26] There is scope for such deliberation – indeed for Oakeshott this is what politics is about – but within a general recognition in a nomocracy that the overall rule of law is non-instrumental, prescribing adverbial conditions.[27] It is not to be determined by considering abstract or universal values. All of this adds further to the case that a social democratic state must lie outside the rule of law because its laws in securing goods and services to individuals as part of a concern with social justice must fall outside the terms of a nomocratic understanding of the rule of law.

However, Oakeshott acknowledges in *On Human Conduct* particularly that both telocracies and nomocracies have been central to the development of Western European political history. The modern European state and the rule of law for Oakeshott are equivocal and ambiguous. Modern European states through many centuries have embodied each of these properties. At various times one has come to dominate the other but they are paired together as Oakeshott says as 'sweet enemies'[28] and they certainly engage different but fundamental aspects of the human psyche, a sense of freedom and individualism on the one side, a desire for belonging and community on the other – these are the twin and opposing roots of nomocracy and telocracy. While Oakeshott himself, clearly preferring nomocracy, leaves the struggle and the resolution of the struggle to history, this is not the case with neo-liberal thinkers such as Hayek, Buchanan, and Rothbard – who seek to provide a strong theoretical or philosophical defence of the neo-liberal version of the nomocratic state and the rule of law.

This still leaves to be explored the relationship between the liberal conception of *Rechtsstaat* and the rule of law on the one hand and legal positivism on the other. Hayek is also a strong critic of legal positivism and his arguments against that position are both more diverse and more elaborate than those of Oakeshott. It is very important at the outset to see how important this issue is for Hayek's position. His social, political, and legal philosophy is a defence of a conception of the *Rechtsstaat* – of a state as embodying and constrained by the rule of law. If, however, the rule of law is identical with a set of non-moral criteria which any mature legal system embodies irrespective of the goals of that system, then the idea of a distinctive form of state – the *Rechtsstaat* – disappears. Hayek is quite clear about this as is shown by his remarks about Kelsen. He says that on Kelsen's view argued, for example, in *Hauptprobleme der Staatsrechtslehre* and in *Der Sociologische und die Juristische Staatsbegriff*, every state with a legal system (and how could it be a state without one) is a *Rechtsstaat* and that the rule of law prevails, of necessity, in every state just because the rule of law has no moral content. It refers only to a procedural process by which law is derived in logical ways from a basic norm (*Grundnorm*). Alternatively, in the view of critics of Fuller, it is law posited by a legitimate source together with the idea that such law embodies – as a set of efficiency criteria only – Fuller's general principles of the rule of law.

So what is the basis of Hayek's critique of the positivist position?

There are several aspects to it. The first, linking back to Oakeshott, is the idea that positivism presupposes that society in which law is embedded is to be seen on the model of an organization or an enterprise rather than as a spontaneous order arising from the unplanned and unpredictable ways over time that innumerable people make use of the limited knowledge and the limited resources that they possess. On Hayek's view the legal positivist tries to obliterate the distinction between rules of just conduct (nomocracy) and the rules of organization (telocracy) and the reason for this is that positivists construe the law as the command of a sovereign which, as it were, determines the nature of the organization over which the sovereign presides.[29] On Hayek's view the positivist posits a central role for power in the legal system as the source of both law and of sanction. This is a point that many positivists would embrace.[30] Positivists sometimes argue that the law and the state constitute a system of power. Hayek argues that this position embodies the constructivist fallacy. Law emerges in many ways, some certainly by legislative action by a sovereign body but very often, and in Hayek's view, the greater part of the time the law emerges through an unintended process as the results of millions of acts of reciprocal activity each of which may have been intended but from which emerges a set of rules which we know as common law. This is not at all the same as saying that law emanates from a locus of power. Hayek allows that the positivist might reply that what makes the common law authoritative is because it is endorsed by whoever or whatever is the sovereign. In Hayek's view this is still a very long way from saying that the content of the common law is in detail sanctioned by sovereign power. It might well be that the sovereign has just said that the common law should be enforced and obeyed without at all determining the content of that law.[31] In Hayek's view the positivist is motivated by the idea that all law must have the same character and that is defined by positivism. Hayek rejects this in favour of a more pluralistic view in which private law and common law which have been closely linked with the emergence of spontaneous orders have their own character and legitimacy.

The positivist mistakenly collapses all order into organization or nomocracy into telocracy. And this collapsing of the distinction is exacerbated because of the positivists' emphasis on public law. In Hayek's view, public lawyers always tend to think of any kind of order as an organizational order – one with a conscious purpose, which is the role of the law to facilitate. On Hayek's view, the contrary is true. Once we understand the importance of spontaneous order then we can see that the idea of the law as the command of the sovereign is defective. It cannot account for the interlinking of private and the common law. An organization and an enterprise need a guiding purpose and a guiding intelligence; spontaneous order does not. As he says:

> What distinguishes the rules which will govern actions within an organisation is that they must be rules for the performance of assigned tasks. They presuppose that there is a place for each individual in a fixed structure determined by command and that the rules each individual must obey depends on the place that he has been assigned and on the particular ends which have been indicated for him by the commanding authority. The rules will thus regulate merely the detail of the action of appointed functionaries or agencies of government.[32]

In Hayek's view many legal positivists look forward to the day when private law, which is largely about the rules to facilitate the spontaneous order of a free market, will in fact become only a kind of limited zone within a more embracing conception of public law – if indeed private law survives at all. He quotes Radbruch on this point[33] when he argues that private law is a 'temporarily reserved and constantly diminishing sphere of free initiative within the all encompassing public law'.[34]

Because socialism and social democracy increase the reach of government into the spontaneous order of society with policies for social justice, social and economic rights, social or positive freedom, and solidarity – they inevitably transform society into an organization and this development displaces private law and the common law by various forms of public law which makes the claims made about the nature of law by legal positivists seem more plausible. Thus, for Hayek the positivist position assumes that society is like an organization with a power centre and from which law emanates in statutes. For Hayek this is a fundamental mistake about the nature of society about which more will be said later.

So in Hayek's view, socialism and social democracy have played a baleful role in transforming order into organization, displacing private law by public law, and replacing common law (which is a species of spontaneous order) by statute law, a process which fits the model of law deployed by legal positivists.

One of the drivers of legal positivism in Hayek's view rests upon a correct insight which positivists have then distorted. If (as positivists deny) the law is law only, and if it is a just law, and if there are no agreed or objective criteria of justice, then the judgement whether *X* is a law or not will turn upon subjective assessments as to whether *X* is just or not. This would make for a kind of legal and moral anarchy. Hence, for the positivists, identification of the law as law has to be separated from justice and indeed any other substantive moral conception. In this context Hayek cites G. Radbruch as saying in his *Rechtsphilosophie*: 'If nobody can ascertain what is just, somebody must determine what is legal'. This, however, has to be done without invoking morality. Hayek agrees with the claim made by positivists that there are no agreed positive criteria for what is just or unjust but there can, in his view, be agreed negative criteria: infringing negative freedom, infringing property, lack of universality in law, etc., and satisfying these negative criteria will be at least partly constitutive of a *Rechtsstaat.* Positivists, in suggesting that moral values are subjective and cannot be used in terms of identifying the law as law, throw out the baby with the bathwater because in his view, as we shall see later in the book, there are compelling negative criteria which law has to fulfil to be law and these do have a moral salience. These issues are complex and important and will be looked at in more detail in subsequent chapters but the important point for the moment is that it is in Hayek's view false to think that law can be literally demoralized so that any state with a legal system is a law-based state or a *Rechtsstaat.* It is a grave defect of socialism and social democracy to assimilate order to organization – a false assumption which favours the account of the law and legal sovereignty given by positivists.

There are two other aspects of Hayek's position which are well worth noting. Firstly the role of common law and secondly the methods to be used to allow the ideals of a *Rechtsstaat* to be realized and the linking of legal positivism to what he regards as the fallacies of constructivism and rationalism in social, political, and legal thought.

To begin with the final point since it follows most clearly from Hayek's contrast between spontaneous order and organization and the nature of the rules appropriate to each. In Hayek's view the legal positivist is guilty of what he regards as the intentionalist fallacy, of seeing all types of order as the product of conscious design and thus requiring a consciously and intentionally constructed legal system to constitute, guide, and develop it. Once this false move has been made, then the way is open for the positivist to argue that what makes the law the law is the exercise of the conscious will of the sovereign appropriate to whatever order it is in positing the law. What makes the law the law is that it is derived from such an authoritative source, and not its content or its purposes. In Hayek's view this is a false sort of constructivism. It is false to what we know about the evolution of human society, the order of which evolved over long tracts of time without law, sovereignty, and legislation as the positivist understands these things.[35] It is also false for epistemological reasons as we shall see in detail later. It is false also for the reasons already given of displacing a spontaneous order more and more by a consciously designed one which, when combined with the deep epistemological problems it faces, poses threats to values such as individual liberty and the conditions necessary for relatively autonomous individuals to utilize their fragmented knowledge in ways that will not only be to their own benefit but indirectly to the benefit of all.

All of these points relate closely to Hayek's view of the importance of the role of the common law in the United Kingdom and more generically to what he calls 'grown law' which has a necessary place in all societies and of which there are many theorists to whom Hayek pays tribute: Coke, Hale, Hume, Burke, Savigny, and Maine, etc. As social groups evolve over history and become more complex and larger, their habits and expectations also develop and these become rules for the group – they become normative for the group not just habits of behaviour. These rules are not invented by a guiding intelligence but are the result of multifarious types of interaction within which individuals use their fragmented and practical knowledge – knowing *how* rather than knowing that – to solve the problems that face them in so far as they can. Out of these interactions habits, norms, and rules develop and expectations are created. These developments are certainly the products of human action, indeed in the individual case intentional action, but the outcomes of these individual intentional actions produce a spontaneous order which is not a matter of design. This is the way the common law or grown law has developed. Such forms of law make more and more explicit what is implicit in the practices of a society as these develop. The common law develops alongside the development of the spontaneous order. At the same time there will be disputes about the law and how the law relates to expectations. These disputes have to be resolved by judges. Judges in such circumstances do not act in arbitrary and discretionary ways. Rather they take the existing state of the common law and also the *rationes decidiendi* from previous cases and adjust them to deal with conflicts in expectations. In doing so Hayek argues that the judges find the law or discern the law implicit in the common practices and ways of life of the particular societies in which they exercise their office.[36] In doing so the judge will seek to make clearer and more coherent a set of grown rules which in some respects may have become inchoate and to develop the corpus of common law and to adapt it to new circumstances and to enable it to accommodate new expectations. In a sense, as Hayek points out, the judge acts and operates with principles – but these principles are derived not from some independent moral standpoint like natural law but rather from an understanding of the deepest ideas in the common or grown law, which in turn have made explicit the ideas that are embedded in the habits, norms, and actions of an existing society. Again for Hayek there is a clear contrast between his understanding of the role of a judge in the common law seeking conscientiously to interpret a corpus of law so that while retaining its identity and integrity it is made relevant to changing circumstances and expectations, and the role of the head of an organization concerned with the arbitration and conciliation of interest, and guided by the overall purpose or dominant aim of the organization. In the case of the common law judges, as Hayek argues, they have no overall aim in view beyond the adjudication in the particular case, utilizing both the law as a *quasi* text and previous decisions. He/she acts in a way that is completely unlike the manager of an organization who conducts himself or herself according to the dominant aim of the organization. Nevertheless

Hayek's approach to the common law and grown law more generally is to argue that its aggregate effect – to which the decisions of judges contribute – is to produce an abstract order of rules of just conduct which will in fact allow individuals the freedom to utilize their fragmentary knowledge more effectively.

Now this is quite a large additional claim. It is one thing to value the common law as an organic product of action rather than design, quite another to argue that it does or can be seen to serve the interests of the growth of a *Rechtsstaat.*[37] Indeed, such a claim might appear at first sight to be rather paradoxical in that the idea of a *Rechtsstaat* as developed by continental liberal thinkers had a very large element of rationalism and constructivism at its heart. It did have an overall aim, albeit an abstract rather than substantive one, namely the legal framework for the operation of a predominantly market society and economy and a free civil society. How does this ambition sit with Hayek's emphasis of the common law as an essential element of the *Rechtsstaat*?

There are various dimensions to Hayek's answer to this question. First of all, he accepts that we cannot just assume that because common law is a spontaneous order all common law will actually lead to the creation or support for a *Rechtsstaat* type of framework without considerable development and adaptation by judges. This point was well made by Carl Menger, a leading neo-liberal thinker and a considerable influence on Hayek in his *Investigations into the Methods of the Social Sciences with Special Reference to Economics.*[38] He points out in commenting on the historical school of law, particularly the work of Savigny, that while the members of the historical school had correctly understood the common law as an organic development – a product of action rather than design – and that it has great value because of this, he also points out that 'Common law has also proved harmful to the common good often enough' and has had to be corrected by legislation. Given this point, he argues that the historical school has made us 'understand the previous uncomprehended advantages of common law' but he goes on to argue that 'never may science dispense with testing for their suitability those constitutions that have come about organically'. He finishes this point rather dramatically by saying that 'No era can renounce this calling.' So Menger's position seems to be that we may well start with the common law which is valuable because of its organic and spontaneous development; nevertheless to attain the legal framework of a free society and a free economy such law may well have to be modified and adapted and this may well require government and legislation. Hayek's mature position, despite a bit of zigzagging during his career, was broadly similar. He argues in *Law, Legislation and Liberty, Vol. 1: Rules and Order*, 'the fact that law that has evolved in this way has certain desirable properties does not prove that it will always be good law or even that some of its rules may be very bad. It does not mean therefore that we can altogether dispense with legislation.'[39] Also, he argues at the same point in the book that the evolution of the common law, gradual as it is, may not be adaptable quickly enough to changes in circumstances.

All of this means that the common law does have to be modified at times so that it works in favour of the *Rechtsstaat*, and this in turn means that the values to do with the rule of law are at the heart of the *Rechtsstaat* ideal and those of the free society and the free economy have to be clear and compelling if they are to serve as the basis for the correction of the negative but still 'grown' features of common law. Not only that but also the moral basis of the *Rechtsstaat* has to have some kind of principled objectivity if it is indeed to be invoked to enable us to modify and modulate through legislation the spontaneous order to be found in common law. In Chapter 2 we shall turn to the different, and not wholly compatible, accounts of this moral basis, scope, and character of the *Rechtsstaat* and the rule of law as a moral and legal ideal. In Hayek's own view as we shall see most aspects of this ideal will be negative: to do with claims about the falseness of certain types of political claims in terms of rights, freedom, justice, community, solidarity, and the like but also negative in the sense that he, unlike some other neo-liberals, does not think that it is possible to develop objective and positive moral conceptions.

Before moving into these arguments, however, I want to address one further issue in Hayek's approach to common law. In his social and legal philosophy Hayek places a great deal of emphasis on the law providing at any one time a framework of certainty and predictability. This is not for him some kind of abstract moral demand but rather is central to the role of the law in addressing the basic circumstances of human life. Given that, as we shall see, for Hayek our knowledge is fragmentary and we need space within which each person can utilize whatever knowledge is available to meet his or her needs and expectations as best he or she can, then this exercise, if it to be successful, requires a stable, free, secure, known, transparent, and predictable environment which only the law can provide. However, there is a big question about whether or not the common law can in fact meet these requirements. Hegel's critique of Savigny's hostility to codification is relevant here since, as we have seen, Hayek rather approves of Savigny. Hegel's view is that transparency and universality are not and cannot be features of the common law in that how a judge at common law will approach a case and how different parties will be treated is far from being clear and predictable. Hegel argues in paragraph 211 in *The Philosophy of Right*[40] that the law has to have the character of 'determinate universality', that is to say it has to be clear and transparent and to apply in a universal way to all of those who fall under the law: property owners, traders, bankers, and citizens in general – whatever the class of those to whom a particular law applies. This knowledge of determinate and universal law is central to the rule of law. In the additional remarks to paragraph 211, he goes on to argue that '[l]aw must be known by thought, it must be a system in itself and only as such can it be recognized in a civilized country', and then in a direct criticism of Savigny, his colleague at the University of Berlin, he goes on to argue that '[t]he recent denial [by Savigny] that nations have a vocation to codify their laws is not only an insult; it also implies the absurdity of supposing that not a single individual has been endowed with skill enough to bring into a single system the endless mass of existing laws'.

The systematization and codification of the law was, in Hegel's view, central to its determinate universality as he makes clear in this paragraph. Only then will it be able to provide the clear and predictable framework within which individuals can act with confidence. This cannot be attained by the common law if it is left uncodified and unsystematized. In some ways Hayek's mature view is not all that different from that of Hegel. In the *Kodifikationsstreit* in Germany to which Hegel contributed and which was provoked by Thibaut – Hegel's mentor in all of this – in his book *Über die Nothwendigkeit eines allgemeinen bürgerlichen Rechts für Deutschland*,[41] published in Heidelberg in 1814, and Savigny in his *Vom Beruf unsrer zeit für Gesetzgebung und Rechtswissenschaft*,[42] published in the same year, the latter argued against codification because he valued the organic growth of the common law – as did Hayek. He did however make an important distinction which is of fundamental importance for the rule of law. He argues that initially law exists in the habits and the consciousness of the community, but as society develops it comes to embody two further aspects. The first aspect is the continuation of the law as part of the habits and practices of the society – what he calls the 'political' aspects of the law; the second aspect is the technical aspect embodied in the science of jurisprudence. The problem with all of this, as Thibaut argued, is that this latter aspect means that in a common law context the understanding of the law – just because it is unsystematized and codified – becomes more complex and the understanding of it has to be in the hands of professional students of jurisprudence and this removes it almost completely from the consciousness of ordinary people. It becomes part of an esoteric science and an esoteric language. The difficulty then comes particularly with the idea of *Rechtsstaat* and the rule of law if an understanding of the rule of law, in a common law jurisdiction the compilation of cases and precedents is removed from the common knowledge of the people. Citizens will not be able to act according to the rules of just conduct if the knowledge of such rules has become esoteric knowledge. At the same time, Thibaut's and Hegel's point was that while systematization is desirable in terms of what we would now call the rule of law, the creation of law with determinate universality does not take place *de novo*, nor is it a case of turning into systematic positive law some general moral framework of law such as natural law might be thought to provide but rather should be a systematization of the common law. Savigny is right to value the common law but wrong to object to its systematization.[43] In some respects, depending on how far Hayek wanted to allow his argument to go we might say that Hayek is more on the side of Thibaut and Hegel here. We start with the common law because that is embedded in the consciousness of the people but we should make that consciousness clear, determinate, and universal and only then can it meet the requirements of the *Rechtsstaat* and the rule of law which in turn facilitate through clarity and universality the conditions necessary for individuals to cope with their limited knowledge and an indifferent natural world.

As I argued earlier for the neo-liberals the rule of law is a moral ideal and, as we have seen, is closely related to ideas about the spontaneous order, the private law, the common law, the negative liberty, the market order, the fragmented and dispersed nature of knowledge, etc. together with the claim that both common law and legislation should be guided more in the direction of the rule of law than has been the case under socialist and social democratic regimes. In Chapter 2

I will discuss some of the fundamental ways in which a liberal account of the rule of law have been argued.

NOTES

1. Rawls, J. A. (1972). *Theory of Justice*. Oxford: Oxford University Press, p. 3.
2. Hayek, F. A. (1976). *Law, Legislation and Liberty, Vol. 2: The Mirage of Social Justice*. London: Routledge and Kegan Paul, p. 15.
3. Oakeshott, M. J. (2006). *Lectures in the History of Political Thought*, ed. T. Nardin and L. O'Sullivan. Exeter: Imprint Academic, p. 484.
4. Oakeshott, M. J. *Lectures in the History of Political Thought*, p. 472.
5. Oakeshott, M. J. *Lectures in the History of Political Though*, p. 472.
6. Oakeshott, M. J. *Lectures in the History of Political Thought*, pp. 472, 488.
7. Oakeshott, M. J. (1975). *On Human Conduct*. Oxford: The Clarendon Press, p. 232.
8. Oakeshott, M. J. *On Human Conduct*, p. 233.
9. Oakeshott, M. J. *On Human Conduct*.
10. Oakeshott, M. J. *On Human Conduct*, p. 131.
11. Oakeshott, M. J. *On Human Conduct*, p. 138.
12. Oakeshott, M. J. *On Human Conduct*, p. 138.
13. Oakeshott, M. J. *Lectures in the History of Political Thought*, p. 487.
14. Hayek, F. A. (1973). *Law, Legislation and Liberty, Vol. 1: Rules and Order*, London, Routledge and Kegan Paul, p. 98.
15. Hayek, F. A. *Law, Legislation and Liberty, Vol. 1: Rules and Order*, p. 106.
16. Oakeshott, M. J. *Lectures in the History of Political Thought*, p. 485.
17. Oakeshott, M. J. (1983).'The Rule of Law', in *On History*. Oxford: Blackwell.
18. Oakeshott, M. J. *Lectures in the History of Political Thought*, p. 489.
19. Oakeshott, M. J. *Lectures in the History of Political Thought*, p. 474.
20. Oakeshott, M. J. *On History*, p. 167.
21. For further discussion see K. Dyson (1980). *The State Tradition in Western Europe*. Oxford: Martin Robertson.
22. Oakeshott, M. J. *Lectures in the History of Political Thought*, p. 490.
23. Fuller, L. (1962). *The Morality of Law*. New Haven: Yale University Press.
24. Oakeshott, M. J. *The Rule of Law*, p. 152.
25. Oakeshott, M. J. *The Rule of Law*, p. 153.
26. Oakeshott, M. J. *The Rule of Law*, p. 156.
27. Oakeshott, M. J. *The Rule of Law*.
28. Oakeshott, M. J. *On Human Conduct*, p. 326.
29. Hayek, F. A. *Law, Legislation and Liberty, Vol. 2: The Mirage of Social Justice*.
30. Kelsen, H. (1957). 'What is Justice?', in *What is Justice? Justice Law and Politics in the Mirror of Science*. Berkeley, CA: Berkeley University Press. For the relationship between his idea of a *Rechtsstaat* and legal positivism, see 'Rechtsstaat und Staatsrecht', in H. Klecatsky, R. Marcic, and H. Schambeck *Die Wiener Rechtstheoretische Schule, Vol. 2*. Vienna (1968). For the full force of Hayek's critique of Kelsen from the point of view of the rule of law and *Rechtsstaat*, see Hayek, *Law, Legislation and Liberty, Vol. 2: The Mirage of Social Justice*, pp. 44–61.
31. Hayek, F. A. *Law, Legislation and Liberty, Vol. 2: The Mirage of Social Justice*, p. 46.
32. Hayek, F. A. *Law, Legislation and Liberty, Vol. 1: Rules and Order*, p. 49.

33. Hayek, F. A. *Law, Legislation and Liberty, Vol. 2: The Mirage of Social Justice*, p. 47.
34. Hayek, F. A. *Law, Legislation and Liberty, Vol. 1: Rules and Order*, p. 91.
35. Hayek, F. A. *Law, Legislation and Liberty, Vol. 1: Rules and Order*, p. 119.
36. Hayek, F. A. *Law, Legislation and Liberty, Vol. 1: Rules and Order*, p. 119.
37. See Shearmur, J. (1996). *Hayek and After*. London: Routledge and Kegan Paul, p. 89.
38. Menger, C. (1985). *Investigations into the Method of the Social Sciences with Special Reference to Economics*. New York: New York University Press, p. 233; and Shearmur, J. *Hayek and After*, p. 44. Overall Shearmur's book is one of the most acute studies of Hayek and I am indebted to him for seeing this aspect of Menger's work.
39. Hayek, F. A. *Law, Legislation and Liberty, Vol. 1: Rules and Order*, p. 88.
40. Hegel, G. W. F. (1952). *The Philosophy of Right*, trans. T. M. Knox. Oxford: The Clarendon Press.
41. Thibaut, A. F. J. (1814).*Über die Nothwendigkeit eines allgemeinen bürgerlichen Rechts für Deutschland*. Heidelberg.
42. Savigny, K. (1831). *Vom Beruf unserer zeit für Gesetzgebung und Rechtswissenschaft*, trans. A. Hayward. London: Littlewood. Reprinted by Ayer Co., North Stratford, New Hampshire.
43. There are interesting insights into these debates and their background to be found in J. Q. Whitman (1990). *The Legacy of Roman Law in the German Romantic Era: Historical Vision and Legal Change*. Princeton, NJ: Princeton University Press.

2

The Foundations of the Rule of Law as a Moral Ideal

In this chapter, I shall sketch the views of a number of either avowed neo-liberals or thinkers who have contributed substantially to the neo-liberal position on the issue of the rule of law as a moral ideal. At this stage of discussion a sketch will be sufficient since the elements of the arguments are considered in much greater detail later on. Central to the ideal of the rule of law is the relationship claimed by neo-liberals between the rule of law and freedom, justice and rights particularly and these will be the focus of subsequent chapters. At the moment, I want to indicate in a broad way the rather different approaches taken by neo-liberal thinkers to the question of the justification of the rule of law as a moral ideal. This is very important because the rule of law in this sense, particularly if expressed in constitutional rules, can put constraints on democratic choices and in particular choices typical of social democracy, for example, in favour of social justice. Given this, it is very important to see how neo-liberal thinkers have in fact argued for the foundational nature of the rule of law and a constitution embodying it.

In *The Constitution of Liberty*, Hayek argues as follows:

> The rule of law, of course, presupposes complete legality, but this is not enough: if a law gave the government unlimited power to act as it pleased, all its actions would be legal, but it would certainly not be under the rule of law. The rule of law, therefore, is also more than constitutionalism: it requires that all laws conform to certain principles.[1]

Clearly, as we have seen, Hayek is not a legal positivist. He sees the rule of law to be an essential requirement of how law *ought* to be, not a characteristic of all duly enacted positive law as it *is*. The rule of law is a political ideal and as such it is reasonable to raise questions about what this ideal means in detail and how it can be justified. Why should the legislator feel bound to conform to the dictates of the rule of law as a political ideal as opposed to the rule of law being the umbrella term for a set of efficiency conditions for any legal system as it is? The answer to this question requires an elaborated moral and political theory to explain why the rule of law should be seen as a compelling moral ideal and the issues surrounding this will be considered in this chapter. Neo-liberals give quite different answers to the question of what is it that justifies the rule of law in this normative sense. We shall look at the different approaches of liberal thinkers to this fundamental question. We shall consider the alternative views of Hayek who argues a case which is based partly on evolution and partly on philosophical principles; James Buchanan (like Hayek a Nobel Prize winner in economics) who holds to a contractarian and, in Hayek's sense, rationalist and constructivist approach; Robert Nozick whose position on this issue is based upon the postulation of a set of basic and absolute rights; Murray Rothbard who invokes natural law to justify the idea of the rule of law; and Ludwig von Mises who focuses on the character of human agency or what he calls the 'acting man' to provide the basis for thinking about these matters.

F. A. VON HAYEK: A STATE OF COMMON LAW?

In Hayek's view the justification of the idea of the rule of law is closely connected to his arguments about the evolutionary emergence of rules, practices, and conventions, more generally some aspects of which were considered in the previous chapter. As we saw, many of the central themes of Oakeshott's account of the distinction between nomocracy and telocracy are paralleled in Hayek's work. There is the same strong emphasis on the non-instrumental nature of law and its separation from purpose; on the generality and universality of law; on the theme that the rule of law is not to secure substantial goods to individuals and groups; and on the fact that nomocracy is closely linked to the growth of individualism in the modern world and an equivalent decline in the salience of community and tribal identification. There is a recognition that in any society there will be an admixture of nomocratic and telocratic rule corresponding to government on the one hand which is nomocratic having no overall substantive purposes, and organizations of all sorts within society which are like Oakeshott's enterprise associations and which pursue whatever the purposes of the organization may be. For Hayek the nomocratic structure and scope of government will form the most basic element of what he calls the 'Great Society' – corresponding to Oakeshott's idea of civil association in many respects. Within a Great Society there will be organizations and enterprises of all sorts constituted by rules which will facilitate the ends for which such organizations are constituted. Government embodying a commitment to the rule of law, however, should not be seen as an organization in the same way at all. For Hayek, the role of government is to act, as he says, like a maintenance squad in a factory. Its function is not to produce goods on its own account but to provide the abstract framework of law within which individuals can freely and non-coercively pursue whatever goods they wish to pursue. There are however some differences from Oakeshott's view and these are significant in deepening the character of the neo-liberal account of law and they also fill out some obscurities and elisions in Oakeshott's position.

The first difference is that whereas Oakeshott's argument for the distinction between telocracy and nomocracy is rooted in a detailed historical understanding and perspective set out at great length in *On Human Conduct* and in *Lectures in the History of Political Thought* as we have seen, Hayek's is much more embedded in a social and economic theory which is certainly partly a general historical and evolutionary account of the emergence of the central features of a Great Society or liberal society under the rule of law together with a more philosophical thesis about the non-instrumentality of law which it has to possess if law is to fulfil the ideal of the rule of law. On the historical side of the issue in *The Constitution of Liberty* he does engage in three historical case studies relating to England, the United States, and Germany. Nevertheless, while this account is important, it is not remotely as thorough and as resourced as Oakeshott's account and is less important in Hayek than the more general theoretical perspective. For Oakeshott such a perspective is embedded within the history that he traces – the political and legal theory is an abridgement of an extant political and legal tradition and its various dimensions – it is not a free-standing theoretical construct. For Hayek the overall stance is much more theoretical. Indeed, in his view, it is necessary to develop an account of the nature of the rule of law from within what he calls an 'Ideology' in *Law, Legislation and Liberty, Vol. 2: The Mirage of Social Justice* where he argues that

> since every social order rests on an ideology, every statement of the criteria by which we can determine what is appropriate law in such an order must also be an ideology.[2]

Hayek wants to provide us with a general social, political, and economic theory (or ideology) of the rule of law which is classical liberal in scope and inspiration.

Central to classical liberalism was, in Hayek's view, an account of the nature of spontaneous order. In Hayek's view we frequently go wrong when thinking about the nature of the social and political order when we think that these orders as we find them have been fashioned by deliberation and design: the assumption that they are made or created orders fulfilling some notion of appropriate design. Rather, in Hayek's view such orders have emerged and evolved over time as the result of countless individuals seeking to cope as best they can in an indifferent natural world with very limited and fragmentary forms of knowledge. These attempts to deal with the practical task of coping with the world and satisfying needs have, over time, yielded practices of all sorts to enable people to cooperate in the same sorts of task. Rules emerge from those practices, first as habits and regularities of behaviour which establish expected or given ways of doing things – but eventually in some areas such rules come to regulate practices or become norms for the pursuit of that practice. Such orders emerge spontaneously, but they do eventually yield rules but they are not made by the rules nor were the rules devised in advance of the practice. It is a matter of a *spontaneous* not a *designed* order. So, what has this to do with a nomocratic order and the purposelessness of law? In Hayek's views such spontaneous orders do not and cannot serve particular purposes since they emerged through countless interactions: They were not created by deliberation to satisfy a purpose. They do not have particular purposes of their own but their existence allows us to pursue many divergent purposes.

In addition, the fragmented and limited nature of human knowledge also means that spontaneous orders cannot be designed because they cover far more circumstances and far more people with a vast diversity of intentions, desires, and means of achieving them to be gathered together into one synoptic deliberative framework. We shall look at this epistemological argument in more detail later but for Hayek 'knowing how' is practical knowledge and activity which in different ways and in the hands of countless different people yields spontaneously created practices which could never have been the result of human design and as such are independent of any purpose with which design might have endowed them. As Hayek has said, such practices serve to facilitate individuals and groups satisfying their needs, whatever they may be. One obvious such spontaneous order is the market economy. It emerged out of the countless acts of individuals who found that economic exchange enabled them to meet their needs far more effectively than they could meet them on their own. People engaged in market activity long before rules emerged to constitute economic exchange into something more formalized like contract law, property law, and the like and equally well in advance of any kind of economic theory to provide a general account of how markets work and to provide an account of the rules and principles characterizing them. Hayek draws an analogy with language and spontaneous social orders. Language arose as a spontaneous order and had an intensely practical purpose; it provides a medium through which we are able to satisfy our own immense variety of individual purposes without it having a designed purpose of its own; it does have rules – of grammar for example – and there can be theoretical treatments of such rules by linguisticians, but these emerge from the practice of speaking a language and were not prior to it. Language embodies habits and regularities (certainly one sense of rules) but rules which come to be seen as regulatory for the language, which can be set out – for example in grammar books – follow much later. Therefore, it is part of Hayek's thesis that a proper understanding of the development of spontaneous orders actually favours the emergence of a nomocratic order or a Great Society with non-instrumental laws constituting it, but within which there could be all sorts of groups and enterprises organized by instrumental rules facilitating the purposes for which such groups came into existence.

As we have seen, Oakeshott traced the emergence of the two political dispositions here in European history. Hayek's argument rests much more on the nature of social development and evolution and on the restrictions imposed on human knowledge. He does, however, have a clear view about how his account of spontaneous order maps out a rather schematic account of history. This account includes the view that the emergence of the Great Society occurred through the breakdown of community life which was small scale and often tribal. As the circle of society widened, people became more and more anonymous to one another. Unlike in a tribal society they no longer shared values and purposes in common and their relationships and forms of cooperation became more complex, and also more abstract as they sought to fulfil their different goals and purposes. Informal relations based upon solidarity were displaced by practices which yielded more abstract relationships, particularly legal ones. Instead of a rich life of interaction in a small scale, face-to-face familial or tribal community, the practical knowledge and its associated actions needed to cope with a larger scale and more anonymous society that yielded an abstract legal order which provided protected domains for individuals to pursue their own goals in their own way without which with their limited knowledge they would not have coped with the circumstances of human life.

Part of the justification and legitimacy of a 'Great Society' and its mode of governance therefore rest upon this account of the growth of modernity. It is less rich than Oakeshott's in terms of historical detail but in another way it is richer in the sense that Hayek's rather thin account of history is supported by a more general theory of human development.

At the same time, however, it still leaves one issue about the justification of the importance of the rule of law in a 'Great Society' unresolved and this issue parallels how can we justify the importance of the rule of law to its critics since giving an answer to the question 'why should we value the rule of law?' might seem to make the rule of law *instrumental* to its justifying purposes or conditions. Hayek believes that he has a straightforward and convincing answer to this question. Ultimately, though, all of these arguments turn upon the plausibility of Hayek's overall arguments for a modern version of classical liberalism which forms the 'ideological' (in Hayek's own terms) framework within which the rule of law has its place. This account of liberalism, as we shall see in subsequent chapters, is subtle and complex and encompasses detailed analysis of freedom, justice, rights, and the general role of government. There is, nevertheless, a very specific answer given by Hayek to the question we are posing at the moment: if law is purposeless what can justify it since any justification is going to have to include the idea of purpose? Hayek's answer to this problem is complex and rather obscure. General laws which do not serve particular ends constitute an abstract order, as Hayek calls it which, in turn, provides the framework for the 'Great Society' or nomocratic order. The order is a spontaneous, unintended achievement of modernity and has arisen through the choices and the application of limited knowledge to specific circumstances of countless individuals over many generations. Given this scenario two things follow: the abstract order is *there* – it is a product of spontaneous human evolution; at the same time it would not have emerged in this way if it did not meet people's practical needs. Picking up this latter point it might be thought that the justification of the abstract order is *utilitarian* in a very broad sense of that term,[3] that is the justification seems to be a type of *rule* but definitely not *act* utilitarianism: that in general the application of the rule maximizes utility even if it does not do so in a particular case.[4] It has to be remembered however, that when assessing the utility of the general role of the abstract order we cannot refer to any specific or particular ends which that order serves. Rather the utility in question is 'the permanent preservation of an abstract order'.

Utilitarianism is usually seen as a telocratic moral and political theory devoted to the maximizing of some end: utility, welfare, preference satisfaction, or whatever, whereas for Hayek the whole point of the beneficial consequences of the abstract order is that it facilitates the achievement of diverse and unknown ends, not some specific dominant end or ends. Hayek's argument looks fine at this point because there is an aim or goal of law after all – the maintenance of the abstract order that will in turn facilitate the pursuit of these diverse and unknown ends. So law is non-instrumental in that it does not serve specific ends but is rather the framework within which specific ends can be realized. However, the argument is muddied to some extent when he also says on the same page that

> these rules ultimately serve particular (though mostly unknown) ends, they will do so only if they are treated not as means but as ultimate values, indeed as the only values common to all and distinct from the particular ends of individuals.[5]

Such a characterization of rules as *ultimate* values cannot be understood straightforwardly on utilitarian grounds. Hayek distinguishes between two senses of utilitarianism. The first, which he rejects, is the one that I have described as utilitarianism based on a dominant goal or end such as pleasure, happiness, or welfare; the other, which he accepts, he sees as an application of the term 'utilitarian' to any critical examination of rules and institutions with respect to the function they perform in the structure of society. Since Hayek is seeking to describe the function that general rules play in constituting an abstract order, he is prepared to accept that his account is utilitarian in this rather general sense. There are however, inconsistencies in his views. As we have seen, on the same page he argues that general rules should not be seen as means but as 'ultimate values' while contrasting the thin form of utilitarianism which he professes to embrace with those who regard all existing values as unquestionable. It is not at all clear how the rules of the abstract order of a great society can both be regarded as ultimate and yet at the same time be given this broad utilitarian justification and whose emergence is, in addition, subject to great historical contingency.

It is very interesting to compare Hayek and Oakeshott on this point of justification. They both argue that in a nomocratic order law should be purposeless. Hayek, though, as we have seen, gives a complex answer to the question of justification. Oakeshott, however, without mentioning Hayek by name, criticizes Hayek's approach in his essay on 'Talking Politics' in *Rationalism in Politics*. The passage is worth quoting in full:

> Finally, the saddest of all misunderstandings of a state as a civil association: that in which it is properly presented as association in terms of non instrumental conditions imposed upon conduct and specified in general rules from whose obligations no associate and no conduct is exempt, but defended as the mode of association more likely than any other to provide and go on promoting the satisfaction of any diverse and proliferant wants. Prosperity may be the likely contingent outcome of civil association, but to recommend it in these terms is to recommend something other than civil association.[6]

Oakeshott endorses Hayek's account of the character of civil association but believes that his broadly utilitarianism justification of such an order – that these general rules will facilitate the achievement of particular purposes – is, as a telocratic justification, deeply flawed.

There is one further feature of the rule of law in Hayek that we need to investigate and that is the generality and the universality of law. The ideas of generality and universality in relation to law need careful unpacking because they seem deceptively simple, embodying the claim that like Kant's categorical imperative law should be general and universal and should apply to all people in similar circumstances. Law is not to be imposed on named individuals as in Bills of Attainder for example, nor is it to be a matter for discretion as to who is to be covered by a law and who is not. Equally law is not universal if it prescribes particular ends or goals since people differ over such things. People have different aims and goals and to legally prescribe or privilege a particular set of goals is not compatible with the universality of law which is crucial to the moral ideal of the rule of law as understood by Hayek. These ideas are also important for Hayek's critique of social democracy and socialism. He argued that the legal system of a social democratic state infringes the principles of generality and universality. First of all, because it is particularistic – securing to individuals goods and benefits which may not be available to others in society on the same terms. It is also bound to be discretionary because it is not possible to write legal rules with sufficient precision to secure to individuals goods which may be in scarce supply such as health, education, and social security. It follows from this that those charged with distributing goods in the pursuit of social justice have to act in arbitrary and discretionary ways since the guidance of laws and rules runs out in allocation to particular individuals in specific circumstances. Then we have to rely on the discretion of officials. The rule of law in a social democratic state will be directed towards achieving certain sorts of moral goals: social justice, community, solidarity, and a classless society. Such goals are not consensually accepted and are not in any sense universal or general, and therefore in so far as the law is geared to achieving these goals it suffers from the same degree of particularity as the ends which the law serves. So, given the significance of universality to the rule of law, it is a central theme of neo-liberalism that social democracy lies outside the rule of law.

The link between the rule of law and universality is also fundamental to Hayek's conception of the rule of law in another respect too. This is in the context of his views on how to make a transition to a more liberal society or one that embodies the ideals of a *Rechtsstaat*. As we have seen Hayek very strongly stresses the role of spontaneous order and tradition rather than a design or deliberate approach to the achievement of a *Rechtsstaat*. For example, in the 'Epilogue' to Volume 3 of *Law, Legislation and Liberty* he says that

> [s]ince we owe the order of our society to a tradition of rules which we only imperfectly understand, all progress must be based on tradition

and

> [T]radition is not something constant but a process of selection guided not by reason but by success.[7]

However, the problem with this is that there is no guarantee that a spontaneous order rooted in a tradition of behaviour, however vivid and dynamic, will produce results favourable to a liberal society and the *Rechtsstaat* ideal. So, do we have to be inert in the face of tradition, and if not how and on what basis can tradition be modulated and modified to serve the emergence of a liberal constitutional order? Hayek is clear that this cannot be done by a positive, substantive political theory because that would then be a species of constructive rationalism of which he is so deeply critical. And it would also have to postulate a set of ends and goals to be pursued which would fit badly with Hayek's critique of such goal-directed political thought. Hayek's own proposal for the development of a 'grown' spontaneously developed legal tradition in such a way as to favour a liberal constitutional and market order is essentially *negative.* It is, as Jeremy Shearmur argues in his important work *Hayek and After*, in the principle of universalizability that we find the negative test for the adaptation of inherited rules and modifications of them.[8] Does the existing inherited rule comply with the principle of universalizability? Does the proposed modification comply with the principle? On this basis we can discover that some inherited law is not capable of being maintained in a universal form without coming into conflict with other rules and laws which do embody this feature. So Hayek argues that

> a negative test that enables us progressively to eliminate rules which prove to be unjust because they are not universalisable within the system of other rules whose validity is not questioned.[9]

Any revised law proposed to fill the gap caused by the repeal of a law because non-universalizable will have to pass the test of universalizability. So, as Shearmur says, Hayek is here offering a 'path to liberal systems of law'. It is possible to move towards a liberal *Rechtsstaat* from any socially inherited system of law, however contextually different the background evolution and traditions of different societies may be, by utilizing the principle of universalizability and in so doing as Hayek sees it without recourse to a constructivist or rationalist political and legal theory because the principle does not presuppose or serve a particular set of goals and purposes. It is also perfectly possible, as Shearmur points out, that from using the test of universalizability in different societies with different traditions we should not expect that there should or could be any *single* path to the achievement of a liberal constitutional order.[10]

This way of looking at universalizability is also linked by Hayek to his evolutionary theory of legal orders. At earlier stages of human evolution laws and rules were constituted by small groups such as tribes which had common shared purposes. In the terms set out in Chapter 1, they were like organizations with a common purpose and the rules of such a society were about achieving that common purpose. However, the processes of modernity have led these boundaries to be broken down in favour of wider and wider forms of society. As this has happened the laws are 'progressively extended to larger and larger groups and finally universalized to the relations between any members of an Open Society who have no concrete purposes in common and merely submit to the same abstract rules they will in the process have shed all reference to specific purposes'.

So the principle of the universality of law has evolutionary roots and is a form of modernity which has accompanied the growing abstraction from shared concrete ends. So part of Hayek's justification of the principle of universalizability rests upon this claimed historical evolution. Generality and universality are part of the nomocratic order and the movement from telocratic to nomocratic orders is part of progressive human development.

Nevertheless, there is also the possibility of a philosophical defence of the principle of universalizability and its role in the law. The defence is heavily indebted to Kant who argued that there had to be a basic rational principle of morality and that this had to be formal. If morality is to be rational, then we need to be able to specify the set of necessary and sufficient conditions for it to be rational. This means that rational morality has to be detached from the varying goals and purposes that people have. We cannot give some of these goals and purposes as such a rationally based privilege over others. Rather, since moral laws should hold for everyone as rational beings, the principles of a rational morality have to be derived from the 'universal concept of a rational being'. Only on this basis can a rational approach to morality be developed. Morality has to be separated from anthropology and from any other empirical account of different human ends and goals. So, from a Kantian point of view, Hayek's anthropological and evolutionary account of law is irrelevant for the purpose of creating a rational ethics. Nevertheless, Kant's approach to universalizability in ethics is central also to Hayek, and not only that but Hayek also sees Kant's work (as do many neo-liberals) as being crucial to a full defence of the *Rechtsstaat* ideal.

So, how powerful a test of morality is the principle of universalizability? On one view of it the principle is in fact rather feeble. It does no doubt preclude having as a legitimate law under the principle of the rule of law one which specifies people by their proper names since that *ex hypothesi* rules out universalizability.[11] Even in this case, however, critics have pointed out that it is always possible to replace proper names with definite descriptions which could potentially apply to large numbers of people but which might as a matter of fact apply only to those whose proper names had been used in the formulation of the original version of the law. Hayek himself accepts this point. But this is in a sense to take the principle of universalizability in a very narrow way. A richer account of the principle would entail two further central aspects. The principle of non-contradiction requires me to consider that if promulgated as a universal law, the principle that I enunciate will also apply to me. If I find that I cannot accept the implications of such a law as it would apply to me, and if there is no relevant difference between me and those to whom I think that the law should apply, then I cannot enunciate the law without contradiction. This may be a powerful principle because it might tell against racism and fascism as Richard Hare famously argued in *Freedom and Reason*. If I enunciate a rule that Jews should be killed, then I have to accept that if research showed that I also had Jewish antecedents then I should assent to the proposition that I too should be killed. Few people other than Hare's 'fanatic' would in fact accept such a principle.[12]

The third aspect of the principle which recommends itself to defenders of the *Rechtsstaat* ideal is that as a formal principle it is neutral between different goals and purposes assuming that such goals can in fact be pursued in a way consistent with formal universalizability. This is very important to neo-liberal accounts of the rule of law because the principle might be thought to imply that a rational system of law which embodies adherence to the principle in fact means that the law has to be formulated in such a way that legal requirements do not conflict with one another and that duties imposed by the law should be compossible (capable of being discharged by all people in similar circumstances) and that rights conferred by the law should also be compossible (capable of being claimed simultaneously by all right holders). If the law does not meet these conditions, then it has to embody discrimination between people similarly situated and this would infringe the principle of universalizability.

These various aspects of universalizability bear directly on Hayek's critique of social democracy and socialism. In Hayek's view, the social legislation of social democracy and socialism contravenes the basic requirements of universalizability because of two features:

1. It secures goods to people in the context of highly specific circumstances: a remedy for this type of ill health, a subsidy to the income of people in situation *X* or *Y*, a subsidized place at university for person in circumstance *X* but not *Y* when there are not good reasons for this departure from universality. It is however dictated by scarcity in the goods – typically health care, education, and social security – which the social democratic state seeks to distribute.
2. Because of this, discretion is at the heart of the application of such social legislation. Discretion moves the law away from universality and it cannot in fact be based on the application of general reasons because the whole point is the circumstances of the particular case. This discretion is unavoidable when applying legislation against a background of scarce resources. Sometimes indeed the giving of reasons for the differential application of laws, rules, and regulations will be abandoned altogether just because the particular case cannot be subsumed under general reasons and some non-rational procedure may well be adopted instead like 'first come first served' or with a more formally randomized procedure for discriminating between people which has nothing to do with the nature of the good being distributed or indeed the difference in the degree of people's need for such a good.

The reference to scarcity in the previous comment leads us to the next reason for Hayek's view that social democratic legislation is outside the rule of law. As stated earlier, a rational and morally legitimate set of rules cannot be in aggregate, inconsistent with one another or non-compossible. There must not be any fundamental conflict between laws in a *Rechtsstaat* because of the consequential discrimination that would entail. This has very profound implications for the neo-liberal view of social democracy and the rule of law. This issue will loom large in the rest of the book but essentially it turns on the idea of what might be called a set of positive rights and positive duties which are seen as legally enforceable and in the case of the duties turning them into strict obligations. Social democracy and socialism cannot, according to the neo-liberal, get away without laying down such sets of positive rights and duties when according to the neo-liberal neither the rights nor the duties are compossible and non-conflictual. If we regard freedom as positive freedom – as not just the absence of coercion and therefore negative but positive, implying some degree of control over personal resources; if we regard social justice as implying that people have rights and entitlements to resources rather than being a purely procedural virtue; if we regard rights as including social and economic rights to material goods and not just as rights to non-interference, then a set of rules securing such goods to individuals could not be compossible because of scarcity. We could not be equally free, simultaneously claiming our freedom; we could not equally exercise our rights simultaneously because of scarcity. If however, freedom and rights are understood negatively – as the absence of interference – then my exercising of my right would be compossible with yours because the duties of others in respect of our negative rights are duties of forbearance – of not interfering, robbing, assaulting, killing, etc. These duties of forbearance are forms of inaction and as such do not run up against scarcity of resources. Positive rights and positive freedom cannot form part of a rational moral basis for society because they offend against universalizability and in doing so bring in their wake the exercise of discretion by public authorities and arbitrariness in the distribution of resources. A neo-liberal *Rechtsstaat* on the contrary will embody a negative conception of freedom, a procedural understanding of the nature of justice, and negative rights to non-interference rather than rights to resources. Such freedoms, justice, and rights can be applied to everyone equally and in ways that make them compossible and non-conflictual. So it is difficult to overestimate the role that the principle of universalizabilty plays in Hayek's thought. When applied to spontaneously generated and inherited rules, it will enable that set of rules over time to be modified in the interests of universality to take us in the direction of a *Rechtsstaat.*

For Hayek the constitutional order of the *Rechtsstaat* requires clear and substantive institutional protection. This corresponds to what we have seen in Oakeshott's work in his distinction between basic nomocratic rules and the actions undertaken by both individuals and governments acting in accordance with such rules. As we shall see shortly this distinction is also crucial to Buchanan's work but in the hands of Hayek it does mean that there is a sharp distinction to be drawn in his view between public and private law. The sphere of public law is vitally important because it is concerned with the rules of just conduct and the protection of liberty and rights and the private domain; but at the same time Hayek is clear that its role should be limited to this task. One of the many baneful features of social democracy and socialism in his view is that the distinction between public and private law becomes blurred and indeed that public law progressively displaces private law. The reason for this is obvious to Hayek because social legislation to meet the alleged need to achieve social justice brings government and law into the sphere of welfare, education, health, social security, and via those into family life too. It displaces private law by replacing private and contractual arrangements by state provision which has to be governed by public law – except that it cannot be in detail, as we have already seen, Hayek argues. Public law is necessary but limited; private law regulates voluntary relations between individuals. Social democracy and socialism threatens this realm of private law by turning these relationships into relationships between individuals and a welfare state and by turning what could have been private deliverers of education, health, and so forth into public bodies.

JAMES BUCHANAN: CONSTITUTIONAL RULES AND CONTRACT

It would be wrong to think that all neo-liberal thinkers take the same view about the fundamental justification of a neo-liberal constitutional order and James Buchanan specifically criticizes Hayek's evolutionary account of the rules of just order on the grounds that there is no good reason for thinking that spontaneous processes as they evolve will in fact produce rules which are consistent with the features of a society embodying the rule of law. He argues this point quite clearly and goes on to make the case that since we cannot rely on evolutionary processes to produce rules embodying the rule of law, we have to move to the idea that such rules have to be given a rational and, in Hayek's terms, 'constructivist' justification.[13] We may well inherit a body of rules that have been formed by spontaneous or evolutionary processes but equally they may well have to be modified by rational considerations and Buchanan focuses directly on how we can in fact justify basic constitutional rules which can then be used as a yardstick by which to reform given rules even if they have arisen as the result of spontaneous processes. In fact, it is reasonable to think that Buchanan has been rather unfair to Hayek in his criticisms because previously I did set out Hayek's own view which is quite close to Buchanan's that there is no guarantee that evolved rules and 'grown' law or for that matter the common law will embody all that is desirable for the rule of law and he argued that they could be modified on grounds of justified liberal principles. In Hayek's view that justification comes through in both a critique of non-liberal accounts of values such as liberty, justice, and rights and a corresponding defence of liberal views of these, and we shall look at these features later. At the present juncture, however, it is more important to contrast Hayek's approach which focuses on liberty, justice, and rights with Buchanan's which does not so directly but rather seeks to derive a liberal framework for the rule of law from the idea of contract. Of course, the idea of contract has played a long role in liberal thought but in Buchanan's case its role is distinctive and in many ways compelling. Buchanan starts from the view that all moral values are subjective and that a good deal of political and legal theory consists in drawing out the consequences of one's subjectively chosen values and then seeking some kind of political, moral, or legal authority for them.[14] Buchanan argues that a strict subjectivist must reject this idea that one's own moral values have a greater degree of importance and authority than anyone else's. It is impossible to build up a case for a philosopher king on the basis of the subjectivity of value. The position of the platonic philosopher king depends on the idea that such a ruler has possession of some kind of objective moral and political truth which grounds the authority of the philosopher king. In an individualistic world within which we recognize the subjectivity of value such an account of moral and political truth is impossible. In Buchanan's view we have to replace the idea of objective truth by that of consensus and agreement as he argues, for example, in *The Limits of Liberty.*[15]

So there are two questions for Buchanan: Is it possible to provide a coherent and compelling justification for a liberal political order against a background of avowed moral subjectivism? Buchanan's answer to the first question is 'yes' and we achieve this through contract. So what framework of law would be chosen by people who recognized that their own values and those of others are subjective? In Buchanan's view there is a close connection between moral subjectivism and the demand for unanimity in the contract. Why should I, with my own subjective point of view, agree to a set of rules whose only authority is that they represent the agreed, but subjective, views of others, but not mine? A non-unanimous contract would mean the imposition of one set of values on another person when there is no authority to these values outside of the contract, and to justify the contract to me it must be unanimous – I must agree to its terms like everyone else. This is clearly a very exacting standard but in Buchanan's view we are able to get quite a long way with it in reasoning about the basic legal order of a liberal society.

So, what do we mean by the basic legal order in this context? In Buchanan's view we have to make a distinction between basic rules or constitutional rules and the actions that are undertaken within those rules once agreed. He draws the analogy with games.[16] Games have a set of rules which define what that game is – they constitute the game. Particular moves within the game such as the particular movements of a rook, pawn, or bishop in chess are made in accordance with the rules if they are not false moves. An indefinitely large number of different games can be played within the rules while at the same time accepting that the pieces are moved in accordance with strict rules. Basic constitutional rules are like this. No doubt the rules of chess emerged in the favoured Hayekian way over time as the result of spontaneous activity with the rules becoming normative only after time. However, constitutional rules have to be given a justification acceptable to all via a unanimous contract. Unlike chess, where to play or not to play is a matter of choice and to ask whether chess itself rather than a particular move within the game is rational or not hardly makes sense, in the case of constitutional rules it is a vital question since all the members of a particular society have to live under the rules. In a world marked by moral subjectivism and individualism these rules can have moral authority over individuals only via the unanimity principle – the fact that they are freely chosen and consented to by everyone. What happens under the rules like the particular game of chess that is played is another matter although, as we shall see, Buchanan has clear ideas about what would be permissible against the background of the basic rules – namely that political action within a liberal set of constitutional rules should be confined to what he calls public or collective goods which cannot be provided by markets which he regards as embodiments of free and subjective choice. This post-constitutional or post-contractual state he sometimes calls the productive state. The job of the constitutional state is essentially protective – to protect individuals in terms of the rules they have unanimously agreed; the role of the productive state is to provide goods and services strictly within the rules agreed as the rules of the protective or constitutional order.

Part of Buchanan's case for the unanimity rule is related to two features of the basic constitutional rules: their generality and their permanence. A critic might argue that it would in fact be impossible to secure unanimity in the rules because individual's subjective interests will always get in the way and these are also likely to change over time. Take Buchanan's own example: as a milk producer, I might favour a rule which would secure a state subsidy for my milk; non-milk producers who are taxpayers would almost certainly disagree. Such a rule could not be a constitutional rule because it would not meet the requirements of unanimity. A constitutional rule would be a much more general one that for example might eliminate all political interference with prices. While adopting such a rule might seem to be against the milk producer's current interests this would not necessarily be the case if the general rule prevented all subsidies to which he or she too would have to contribute as a taxpayer. It might indeed be the case that given that tax would not have to be imposed to finance politically generated subsidies the milk producer might actually be better off under such arrangements than under ones where he was a recipient of one subsidy and a contributor for others. So the general nature of a constitutional rule is, in general, far less of a direct challenge to individual interests compared with a more specific rule. The same point applies to the permanence of rules. If constitutional rules are to be in place for a significant period of time and, as constitutional rules, it is difficult to see how they could fail to be, then the effect in the long term on an individual's interests is much more difficult to assess and, as such, may not be directly challenged by subjective interests or challenges to those interests when the rule is at the stage of adoption. They are, indeed, decided almost under a veil of ignorance about how over time they would or would not affect subjective interests. In this way, for Buchanan, the question of how unanimity in the choice about basic rules and their interaction with subjective interests is rather similar to Rawls' position.

So Buchanan argues that we have to distinguish between the case for basic constitutional rules and arguments about which policies should or should not be pursued within these rules by political action. The basis of the constitution is unanimity, and political action is legitimate only when it is compatible with such basic constitutional rules. Buchanan accepts that political action within unanimously agreed rules does not itself have to be sanctioned by unanimity. There is, in his view, a deep reason for this. Many of the goods to be provided within the productive state will be public goods, mechanisms, and rules to remedy market failures. Individuals from their own subjective point of view may well have reasons and, indeed, incentives for not contributing to the production of public goods and remedies for market failures. This is intrinsic to the idea of public goods. A public good is a good which is widely regarded as desirable – for example clean air or national defence. A public good, in addition, is a good that can only be produced by collective action and cooperation. At the same time the good cannot be partitioned, that is to say its benefits cannot be confined to those who either want it or cooperate in its production. Non-cooperators cannot be excluded from the benefits of the public good or may only be excluded at disproportionate expense. Because everyone may then have a subjective interest in not contributing since they cannot be excluded from the benefit, the scope of freeriding would be such that the market will not be able to produce such goods. Such goods, if widely enough desired, can only be produced by collective action outside the market, using coercion as a last resort – usually through the tax system. In a liberal order most goods will be produced and exchanged through the market and through free trade, but there are desired public goods and if unanimity fails, which it is almost certain to do, for the reasons given, then they have to be produced coercively. If there had to be unanimous agreement on public goods, then, despite being widely desired, they would not be produced. This might look to be utterly inconsistent with a constitutional order based on unanimity of the sort for which Buchanan argues. This is not in his view the case. If there are goods which are widely wanted and which free exchange and the market cannot produce, then in his view at the constitutional level it would make sense to introduce a rule, subject to the unanimity requirement, which would sanction a less-than-unanimous rule for the production of public goods so long as such goods met the strict criteria for their being public goods. Thus, in Buchanan's view there could perfectly well be a unanimously agreed rule at the constitutional level sanctioning less-than-unanimous agreement to the production of public goods. So given that the constitutional rules which bind the productive state will have the features of generality and permanence what will they be and what would in fact justify them? This is a very serious issue because these rules may well prevent democratic majorities in a liberal state from pursuing what they want to do. So the justification of constitutional rules has to be powerful enough to block such democratic claims and such a justification has to be consistent with moral subjectivism as Buchanan describes it. Buchanan's subjectivism will not allow him to adopt a consequentialist or telocratic view of the justification of constitutional rules. Any such consequentialist view will have to assume that there is some kind of valued outcome – greater social justice, greater social solidarity, greater social freedom, rights of various sorts, or the maximization of welfare – which is the job of constitutional rules to facilitate. This, however, implies that values such as these have some sort of objectivity or transpersonal moral cogency. If, however, morality is radically subjective, then this cannot be so. Buchanan argues, however, in *The Reasons of Rules* that a political order cannot and should not be seen as a means or an instrument to some sort of external end or goal of discovery. His point is clear and unambiguous:

> The state does not emerge to protect 'natural rights'. Nor does it reflect or represent the working out of some cosmic force, some will of God or gods. More important, the state does not exist as an organic entity independent of the individuals in a polity. The state does not act as such, and it cannot seek its own ends or objectives. Social welfare cannot be defined independently since, as such, it cannot exist.[17]

So justice, for example, is not to be understood as a moral requirement antecedent to agreed consensual rules, acting as a constraint to an agreement to a possible set of constitutional rules. That would be to import into the fundamental constitutional structure a moral ideal of a particular sort for which some kind of moral authority is claimed prior to the process of consensual agreement over rules being reached. This is inconsistent with Buchanan's subjectivism. Rather, justice has to be seen as the *product* of rules not the moral *precursor* to rules. It is, as Buchanan argues, not justice that can be seen to provide an independent norm on the basis of which a set of rules might be constructed. In a situation of moral subjectivism it is only unanimous consensus building that can in fact perform this role. It is consensus that performs the basic normative function. As Buchanan puts the point, rules set the terms of justice, not the reverse. This leads to a very important point about the rule of law as a moral ideal from Buchanan's perspective. There could be many sorts of rules that could be created out of unanimous consensual agreement and therefore different understandings of justice internal to such rules. This means that justice has to be understood *contextually*. There cannot be an abstract and universal ideal of justice to underpin the idea of the rule of law detached from any contextually based set of rules which give a particular conception of justice its meaning and justification. It follows that such an ideal cannot be used as some kind of Archimedean point from which to evaluate the justice or otherwise of particular sets of rules agreed on a constitutional basis for a given political order.

Given these anti-consequentialist and anti-telocratic points it might be thought that Buchanan is in rather a quandary. If he cannot appeal to some kind of moralized end state as a justification for a set of rules, what is it then that justifies them? He has already ruled out Hayek's response to this question in terms of a theory of evolution of rules. So what function do such rules play and how can we understand their function in non-telocratic terms?

Perhaps the best way of understanding Buchanan's response to this is to say that constitutional rules provide, in particular contexts, prudential responses to basic issues in what might be thought of as 'the human condition'. He argues that a pre-constitutional form of anarchy would have a very great deal to commend it from an individualist and subjectivist perspective because a person would be free to act as he or she desired only subject to possible conflict with others and would be free to possess holdings and possessions of all sorts as the objects of desire with no limits on acquisition at this pre-constitutional stage. Equally there would be no limits to trade and exchange if such acts were seen to be of mutual advantage.

Nevertheless, in Buchanan's view, there would undoubtedly be conflicts between persons over possessions and property. He rejects any kind of romantic version of anarchism which assumes either a natural harmony between the desires of persons or, for that matter, assumes a very high degree of altruism so that conflicts would not arise. We would have to struggle and fight for our own private spaces to follow our own desires and interests in such a world. Unanimously agreed rules are the way out of this situation. But the fact remains for Buchanan that we live in a morally anarchic world in which values are subjective and the only set of rules or norms that could have legitimacy in such a world are those that are unanimously agreed. Given this moral subjectivism, the set of basic rules – subject to contextual variation, will define both the scope and the boundaries of the private spaces within which we can act freely. This means that for Buchanan, whatever the variations may be, the rules will essentially be about the protection of negative liberty: liberty as freedom from coercion. Freedom in this sense, in Buchanan's view, can be regarded as somehow fundamental and morally neutral between different conceptions of value. It is by being free from coercion or negatively free that I am able to pursue whatever my conception of the good may be from my own subjective point of view.

Does this imply that Buchanan is then arguing that basic or constitutional rules do in fact have a substantive telocratic justification, namely the protection of negative freedom? Does not this break his own constraints on importing subjective value into the justification of political arrangements? Surely the facilitation of negative liberty is as goal directed as any telocratic aim? The most obvious response to this would be to argue that negative freedom is not a moralized condition. It is not itself a substantive value and therefore part of the world of moral subjectivism. A is free if he or she is free from the coercion of B who might otherwise coerce him into doing what he would otherwise not do or into not doing what he otherwise would do. This situation, it might be argued, is wholly empirical and non-moralized. Therefore, on this view, if private space is to protect negative liberty, it is to protect a realm which is not in itself moralized, although what we do within the space thus constituted will in fact be moralized since it is the private space within which we pursue our subjectively chosen ends.

This claim will be subject to further examination and analysis later in the book. But there is a second point on which Buchanan puts even more weight. This is the claim that negative liberty is not like one value among others and subject, therefore, to different subjective interpretations and controversies, but is rather part of what is in fact entailed by individualism and subjectivism which, as we have seen, Buchanan regards as central to the understanding of the human condition in modernity. The argument goes as follows. If there are no agreed values to constrain individuals, then the individual in this anarchical position is negatively free in that situation. It is because of the inconveniences of the conflicts that arise between negatively free persons that we need consensually agreed rules to constrain negative liberty. So in this sense negative freedom is part of the conceptual structure used to characterize the anarchical world prior to constitutional rules. It is not some specific and controversial value among others but part of what individualism and subjectivism entail. Thus, in Buchanan's view to see the reasons for rules as dealing with this pre-constitutional anarchy and as a prudential reaction to the situation created by individualism, subjectivism, and unlimited negative liberty is not to invoke some sort of thick telological justification.

We now need to consider a further aspect of Buchanan's argument about constitutional agreement, namely the link between such a unanimous agreement and Pareto optimality. In the example of trade between two people, a free trade between them would be Pareto optimal because in moving from situation A (the pre-trade situation) to B (the post-trade situation) at least one person would be better off and neither would be worse off, otherwise such a unanimous trade would not have taken place. In Buchanan's view, constitutional agreement closely mimics the trading example. There is an intimate relationship, in his view, between unanimity and Pareto optimality under which situation *X* is to be preferred to situation *Y* if in the move from *Y* to *X* at least one person becomes better off and no one is made worse off. If there is the prudential need to create constitutional arrangements to define the space within which individuals are negatively free to act, then such arrangements are Pareto optimal. Each person engages in the agreement because, as a unanimous agreement, no one is worse off and the assumption is that for any individual he or she would be better off under a constitution than they would be under anarchy and certainly not worse off. Therefore, given Buchanan's austere idea of eschewing any moral basis for the contract other than unanimity, we have to ask the question as to whether or not Pareto optimality itself embodies morally controversial assumptions because, if it does, then it would undermine Buchanan's idea that the basic constitutional contract could be seen as morally neutral.

In this context there is a standard argument due to Rowley and Peacock in *Welfare Economics: A Liberal Restatement*[18] and Rothbard in *The Ethics of Liberty*[19] that in fact Pareto optimality does involve an implicit moral endorsement of the status quo, since a move from the status quo *Y* to new position *X* would always be difficult to arrive at under unanimity. So, for example, if existing property rights would be recognized under a constitution, as they would be for Buchanan, then it would be highly likely that an attempt under a social democratic regime to move to what it regarded as a more just distribution of resources would not be Pareto optimal since while some people would be made better off, the existing property owners would be made worse off. Buchanan's answer to this sort of Pareto default position in favour of the status quo is in terms of his critique of end state values. The proposed move from the status quo is justified in terms of an end state value such as social justice and we have seen why he is opposed to that. At the same time the status quo is not defended because it embodies some end state value such as a morally based view of the importance of property rights. The status quo in terms of rights is justified, if it is, because it embodies unanimity; equally a move away from the status quo would also have to reflect unanimity and this unanimity, if it is arrived at in either case, has to be through a consensual agreement between people using their own subjective judgements and not grounded in claims about end state values. So the status quo is not valued because it embodies an end state set of principles, nor is the move away from it. If we are to be true to individualism and subjectivism, the only question at the constitutional level is whether the move from *Y* to *X* is or is not Pareto optimal, or at least superior, for each person considered individually. Or to put the point in the same way as Buchanan sees it: Is it unanimous?[20] The individual and his or her subjective point of view is privileged both epistemically and morally for Buchanan and this underpins both the unanimity rule at the constitutional level and his use of Pareto optimality. In his view from these assumptions a basic constitutional order can emerge although, as he says it, may take different forms in different contexts. Again there is in his view a deep reason for this.

Obviously, given his strictures on the predilection of philosophers to act as philosopher kings, given that for him there is no 'truth' outside of agreement and given that justice is internal to a given set of agreed rules, it would be wholly paradoxical were Buchanan to try to specify in any detail the types of rules to be agreed. Nevertheless he does believe that rational contracting parties seeking to achieve unanimity over basic rules would in fact fix upon a mix of different sorts of constitutional rules. These are as follows:

1. Limits on the behaviour of any person in relation to any other. If there were no such limitations, then the contractual agreement would not in fact take us beyond anarchy. Such rules will define the scope of mutual non-coercion and as basic rules rooted in unanimity they would be legitimately enforceable.
2. A set of basic constitutional rules will define rights over stocks of goods and personal endowments and skills. These are central features of a person's liberty which constitutional rules are supposed to preserve. In anarchy, I may 'own' various sorts of external goods through either acquisition or trade. As a free person I shall require, as will everyone else, agreements to protect my rights to what I have acquired up to that point since the advent of a constitutional order will provide the legal framework of subsequent forms of acquisition, exchange, trade, contract, and the like. This point links back to the issue of Pareto optimality in that the pattern of property ownership prior to constitutional rules is not defended by Buchanan because it embodies some desirable end state but rather because those forms of property are owned by individuals who have used their individual liberties at the pre-constitutional level to come to possess whatever they do possess. They cannot be dispossessed of them because some basic principle of justice has been infringed and because there is no such principle prior to agreement. If there is to be a move away from such protected forms of ownership it has to be *via* unanimous agreement. Similarly, as a free person, I will require an agreement which protects not just my assets but my endowments in my person – my abilities and the like so that they are guaranteed to be seen as my own rather than as some sort of collective asset to be used in the pursuit of some kind of end state such as social justice.
3. A constitutional contract as well as placing mutually agreed limits on behaviour and securing the rights of ownership must also set out the terms and conditions of enforcement, namely the operation and the limits of the protective state established by unanimity as the enforcement agent.

4. The final point of the mix has to do with the productive state sanctioned and brought into being by the protective or constitutional state. To put the point more conventionally, part of the contract will have to do with the limits on constitutional government. The productive state will be concerned with the production and the financing of public goods including the law and remedies for market failures where market or non-governmental solutions are not available. Buchanan argues that such rules will include:
   (i) A clear account of the allowable range over which collective action may take place.
   (ii) Restrictions in the type of goods that may be collectively produced.
   (iii) A dividing line between the public and private aspects of the economy.
   (iv) The circumstances under which it is allowed to move from unanimity in the production of public goods and remedies for market failure.

While it is possible in Buchanan's view to set these broad parameters, and indeed to argue for the efficiency of certain types of rules, he cannot go further partly because, as we have seen, he believes that context, circumstance, and environment play a large part in determining what type of rules will be agreed, but primarily because of his belief that such rules cannot be set down by philosophical fiat. Unanimity is the key to the establishment of rules not the philosopher generalizing his or her own subjective values.[21]

All of these rules leave the issue of what practical importance Buchanan's theory might be thought to have in terms of looking at and evaluating existing societies and their constitutional orders. In this sort of context Buchanan argues that we have to focus on a set of issues:

1. Does the constitutional order embody a set of rules that could have been agreed by all under conditions of unanimity or do the rules seem to favour one group identified in terms of religion, culture, gender, ethnicity, or whatever? This has nothing to do with endorsing an end state principle in Buchanan's view – for example, multiculturalism – but rather has everything to do with what unanimity could plausibly be regarded as requiring.
2. Is there a clear demarcation between basic constitutional rules on the one hand and normal politics and public policy formation on the other?
3. At the constitutional level, are the rights to be protected based on negative liberty, which, as we have seen, is closely involved in the idea of subjectivism and individualism?
4. Is collective action in a given state limited to the provision of public goods and the remedying of market failure?
5. Is the fundamental legitimacy of the state seen to depend on the mutual agreement of free people rather than on religious, ideological, or philosophical positions which ultimately reflect the choices of a limited number of citizens and which have no authority over those who reject them?

Thus, for Buchanan, the economic market which is, in a sense, the institutional embodiment of value subjectivism, requires a constitutional order and indeed his approach is sometimes called 'constitutional economics'. A liberal political order knits together a constitutional order sustained by the agreement of free individuals, while the market provides a framework for the free play of voluntary and subjective preference. It has to be said, however, that he is not at all high-minded about how a change from an existing order to a more liberal one might be effected. It does, of course, have to embody unanimity but that can be achieved not just, for example, by reasoning about it or for that matter applying a negative test to existing laws as Hayek advocated in respect of the principle of universalizability. Rather he thought that unanimity might come through negotiations that could include compromise, side payments, compensation, bribes, exchange, and trade-offs![22] These sorts of processes are not usually associated with neo-liberal conceptions of politics but for Buchanan the important thing is in fact the achievement of unanimity by voluntary rather than coercive means and all the means mentioned are voluntary and may therefore be admitted as legitimate.

ROBERT NOZICK: LIBERALISM AND RIGHTS

For Buchanan the foundations of a liberal constitutional order are to be found in unanimous agreement not in being based on some kind of philosophical foundation. Those who are parties to a unanimous constitutional agreement may well come to agree on what rights should be protected by the constitution and upon the nature of claims to justice and the scope of coercion. These values, however, emerge from the nature of the agreement itself. They do not act as antecedent constraints on the sort of agreement that might be concluded. The agreement does not track a set of objective values nor is it based upon them. This, however, is precisely not true of Robert Nozick whose work has exercised a great influence on the development of liberal political thought over the past thirty years. Nozick is in a way as much of a contractarian as Buchanan (and thus in contrast to Hayek), but for Nozick there is one central value that is prior to and provides the fundamental constraint on the nature and role of contract and this is the idea of rights. Rights, for Nozick, are fundamental, absolute, and basic and the scope of the state is to be circumscribed by agreements about how to protect these basic rights. The argument is clear and forthright:

> Individuals have rights, and there are things no person or group may do to them (without violating their rights). So strong and far reaching are these rights that they may raise the question of what, if anything, the state and its officials may do. . . . our main conclusions about the role of the state are that a minimal state, limited to the narrow functions of protection against force, theft, fraud, enforcement of contracts and so on is justified.[23]

The state has legitimacy only if it protects and secures basic rights and acts in accordance with such rights. It does not legitimately serve any end state, goal, or purpose such as social justice or social solidarity or, for that matter increased material wealth, and for Nozick rights are not in any sense end state principles or telocratic principles. Nozick's view about the nature and scope of rights will be considered in Chapter 5 in the context of a discussion of neo-liberal ideas about rights more generally. What will be the focus for the moment will be his argumentative strategy in trying to secure the basis for a neo-liberal nomocratic state protecting basic rights and limited government.

Nozick's strategy might be understood in the following way: it embodies a kind of internal critique of anarchism with the claim emerging from that critique of the view that a limited government is necessary for rights protection; a critique of a more extensive state with particular emphasis on a critique of a redistributive state, that is to say one pursuing social justice as an end state; a critique of a state designed to meet basic needs; and a critique of a state providing for the embodiment of some kind of substantive religious, cultural, or moral ideal.

So, if Nozick regards rights as fundamental, what is the case for those rights and why do those rights entail a state that is an advance on anarchy but also entails a state which is categorically different from one pursuing some specific end? Why do rights entail a nomocratic rather than a telocratic state? The question of the justification of rights is basic here because there is a need to meet the challenge of Buchanan that to regard some particular moral conception such as rights as foundational is incompatible with what flows from the idea of the subjective nature of value.

It has to be said that Nozick could have set out his arguments in favour of the basic right to inviolability in a more direct and clearer way and he has been accused as the result of his failure to do so of formulating a liberalism without foundations – that is to say for invoking a foundational principle, namely rights, but failing to provide a strong moral case for these postulated rights. Again some of the issues here will be treated more fully later, but for the moment, it might be argued that this view of Nozick is, in fact, rather harsh and that there are in fact two basic arguments presented in favour of the right to inviolability which he invokes. One is positive the other negative but both arguments are linked in their rather different ways to the idea of the separateness of persons which Nozick regards as the crucial idea underpinning his case for a right to individual inviolability.

The positive argument is that there are in the world only individuals with their own individual ends or goals or purposes. Pursuing these goals gives point and meaning to the lives of individuals. There is no objective or antecedent background whether moral, religious, or metaphysical which can provide this meaning. It is down to individuals to give their own lives meaning and they do this in pursuing what they regard as valued goals. So far it might be thought that Nozick's position is very similar to that of Buchanan in which both recognize that the question of value is ultimately subjective. Nozick, however, wants to go on and draw a substantive moral conclusion from this which is foundational to his view of rights and the minimal state, namely that the separateness of existence and the values which people subjectively hold mean that they should be treated as inviolable – that things should not be done to them without their consent. It is certainly wrong to interfere with someone else's life based upon some kind of end state value – political, moral, or cultural – with which an individual may well disagree. Such interference is legitimate only if it is subject to the consent of the individual and this is what a right to inviolability means.

The negative account of rights depends on the claim that any attempt to coerce a person (to impose on or to interfere with him or her without his or her consent) depends on end state social values like social justice, social or cultural solidarity, and religious loyalty or religious identity. For Nozick such end state principles have no collective moral legitimacy. Of course, an individual in pursuit of his or her own values may endorse end state values of their own and choose to join groups which seek to embody in the life and behaviour of the group whatever the goal or purpose of the group may be. However, such end state values have no broad social and political legitimacy such that they can be invoked to interfere with someone without that person's consent. It is morally illegitimate to impose on an individual duties and obligations to which he or she has not consented in the name of end state values with spurious legitimacy in that they do not reflect the values of all the individuals in a society and which give those individuals a sense of meaning in their lives. Hence, the idea of the separateness of persons and their value provides the negative case for the fundamental nature of a right to inviolability.

For Nozick rights impose side constraints on others. That is to say constraints on their actions. I am free to exercise my freedom so long as in so doing I do not infringe the basic rights of others to inviolability. Nozick sees a close link between his account of inviolability and the Kantian idea of respect for persons, that each person should be treated as an end in himself or herself and not as a means to the ends of others.[24] Given that, the imposition of an end state set of values on me when I disagree with such values is in fact to treat me as a means to the ends or goals of others. So, on Nozick's view, the principle of inviolability and the basic rights that flow from it is another way of talking about the fundamental principle of respect for persons but this principle derives, for Nozick, from the fundamental separateness of persons and the subjective nature of their values. Hence, there is both a similarity and a big difference between Buchanan and Nozick. They both agree on the separateness of persons and the subjectivity of value, and they both agree on the illegitimacy of the enforcement of end state values. However, for Nozick, unlike for Buchanan, this can lead directly to the claim that there can be a foundational principle for political morality, namely rights to inviolable treatment; whereas for Buchanan rights and justice arise from rules which in turn emerge through unanimous agreements at the level of constitutional deliberation.

In the case of Nozick it follows that the rule of law is concerned with the protection of basic rights. This is the fundamental function of both the state and the law. Legal rules which go beyond this and seek to impose end state-based principles and policies deriving from such principles fall outside the rule of law. So while Nozick's account of the basis of a liberal constitutional order is very different from that of both Hayek and Buchanan, what they share in common is the commitment to the close link between the rule of law and a nomocratic order and they all see the rule of law as a moral ideal which only some systems of positive law will in fact embody, namely those of liberal states with strongly limited governments.

So what does the protection of rights actually mean in practice for Nozick? The first thing to be said is that he does not believe that anarchy can in fact provide sufficient rights protection. While it may be true that in an anarchical situation individuals could either bind themselves together into protective associations or they could voluntarily choose to employ private security firms to protect their rights, Nozick argues that in fact the dynamic of this situation will lead to the emergence of a dominant protection association in a geographical area and that this is to all intents and purposes the same as the state which according to the classical Weberian definition has a monopoly of violence and coercive power in its territory. The fundamental reason why the dominant protection association will emerge and serve the same function as the state is that for individuals the main thing at stake in anarchy is the protection of their individual rights. If protection associations compete in providing such protection and one does it more effectively than others (and it is difficult to see that over time there would be more than one in a specific geographical area), then every individual has an overwhelming interest at stake in joining the most successful protection association offering protection for rights. Hence, there is a dynamic at work which will lead people with a basic interest in the protection of their rights to voluntarily choose the protection offered by the dominant association and there are good reasons for thinking that such a body is in fact a state.[25] So for Nozick anarchy is not in fact a stable framework within which individuals could in fact enjoy their rights or be treated inviolably.

Individuals are inviolable and this right to inviolability places side constraints on the actions of others and on the individual concerned. This means that an individual has a moral right to free action so long as exercising this freedom does not infringe the similar rights of all others. Part of this free action will involve coming to own property and so a liberal constitutional order has to provide a clear basis for the ways in which property rights could be exercised without infringing the inviolability or the rights of others. In Nozick's view this requires an account of justice in acquisition – in the first ownership of material and other sorts of goods and then subsequently justice in transfer – that is to say the transfer of goods to others through economic exchange, voluntary gift, or bequest. Nozick gives an account of justice in acquisition that he believes is consistent with preserving the rights of others who might be thought to be disadvantaged by such acquisition. The issue of justice in transfer is essentially about the processes whereby transfer and exchange can be affected by voluntary and non-coercive means.

The important point at this stage of the argument of this book is that essentially Nozick's account of justice in respect of exercising rights is a procedural one. Justice is not about implementing some end state set of principles which could very well infringe inviolability if this implementation was done coercively, that is to say without consent. Rather justice is about the rules for mutual non-coercion and these rules are embodied in the basic legal principles of a liberal constitutional order. Any alternative to this through, for example, a social democratic distributive state, would not only appeal to illegitimate end state principles but would also in a sense deny the separateness of persons. It assumes that society is some kind of entity which can have ends, goals, and purposes of its own, and also a good of its own (a common good) which justifies imposing non-consensual rules on individuals and in so doing denying the importance of the values which give a sense of meaning to individual lives.

It is very important to see how thoroughgoing Nozick's rejection of telocratic approaches to politics is. As we have seen this is a feature of both Hayek and Buchanan (although as we saw there are very distinct wobbles in Hayek over this). Nozick is, however, very thoroughgoing in respect of this issue. For him the crucial point is that the state is there to protect basic rights and it has no legitimate function beyond that. Thus, the crucial question to ask about a liberal constitutional order is whether it does protect those rights. What ends individuals then pursue alone or with others is not a matter of political or legal concern so long as in pursuing these goals individuals or voluntary groups respect the side constraints that the rights of others place on their behaviour. It is definitely not part of Nozick's fundamental argument that a liberal legal order which protects property rights and free exchange in markets will make us better off than we would be, for example, under socialism or social democracy. If this proved true for Nozick, a society A which protected basic rights would be preferable to society B which did not but was materially far richer. In a sense for Nozick this is a wholly academic question (in the bad sense) because he accepts arguments from Hayek and others that markets and entrepreneurship will in fact help us to cope more effectively with our environments than any alternative, but there is nothing in his theory to say that once a constitutional order has been established individuals will in fact choose to act in entrepreneurial and utility maximizing ways. These are choices to be made by individuals. The only constraint is the procedural one of respecting the rights of others and the side constraints that flow from that. So, in a way, Nozick would have some sympathy for Oakeshott's criticism of Hayek for seeking, at least in part, to justify a nomocratic order on the grounds that it would make us better off. While Oakeshott would deplore the rather ahistorical rationalism of Nozick, nevertheless they do share the view that the fundamental justification of a nomocratic order cannot rely on the implicit importation of some overall goal or purpose such as greater material wealth.

MURRAY ROTHBARD AND NATURAL LAW

We shall now turn to the work of Murray Rothbard. The emphasis will be on what might be called argumentative strategy at this stage. The aim is to get some grip on his overall argument in favour of a liberal, or from his perspective, a libertarian or anarchist conception of the rule of law and what would ground such a conception of the rule of law. The central element of Rothbard's justificatory strategy is his utilization of the doctrines of natural law as a basic foundation for his ideas on the rule of law and politics. Indeed, it could be argued that in a weak and very general sense most liberal thinkers who write about the rule of law as an ideal in fact appeal to the idea of natural law – to a set of objective and shared values which the rule of law should ideally embody. We should not be at all surprised about this, as some of the central founding fathers of liberal political thought and most notably John Locke have in fact rested their liberalism on natural law. Nevertheless we can see why many liberals today do not immediately think of an affinity between liberalism and natural law, as for example Christopher Wolfe has pointed out in his *Natural Law Liberalism*.[26] The reason is that many contemporary liberals start from assumptions about either moral pluralism or moral subjectivism – the view that people differ significantly in their personal conceptions of the good and, as we have seen, a thinker like Buchanan has been able to erect a whole theory on this basis. However, natural law thinkers stress the idea that there are in fact objective goods and bads and that an account can be given of the objective goods for human life which will facilitate human flourishing and of a form of politics to embody the conditions for the achievement of such goods. One other reason why many contemporary liberals have been wary of looking to natural law for foundational principles for liberal politics is that natural law is often thought to require in its turn a metaphysical or religious view to underpin it. Such views for a thinker such as Buchanan are just as controversial and our beliefs in them are just as subjective as any other in a modern society. Rothbard, however, would defend his view of natural law as not making stringent demands in terms of its own foundations and yet providing a more secure foundation for a liberal or libertarian position than for example Hayek's evolutionary approach, Buchanan's moral subjectivism or Nozick's foundationless rights or for that matter any 'system' utilitarian basis for liberalism which as we have seen, on occasion, Hayek himself invokes.[27] In Rothbard's view natural law is discoverable by *reason* and he is quite able to cite theological defenders of natural law preeminent amongst whom is Aquinas who argues the same thing. For Aquinas certainly the natural law was capable of being found *via* faith and revelation but it could equally well be found *via* reason.

The problem here, though, is that in modernity, and particularly after the critique of David Hume, reason has been confined to a purely *instrumental* role. The idea here is that the ends, goals, and goods of human life are chosen by individuals, basing such choices on their desires, passions, and emotions; they are not discovered by the exercise of reason. The role of reason is that, given these subjectively chosen ends, what are the most efficient means of achieving such ends? Ends are, in a sense, expressive and reason is instrumental to the attainment of ends chosen by non-rational means. Given that for natural law thinkers ends could be established by reason one can see quite easily how Hume's argument has been seen to be fatal to the assumptions of natural law by post-Humean critics.

As Rothbard points out, Hume's philosophy was held to be fatal to natural law theories not just for his account of the instrumental role of reason but also because of his argument in favour of the fact-value dichotomy.[28] Here the argument is that since no normative conclusions (statements about what *ought* to be the case) can follow from purely factual premises, there is a fatal flaw at the heart of natural law because the goods allegedly discovered by reason in natural law theory will in fact be inferred (fallaciously according to Hume) from a set of factual premises about our nature as human beings.

From the natural law perspective, however, there can be a rational basis for discovering what sorts of goals and purposes will lead to human flourishing and fulfilment and this will depend on finding out about our own natures. We can arrive at a rationally grounded set of human goods from an understanding of the elements of our own nature. Again, pluralistic and subjectivist thinkers will reject the idea that there is some kind of basic unchangeable core to human nature which is sufficiently rich and uncontroversial to provide a basis for an account of distinctive human goods. Either our account of human nature in order to be non-controversial will have to be too general or thin to support a set of thick and elaborated human goods; or if it can support such a set, then the account of human nature on which it is supposed to rest will itself be too contested and controversial to be a secure foundation for any normative structure. An example will make this point clearer. We might all agree, for example, that it is part of our nature to have certain sorts of needs, wants, desires, and interests and that, as such, these might be regarded as natural. However, from the mere factual listing of these features nothing of normative significance can follow (for the Humean) not only because of the fact-value dichotomy, but also because in order to derive an account of human goods even assuming that this was possible, it would be necessary to put such needs or desires or wants or interests into some kind of hierarchy – that some are more important than others. Given such a hierarchy, then it might be possible to draw out normative conclusions which might be thick enough to have some practical import, but this is possible only because we think that the ranking of the characteristics of our nature is in some sense obvious and uncontroversial – which is untrue since it would be extremely controversial. Secondly, in producing such a hierarchy or ranking we would almost certainly be using some kinds of moral assumptions so that in fact moral values enter not as a *conclusion* to determining our nature and what we need to flourish given the sort of people that we are, but would enter into the ordering of an account of our nature itself. This would certainly mean that we could derive moral conclusions from such an account of our nature but only because moral *premises* have been built into the account of human nature from which the conclusions have been drawn.[29] So, for example, we might well agree that such and such a need is part of our nature and that its satisfaction is urgent but we will not necessarily agree that the urgency of its satisfaction is morally more important than some other need or interest or desire which would have to be sacrificed to meet this urgent need. If we argued that the urgency itself was of some intrinsic moral importance, thus making its satisfaction more important than these other desires or interests or needs, then we would have already imported moral values into our account of what is supposed to be a factual account of our nature. In this way natural law is thought to be intensely problematic particularly for liberals who not only favour but in some cases want to build their own theories of liberalism on a basis of moral subjectivism.

Rothbard rejects such criticisms and he clearly believes that natural law has to be foundational for liberalism. However, our main interest at the moment is his argumentative strategy and so far it is rooted in this contentious claim that we can arrive at a view of the rational good for humankind by reflecting on human nature – its powers and capacities. As such, Rothbard regards natural law theory as being intrinsically radical because natural law gives us a set of rationally founded values in terms of which we can judge any status quo or prevailing state of affairs.[30]

He argues that the idea of natural law is allied to that of natural rights and this is so partly in relation to the idea of liberty. In a Robinson Crusoe type of situation where a person is abstracted from other persons and social networks it would be part of the nature of that person to have a sense of his or her absolute freedom – if by freedom we understand freedom from interference rather than power and capacity which are obviously limited by nature.[31] Crusoe is, however, free in an absolute sense in that there is literally no one to coerce him. He, therefore, also has freedom over his own body and the goods which he has come to possess during his time on the desert island. This follows from the same understanding of the nature of freedom (which is a theme of Chapter 3). So freedom in a pre-social sense – free of links to social networks – implies a freedom to do whatever I want to do and to come to possess whatever I want to possess. In Rothbard's view an individual in these circumstances will also learn some of the facts about external nature – about the character of the natural objects and creatures with whom he shares the island and will utilize such knowledge in his own exercise of freedom. He will also learn things of a more general nature – that with regard to some sorts of consumption goods he will have to produce before he can consume. In these circumstances an individual will come to know his own nature and how that nature relates to the world and one of the fundamental aspects of that is a sense of the basic nature of freedom or liberty.[32] So for Rothbard the next important question is what difference does interaction with others make to this one-person analysis? For Rothbard the most fundamental aspect of human interaction in relation to natural law is the realization that talents and attributes are unevenly distributed and therefore that one can achieve far more of one's own ends by exchange than one could by pursuing one's own talents and attributes alone. Secondly, one realizes that natural resources are not evenly distributed either, so being located in one geographical area rather than another one can increase the capacity for varied consumption by exchange. In both cases these are natural facts or as he would prefer to say natural laws about the human situation which combined with the idea of freedom as freedom from coercion indicates the fundamental importance of free exchange – free in the sense of uncoerced exchange. It is also part of this natural set of laws that it is to each individual's benefit to concentrate on what he or she is relatively good at. I may be good at both *X* and *Y* but I can gain more if I concentrate on *X* rather than

Y and concentrate on exchanging my surplus *X* for some of the *Y* that you produce. This is the basis for Ricardo's Law of Comparative Advantage,[33] which means that in a system of free exchange or what Rawls calls a system of natural liberty,[34] the strong do not in fact crush the weak because the weaker will be able to exchange with the stronger, and also because it is in the interests of both parties to do so. In this sort of situation we are able to do far more by way of exchange than we could ever achieve each by himself or herself. It also follows for Rothbard that it is not just individual goods that are being exchanged but rather property rights. I have property rights in my *X* – let us say the fish that I have caught; I exchange with you and you have property rights in your wheat which you exchange with me. So a market is not just an exchange of goods but of property rights.[35] This same simplified model can also explain the emergence of a medium of exchange – money or its equivalent – just because it facilitates the growth of exchange and the satisfaction of wants. Rothbard goes on in the same sort of way to explain the emergence of the capitalist. The main point about all of this narrative is that it provides a schematic explanation of the spontaneous emergence of the elements of freedom, property, a free market, free exchange, the division of labour, and the social relationships of capitalism. This is important for Rothbard because it shows in his view that in a state of natural liberty none of the goods to be consumed were 'distributed' by some sort of agency – the state typically – but rather emerged spontaneously out of the natural circumstances and opportunities of human life. There is, therefore, for Rothbard a sort of rational narrative[36] that can be told about this which does reflect the natural law or the natural circumstances of human life and the opportunities which people with our natures as we can rationally know them will in fact create out of these circumstances.[37]

In Rothbard's view, it is perfectly possible, given the right circumstances, to think and to have absolute freedom in society. The reason for this is that we should not think say of a rule which prevents one person from invading the property of another as a restriction of freedom understood as the absence of coercion because what is being limited is not the person's freedom but his power of action: '[I]f we define freedom again as the absence of invasion by another man of any man's person or property, the fatal confusion of freedom and power is at last laid to rest.' For Rothbard, our powers are always limited by nature and by other men, and this fact is part of the natural circumstances of human life and of the natural law, but constraints on power are fundamentally different from constraints on freedom. Rothbard himself draws the conclusion from his argument that his view of freedom, exchange, and the rest is in fact only compatible with an anarcho-capitalist type of economic order where that order will arise spontaneously and will be neither be brought into being, sustained, or protected by the state, but to look into that alternative for the moment would take us too far afield. What is important for Rothbard in relation to a book on neo-liberalism is that for him the free market, freedom, rights, property, and free exchange have a rational basis and are in accordance with our nature and thus constitute a rational set of goods for human life. His view is that they may be best secured by an anarcho-capitalist society but it would be open to a liberal who was convinced of the need for some kind of rationalist foundation for liberalism to stop short of that point in Rothbard's argument and to claim alternatively that there can be a rule of law in a liberal society which acts to facilitate these goods which are not just a matter of personal choice or of unanimous agreement but rather reflect in a rational way the natural circumstances of human life. One of Rothbard's interesting arguments about the rule of law is in fact to endorse Randy Barnett's critique of Fuller's conception of the rule of law. Barnett argues that Fuller, while recognizing the importance of the idea of the rule of law in *The Morality of Law* did not go far enough and if he had gone further would in fact have pointed up the fundamental contradiction between the role of the state and the rule of law. Fuller argued that the rule of law means that the state should stick to the procedural rules in formulating and promulgating law. This is what the *Rechtsstaat* means: a state that follows its own procedural rules and does not stray beyond them or seek to rule outside of them. It is a state under the law or constrained by law. Barnett, however, argues that Fuller should have gone much further and argued that the rule of law means that the state should be governed by the *substance* of its own laws not just by its own procedures. The rub here is this for Barnett and Rothbard: the state in terms of substantial law will have many laws protecting property from removal by force and without consent and yet in taxation the state uses its coercive power to remove property from people which they undoubtedly own by coercion and without their consent. The state cannot therefore live in accordance with the principles embodied within its own substantial laws and this is what Rothbard calls the inner contradiction of the state.[38] Given that neo-liberals favour the idea of a *Rechtsstaat*, this is a major challenge. Can a *Rechtsstaat* only ever be a formal one, being constrained by its own procedural rules or could a *Rechtsstaat* ever be a substantial one acting within its own laws and the basic principles on which those laws are predicated? This is a basic challenge to neo-liberals. Rothbard thinks that it cannot be met and he takes the anarcho-capitalist option. The answer has to lie in the idea of legitimate coercion which will have two aspects: the first is that coercion is applied consistently with the rule of law and according to general rules; more substantially, though, will be the account of what constitutes legitimate coercion with the emphasis on legitimacy. An answer to what is legitimate coercion will require us to look into the whole range of neo-liberal political and legal theory because the exercise of coercion will be rendered legitimate if and only if it serves legitimate purposes and this takes us to the heart of the neo-liberal theory of what the state is for and how such function or functions can be justified.

LUDWIG VON MISES: AGENCY AND PRAXEOLOGY

The final thinker whose work I want to discuss in this chapter on the foundations of the rule of law as a moral ideal is Ludwig von Mises who is one of the foremost twentieth-century neo-liberal thinkers. His book *Human Action: A Treatise on Economics*[39] is one of the foundational texts for modern forms of neo-liberalism. Von Mises is also one of the most methodologically self-conscious of neo-liberal thinkers, so part of this discussion will focus on methodological issues and part on matters of substance. Mises takes what he calls a praxeological approach to issues of political and legal thought and particularly to economics. He is rather scathing about both jurisprudential and political science approaches to the issues we have been discussing so far and argues strongly for the superiority of the praxeological approach. The basic category in his account is that of human action, and praxeology is the science of the means to be engaged in pursuing the ends of human action whatever they may turn out to be. He agrees, for example, with Buchanan that the ends of human action are subjective and that no one can substitute his or her judgement for that of anyone else in relation to the ends, goals, or purposes of an individual's life. He rejects the idea that all human action is directed at some kind of overall goal – happiness or welfare or whatever. In Mises' view this is not the case. Human action is undertaken to remedy some subjectively perceived unease in life.[40] There can be no general theory of that unease which would provide some kind of generic account of basic reasons for action. The unease is personal and specific and individuals act to remedy the unease whatever it may happen to be. Sometimes they are successful in removing the unease through their actions, sometimes they are not. Praxeology is the science of means – that is to say of the means used in action to achieve some subjectively determined end. It is not and cannot be a science of ends. There cannot be a normative science if ends are determined by individual subjective choice. There can, however, be a science of means to these self-chosen ends. However, this is not to be regarded as an empirical science in the standard sense. Rather praxeology consists in a set of what philosophers call 'synthetic a priori propositions', that is to say propositions which are necessarily true but which also tell us important truths about the world. In making this case, Mises was arguing against the prevailing logical positivism of his day. Positivists argued that there were in fact no synthetic a priori propositions. Only the truths of mathematics and logic could be a priori and necessarily true. Their necessity was bought at the cost of accepting that the necessity was due to definition and the consequences of definition rather than informing us about the nature of the world. Thus, to take a simple example 'All bachelors are unmarried men' is necessarily true, but its necessity lies in the fact that it is drawing out the consequences of definitions not telling us about the world. Sometimes, as for example in mathematics, because of the complexity of the definitions employed the remote consequences of those definitions may be both complicated to work through and be surprising, but it is a surprise within a system of definition; it is not a surprising discovery about reality.

Mises rejects this view of necessity and the a priori. He argues that definitions embody claims about, or characterizations of, reality and therefore the process of working out the consequences of definitions tell us essential truths about the world as the definitions themselves capture an essential aspect of the nature of reality. He is not at all coy about these claims. First of all he devotes a book, *The Ultimate Foundations of Economic Science*, to the elaboration of this view about synthetic a priori propositions but to take a rather substantial example from *Human Action* he argues that the whole of monetary theory consists of such propositions. I will quote from this passage since it is crucial to the understanding of Mises' whole approach to the justification of the market economy and the framework of liberal institutions which should surround it:

> In the concept of money all the theorems of monetary theory are already implied. The quantity theory does not add to our knowledge anything which is not virtually contained in the concept of money. It transforms, develops, and unfolds; it only analyses and is therefore tautological like the theorem of Pythagoras in relation to the concept of the rectangular triangle. However, nobody would deny the cognitive value of the quantity theory. Theory and the comprehension of living and changing reality are not in opposition to one another. Without theory, the general aprioristic science of human action, there is no comprehension of the reality of human action.[41]

Indeed, he goes on to claim in the same context that '[t]he theorems attained by correct praxeological reasoning are not only perfect and incontestable, like the correct mathematical theorems. They refer, moreover, with the full rigidity of their apodictic certainty and incontestability to the reality of action as it appears in life and history. Praxeology conveys exact and precise knowledge of real things.'[42]

This is a very considerable claim. In the specific case of monetary theory in Mises' view praxeology would show, in some sense, that monetarism is incontestably true. It is not one hypothesis among others to be settled by looking for evidence that would refute it but follows from unpacking what is captured about the world in the definition of money. However, more generally, Mises is resting his case for the market economy and a liberal legal and political order on a set of what he takes to be incontestable truths.

He tries to explain that there is a difference between praxeology as the science of means to ends and the science of the natural world in that *things* are only *means* in relation to some kind of human project or purpose. Praxeology is not a rival to natural science as a science of things but rather it looks at things given significance 'as means to ends in human thought and action'. Goods, commodities, wealth, and all the other notions of conduct are not elements of nature, they are elements of human meaning and conduct. 'He who wants to deal with them must not look at the external world, he must search for them in the meaning of acting men.'[43] Praxeology is not a normative science because the ends of human life differ fundamentally between persons and are 'not open to examination from any absolute standard. Ultimate ends are ultimately given, they are purely subjective'. So how can praxeology contribute to the foundations of neo-liberalism and ideas about the rule of law as a set of moral ideals? The answer lies in the fact that the aprioristic reasoning of economics can unmask false views which may well underpin alternative views of politics, economics, and the law. The falsity of these views will, however, not turn on their normative falsity established by a critical normative argument, but rather through the failure to establish proper means to the achievement of subjectively chosen ends. So, for example, as we have seen, he argues for the certainty of the quantity theory of money and all that follows from that. Given that, as we shall see, social democracy has often been seen to be a very fortunate combination of a set of moral ideals with a set of Keynesian means to achieve these ideals, the establishment of the certainty of the quantity theory of money would undermine the Keynesian means which are often regarded as essential to the achievement of social democratic goals. Mises also points out that foreign exchange controls have been an instrument of socialism and social democracy but that there are strong praxeological reasons for rejecting these as a means. The most obvious example of this negative approach is given partly in *Human Action* and partly in his *Socialism*[44] in which he argues that economic calculation under planning will prove to be impossible because of the lack of prices determined through normal market exchange. These prices are essential to the communication of demand to potential suppliers and yet they are absent in a planned economy. Hence, the result of his argument is that an indispensable means to the end of socialism, namely central planning, will prove disastrous. The point here is this. There may well be a range of possible political ideals and ideologies, and these are subjectively chosen and are beyond rational scrutiny. What is within rational scrutiny is the range of means adopted to achieve these ends and ultimately Mises' position is that only free market economics will provide the means which human beings need to attain the wide and subjectively chosen ends which they endorse, and along with the market there has to be a legal system which will facilitate market exchange rather than continually attempting to displace it.

This argument about means becomes particularly cogent if a political position or ideology rests entirely on the availability and effectiveness of a given set of means. If those means are shown to be irrational or unsustainable by praxeological argument, then it follows that the political position indissolubly linked to that set of means also has to fall. This is what, some have argued, was seen (prematurely as it turns out) to have been the effect on social democracy of the eclipse of Keynesianism in the 1970s onwards. It was assumed that Keynesian demand management techniques and the role of the state that these implied were essential for the intellectual coherence of the social democratic position. If you can only will the end if you will the means, and if the means are not available or can be demonstrated to be irrational, then the ends themselves become impossible to attain and thus irrational if the means in question are the only ones available. Thus, the eclipse of Keynesian means, it was held, meant that social democratic ends were unobtainable.

It is worth dwelling on Mises' idea of human action for the moment. This is the central category of his social thought and in a sense his argument is that all the a priori propositions in fact emerge from reflecting on what he calls 'acting man'. Acting man or perhaps more idiomatically these days the 'human agent' chooses his or her ends and assembles means to achieve those ends. He or she cannot be mistaken about ends since they are non-cognitive; he or she can, however, be mistaken about means as the previous argument shows. Means are chosen against a background of scarcity which is also a clear and incontestable feature of the human condition. Also the human agent is an egoist, that is to say acts out of self-interest. Given his or her choice of ends, he or she will then act in a self-interested way to achieve those ends. So in order to keep his methodological assumptions on track, Mises has to take the view that scarcity and self-interest are part of the structure of synthetic a priori propositions out of which praxeology is constructed. There are, however, other contestable or controversial assumptions on which his argument puts weight. He assumes, for example, that while values are subjective there will in fact be a very large measure of agreement about which values will be chosen. This is very important to Mises' defence of liberalism, as Norman Barry has rightly noted.[45] Given that all his arguments about political and legal orders have to be praxeological or, as Barry says, technological and cannot focus directly on ends, we have to answer the question of why it is that liberalism is the best or only technology for the achievement of the diverse range of goals that individuals have. One way of making this claim more manageable is to say that in fact there will be a great deal of congruence between goals and, therefore, only one set of means is essential to achieving them, that is, the liberal set. However, it is not at all clear that Mises can reasonably include any such assumption into his claim to be operating at a wholly a priori level. Without this assumption there can be no reason for thinking that the liberal market order is in fact the best means to realizing these ends.

It is important to distinguish between Mises' approach and that of Rothbard. As a natural law thinker, Rothbard also takes himself to be building up a neo-liberal, or to be more precise in his case, libertarian theory, on the basis of a set of a priori truths about human nature which then generate the natural law truths on the basis of which he can erect his theory. However, while Mises too is arguing on the basis of synthetic a priori propositions, the difference is that for Rothbard the natural law derives an account of a set of human goods from an account of human nature; whereas Mises is arguing a case about *means* not about *goods*. Of course, it may well be that the undermining of a particular set or sets of means will lead us to revise and reconsider the view of the human good which we believed could be brought into being by those means; nevertheless, the theory is not about the goods themselves whereas that of Rothbard's is. In addition, there are some ambiguities in Mises about what are to be seen as means and what are to be taken as ends. Individual negative freedom has often been taken to be one of the ends of liberalism, one of its basic values. However, Mises treats it at some length in *Human Action*, which is a book of praxeology or the science of means. The same is true of property. It seems that these have to be seen as essential means to a liberal state but are not themselves liberal ends or goals. The liberal end or goal cannot be rationally evaluated according to Mises' theory of value: It is subjective and personal. What can be subjected to rational deliberation is freedom as a means to the achievement of a liberal state. But what then are the guiding ends, goals, and purposes of a liberal state? Is it just the way and perhaps the only way to accommodate moral subjectivism along with increasing material wealth? Despite his voluminous writings Mises is rather unclear about this point. It is also quite basic as to whether he sees freedom as a means or an end. If freedom is a goal of liberalism, then it will be a value-laden idea since goals embody subjective values. If it is value-laden then it will also be subjective. If it is to be seen as a means, then not only can it be seen in purely empirical terms but it has to be since means cannot have values built into them, otherwise they could not be part of the synthetic a priori reasoning which praxeology is. As we saw earlier in this chapter, Hayek too was ambiguous about whether freedom was to be seen as a means or an end. For quite different reasons Mises seems to be caught up in the same sort of ambiguity. This question about whether or not freedom can and should be demoralized is a central theme of Chapter 3.

NOTES

1. Hayek, F. A. (1960). *The Constitution of Liberty.* London: Routledge and Kegan Paul, p. 205.
2. Hayek, F. A. *The Constitution of Liberty,* p. 21.
3. Hayek, F. A. *The Constitution of Liberty,* pp. 158–9.
4. Hayek, F. A. *The Constitution of Liberty,* p. 159.
5. Hayek, F. A. *The Constitution of Liberty,* p. 159.
6. Oakeshott, M. J. (1991). 'Talking Politics', in *Rationalism in Politics and Other Essays.* Indianapolis, IN: The Liberty Fund, p. 457.
7. Hayek, F. A. (1979). 'Epilogue' to *Law, Legislation and Liberty, Vol. 3: The Political Order of a Free People.* London: Routledge and Kegan Paul, p. 166.
8. Shearmur, J. (1996). *Hayek and After: Hayekian Liberalism as a Research Programme.* London: Routledge and Kegan Paul, p. 95. There is a significant difference of interpretation here from that given by another leading Hayek scholar, John Gray in the third edition of his *Hayek on Liberty* where he argues that Hayek envisages a common law *Rechtsstaat* and he then argues that 'We are left with no leverage in Hayek's account which might be used against the outcomes of the historical process. Instead, it seems, we are bound to entrust ourselves to all the vagaries of mankind's random walk in historical space.' Gray, J. N. (1998). *Hayek on Liberty.* London: Routledge and Kegan Paul, pp. 69–70. On Shearmur's interpretation, the principle of universalizability provides something of a check against the point made by Gray. It has to be said that as we shall see Buchanan too shares Gray's view. I am, however, inclined to Shearmur's view of this.
9. Hayek, F. A. (1976). *Law, Legislation and Liberty Vol. 2: The Mirage of Social Justice.* London: Routledge and Kegan Paul, p. 54.
10. Shearmur, J. *Hayek and After,* p. 95.
11. Hayek, F. A. *Law, Legislation and Liberty, Vol. 2: The Mirage of Social Justice,* p. 54 and *The Constitution of Liberty,* p. 154.
12. Hare, R. M. (1963). *Freedom and Reason.* Oxford: The Clarendon Press.
13. Buchanan, J. (2000). *The Limits of Liberty.* Indianapolis, IN: The Liberty Fund, pp. 37–8 and *The Reason of Rules.* Indianapolis, IN: The Liberty Fund, p. 13.
14. Buchanan, J. and Brennan, G. (1985). *The Reason of Rules.* Cambridge: Cambridge University Press, p. 44.

15. See Buchanan, J. *The Limits of Liberty*, chapter 1.
16. Buchanan, J. and Brennan, G. *The Reason of Rules*, chapter 1.
17. Buchanan, J. and Brennan, G. *The Reason of Rules*, p. 27.
18. Rowley, C. K. and Peacock, A. T. (1975). *Welfare Economics: A Liberal Restatement*. London: Martin Robertson. See pp. 10 and 167.
19. Rothbard, M. (2002). *The Ethics of Liberty*. New York: New York University Press.
20. Buchanan, J. and Brennan, G. *The Reason of Rules*, p. 151.
21. These lists are extrapolated from various places in Buchanan, J. *The Limits of Liberty*, and *The Reason of Rules*.
22. Buchanan, J. and Tullock, G. (1962). *The Calculus of Consent*. Ann Arbor, MI: University of Michigan.
23. Nozick, R. (1974). *Anarchy, State and Utopia*. Oxford: Blackwell, p. 9.
24. Nozick, R. *Anarchy, State and Utopia*, p. 32.
25. Nozick, R. *Anarchy, State and Utopia*, p. 25 ff.
26. Wolfe, C. (2006). *Natural Law Liberalism*. Cambridge: Cambridge University Press.
27. Rothbard, *The Ethics of Liberty*, in which he deploys strong critiques of both Hayek and Nozick from the natural law perspective (see chapters 28 and 29).
28. Rothbard, *The Ethics of Liberty*, pp. 7, 13, 15, 169–70.
29. Plant, R. (1991). *Modern Political Thought*. Oxford: Blackwell, chapter 2.
30. Rothbard, M. *The Ethics of Liberty*, chapters 1 and 2 on reason and nature, respectively.
31. Rothbard, M. *The Ethics of Liberty*, pp. 42–3.
32. Rothbard, M. *The Ethics of Liberty*, pp. 29–37; 47–50, 72.
33. Rothbard, M. *The Ethics of Liberty*, p. 36.
34. Rawls, A. (1972). *Theory of Justice*. Oxford: Oxford University Press.
35. Rothbard, M. *The Ethics of Liberty*, p. 41.
36. Rothbard, M. *The Ethics of Liberty*, chapter 6.
37. Rothbard, M. *The Ethics of Liberty*, p. 31.
38. Rothbard, M. *The Ethics of Liberty*, op. cit. p. 179. The reference to Barnett is Barnett, R. (1976). 'Fuller, Law and Anarchism', in *The Libertarian Forum*, February 1976.
39. Mises, L. von. (1996). *Human Action*. New Haven, CT: Yale University Press.
40. Mises, L. von. *Human Action*, p. 13.
41. Mises, L. von. *Human Action*, p. 38.
42. Mises, L. von. *Human Action*, p. 39.
43. Mises, L. von. *Human Action*, p. 92.
44. Mises, L. von. (1981). *Socialism*, Indianapolis, IN: The Liberty Fund.
45. Barry, N. (1987). *On Classical Liberalism and Libertarianism*. New York: St Martin's Press, chapter 4.

3

Freedom, Coercion, and the Law

The ideas of freedom and liberty – terms which will be used interchangeably in this study – are central to neo-liberal social, political, economic, and legal theory. Indeed, neo-liberalism is often portrayed as the theory of the free society and therefore the nature of liberty is crucial. But while it is crucial, the idea of freedom in general and within neo-liberal thought in particular is highly complex and controversial. It is central to the neo-liberal project that freedom has to be made compatible with the rule of law as we have seen neo-liberals understand it. Given that the rule of law has to be nomocratic, independent of purposes and goals, universal, and applying to every citizen equally, the central claim made by neo-liberals about liberty is that it has to be seen as negative liberty. That is to say it is freedom *from* rather than freedom *to*. It is about freedom from coercion rather than freedom to in the sense either of having powers and capacities or pursuing particular kinds of goals. As a nomocratic state and its laws have to be seen as independent of purposes, freedom also has to be similarly independent and this can only be achieved by negative freedom. We now need to explore these claims in more detail.

Any comprehensive account of freedom will have to address the following issues:

(1) An analysis of the meaning of freedom.
(2) The nature of the link between freedom and coercion and thus the nature of coercion and in particular the role of intention and agency in coercion.
(3) The nature of the agent to whom freedom is ascribed and the relationship, if any, between that agent's subjective desires and inclinations and liberty.
(4) The nature of the value of liberty: Why do we think of freedom as being of value to us?
(5) The relationship between freedom and the rule of law – a particularly important aspect of freedom from a neo-liberal perspective.

On the whole my account and critique of neo-liberal accounts of liberty in this chapter will focus mainly on Hayek. This is largely because he is such an influential neo-liberal thinker and because, as its title *The Constitution of Liberty* implies, Hayek's book provides the most extensive account of freedom in the various aspects noted earlier. This analysis has been enormously influential in the development of the neo-liberal views of freedom.

I shall begin the analysis with a broad sketch of Hayek's views and then discuss them in more detail. Since the detail is complex, it is essential to have the importance of his overall idea in mind to enable us to see how the more complex detail fits into the general theory.

Hayek is usually regarded as being a proponent of negative freedom. That is to say that freedom is the absence of coercion and constraint, as opposed to positive freedom in which freedom is understood as the capacity or power to do things or the view that one is only free when pursuing particular sorts of goals.[1] There is certainly a great deal of support in Hayek's writing to sustain this judgement but as we shall see, the picture is not wholly clear-cut.

At the beginning of chapter 1 of *The Constitution of Liberty* Hayek states that 'the task of a policy of freedom must therefore be to minimize coercion or its harmful effects even if it cannot eliminate it completely'.[2] Freedom is the absence of coercion, and coercion has to be understood as an *intentional* action by a human agent. The importance of this point cannot be overstated because it is used to block two possibilities. The first is that natural processes cannot give rise to coercion however far they may limit the freedom of action of an individual. The snowstorm prevents me from doing what I want to do – say going to the cinema – but it is not a form of coercion because it is unintended. Secondly, there are human processes which may restrict the options available to an individual but, because they are not intentional, they are not coercive. So, for example, as a result of the operation of the market, I may end up very poor and the options open to me may thus be very limited. This is not, however, coercive since my poverty is the result of the unintended aggregate outcomes of market behaviour. Individuals buying and selling in a market act intentionally but the overall effect, the 'distribution' of income and wealth as the result of that buying and selling, is not intended. Hence, the restriction of options available to the poor person in the example given is not a case of coercion because such an outcome is not intended.

Indeed, the argument about options goes further than this for Hayek and, as he argues in *The Constitution of Liberty*, 'the range of physical possibilities from which a person can choose at a given moment has no direct relevance to freedom'. This is a very important claim to which we shall return shortly.

Freedom in its correct sense of the absence of coercion has, in Hayek's view, to be distinguished very clearly from freedom or liberty as a power or an ability to do something. The assimilation of freedom to do *X* with the ability to do *X* is for Hayek a fundamental muddle.[3] It also has baleful political consequences in his view in that the assimilation of freedom and ability has allowed socialists, social democrats, and New Liberals[4] to argue that the state has a duty to secure to individuals resources to enable them to do things which otherwise they could not do and to defend such a policy in the name of extending freedom. Therefore, the assimilation of 'free to' with 'being able to' has to be resisted. This assimilation is one form of positive freedom, moving from the absence of coercion to freedom as the power or ability to do various things, whereas for Hayek freedom should be seen as a negative concept:

> It is to this class of concepts that liberty belongs: it describes the absence of a particular obstacle – coercion by other men. It becomes positive only through

> what we make of it. It does not assure us of any particular opportunities but leaves it to us to decide what use we shall make of the circumstances in which we find ourselves.[5]

So what is the basis for the sharp distinction between freedom and ability or power?

The central argument is that they must be categorically different because no one is able to do all that they are free to do. I am free to do anything that I am not currently prevented from doing by the intentional action of another person. This range of options open to me is indefinitely large. However rich or powerful or intelligent I am, in other words whatever my powers and capacities may be, I am unable to do all that I am free to do. Thus, freedom and ability cannot mean the same thing because if they meant the same thing, then exactly the same considerations would apply to them in each case. Freedom is the absence of coercion. It has nothing to do with the options and choices that I make within the free space that is secured to me by the absence of coercion. It has nothing to do with my abilities and capacities. This point is made clearly and trenchantly by Murray Rothbard when he argues:

> Each man's power, then, is always necessarily limited by the facts of the human condition, by the nature of man and the world; but it is one of the glories of man's condition that each person *can* be absolutely free, even in a world of complex interaction and exchange.[6]

I am free when I am not coerced. What I am then able to do has no bearing on the definition of freedom – a definition which is essential for the nature of the rule of law in a free society.

Because coercion implies that my own will becomes subordinate to that of another person such that I am prevented from doing what I would otherwise do or be required to do what I would otherwise not do, it follows that the best way of defending freedom as the absence of coercion is by securing an area of individual 'private sphere'.[7] The argument here is in favour, as Hayek puts it, of 'some set of circumstances in his environment with which others cannot interfere'.

This conception of liberty has to be understood in contrast to other forms of what are frequently called freedom. In particular, Hayek contrasts his own idea of personal liberty with the idea of political freedom. That is to say 'the participation of men in the choice of their government, in the process of legislation and in the control of administration'. However, in Hayek's view political freedom in this sense, while it may in certain situations be consistent with personal freedom in his sense, does not require it. People may, under a system of political liberty vote to constrain or even eliminate personal liberty as he understands it.

Equally personal liberty does not necessarily entail political liberty.[8] Someone, say who is a resident alien in the United States, may well experience a high degree of personal freedom while being denied formal political participation. Hayek points out that there is an historical affinity between personal liberty as he understands it and political liberty in the sense that national movements for political liberty have been concerned with the removal of the coercion of another power. In that sense there is something conceptually in common between political and personal liberty and he points out that in the nineteenth century many defenders of a liberal view of personal freedom were also in favour of national liberation movements in Europe,[9] but, in his view, it is necessary to 'keep the two conceptions clearly apart'.

Hayek also wants to distinguish between personal liberty and what he variously calls 'inner', 'metaphysical', or 'subjective' freedom. He admits that in spite of a ready similarity between these aspects of freedom and personal liberty as he sees it, they should be kept apart. By inner freedom and its cognates Hayek is referring to the fact that a person may be inhibited from reaching his or her own chosen goals by aspects of his or her own internal psychology. These could include emotional inhibitions, weakness of will, neuroses, obsessions, and the like.[10] The removal of these inhibiting factors has often been seen as a form of liberation. For Hayek, however, this is quite different from personal liberty which is about whether another person is able to impose his or her will on an agent and get that agent to do or refrain from doing something.

Part of any comprehensive account of freedom will also have to address the nature of the agent to whom freedom is ascribed. Hayek clearly regards personal liberty as depending on a rule-governed relationship between agents. Within this rule-governed framework the free person will be free to 'follow his own plans and intentions' and to be directed 'towards ends for which he has been persistently striving rather than towards necessities created by others in order to make him do what they want'. Picking up the earlier theme about the lack of a necessary link between freedom and a specific range of choice, Hayek argues that

> whether he is free or not does not depend on the range of choice but on whether he can expect to shape his course of action in accordance with his present intentions, or whether somebody else has power so to manipulate the conditions as to make him act according to that person's will rather than his own.[11]

So the agent has to have the capacity to choose and to follow through patterns of intentional action. This does not mean for Hayek that there has to be a range of morally or culturally valued choices and options open to the person; nor does it mean that the agent has to have some right to resources to be able to follow through and act on these intentions. Both these possible aspects of personal liberty are rejected by Hayek because they would be forms of positive freedom. Indeed the point goes deeper than this. If we believe that freedom involves having before us a range of morally or culturally significant choices, then a theory of the free society would have to endorse some list of such approved choices.[12] This would however mean that the law in such a society would be about facilitating the achievement of this set of significant choices but that would make the law non-nomocratic. It would be about securing particular goals and values. In addition, we need to recall that neo-liberals are typically moral subjectivists who do not think that it is possible to provide a cognitive basis for a set of normative claims. The same point would apply to the number of choices available to a person as well as the quality of such choices. Who is to determine at which point the number of choices open to a person makes that person a free agent whereas below that threshold the person is unfree? In the neo-liberal view such judgements are foolish and unsustainable in rational terms.

Hayek links the capacity of a person to be an agent with an account of what is wrong with coercion. He stresses in this account the way in which coercion undermines this capacity and he puts the point in a very strong way.

> By 'coercion' we mean such control of the environment or circumstances of a person by another that, in order to avoid greater evil, he is forced to act not according to a coherent plan of his own but to service the ends of another. . . . Coercion is evil precisely because it thus eliminates an individual as a thinking and valuing person . . . [13]

We shall need to revisit this account when we turn to the critical analysis of Hayek's view of coercion in Chapter 10, but it is interesting to note at this stage in the exposition the emphasis on 'a coherent plan', the prevention of which is coercion.[14] There are different links here with his account of 'inner freedom', and how inner freedom is different from 'personal freedom' which, as we shall see, will cause Hayek problems with the coherence of his account. As Kukathas has pointed out, Hayek's view of what is wrong with coercion is strikingly Kantian with its emphasis on the agent pursuing a rational and coherent plan of life rather than becoming a tool of others.[15]

There is a big issue here to which we shall return – but to explain the point for the moment. In his account Hayek often refers to coercion as being subject to the arbitrary will of another.[16] However, since we do not live in a community of saints it is overwhelmingly likely that an individual will often strive to make another the instrument of his or her will and then act in a coercive manner. This mutual coercion can only be controlled by the state and law:

> Coercion, however, cannot be altogether avoided because the only way to prevent it is by the threat of coercion. Free society has met this problem by conferring the monopoly of coercion on the state and by attempting to limit this power of the state to instances where it is required to prevent coercion by private persons.[17]

But if part of the evil of coercion is that between private individuals it is the use of *arbitrary* power, what is it that makes the coercion of the state non-arbitrary? Basically his answer is that the laws of the state that threaten coercion should be of a wholly general and abstract sort. This is in fact quite a complex idea in relation to coercion and involves a number of distinct elements.

These may indeed be features of law, but what is it that makes the threatened coercion of the law non-arbitrary? The answer is purely its generality and its abstract nature. It is non-arbitrary in that it does not specify prohibitions and penalties for specified individuals; it is non-arbitrary in that it protects the private spheres of all equally; it does not prescribe a set of arbitrarily chosen ends, goals, purposes, or coherent plans of life giving these some kind of legal privilege. Hayek contrasts law in his understanding of it with a conception of law which sees it as a set of commands: 'The ideal type of command determines uniquely the action to be performed and leaves those to whom it is addressed no chance to use their own knowledge or follow their own predilections.'[18] Law on the other hand provides merely additional information to be taken into account in the determination of the action.

Behind this remark lies the idea that I, as a potential coercer of another, will find that if I invade the private sphere of another, I shall be punished. This is not to give legal endorsement to the content of the choices made by the individual in his or her particular private sphere, but rather an equal threat of punishment for any interference in any private sphere (as long as the person in that private sphere is not coercing someone else). Hence, so far we could say that the generality and abstract nature of law ensure that it is not arbitrary between individuals.

However, Hayek makes a further claim in this argument which is not perhaps endorsed by other neo-liberal thinkers, most of whom would probably go along with Hayek up to this point. The argument here is about the relationship between the law, in Hayek's understanding of it, and the nature of rationality. Recall what Hayek says:

> When we obey laws, in the sense of general abstract rules laid down irrespective of their application to us, we are not subject to another man's will and are therefore free.[19]

So long, therefore, as an individual acts in accordance with the law, he or she is free. However, Hayek also seems to argue that the non-arbitrary nature of law lies not only in its generality and its abstract nature, but also in its spontaneous and unplanned and unintended growth over time. The spontaneous growth of a legal order means that it is not the instrument of a particular will whether of an individual (like an absolute monarch or a dictator) or of a particular legislature at a particular time, but is an organic growth.

In his 'Epilogue' to the third volume of *Law, Legislation and Liberty*, Hayek focuses on the link between the growth of reason and spontaneous development. He argues that human practices are neither natural (i.e. given a part of the natural order as some natural law thinkers and theorists might hold), nor are they context-free rational inventions. They are, he says, created by a process of winnowing and sifting 'directed by differential advantages gained by groups from practices adopted for unknown and perhaps purely accidental reasons'.

This means that mind and culture develop concurrently through the process of spontaneous adaptation and adjustment. This is also true of the exercise of reason.[20] People learned to do the right thing without comprehending that it was the right thing. Rules of conduct emerge in the same way and by the same processes. Freedom has also developed in the same way.

> Freedom was made possible by the gradual evolution of the discipline of civilisation which is at the same time the discipline of freedom. It protects him by impersonal abstract rules against arbitrary violence of others.[21]

Once we abandon the dichotomy between nature and reason and we see rational practices arising out of the adaptation of traditional forms of behaviour, then we can see the emergence of abstract and general rules which by the threat of coercion prevent the mutual coercion of private individuals as being rational and non-arbitrary. In this sense Hayek can give backing to his idea that when we obey abstract and general laws we are free because they are not the product of arbitrary will.

There are two further issues to be discussed to complete this broad outline of Hayek's theory of liberty. The first is his answer to the question of what it is that makes liberty valuable to us; the second and, as we shall see is a related point, is his view of the relationship between freedom and markets.

So what is for Hayek the value of liberty? It could, of course, be argued that freedom is an intrinsic good in some sense, or possibly an absolute good. It seems clear that such claims would be complicated to explicate since terms such as intrinsic or absolute are notoriously difficult to clarify in the context of values, but nevertheless they have a point in this discussion because they throw into relief the alternative claim that freedom is in fact an instrumental value. The point incorporated into this latter claim is that freedom is not a good in and of itself; it is, rather, valuable in human life because it serves other purposes which we find either valuable in themselves or in some sense fundamentally valuable.

So, for Hayek, is freedom a good in itself, whatever that might mean, or does its value lie in its role in facilitating other values or our ability to deal with the basic circumstances of human life? Given that for Hayek freedom is the absence of coercion, then an account of why freedom is valuable to us would also be an explanation of why coercion is wrong. This is a crucial issue because the defence of freedom puts a constraint on the actions of others when they are tempted to act coercively, and so an account of the value of freedom and the disvalue of coercion is crucial to the coherence of the argument. It has to be said, however, that Hayek's argument here is ambiguous – an ambiguity which will be more fully analysed in the second part of this book.

In chapter 4 of *The Constitution of Liberty* he makes a clear case for saying that freedom is a non-instrumental value[22] and there is an endorsement of the idea of liberty as an intrinsic value when he says:

> Like all moral principles, it demands that it be accepted as a value in itself, as a principle that must be respected without our asking whether the consequences in the particular instance will be beneficial.[23]

He then goes on to say in a point which we shall look at more fully later:

> We shall not achieve the results we want if we do not accept it as a creed or prescription so strong that no considerations of expediency can be allowed to limit it.[24]

This reference to consequences or results should give us pause for thought in that if freedom is, as he says, a value in itself – what is the link in Hayek's mind between this and results or consequences? It begins to look as though freedom is valuable because it facilitates beneficial consequences and is therefore instrumental to the value of those consequences. So what might these be?

Earlier in *The Constitution of Liberty* Hayek seems to have produced an instrumentalist and consequentialist view of freedom which is crucially connected to his account of the limitations on reason for which he argues in his epistemological work, *The Constitution of Liberty*, and in his critique of planning. The passage which follows is an account of the limited, fragmented, dispersed, context-orientated, and habitual nature of knowledge and is critical and is worth quoting in full. The process to which he refers in the opening sentence below is the process by which an individual uses the specific knowledge which he or she has in order to find the 'better way' for that person in those circumstances.

> What is essential to the functioning of the process is that each individual be able to act on his particular knowledge, always unique, at least so far as it refers to some particular circumstances, and that he is able to use his individual skills and opportunities within the limits known to him and for his own individual purpose. We have now reached the point at which the main contention of this chapter will be readily intelligible. It is that the case for individual freedom rests chiefly on the recognition of the inevitable ignorance of all of us concerning a great many of the factors on which the achievement of our ends and welfare depends.
>
> If there were omniscient men, if we could know not only all that affects the attainment of our present wishes but also our future wants and desires, there would be little case for liberty. . . . Liberty is essential in order to leave room for the unforeseeable and unpredictable; we want it because we have learned to expect from it the opportunity of realising many of our aims.[25]

This looks quite a long way from the claim that freedom is valuable in itself. It is now of value because it resolves the problem of our ignorance. Being in possession of a sphere of private life free from coercion enables me to utilize my knowledge in the particular circumstances in which I find myself to realize some good for me or to find what Hayek calls 'the better way'. Coercion is bad because it prevents this happening. We shall reserve judgement for the moment on whether these two seemingly very different views on the nature of liberty pull Hayek's social, political, and legal theory in different directions. But it is worth just putting the contrast in a rather stark way. The idea of freedom as a good in itself seems to be indicated when Hayek argues:

> Coercion is evil precisely because it thus eliminates an individual as a thinking and valuing person.[26]

This theory sees freedom as part and parcel of human agency – the ability to construct and carry forward what Hayek calls a 'coherent plan of his own'.[27] Freedom is an intrinsic part of moral agency. On the alternative view, freedom is that set of conditions rendering us free from coercion within which we can utilize our limited knowledge for both individual and social benefit. We shall have to see how coherent these two views can in fact be made.

I shall now move on to link the idea of liberty to that of markets. Some aspects of this relationship will only become clear later once I have discussed in full Hayek's account of markets. There are, however, even at this stage obvious links.

First of all, as we have seen, for Hayek freedom presupposes 'that the individual has some assured private sphere, that there is some set of circumstances in his environment with which actions can not interfere'.[28] Within such a private sphere, utilizing his knowledge and circumstances and pursuing a coherent plan relative to that knowledge and set of circumstances an individual can possess, buy, and sell how he or she sees fit. This is just an aspect of free activity. That is to say engaging in market exchange is an exercise in free action in the same way as engaging in any other voluntary activity like joining a club or a church. So freedom, at least at this stage of the argument, does not, as it were, entail markets; it does however, provide the uncoerced space within which market exchange can occur as one form amongst others of free activity. This is certainly a view of the relationship between freedom and markets endorsed by Buchanan and Mises.

The second link between markets and freedom ties this relationship together more closely. As we have just seen in what I have called Hayek's instrumental justification of liberty, freedom is essential for the utilization of dispersed, fragmented, and habitual or tacit knowledge. The market provides the mechanism within which such knowledge can be deployed most effectively. A market is essentially both a coordination mechanism and an information providing system. It provides a mechanism whereby through free production and exchange individuals can use the resources available to them, whether they are intellectual or physical, to meet their own wants and desires and to meet those of others through exchange. It is an information providing system in that prices which represent how others value what A has to sell allows A in his protected private sphere to determine how and whether he or she can exchange on the terms indicated as being available for his or her product. Market value does not represent some metaphysical value such as a 'just' price, nor does it track some moral value such as social justice. Rather a price is an aggregate of individual evaluations of the worth of something. To interfere in this sphere of freedom in pursuit of some kind of collective moral ideal like equality or social justice would have the effect of distorting or in extreme cases destroying both the informational and coordinating aspects of markets.[29]

This also in Hayek's view links up to the twin ideas of freedom and responsibility. As he argues the free individual has the opportunity and the burden of choice and this means that he must bear the consequences of his actions.[30] This relates to the role of freedom and markets in the following way: in a market, using limited knowledge against the background of specific circumstances, the individual will be involved in production and exchange and he or she will do this in a free market which embodies the price which the service or good being offered will actually fetch. Hence, whether they are successful or unsuccessful will depend largely, although (as we shall see later in Chapter 4) not entirely, on their own efforts. They are free to make these efforts or to abstain, and subsequent success and failure will be their responsibility. This contrasts with a regime in which a person's status and security do not reflect his or her own efforts but rather a political or collective scale of values such as one that might be informed by values such as social justice, just deserts, or equality. Freedom means taking responsibility for one's place in society and this will be determined by success or failure in a free market not by a political mechanism which protects individuals from the circumstances of liberty and in particular the consequences of their own actions. Thus,

> [i]t is of the essence of a free society that a man's value and remuneration depends not on capacity in the abstract but on success in turning it into

> concrete service which is useful to others who can reciprocate. And the chief aim of freedom is to provide both the opportunity and the inducement to insure the maximum use of knowledge that an individual can acquire. What makes the individual unique in this respect is not his generic but his concrete knowledge, his knowledge of particular circumstances and conditions.[31]

Here we see the clearest possible link between the instrumental view of freedom as the means of facilitating the use of limited knowledge and the free market and the individual degree of freedom and responsibility that go with that.

This does not, of course, exhaust Hayek's account of the moral nature of markets which will be the subject of explicit and detailed focus later in this study. However, before we leave the topic I want to discuss the relationship between freedom and property. Given that Hayek has argued for an indissoluble link between freedom, the absence of coercion and what he calls 'an assured free sphere' he goes on to argue that the protection of such a free sphere depends crucially upon property. It is in his view 'an essential condition'.

> The recognition of property is clearly the first step in the delimitation of the private sphere which protects us against coercion.[32]

The reason for this is as follows: We are only able to act freely in carrying out 'a coherent plan of action' if we are certain of our exclusive control of some material objects.[33] However, Hayek rather quickly changes this argument which might, as it stands, imply that equal negative freedom requires individual positive rights to property on an equal basis. In fact he goes on to say that in a modern society what matters is not in fact individual ownership so much as the fact that the material means necessary for a person 'to pursue any plan of action' should not be all in the exclusive control of one other agent. So he argues:

> It is one of the accomplishments of modern society that freedom may be enjoyed by a person with practically no property of his own (beyond personal belongings like clothing – and even these can be rented) and that we can leave the care of the property that serves our needs largely to others.[34]

So, there is rather a rapid shift in Hayek's view here. There is, however, one further point relating to property, liberty, and the rule of law in the sense of nomocratic abstract and general laws. Under, for example, a social democratic regime, it might be though that a link between property and freedom, if it were to be regarded as plausible, might lead such a state to secure to individuals through the law particular bundles of material goods which were to be regarded as the necessary conditions of free action (as Hayek himself first argued that they were). This might be done by a set of entitlements or social and economic rights. Such an approach would however, in Hayek's view, contradict the nomocratic and general nature of law as well as giving a person a status and a degree of security outside the market mechanism by political action which as we have already seen Hayek regards as being incompatible with a proper understanding of the relationship between freedom, markets, personal responsibility, and the rule of law. In Chapter 4, on social justice, we shall study in more detail the neo-liberal views on this particular point. Hence, given that Hayek takes up the position that he does that property whether owned or rented is essential for the protection of an assured free space,[35] and that the resources necessary for action are not all owned by one person or institution such as the state, how does he explain how this protection can be secured while avoiding the social democratic approach of securing a 'fair' share of basic goods to all citizens? His answer to this lies in the law of contract. The law of contract is general and nomocratic in that it does not serve directly the ends of particular individuals or groups but facilitates myriad individual ends for which individuals contract:

> The whole network of rights created by contracts is as important a part of our own protected sphere, as much as the basis of our plans as any property of our own.[36]

This is a crucial move in Hayek's philosophy between arguing for the direct ownership of property as 'an essential condition' of freedom and the protected private sphere and then ending up with the position cited above. As we shall see later in the book the issues at stake here have wide ramifications.

This then completes the overall sketch of Hayek's view of liberty and we shall now move on to a closer analysis of some of the component parts of these arguments which have been so critical in underpinning the whole approach of neo-liberal political, social, economic, and legal philosophy.

First of all, I want to turn to an analysis of the ideas of freedom and coercion. Freedom for Hayek is the absence of coercion and the prevention of coercion by one private individual or through the threat of coercion by the state through the law. Hence, for Hayek freedom is a product of law.

At this stage of the discussion I want to concentrate most on the idea of coercion. A clear and convincing account of coercion is vital if Hayek's account of freedom and his vision of a free society are to have purchase. I shall start the analysis by looking at a particular conception of negative liberty. Hayek claims to be defending negative liberty and it is useful to have before us what has sometimes been called the 'pure' theory of negative liberty or in the view of its detractors, 'crude' negative liberty. On this view coercion is a matter of the coercer A making it impossible for B to do *X* which is what he or she wants to do or to refrain from doing *Y*. This idea of liberty, which is to be found in chapter 14 of Hobbes' *Leviathan*, treats coercion as an obstacle which impedes or prevents or renders impossible what someone would otherwise do.

On the face of it at least, this view has a number of advantages. The most obvious one is that it seems to make what we are to understand as coercion to be a matter of objective fact. Whether A makes it physically impossible for B to act is an empirical issue. It raises no normative considerations. Laws directed at preventing coercion would therefore have a wholly factual objective, namely removing the intentional coercion involving one person making it impossible for another person to act. We would have a clear answer to the question of whether B is free to do *X* or whether A is coercing him or her since impossibility is a physical state of affairs. This would mean that the question of freedom and coercion would not be involved in subjective judgement as to whether B feels coerced or made unfree by A in respect of doing *X*. Whether he or she is coerced or not is a matter of fact, not to be interpreted against an understanding of what B's beliefs and desires happen to be.

In terms of an account of the rule of law such a conception of coercion has a lot to recommend it because it would mean that preventing coercion would not be arbitrary. It would be concerned with coercion as impossibility which is an objective, empirically determinable state rather than with psychological judgements which could vary from person to person. The rule of law has to take coercion in an objective way and it cannot make it relative to the perceptions and feelings of the person who claims to have been coerced.

However, it might be said that such an account of coercion is far too restrictive and does not chime with our own experience because we may see our actions as being constrained by threats rather than impossibility or prevention. In addition, given that in Hayek's view it is the function of the law to use coercion to prevent the coercion of one person by another, how can the law be coercive on the account of pure negative liberty? The law works through *threats* of punishment not by making it impossible for me to do something. So, if we were to abandon this pure idea of negative liberty of freedom as unpreventedness and came to regard threats as coercive, then it is difficult to see how the objectivity of the idea of coercion and thus objectively determinated sphere of freedom could be preserved. To regard a threat as coercive seems to imply some reference to individual psychology and an individual's own scale of values. One person may find a threat so intimidating as to deter him or her from the action he or she would otherwise do, another person faced with the same threat might not feel intimidated at all. So while it may seem eminently plausible to move from a strict account of coercion as impossibility, this move is at the cost of making the idea of coercion much less determinate compared with the case of impossibility. This in turn would have some effect on the scope of law which is there to prevent coercion. If, however, coercion depends on psychological states and beliefs, then the scope of law might be thought to be less determinate unless we thought that there were beliefs, interests, desires, or needs which all rational persons share such that to threaten these would always be coercive and the reason for that would depend on these 'facts' of philosophical anthropology rather than the variable beliefs of individuals. So from this perspective a broader conception of negative liberty to include threats (not to mention offers) might maintain the objectivity of the idea of coercion by means of reference to such a theory of human nature and human purpose. This would not, however, look to be acceptable to a nomocratic theory of law since such accounts of human nature and value are going to be controversial, normative, and ungrounded.

Let us now consider the role of intention in coercion. In terms of the pure theory of negative liberty A's coercion in rendering it impossible for B to do *X* has to be seen as intentional. There might be all sorts of things which prevent B from doing *X*: he/she may be physically incapable of doing *X*; *X* may be a practical impossibility; or there may be physical constraints to do with time and place which prevent him or her doing X. This form of impossibility which does not depend on human agency would not be coercion. Coercion on the pure theory comes in through human agency and intention. This, however, is not as clear as it might seem. There are a lot of questions about intention: the proximity of the coercer to the coerced person; intention versus foreseeability; acts and omissions; and the relationship between moral responsibility for coercion and causal responsibility. These questions are raised by Hayek's own treatment of these issues and will be considered in the critical evaluation of these things in Part II of this book. All that needs to be pointed out at the moment is that even the pure theory of negative liberty contains very complex issues which become even more salient in a theory such as Hayek's which does not defend such a pure theory of negative liberty.

There is one final point worth making about Hayek in relation to the pure theory of negative liberty and that is the idea of impossibility which is at the heart of this position's account of coercion. It seems clear that Hayek adopts a much looser view of coercion than the advocate of pure negative liberty. His account of coercion incorporates the depiction of coercion as impossibility, but in his view it involves a wider set of constraints. Recall that he defines freedom as a state in which 'a man is not subject to coercion by the arbitrary will of another or others'. Let us put on one side the issue of arbitrariness of the will for the moment and concentrate on coercion. He clearly wants to distinguish between coercion and direct, inescapable, physical force when he argues in *The Constitution of Liberty* that a person subject to coercion still retains the capacity for choice in those circumstances. The passage involved is worth quoting in full:

> It is not that the coerced does not choose at all; if that were the case we should not speak of his 'acting'. If my hand is guided by physical force to trace my signature or my finger pressed against the trigger of a gun, I have not acted. Such violence, which makes my body someone's physical tool is, of course, as bad as coercion proper and must be prevented for the same reason. Coercion implies, however, that I still choose but that my mind is made someone else's tool, because the alternatives before me have been so manipulated that the conduct that the coercer wants me to choose becomes for me the least painful one. Although coerced, it is still I who decide which is the least painful evil under the circumstances.[37]

Therefore, physical force and violence, which would be the paradigm case of coercion for the defender of pure negative liberty, are certainly restrictions of freedom for Hayek but have to be distinguished from coercion. The reason being that coercion is about *action* rather than just *physical movements*. If I have no choice I do not act. The man who signs with a gun held to his head is behaving not acting; he is more like a robot rather than an agent. There seems to be some running together of these points about coercion and action when he argues at page 139 that 'coercion is the control of the essential data of an individual's action by another'.

All of this clearly differentiates his view of coercion from that of the defender of pure negative liberty. As we saw, one of the points in favour of the pure theory from a neo-liberal perspective on the rule of law is that it provides a non-normative and non-subjectivist account of coercion. Given that Hayek moves beyond this account of negative freedom, we have to ask whether in his own account this essential feature of coercion can be retained. This will constitute a major theme in Chapter 10. In the passage just cited, Hayek talks about the 'essential data' of an action. What are we to understand by this? If the language is to be understood precisely I think that it must mean an action's constituent parts and this includes bodily movement since all actions are constituted out of such bodily data. Even the action of remaining stationary so as not to alert a burglar depends on the physical state of the body for its performance. So if bodily data are essential for actions and if coercion involves the control of bodily movements, then it becomes very difficult to see what the difference is between coercion in this sense and the forcing of bodily movements of the type that Hayek wanted to distinguish from coercion in the passage previously cited. It may be that we can make some progress here by considering what Hayek means by 'inner freedom'. In his account of freedom and coercion outlined earlier Hayek wanted to distinguish personal freedom or individual liberty from political freedom on the one hand and what he called inner freedom on the other. By inner freedom Hayek means the capacity that a person has to follow purposes of 'his own considered will, by his reason or convictions' and not to act on momentary impulse or circumstance. In terms of inner freedom my own weakness of character, my own lack of foresight, or my own obsessions and neuroses, may impede my liberty to achieve the goals that I want to achieve. For Hayek, however, this has nothing to do with personal or individual freedom, which is understood as the absence of coercion and the possession of an assured private sphere. There is, however, a link between this inner freedom and freedom as the absence of coercion and it is at least implicitly recognized by Hayek. If coercion goes beyond physical impossibility, as Hayek clearly thinks that it does, then difficulty here is that if coercion is a matter of individual perception related to what Hayek calls 'inner strength',[38] then the idea of coercion and the idea of freedom, since that is the absence of coercion, would no longer have the objectivity which they seemed to have under pure negative liberty. If the state is to use the threat of coercion to prevent coercion between private individuals, then this claim becomes problematic and inexact if coercion is essentially perceptual and evaluative. In the views of some philosophers, it is of vital importance to distinguish between 'being free' (objective fact) and 'feeling free' (perceived and evaluated situation). On the neo-liberal account of the rule of law, the role of law is to secure mutual non-coercion and it can only do this in a universal, equal, and abstract way if it does not incorporate subjective perceptions of coercion. Once we move away from the idea of impossibility and prevention, this view becomes much more difficult to sustain.

Hayek's solution to the problem, as set out with extreme brevity in *The Constitution of Liberty*, is to claim that as far as social philosophy is concerned he is taking into account coercion in respect of what he calls 'the normal, average person' and in his view this means that coercion will be seen in terms of the following: 'threat of bodily harm to oneself or those dear to one; or damage to a valuable or cherished possession'.[39] Now, this is no doubt a sensible move to make in the argument, but it seems pretty clear that Hayek's list against what sorts of goods and aspects of the coerced person's life the normal or average person would regard as coercive appears rather perfunctory and underdetermined. The point is partly that Hayek's list is far from being plausibly exhaustive, and partly this means that it may be indeterminate and controversial. Does it for example include needs? In *The Constitution of Liberty* Hayek himself produces an argument in the context of coercion which could easily be extended to show that even on Hayek's own terms, needs have a part to play in the list of what might be thought of as the normal average person's basic interests – interference with which would be coercive on Hayek's own view. He takes the case of a monopolist who owns the only remaining spring in an oasis.[40] If the monopolist required people to pay a very high price to buy water from him to survive, then this for Hayek would be a clear case of coercion. The reason is twofold: first of all the water is, to use Hayek's term, 'an essential commodity' and one way of describing an essential commodity would be that it meets a basic need and therefore withholding that 'indispensable supply' would be coercive. The second reason why the action of the monopolist would be coercive is that there are no alternative suppliers of the good to meet this basic need. However, the behaviour of a monopoly provider would not be coercive if, for example, he was the only supplier of beads at the oasis. Beads are not an essential good. Therefore, the coercion resides more in the withholding of the goods to satisfy basic needs rather than in the monopoly on its own. Other types of monopoly may be undesirable but they are not coercive because they do not have this link to basic needs. So, taking our guide from this example and using Hayek's language about coercion being the control of the data of an individual's actions, it would be possible to argue that the satisfaction of basic needs is an essential datum for any action whatsoever. If the denial of satisfaction by those capable of supplying such means satisfying basic needs can be coercive, then the satisfaction of them may be seen as part of freedom on Hayek's views of the link between freedom and coercion. This, as we shall see later, would take us some way from the normal approach of neo-liberals. So for example, given Hayek's own emphasis on the nature of freedom involving following a coherent plan of life, why does freedom not involve access to these resources which are the 'essential data' to that achievement? Indeed, Hayek himself argues at page 136 that I am indeed coerced by someone who refuses me goods and services 'which are crucial to my existence or the preservation of what I most value'. Hayek, as we have seen, has argued that pursuing a coherent plan of life is crucial to what it is to be a thinking, valuing human, and as such it could certainly be argued that the satisfaction of needs is essential to freedom. This would, however, turn Hayek's theory from a negative to a positive theory of freedom.

This point can be taken further by looking further at other aspects of Hayek's account of coercion. As we have seen, for Hayek coercion has to be compatible with choice. The problem with coercion is that the ends for which I act are in the hands of another and I act according to this evil to avoid a worse evil. As we saw earlier, Hayek rejected the view that freedom involves the possession of a particular range of options, but as we have seen in the argument developing he has come to accept that there is in fact a link between freedom and particular sorts of options. Certain types of goods are more significant than others in human life and being unable to choose those goods is implicitly for Hayek a restriction of liberty. There are two aspects to this. First of all, as we have seen, Hayek regards certain sorts of goods to be indispensable for human life and for the pursuing of a coherent plan of life and to be a thinking and valuing person. Hence, these goods are always going to be highly significant for freedom.[41] Secondly, the goods which are essential to freedom for a particular individual are going to be those which are central to his or her rational and coherent plan of life.

There is a final issue to discuss at this juncture and it has to do with the question of what is so bad about coercion, or wherein lies the evil of coercion? Hayek has a very clear answer to this question because he says quite clearly that

> [c]oercion is evil precisely because it thus eliminates an individual as a thinking and valued person and makes him a bare tool in the achievement of the evils of another.[42]

He had previously defined coercion as 'such control of the environment or circumstances of a person by another that, in order to avoid greater evil he is forced to act not according to a coherent plan of his own but to serve the ends of another'.[43]

Given that coercion prevents the following of a coherent plan of life it would seem reasonably natural therefore in today's idiom that coercion is wrong because it restricts autonomy. Freedom as the absence of coercion (negative liberty in Hayek's version of it) is valuable because it facilitates autonomy. It is his account of the relationship between autonomy and material goods on which I want to focus. We have already seen that for Hayek an autonomous life in terms of its negative liberty aspect means that very great importance is attached to the preservation of life and loved ones and cherished or valuable aspects and attachments. Interference with these aspects is coercive. We have also seen in the oasis example that there are goods essential to my existence the lack of access to which may, if another agent is involved in denying that access, threaten my freedom. I have suggested that a critique of Hayek, wanting to transform and develop his work, could well build upon these points. Nevertheless, Hayek's view here is complex and we need to look at his approach to freedom and employment contracts. This is very important partly because as he has argued in relation to personal control over material goods this does not require direct ownership but may be secured, for example, by a rental contract and partly because many socialists, social democrats, and social liberals have in fact focused on the idea that in a free market there is great danger that the contractual relationship may be unfair, exploitative, and coercive. So it seems reasonable in discussing Hayek's account of coercion to consider what he says about this fundamental issue.

We have just looked at the case of monopoly in relation to essential goods to meet basic needs. However, where there is no monopoly in other sorts of goods in terms say of an employment contract, then agreeing to such a contract even if very disadvantageous or harmful to me is not coercive because there are other suppliers of work with whom I could sign a contract. Where there is more than one source of work, a particular employment contract cannot be coercive. (It is worth noting at this point that this rather runs against Hayek's argument cited earlier that the range of options open to me has nothing to do with liberty.) 'So long as he (the employer) can remove only one opportunity among many to earn a living, he cannot coerce, though he may cause pain.'[44] The crucial point here is that there are other options open to me so the contract is not coercive. So coercion, or the absence of it, will crucially depend on the assessment of the number of options open. Hayek expresses confidence that significant numbers of options will still be open in a competitive market economy for this not to be a problem. He does, however, say that for an employer to insist on conditions in addition to those set out in a contract may well be coercive against certain sorts of backgrounds particularly in circumstances of high unemployment which has occurred, let us say, since the contract was entered into.[45] However, in general he does not see the sphere of contract as a likely site for coercion. His position has a startling simplicity. He argues that outside of the oasis type of case the withholding of a benefit from me by the intentional action of another is not coercive. The fact that A has withheld this benefit from B – such as an offer of employment – has changed the context in which B exercises his or her autonomy. It may have reduced the options open to B to 'distressingly few'; nevertheless this action does not coerce, even though B has to act under 'great pressure'. He goes on to say:

> Even if the threat of starvation to me and perhaps to my family impels me to accept a distasteful job at a very low wage, even if I am 'at the mercy' of the only man willing to employ me, I am not coerced by him or anyone else.[46]

Why is this so? There are two reasons: The fact that even though my plans and my capacity to follow a coherent plan will now be truncated it is still my own, and not some other, will that guides my action. He then goes on to say:

> [S]o long as the act (of withholding the benefit) has placed me in my predicament is not aimed at making me do or not do specific things, so long as the intent of the act that harms me is not to make me serve another ends, its effect on my freedom is not different from that of any natural calamity – a fire or a flood that destroys my house, or an accident that harms my health.[47]

Coercion is a threat of an action or the action itself which displaces my own ends by another's. It is not coercive to make an offer say of employment on very disadvantageous terms to me which I am compelled to accept to avoid starvation – in the case cited by Hayek. Such an approach implies that *threats* are coercive and *offers* are not. It also implies that there is a clear and categorical distinction to be drawn between threats and offers – even offers which in the extreme case cited by Hayek can hardly be refused. There is, however, a very considerable literature disputing the basis of such a distinction and the implication of that literature is that, at the very least, Hayek's argument here needs to be made much more sophisticated before we can assume that there is such a categorical difference between coercive threats and uncoercive offers. One reason why defenders of pure negative liberty want to argue that offers cannot be coercive is that it would make the idea of coercion too subjective. What might be seen by person A in situation *X* to be a very onerous and therefore potentially coercive offer may be seen by B in situation *Y* in a different light. Of course, such defenders of pure negative liberty take the same view of threats. See for example Steiner's argument:

> Interventions of an offering or a threatening kind effect changes in an individual's relative desires to do certain actions. But neither the making of threats nor that of offers constitutes a diminution of personal liberty.[48]

Because of the link between threats, offers, and desires, to assume that either or both could infringe liberty is to make liberty wholly subjective and to confuse 'being free' with 'feeling free'. However, it is not open to Hayek to use this argument in relation to the non-coerciveness of offers since he has already argued that coercion is to be seen largely in terms of threats. So in order to argue that the offer made in the example he gives set against the background of potential starvation for the agent and his or her family he has to distinguish between threats and offers on other grounds.

His argument is partly to do with ends or goals and purposes and partly to do with intention. A coercive threat is such because the threat is to displace my own will, my own purposes, or my own values as the controlling force in my life, and to replace it by the will of another. As a result of a coercive threat I shall not be able to act on a coherent plan of life. An offer in Hayek's view is different – as long as the intent of the offer is 'not to make me serve another person's ends'. This is quite ambiguous, as any offer by A to B is going to invite B to perform some service to A and thus will in *that respect* serve A's ends. Presumably, Hayek means that an offer is coercive when a substantial portion of B's purposes are replaced by A's and that A's ends then dominate B's. There is, of course, then a question of how any offer does or does not do this and how that is to be determined – so reducing the question of whether an offer is coercive or not to a subjective perception of how extensively the terms of the offer will affect B's own goals and coherent plan of life – in other words affect his autonomy.

As we saw earlier in this chapter Hayek does link liberty with essential goods in his oasis example so, given his current example about avoiding starvation through concluding a harsh contract, why does not he regard such a contract as coercive. After all it is the potential absence of a necessary good, namely food, that leads the individual to conclude the contract. His answer to this brings into play the central role of intention in his account of coercion. In the oasis case the well owner is intent on denying the supply of a necessary good except at exorbitant cost. It is this fact that makes it a case of coercion. The present example about the employment contract is one equally concerned with a necessary good – the absence of starvation. The crucial difference for Hayek is that the absence of food is not the result of the behaviour and intention of the person offering the contract. In the oasis case the withholding of an essential supply to meet a basic need would be an intentional act; in the present case it would not. Therefore, the situation we are considering would be coercive only if the poverty of the individual was caused by the intentional action of another. This raises the question of the appropriate description and identification of the intention which is by no means a simple matter.[49]

The question at stake is whether and if so in what way poverty can be regarded as coercive and thus a form of unfreedom. In Hayek's view it can, if it is caused intentionally by another. If, however, it is caused by non-intentional forces such as famine, damaged harvests, etc., then poverty makes me unable to do things, but is not coercive or a form of unfreedom. So in a free society with a very large role for the market, would the poverty which some would experience as a result of market exchanges be a form of coercion and unfreedom? For Hayek the answer to this question is 'no' because while it is true that in a market millions of people buy and sell they do this intentionally, nevertheless the overall, aggregate outcomes of all this economic activity is not intended by anyone. The distribution of income and wealth that arises as the aggregate outcome of market exchange and the place of the poor in that distribution is not an intentional result or outcome. Therefore, poverty that is not caused as part of the deliberate intention of another is not unfreedom and it does not mean that the poverty acts as a form of coercion upon a person when, for example, he or she may conclude (for himself or herself) a tough employment contract.

This position raises some serious questions about the role of intention in distribution and the relationship, for example, between intention and foreseeability, intention and acts and omissions, and the way in which human agency can be identified in complex processes. However, these questions are more at home in Chapter 4 on social justice.

NOTES

1. Hayek, F. A. (1960). *The Constitution of Liberty.* London: Routledge and Kegan Paul. p. 421.
2. Hayek, F. A. *The Constitution of Liberty*, p. 12.
3. Hayek, F. A. *The Constitution of Liberty*, pp. 16–17.
4. See for example, Carter, M. (2003). *T. H. Green and the Development of Ethical Socialism.* Exeter: Academic Imprint; Leighton, D. P. (2004). *The Greenian Moment: T. H. Green, Religion and Political Argument in Victorian Britain.* Exeter: Imprint Academic; Richter, M. (2004). *The Politics of Conscience: T. H. Green and His Age.* London: Weidenfeld and Nicholson; Vincent, A. and Plant, R. (1981). *Philosophy, Politics and Citizenship.* Oxford: Blackwell; and Wempe, B. (2004). *T. H. Green's Theory of Positive Freedom: From Metaphysics to Political Theory.* Exeter: Imprint Academic.
5. Hayek, F. A. *The Constitution of Liberty*, p. 19.
6. Rothbard, M. (2002). *The Ethics of Liberty.* New York: New York University Press.
7. Hayek, F. A. *The Constitution of Liberty*, p. 13.
8. Hayek, F. A. *The Constitution of Liberty*, p. 14.
9. Hayek, F. A. *The Constitution of Liberty*, p. 15.
10. Hayek, F. A. *The Constitution of Liberty*, p. 15.
11. Hayek, F. A. *The Constitution of Liberty*, p. 13.
12. Hayek, F. A. *The Constitution of Liberty*, pp. 12 and cf. 17.

13. Hayek, F. A. *The Constitution of Liberty*, p. 21.
14. Hayek, F. A. *The Constitution of Liberty*, pp. 134, 140–3.
15. Kukathas, C. (1989). *Hayek and Modern Liberalism.* Oxford: The Clarendon Press, p. 143.
16. Hayek, F. A. *The Constitution of Liberty*, op. cit., pp. 12 and cf. 139.
17. Hayek, F. A. *The Constitution of Liberty*, p. 21.
18. Hayek, F. A. *The Constitution of Liberty*, p. 150.
19. Hayek, F. A. *The Constitution of* Liberty, p. 153.
20. Hayek, F. A. (1979). *Law, Legislation and Liberty*, Vol. 3, *The Political Order of a Free People.* London: Routledge and Kegan Paul, p. 157.
21. Hayek, F. A. *Law, Legislation and Liberty*, Vol. 3, *The Political Order of a Free People*, p. 157.
22. Hayek, F. A. *The Constitution of Liberty*, p. 68.
23. Hayek, F. A. *The Constitution of Liberty*, p. 68.
24. Hayek, F. A. *The Constitution of Liberty*, p. 68.
25. Hayek, F. A. *The Constitution of Liberty*, p. 29.
26. Hayek, F. A. *The Constitution of Liberty*, p. 21.
27. Hayek, F. A. *The Constitution of Liberty*, pp. 20–1.
28. Hayek, F. A. *The Constitution of Liberty*, p. 13.
29. Hayek, F. A. *The Constitution of Liberty*, p. 97.
30. Hayek, F. A. *The Constitution of Liberty*, p. 71.
31. Hayek, F. A. *The Constitution of Liberty*, p. 81.
32. Hayek, F. A. *The Constitution of Liberty*, p. 140.
33. Hayek, F. A. *The Constitution of Liberty*, p. 140.
34. Hayek, F. A. *The Constitution of Liberty*, pp. 140–1.
35. Hayek, F. A. *The Constitution of Liberty*, pp. 140–1.
36. Hayek, F. A. *The Constitution of Liberty*, pp. 140–1.
37. Hayek, F. A. *The Constitution of Liberty*, p. 138.
38. Hayek, F. A. *The Constitution of Liberty*, p. 138.
39. Hayek, F. A. *The Constitution of Liberty*, p. 136.
40. Hayek, F. A. *The Constitution of Liberty*, p. 136.
41. Hayek, F. A. *The Constitution of Liberty*, p. 21.
42. Hayek, F. A. *The Constitution of Liberty*, p. 21.
43. Hayek, F. A. *The Constitution of Liberty*, p. 136.
44. Hayek, F. A. *The Constitution of Liberty*, p. 136.
45. Hayek, F. A. *The Constitution of Liberty*, p. 137.
46. Hayek, F. A. *The Constitution of Liberty*, p. 137.
47. Hayek, F. A. *The Constitution of Liberty*, p. 137.
48. Steiner, H. (1970). 'Individual Liberty', *Proceedings of the Aristotelian Society.*
49. For a discussion of some of the complexities here, see Anscombe, E. (1963). *Intention*, 2nd edn, Oxford: Blackwell.

4

Social Justice: A Mirage?

Earlier in this book there was a discussion of the relationship between justice and the rule of law in neo-liberal thought. The aim of this chapter is to focus on the issue of social or distributive justice, sometimes called 'economic justice'. Among neo-liberal thinkers there is a very strong opposition to the claims of social justice which are regarded as being illusory or a mirage. This issue is an absolutely crucial one for the intellectual coherence of neo-liberalism and for its conception of *Rechtsstaat* – that is to say the conception of a state which would embody the rule of law as a moral ideal as understood by neo-liberal thinkers. In the neo-liberal view, the welfare state has grown up in European societies under the pressure of claims about social justice. It is, however, an essential theme of neo-liberal thought that a socially just version of the welfare state cannot be made compatible with the rule of law. This is denied by social democrats such as Gustav Radbruch who argued in his *Rechtsphilosophie*:

> The socialist community would also be a Rechtsstaat, although a Rechtsstaat governed not by commutatitive justice but by distributive justice.[1]

The neo-liberal denies this possibility, and the denial is rooted in the critique of the idea of social justice. There are many aspects to this critique set out by different neo-liberal authors, so, as with the first chapter devoted to freedom, I shall try first of all to set out as fairly and as sympathetically as I can the main aspects of the critique of social justice.

The first element of the critique is most comprehensively developed by Hayek and draws upon his idea of the rule of law. It will be recalled that for Hayek the law should not be telological but rather nomocratic. That is to say that as a set of universal, abstract, and predictable rules, the law should set the framework for action with which individuals are able to pursue their own goals and purposes and in doing so not engage in the coercion of others. It is not the function of law to serve a set of goals or purposes or a hierarchy of goods and purposes. The rules governing an organization will typically facilitate the achievement of certain aims – namely those that the organization is set up to achieve but, as far as society is concerned, there are no such overall goals and purposes and there would be a grave danger of authoritarianism and, indeed in Hayek's view, totalitarianism were any such goals to be pursued.[2] However, social justice is precisely about the achievement of an overall goal, namely a particular pattern of distribution of economic and social resources. Below this overall goal there will be subordinate goals set out either as law or policy which will be instrumental to the achievement of that overall aim.

Such an overall distribution of resources might, for example, be one based on merit or desert, or it might be based upon need or equality – the key point though, is that in a state the aim of whose policy is social justice the law will be telocratic and not nomocratic. If as neo-liberals clearly think nomocratic law is the most desirable form of law, then in so far as social justice requires telocratic law it will require a set of bad laws.

A regime based on social justice would not only contravene the principles of the *Rechtsstaat* and nomocratic law in the way indicated, but in other ways too. These include the following aspects. First of all if it is the job of law to secure to individuals a particular bundle of goods in the interests of social justice, then this is going to entail that the law applies unequally between people. On the neo-liberal view of nomocratic law aimed at preventing mutual coercion, it is perfectly possible to believe that the law will apply equally to all and can be equally obeyed by all because the law requires abstinence from action – namely acts of coercion. Forbearing to coerce does not run up against the limits of scarcity. However, if it is assumed under the influence of social justice that the law has to secure particular sets of goods to individuals as part of their just share or distribution then, because such goods will involve scarcity, there can be no guarantee that each individual will in fact receive his or her just share. This contrasts very unfavourably with the achieved position of equal protection against coercion in the context of nomocratic law.

If it is assumed that goods are to be distributed equally under an egalitarian conception of distributive justice, then the position is considerably worse. As Hayek points out in *Law, Legislation and Liberty: The Mirage of Social Justice*:

> There is, of course, a great difference between governments treating all citizens according to the same rules in all the activities it undertakes for other purposes and the government doing what is required in order to place the different citizens is equal (or less unequal) material positions. . . . Since people will differ in many attributes which governments cannot alter, to secure for them the same material position would require that the government treat them very differently. Indeed, to assure the same material position to people who differ greatly in strength, intelligence, skill, knowledge and perseverance as well as their physical and social environment, government would clearly have to treat them very differently to compensate for these disadvantages and deficiencies it could not directly alter.[3]

Therefore, again on this view, a state of social justice would not be compatible with the *Rechtsstaat* ideal of equality before the law.

There is a further point about social justice and the law which will be taken up further in the chapter on bureaucracy but it is that social justice is about fair or just shares of social goods for individuals – goods such as health, education, benefits, etc. If the job of the state is to produce particular outcomes for particular people to ensure them a 'just' share, then considerable arbitrary power has to be put into the hands of those who administer the welfare system. It is arbitrary in a number of ways according to the neo-liberal, as we shall see later. For the moment, in the context of the rule of law, it might be regarded as arbitrary in the sense that it is not possible to write rules of law which could in fact procure particular outcomes for particular people. This fact, along with the fact of scarcity, will mean that there will be a very clear limit to the extent to which administrators of the welfare system can in fact stay true to the rule of law.

The final point in relation to the *Rechtsstaat* and nomocratic law is more complex in some ways. It is that if a particular form of distributive or social justice – say distribution according to merit is going to overlay the market economy – then this will completely distort the role of the market as an information exchange via the price system. Instead of a good or service commanding a market price which reflects a multitude of valuations of people each from their own subjective view, price and value will be a politically determined distribution of at least some sort of goods independently of free market exchange. This will displace the fact that what a good or service is worth will depend on what other people are prepared to pay for it. In this context, from a neo-liberal view, the consequences are dire:

> Once the rewards the individual can expect are no longer an appropriate indication of how to direct their efforts to where they are most needed, because these rewards correspond not to the value which their services have for their fellows, but to the moral merit or desert the persons are deemed to have earned, they use the guiding function they have in the market order and would have to be replaced by the commands of the directing authority.[4]

Not only would this be a great threat to liberty, it would also be fundamentally incompatible with the generality and abstract nature of the rule of law in the absence of market signals which operate at a macro level on individual motivation. The administrative aim of the state would have to allocate benefits and burdens to individuals based on expediency or perceived efficiency and this again would not be compatible with the ideal of the rule of law.

There are, in addition, other aspects of the critique of social justice which do not have this internal relationship with the rule of law. The first is an argument about moral diversity. There is a range of possible distributive principles: merit, need, equality, contribution to society, etc. To appeal to social justice as a guiding principle without specifying the particular distributive principle to be involved does not take us anywhere. One way of putting this point following Rawls' terminology is that there is a concept of social justice which is general and indeterminate such as 'to each his or her due' but that has to be turned into a specific conception where 'due' is interpreted in terms of need, merit, equality, or whatever. The problem is that these different conceptions will yield potential distributions which are not compatible with one another. Take the simplest example: Distributing a cake at a family tea according to need (where one family member has missed lunch) will yield a different sized slice to one based on desert (where another family member has just passed an examination). So we cannot embrace all of the conceptions simultaneously. We have to have a mechanism to determine which principle of distribution will prevail over others. Alternatively, we might think that while they are not all compatible, they each have a place in thinking about distribution – perhaps depending on what sort of good it is. Then, however, we need to look for agreement about what sort of goods should be distributed according to what kind of principle and the point at which one principle and one good gives way to another – for example, when do we stop meeting needs and move on to deserts? John Gray, when he was more sympathetic to neo-liberalism than he now is, had a particularly good and trenchant account of what he regarded as the insoluble dilemmas here. He is speaking about needs but the point would apply to merit and other distributive principles too. He is pointing out that distributive principles are part of broader moral frameworks which may well compete and will almost certainly be incommensurable:

> The objectivity of basic needs is equally delusive. Needs can be given no plausible cross cultural content, but instead are seen to vary across different moral traditions. Even where moral traditions overlap so as to allow agreement to be reached on a list of basic needs, there is no means of arriving at a schedule of urgency among conflicting basic needs.... There is an astonishing presumptiveness in those who write as if dilemmas of the sort can be subject to morally consensual resolution. Their blindness to those difficulties can only be accounted for by their failure to take seriously the realities of moral pluralism in our society or . . . to their taking as authoritative their own traditional values.[5]

Therefore, on this view not only would the law in a state seeking social justice necessarily be telocratic but the goal, end, or purpose of that law would be endlessly controversial. The controversies would be between principles (e.g. need and desert), but also within each of these as Gray's passage indicates there are deep controversies. If freedom is to be free from arbitrary coercion as it is for Hayek, then a set of laws which require one distribution rather than another is going to be arbitrary in respect of the preferred principles of distribution. Of course, it might be argued that there is a ready answer to the question, namely a democratic state; however, this response will be looked at later when we discuss the neo-liberal approach to democracy and the scope of democratic decision-making.

It is central to neo-liberalism that justice and injustice can only occur in the context of human intentional action. A natural event like the weather, though it might devastate someone's life, does not cause injustice since it was not the result of an intentional process. To suffer from a genetic disorder is not an injustice, even though it might have dire consequences for the individual just because it is not the result of intention. (Both of these examples, of course, presuppose that God is not intending to cause havoc with the weather or genetic pattern in a particular family.) Therefore I can certainly cause injustice by any act of intentional coercion in which I am involved and the law is there to protect individuals from such injustice by the negative device of requiring individuals to abstain from such acts. This argument is then used to undermine the whole case for social justice in the following way: A concern with social justice is usually inspired by recognizing poverty and deprivation. Poverty and deprivation in the context of a relatively rich society is regarded as unjust and as needing collective state action to rectify. Such are typically the views of those with a belief in social justice.

However, this presupposes that the poverty and deprivation are injustices but these in turn, on the argument presented earlier, have to be shown to arise from intentional action. The claim of the neo-liberal is that this is not the case, that in the words of H. B. Acton, poverty and 'deprivation are evils but they are not injustices'.[6] The detail of the argument works out in the following way: In a market millions of people are involved in buying and selling and they do so (usually) intentionally. So each act of exchange is intentional. To be sure, injustice can arise at this individual level. I may coerce you into an exchange, for example, or I can wrongly deprive you of your resources by fraud, cheating, embezzling, and the like. All of those are injustices because they follow from the intentional action of one individual towards another. However, the aggregate outcomes of markets where some grow rich, others grow poor, some prosper, others fail are an *unintended* consequence of market behaviour. We are misled by our language into thinking that overall market outcomes are intended – we talk glibly, for example, about the 'distribution' of income and wealth which might be thought to imply an intentional process of distribution. But this is a fundamentally flawed idea. There is no intention, and there is no distributor. The 'patterns' of income and wealth are an unintended consequence of countless forms of individual behaviour. It is an aggregate consequence of millions of different and diverse intentional acts and this aggregate outcome is not intended.

Since they are not intended, the outcomes cannot be regarded as being either just or unjust because, as we have seen, injustice and justice are direct consequences of individual behaviour. Market outcomes, from this point of view are, to use Fred Hirsch's felicitous words 'in principle unprincipled'.[7] Since these outcomes are unintended they cannot be unjust and we do not have collective responsibilities to rectify them. It is certainly a central duty of the state and the rule of law to protect people from injustice but there is no moral case for saying the injustice can be seen in the overall 'distribution' of income and wealth in society. This argument strikes at the very heart of the rationale for the social democratic state which is usually seen as having its *raison d'etre* the achievement of social, distributive, or economic justice.

This argument about intention applies to the one put forward by social democrats which says that the outcomes and markets have to be rejected as unjust because of injustice to be found in the fact that people's starting points are so disparate. There is a fundamental issue here. Those who believe in social justice endorse the idea that a just economy is one which produces a pattern of distribution which reflects the preferred distributive principle – merit, equality, or need, for example. The role of government is to use its power intelligently to produce outcomes that approximate to the pattern. Social justice consists of securing that pattern as far as possible. The alternative view, central to neo-liberalism, is that justice is not about *patterns* but about *process*. If we have a system of voluntary exchange in a free market and each exchange is uncoerced, then the outcomes for all via that proviso are to be accepted – just that, not as fair or as just because that implies an intentional outcome. The outcome will not embody any pattern but the uncoerced nature of the individual exchanges which have led to that outcome secure its legitimacy. Now, of course, the critic will immediately fix on the argument that in fact the process is not fair, nor are all exchanges uncoerced because in terms of the starting points of the process individual's resources and holdings will be vastly different. These differences in their turn will mean that the rich will be able to coerce the less well off in respect of employment contracts and other forms of exchange.

There is, however, a ready response to this sort of argument. The first is to do with initial holdings. To argue that those should be justly arranged in order to ensure that the subsequent processes of exchange are fair presupposes that the initial set of holdings possessed by an individual is itself the result of an intentional process and subject to moral critique in respect of social justice. However, assuming that initial holdings and acquisitions are acquired without injustice towards identifiable individuals as the result of fraud or coercion, then the initial holdings of an individual are not susceptible to assessment in terms of social justice or injustice. In the same way as the 'pattern' of income and wealth emerging from market transactions is neither just nor unjust so is the pattern of initial holdings. We cannot regard a process of market exchange leading to a particular aggregate outcome as unjust because starting points are also unjust. Only if they arose because of coercion or fraud would this be so. Indeed, in the view of a thinker such as Hayek we do not need a theory of initial holdings at all. What we have to do is to ensure the negative rule of law – protecting the person from injustice in the sense of coercion by others – is in place and then whatever resource an individual starts with is legitimately held. Although the outcome is the same in this respect Hayek differs somewhat from Robert Nozick who in *Anarchy, State and Utopia* develops a sophisticated account of justice in acquisition and justice in transfer.

The other counter argument to the process approach to justice which I mentioned at the beginning of this discussion also fails for the neo-liberal. The argument is that we cannot accept the outcomes of free market exchange relationships as being legitimate because as the process carries on many of the exchanges will be coercive because of the disparities of income and wealth of the exchanging parties – not least reflecting initial disparities in holdings. However, as we saw in Chapter 3, the neo-liberal account of coercion blocks this line of criticism.

Therefore, given that the question of initial holdings does not (usually) give rise to issues of justice for the neo-liberal, and given that market inequalities are not coercive, it follows for the neo-liberal that the process of market exchange produces legitimate results. We should abandon concern with the pattern at the end of the process and accept the legitimate outcomes arising from just, non-coercive, processes.

The same sort of argument also applies to the neo-liberal case in respect of equality of opportunity. In the neo-liberal view inequality of opportunity is unjust if it arises as the result of the intentional preventing of A acquiring X or the coercion of A in respect of X. Therefore, the removal of intentionally imposed barriers to people being recruited for offices or access to basic goods is a legitimate role for government to take on. In the case of the market or process argument we have been looking at, both at the beginning of a process (however artificial that idea may sound) and while the process is proceeding equal opportunity in the sense defined is for the neo-liberal necessary to make the process fair because the denial of equal opportunities in the respect we are currently considering is a form of coercion and thus unjust.

At this point we need to consider the claim that markets are hard on discrimination. For instance, Cass Sunstein in summarizing an argument with which he disagrees puts the point very well:

> Markets, it is sometimes said, are hard on discrimination. An employer who finds himself refusing to hire qualified blacks and women, will in the long run, lose out to those who are willing to draw from a broader labour pool. Employer discrimination amounts to a self-destructive 'taste', self destructive because employers who indulge that taste add to the cost of doing business. To put it simply, bigots are weak competitors. The market will drive them out.[8]

However, in the view of the neo-liberals this is a very far cry indeed from equality of opportunity understood as a policy, the aim of which is to secure to individuals particular bundles of goods without which they are assumed not to enjoy equality of opportunity.

In *Anarchy, State and Utopia* Nozick makes the argument that if we move away from the idea of removing prohibitions on action as the core of equality of opportunity we shall move into saying that people need resources to improve their opportunities. However, he points out that this must involve worsening the position of some people from whom resources are, in his words, seized via the tax system in order to improve the opportunities of others. But Nozick argues, if those holdings have been justly (i.e. non-coercively) acquired, then they cannot legitimately be taken for this, in any case, morally unjust purpose. He argues that the only legitimate means to this end, even assuming it is regarded as legitimate, is to convince individuals to *choose* 'to devote some of their holdings to achieving it'.[9]

The removal of intentionally imposed restrictions is on a par with the argument about freedom in Chapter 3. The removal of coercion is essential to liberty, so the removal of intentionally imposed restrictions on behaviour – equal opportunities in the neo-liberal sense – is therefore part of the liberty of a free society. However, to secure to individuals particular sets of resources to enable them to compete in market processes more equally, however, is on a par with treating liberty as a *power* or *ability* and we saw earlier the neo-liberal objection to that. So from the neo-liberal point of view, the market is a fair process yielding legitimate outcomes if it embodies equality of opportunity in this limited sense. It does not require that the greater material equality should be secured to people who engage together in market processes as a condition for the legitimacy of such processes.

There is a further critical aspect of the idea of equality of opportunity from a neo-liberal perspective and it is clearly stated by Nozick. His argument is that we are misled by metaphors when thinking about equality of opportunity, particularly the metaphor of life as a race or a competition for some prize or other. This is, however, deeply misleading in his view. It is not the case that life is a single race for a single prize which someone has established. In a free society there are a wide variety of goals which might or might not be pursued and there are different, independent people pursuing them in particular circumstances and contexts. It is not possible to overlay this view completely with a political project of securing a one-dimensional view of equality of opportunity.[10]

From a socialist or social democratic perspective it would be the job of government to ensure that the distributive pattern required by the patterned principle of social justice should be maintained. The neo-liberal will, however, argue that this leads inevitably to a link between freedom and social justice because, as Robert Nozick argues, 'liberty upsets patterns'.[11] Liberty for the neo-liberal is the absence of coercion and within the sphere within which an individual is free from coercion he or she will be able to behave as he or she sees fit. Some of this free action, for example, in gifts, bequests, and the like may well upset any patterned outcomes legitimated by the patterned principles of justice whatever they might be. So the maintenance of a pattern of social justice may well be incompatible with some sorts of individual liberty. Indeed, in the context of gift and bequest there may be liberties which bear a close relationship to family and friends. Gifts to children is a good example. Freedom to spend money on private education, private tutors, gifts of money, etc., may all give a child advantages which other children lack. They are all forms of free action but the effect of these gifts may well be to favour this child in a way the effect of which, when the aggregate consequences of these actions are taken into account, may well disturb the patterns of distribution underpinned by a particular distributive principle. Therefore, the claim is because liberty disturbs patterns in a socially just state, government will constantly have to search for ways to limit that form of liberty, the exercise of which may well undermine the form of social justice in question. Therefore, on the neo-liberal view there cannot be a reconciliation between ideals of liberty and social justice. As we saw earlier, the neo-liberal view of freedom and coercion, ostensibly at least, makes it impossible to effect a reconciliation on the grounds that since liberty involves or includes certain sorts of basic resources, equal liberty requires at least a just or fair distribution of those goods. This argument is blocked by the claim that liberty is one thing, ability resources and opportunities are another. This argument comes to the foreground again at this point to resist the idea that there can be a bridge between liberty and social justice.

There are two further arguments which have been important in the context of social justice. The first is that unpleasant jobs on which society relies may pay very poorly and this is unjust. The second, a slightly different point, is that of rent of ability, that is, the pay level that may be necessary to induce people to take on jobs either because they are unpleasant or because they involve a very great deal of training and responsibility. Hayek's answer to those points is essentially the same. That is to say he points out again that the value of a service is wholly dependent on the valuation of the person or persons to whom the service is rendered. There is no meaningful sense of value independent of this. To think otherwise would be to take the view that the supplier of the service 'merited' or 'needed' a level of remuneration separate from the perceived value of the service. Given the neo-liberal critique of these ideas, it follows that the value of a service is to be revealed by the market price of offering that service whether the price is high or low. Justice or injustice does not come into the picture in a market context.

Much the same argument is deployed in relation to the case to be made for those doing jobs which require more training and which embody more risk and more responsibility who would be suffering an injustice if they were not paid more, almost, as it were, in compensation for these factors. Again, however, Hayek argues that the value of those services should be settled by the market price. This may well increase if few people want to do the jobs because of training and responsibility, etc. These are valued services, and if there is a shortfall the price will rise. This can be represented as a market driven 'rent of ability' rather than a spurious matter of social justice and a concern of government.

There is a further argument about social justice which has to be considered. As this neo-liberal view, which can be found in Mises' *Socialism* and in Nozick's *Anarchy, State and Utopia*, his socialist or social democratic approach to social justice is fundamentally misguided because it presupposes that production and distribution are two quite different things. As Mises puts the point:

> The socialist community is characterised by the fact that there is no connection between production and distribution.[12]

Nozick argues that this view treats goods and services as being like 'manna from heaven'. It sees things as goods to be distributed and that the distribution is to pay no particular attention to the process of production whereby these goods are created. In the view of Nozick and Mises this is a fundamental error. In the case of incomes Mises argues that they are normally fixed in economic transactions and exchanges which are in his words 'indissolubly tied' to production. We do not first produce things and then distribute them. Income and wealth reflect what goes on in the process of production and most importantly the property rights embodied in these processes. These cannot be altered without altering the processes of production and their accompanying property rights. It is, however, a central theme of social democracy that there can be just this disjunction between production and distribution. A very similar point is made by Robert Nozick when he argues that the processes of production create entitlement in those goods including income and wealth that are produced by this process.

Assuming that the activity of production is uncoerced for those who take part in it then there is no reason to think that these entitlements which arise out of production and property rights are illegitimate or that the aggregate patterns of entitlements emerging out of such processes of production are socially unjust even if meaningful content could be given to this idea.

This point is argued by Nozick in the following way:

> [W]hoever makes something having bought or contracted for all other held resources used in the process... is entitled to it. The situation is *not* one of

> something getting made and then there being an open question of who is to get it. Things come into the world already attached to people having entitlements over them.[13]

So long as I act within my own rights and do not infringe those of others – given Nozick's view of coercion – then this non-coercive outcome is legitimate. Without deploying a large-scale theory of rights, Mises' point is very much the same. In the non-manna-from-heaven-world, in which things have to be made or produced or transformed by people, there is no separate process of distribution for a theory of distribution to be a theory of. Interestingly enough, Karl Marx makes the same point in criticism of social democracy in a *Critique of the Gotha Program*.[14]

The final point to be made about the case against social justice is the critique of the word 'social' in legal and political philosophy. This is a point particularly developed by Hayek and echoed by other neo-liberals. There are several strands to the argument.

First of all, Hayek argues that in its origin the word 'social' like 'national', 'tribal', or 'organizational' merely means pertaining to the organization of society. So in a sense any shared activity or practice that is part of society can be called social. Usually, however, these terms would be redundant. A 'social language' would be a pleonasm since language is inherently social and to qualify it by the term 'social' adds nothing to it. The same, he argues, applies to justice. Justice is social in that it is about how one person relates to another – in Hayek's view by not coercing them. It is a term that presupposes social relationships and interaction in just the same way as language does. However, referring to 'social language' in that case does not do harm, but in the case of justice it does, because people come to believe, through the use of such a concept, that society has a responsibility to ensure just shares in the social product and that society agrees to hold itself responsible for the particular material position of all its members.[15]

It has also led, in Hayek's view, to the anthropomorphism of society – that 'society' has responsibilities and can be held accountable for material well-being. As we have seen however, for Hayek there is no central distribution of resources to be identified in a market economy and as collective responsibility for market outcomes.

> Society has simply become the new deity to which we complain and clamour for redress if it does not fulfil the expectations it has created.[16]

Against this Hayek points out that when we complain about the outcome of the market as being unjust, we do not really assert that someone has been unjust (as is the case of individual coercive exchange or fraud) and he argues that there is really no answer to the question of who has been unjust?

These arguments about the meaning of 'social' in the context of social justice (and also social democracy, in Hayek's view) mirror deeper methodological issues in Hayek's thought and that of other neo-liberals, namely other commitments to some form of methodological individualism.

At the heart of the neo-liberal case, therefore, is the claim that it is not in fact possible to reconcile a *Rechtsstaat* and a regime of social justice. A regime of social justice must, of necessity, undermine the rule of law.

There has been a long-running debate about this issue by legal scholars in Germany. For example, E. Forsthoff argued in 1968 in *Rechtsstaatlichkeit und Sozialstaatlichkeit* that half a *Rechtsstaat* and half a *Sozialstaat* would not produce a *sozialer Rechtsstaat.*

> Rechtsstaat and Sozialstaat are based on different and incompatible principles: one is a formal legal conception; the other is a political and policy-oriented conception. The actions of the latter cannot be brought within the rule of law found in the former.[17]

Hayek and other neo-liberals see social justice as atavistic, as a kind of nostalgia from an earlier type of society in which there was an acknowledged social and political purpose, an overriding end to be pursued. This end allowed for the possibility of society directing individuals and groups to do things to contribute to and facilitate the achievement of this overall purpose. In such a society ideas of merit and of common needs could be fixed by the overall *telos.* But, in an open, nomocratic society with no overall ends, with the law having the role of facilitating the achievement of private ends, then these common moral values make no sense. We should embrace modernity in the Great Society and abandon the atavistic concern with social justice.

There are, however, two more points to note at this stage of the argument although their further elaboration and analysis will be delayed until the chapter on the critique of the welfare state and the chapter on rights, respectively. Neo-liberal thinkers are very concerned about what they take to be the political consequences of a state with social justice as its goal. These consequences, it is claimed, involve a very great increase in bureaucracy as the major public instrument for the promotion of social justice with the associated claim that such bureaucracy is not benign, but involves a great deal of necessarily arbitrary power and the opportunity for self-interested and rent-seeking behaviour by bureaucrats. A state of social justice would also bring into being an array of interest groups each seeking on behalf of itself or the groups it represents to push what from its point of view are 'just' entitlements of such a group. This is particularly going to be the case where there are (and can be) no agreed criterion for social justice from a neo-liberal perspective. In such circumstances there will be no moral restraint on what groups may claim for themselves.

The final point is the critique of the idea of social rights: That in a socially just state, such a state would confer a set of welfare rights on individuals which would define their just entitlements. In line with the previous points, this issue raises concerns that go beyond social justice and lead us to the neo-liberal approach of rights and bureaucracy, respectively.

NOTES

1. Radbruch, G. (1950). *Rechtsphilosophie.* Stuttgart: Köhler Verlag, p. 87.
2. Hayek, F. A. (1944). *The Road to Serfdom.* London: Routledge and Kegan Paul.

3. Hayek, F. A. (1976). *Law, Legislation and Liberty, Vol. 2: The Mirage of Social Justice.* London: Routledge and Kegan Paul, p. 82.
4. Hayek, F. A. *Law, Legislation and Liberty, Vol. 2: The Mirage of Social Justice,* p. 82.
5. Gray, J. (1983). 'Classical Liberalism, Positional Goods and the Politicisation of Poverty', in A. Ellis and K. Kumar (eds.), *Dilemmas of Liberal Democracies.* London: Tavistock, pp. 181–2.
6. Acton, H. B. (1993). *The Morals of Markets,* ed. D. Gordon and J. Shearmur, Indianapolis: The Liberty Fund, p. 116.
7. Hirsch, F. (1977). *The Social Limits to Growth.* London: Routledge and Kegan Paul.
8. Sunstein, C. (1997). *Free Markets and Social Justice.* Oxford: Oxford University Press, p. 151.
9. Nozick, R. (1974). *Anarchy, State and Utopia.* Oxford: Blackwell, p. 235.
10. Nozick, R. *Anarchy, State and Utopia,* p. 235.
11. Nozick, R. *Anarchy, State and Utopia,* p. 235.
12. Mises, L. von. (1981). *Socialism.* Indianapolis: The Liberty Fund, p. 134.
13. Nozick, R. *Anarchy, State and Utopia,* p. 160.
14. Marx, K. *Critique of the Gotha Program* in *Collected Works of Marx and Engels,* Vol. 24. London: Lawrence and Wishart, 1989, pp. 87–8.
15. Hayek, F. A. *Law, Legislation and Liberty, Vol. 2: The Mirage of Social Justice,* p. 78–9.
16. Hayek, F. A. *Law, Legislation and Liberty, Vol. 2: The Mirage of Social Justice,* p. 69.
17. Cited in Dyson, K. (1980). *The State Tradition in Western Europe.* Oxford: Martin Robertson, p. 127.

5

Neo-liberal Rights

In this chapter I shall look in detail at rights-based theories, and in so doing I shall concentrate on four aspects of such theories. The first is concerned with the grounding of such rights claims; the second with the sorts of rights which are thought to be entailed by such grounding; third, I shall look at the very important issue of whether or not a theory of rights can add anything significant to the account of coercion which I discussed earlier; and finally I shall look at the claim shared by all neo-liberals namely that social and economic rights are not genuinely rights.

In the context of grounding rights I will consider two approaches each of which has been influential in the development of neo-liberalism, although the authors of these theories, probably in the case of Robert Nozick and certainly in the case of Murray Rothbard, would dissent from such a label.

Nozick's theory of rights provides a very important alternative to seeing the justification of the free market and limited government in terms of efficiency and utility. We found such an argument in at least one strand in Hayek's justification for markets when he argued that the market plays an essential role in enabling us to deal with the dispersed and fragmented nature of knowledge. Without the market we would face severe constraints on our ability to act effectively. Competitive markets solve coordination problems; they indicate relative values of goods and services, and they are discovery mechanisms. The justification for the market and for its continuing legitimacy therefore rests upon the facts about the human situation. It is important not to under-appreciate what is being argued here. These problems in the human condition are, in one sense contingent – no God ordained that things should be like this – in another sense, however, they are not contingent in that from the point of view of the market protagonist these features relating to the nature of knowledge cannot be remedied or displaced by any mechanism ranging from computers to central planning. They are endemic features in human life. Therefore, when it is claimed that a Hayekian type of justification of market institutions has a strong utilitarian element, it is utilitarian in a sense rather unlike the assessment of other social practices and institutions by utilitarian or consequentialist criteria. Overall the market is much more efficient than alternatives but that is not so because it provides the means of satisfying a group of current preferences, even though it does do this. Rather its efficiency goes a very long way beyond meeting a set of current preferences; it is rather a condition for securing a remedy for the natural circumstances of human life in providing an abstract order within which we can utilize whatever limited knowledge we have got.

Rights-based theories, on the contrary, are thought by the proponents to produce a very different basis for the justification of the market. On the rights-based view, which is taken to involve an absolute set of demands, the market and very limited governments, in the case of Nozick constitute the only set of institutions which will satisfy the basic moral imperatives embodied in rights. So, at least theoretically a market order and a *Rechtsstaat* could still be regarded as legitimate even if it did not actually increase wealth and preference satisfaction or the utilization of knowledge. Its legitimacy would lie in the fact that it protects basic rights.

There is another sense too in which the utilitarian and the rights-based approach differ quite fundamentally in their approach to the understanding of market institutions. On the conventional basis of comparison, the utilitarian approach is oriented to outcomes, for example, whether the market maximizes welfare and efficiency relative to other real-world alternatives. While such an approach may well eschew looking at markets in terms of social justice, which is another end state or outcome-based framework for evaluation, it does share with such an approach to patterned principles of social justice, a concern with *outcomes*.

On the other hand, a rights-based approach both justifies markets in general and assesses particular market exchanges in terms of *process*. So, in the process of exchange, does the definition of property rights, does the framework for contract, etc. transgress basic rights or not? If the processes are just – in the sense of being consistent with and not transgressing rights – then the outcomes are legitimate and are not to be further assessed in terms of other criteria such as utility, welfare creation, and certainly not social justice. Rights, to use Nozick's terminology, put side constraints on an individual's action and the individual must act within such constraints for his or her behaviour to be just. Therefore, justice plays a role in the justification of markets, but emphatically not in the outcome and patterned sense of social justice. Rather justice is a matter of process and the process is just if it occurs within the side constraints embodied in individual rights.

We shall now look briefly at Nozick's and Rothbard's rights-based theories because each theory reveals interesting insights into the normative framework within which markets operate.

While Nozick has a very strong theory of rights, the implications of which are argued with great verve and rigour, he is often regarded as having failed to produce a convincing account of the normative basis for the set of rights that he endorses – producing, in effect, a 'libertarianism without foundations'.[1] If this were true, it would be a serious defect in his theory since his account of rights and their relation to the market order would lack conviction to the extent to which they would lack grounding. It would be open to the critic merely to say that he or she did not share Nozick's intuitions about rights, their nature, and their scope and thus did not feel compelled to accept the legitimacy of the market order based upon these controversial rights. So, there is a clear connection between rights and the grounding offered (or not) for such rights. As we shall see, this is true also of Rothbard. In addition, the scope of rights, for example whether they are negative or positive – requiring resources – is very heavily influenced by what are taken to be the compelling reasons in favour of rights in the first place.

It is, I believe, a mistake to think that Nozick does not provide an account of the basis for the rights that he advocates. He is certainly his own worst enemy here since he does not set out his reasoning in one place, nor does he offer much in the way of elaboration of his views. Nevertheless, it is possible to construct an argument which underlies Nozick's position and it goes like this. It is essentially focused on our separateness as persons and the idea of inviolability that flows from that. Rights place side constraints on the behaviour of others.[2] If I have a right to *Φ* then others have a duty, a constraint which ought to inhibit them from interfering with my *Φ*ing. They will act unjustly and infringe my rights if they prevent me from *Φ*ing. In Nozick's view those side constraints and, correlatively, rights 'reflect the fact of our separate existences'.[3] Nozick also puts the point in terms of the Kantian argument about respect for persons and treating individuals as ends in themselves and not as means to the ends of others. This Kantian theme becomes clearer in the section of *Anarchy, State and Utopia* entitled 'What Are Side Constraints Based Upon?'. Here he links the point about the separateness of persons, treating them as ends and not just as means, with the idea of moral agency and the idea that life has a value to an agent who is a:

> [B]eing able to formulate long term plans for its life, able to consider and decide on the basis of abstract principles or considerations it formulates to itself and hence not merely the plaything of immediate stimuli; a being that limits its own behaviour in accordance with some principles or picture it has of what an appropriate life is for itself and others and so on.[4]

This is linked by Nozick to the idea of the meaning of life because a person's shaping his life in accordance with some overall plan is his way of giving meaning to his life. He adds, though, that only a being with the capacity to so shape his life can have or strive for a meaningful life. The contrast for Nozick is with end state or goal directed or patterned political principles. Such end state principles whether of a utilitarian sort – maximize aggregate utility – or of social justice – distribute the social product according to a particular principle (desert or whatever) – are bound to involve breaching such side constraints and will involve treating individuals as means to the ends of others as embodied in the end state principle. At the very best such end state principles can only enjoin us to minimize the extent to which we use others as means. It would be as if, according to Nozick, Kant's categorical imperative in its second formulation enjoined us to 'act as to minimize the use of humanity simply as a means' rather than his own formulation. 'Act in such a way that you always treat humanity, whether in your own person or in the person of any other, never simply as a means, but always at the same time as an end.'[5] In Nozick's view, a political and economic order consistent with the principle of respect for persons, with the principle of inviolability and with respecting the facts of our separate existence will require a very limited state and a free market economy and certainly not one constrained by end state principles whether of a utilitarian or socially just kind. Outcomes of transactions which are entirely voluntary and uncoerced will be legitimate and just because they have arisen out of a procedurally just process. No doubt an individual may *choose* to use his resources to help someone else or a group of people, but what is not legitimate for Nozick is to infringe side constraints and inviolability in the interests of some social value whether it be utilitarian or social justice. The reason for this is clear for Nozick:

> [T]here is no *social entity* with a good that undergoes some sacrifice for its own good. There are only individual people, different individual people, with their own individual lives using one of these people for the benefit of others, uses him and benefits the others. . . . Talk of an overall social good covers this up (intentionally?). To use a person in this way does not sufficiently respect and take account of the fact that he is a separate person, that this is the only life that he has.[6]

So for Nozick a utilitarian defence of limited government and the free market is on very weak ethical grounds because it can indeed justify significant violation of rights and indeed, if the utilitarian calculus changed, could always justify extensions of government power and coercion which would mean that one individual was being used for the good of another. Nozick and Hayek both accept that 'society' should not be anthropomorphized but Nozick uses that insight together with a rigorous insistence on the moral importance of the separateness of persons to provide a radical justification for his own approach – a deontological justification of the market order, the only justification consistent with taking the separateness of persons seriously.

Given this basis for rights, for the purposes of this book, we need to look briefly at three details of it: Nozick's view of justice in acquisition; justice in transfer; and the relationship between rights, justice, side constraints, and coercion. I shall then draw these theories together in relation to Nozick's place within neo-liberal thought.

If a person is inviolable, then he or she has an absolute property right in his or her own person, powers and capacities, and labour, which consists of physical movements in his or her body. Given this point, Nozick next has to explain how using my powers and capacities through my labour I can come to have a private, unquestionable property right in unowned things. Nozick's answer here is a variation of Locke's labour theory of property – that it is the action of *mixing my labour* with unowned goods that yields the idea of property right in those goods.

Nozick's arguments on this point are quite difficult to assess because in the course of his discussion of the Lockean theory which he endorses, he brings forward some cogent and amusing objections to Locke's theory which he then proceeds to ignore. The central issue to be addressed here is as follows:

1. Human beings are inviolable.
2. Inviolable persons own their persons and their labour.

3. Person A mixes his labour which he owns with *X* which is unowned.
4. A has a property right in *X*.

Assuming that there is a clear line of argument from (1) to (3), how do we get from (3) to (4)? On Locke's view it is because of some kind of incorporation of *X* into A through the process of labour. In some cases, this incorporation is exact and literal, as it would be in the case of using an animal for food as in Locke's own example of how the venison nourishes the 'Wild Indian'. In killing and eating the animal, the hunter incorporates it into himself and this becomes part of him and on the argument about self-ownership, part of his property. However, most property is not literally incorporation of the unowned resource into oneself. Locke wants to argue that it is mixing one's labour with the thing which is analogous to incorporation. This argument as it stands, however, is not sufficient to justify the idea that mixing labour creates an exclusive property right in something. Nozick is very good at specifying the sharp questions which can be asked about this argument. They are as follows:

1. What are the boundaries of what labour is mixed with? We only labour on parts of objects. Why does mixing labour entail a right in the whole of the object?
2. Why does mixing my labour which I own with something which I do not own, lead me to own the thing rather than losing what I own, as opposed to gaining what I don't?
3. Why should mixing one's labour with something entitle you to the whole of that thing as opposed to the added value which one's labour has created? If my labour adds to the value of something I might certainly be thought to have a right to that added value, but why do I have a right to the total object rather than the added value?

Nozick raises these questions about the idea of mixing labour with something leading to a property right, but he does not try to answer them and in fact moves on to discuss the proviso that my original acquisition of property should not worsen the position of others, or in Locke's famous phrase, leaves as much and as good for others. The reason why he moves on to this issue seems fairly clear. Given the difficulties involved in the transition from A mixing his labour with *X*, to A owns *X*, it then might seem plausible to argue that attention should be moved to the question of how anyone could object to this move, and in Nozick's view the only ground for objection is that in coming to own *X*, A worsens the position of others. To use his own example, if I appropriate a grain of sand from Coney Island, leaving aside the question of mixing my labour with it, the only real objection to my appropriating it is whether it worsens the condition of others, which in his view it clearly does not. So attention moves away from the metaphysical issue of whether labour creates a property right by some mysterious process to the question of whether this appropriation worsens the position of others. If it does not, there can be no objection to the assertion of my property right however obscure the metaphysical basis of that might be.

So the problem becomes: Does a system of private property rights worsen the position of others when there are a few if any unowned resources in the world left to appropriate? In Nozick's view the proviso that property acquisition should not worsen the position of others can be understood in two ways:

1. It could be that as the result of my acquisition other people can no longer acquire that sort of property and those sorts of resources.
2. It could mean that while others can no longer appropriate, they can still have access to and use those resources.

That is to say, is the position of others worsened if they are unable to appropriate, or if they are unable to satisfy their needs in relation to those resources? This second interpretation is the one proposed by Nozick and he argues that 'no one can legitimately complain if the weaker provision is satisfied'.[7] The reason why Nozick takes this view is that while a system of private property rights may well mean that others no longer have the right to appropriate, they can still benefit from being excluded from such ownership because private property will yield all sorts of advantages even to those excluded from the possibility of appropriation, and according to the weaker criterion therefore their position will not be worsened and hence no basic right is violated. The reasons why Nozick takes this view are the result of what he takes to be the beneficial effects of private ownership, which he argues are as follows:

1. Private ownership increases the overall social product by putting resources into the hands of those who can use them most efficiently and profitably.
2. Private ownership encourages experimentation because with separate persons controlling resources, there is no one person or small group whom someone with a new idea must convince to try it out.
3. Private property leads to expertise in risk bearing because such a system requires that each person should bear the costs of the risks they run in business.
4. It protects future generations by leading some to hold back resources from current assumptions for future markets.
5. It provides protection for unpopular persons in the labour market because in a private property system there are many different sources of employment.

In Nozick's view, therefore, a free market and the private ownership of resources will not run up against the Lockean proviso so long as the proviso is understood as being that the position of others no longer at liberty to use the thing is thereby worsened. It is clear how close Nozick is here to Hayek's claim that the private market is superior to other forms of social organization because of the trickle-down effect, or the benefit that all will receive over time in absolute terms from the operation of the twin institutions of private property and free markets. This argument is crucial to the defence of free markets as opposed to state redistribution. Indeed, as with much else in liberalism this argument too goes back to Locke when he argued in the *Second Treatise* that the day labourer in England is better off than the king in an American tribe. What matters is not inequality, but the level of basic welfare. In the view of Nozick and Hayek, following Locke, the poor are better off in a private property or free market society than they would be under any other alternative and in Nozick's view this satisfied the requirement for the legitimacy of private appropriation, coupled with the fact that any other alternative – say, a state-directed system of redistribution and social justice – would infringe rights and inviolability.

It should be made clear, however, that Nozick is not offering this argument as a utilitarian justification of a market structure as opposed to a socialist one. Rather the argument is designed to show that those who do not own property and are excluded from the opportunity of doing so by initial acts of appropriation cannot complain that their rights have been infringed. This would be a legitimate argument only if their position had been worsened. However, the argument above is designed to show that under a private property and free market regime their position under the weak version of the Lockean proviso will not be worsened and will be better than it would be under any other alternative.

Therefore, having argued that inviolability and self-ownership, subject to his account of the Lockean proviso, produces a set of property rights and that such acquisitions are just, we need in addition some account of justice in transfer.[8] In the same way as Nozick has argued that just acquisition does not violate rights and does not infringe side constraints so, to be consistent, he has to explain how justice in transfer can be justified in the same way since 'whatever arises from a just situation by just steps is itself just'.[9]

Nozick points out in his book that he is not proposing a full account of justice in transfer, but the thrust of his argument is clear enough and is two-fold. First of all it is the argument that transfer is just when it is voluntary and not coerced, when it is not the product of fraud, theft, or embezzlement – when in short it is compatible with the side constraints which embody the principles of inviolability. The second element is a critique of the views of opponents of free transfer, basing their critique on patterned or end state or time slice principles. The basis of Nozick's approach to this critique is already obvious and consists in several claims:

1. We cannot interfere with free exchange because to do so would maximize some social values such as utility or social justice. Society is not the kind of entity which can have values in such a way as to justify interfering with rights and side constraints.
2. Interfering with free exchange will have to be ubiquitous because 'liberty upsets patterns'. The maintenance of a patterned principle of distributive justice will require constant interference with capitalist acts between consenting adults.
3. The argument that there can be no moral balancing act between us. The good is what it is for each individual. There is no overall good in terms of which such a balancing act could then be justified or achieved.

We need now to look at Nozick's account of coercion since both justice in acquisition and in transfer rely on their uncoerced nature in order to be legitimate. Most of what is important in the discussion is to be found in the section on 'Voluntary Exchange' in *Anarchy, State and Utopia*[10] and what is central to this account is Nozick's link between coercion and rights. It will be recalled that some neo-liberal critics themselves regarded Hayek's account of coercion as loose and as giving up a hostage to fortune for critics of neo-liberalism. Nozick and, as we shall see, Murray Rothbard both want to produce a more coherent and sophisticated account of coercion by limiting it to rights in a way that Hayek did not.

However, at the start of the discussion it is worth pointing out that in his book *Philosophical Explanations* Nozick agrees with Hayek that coercion has to be linked to intentional interference. He points out that I may be kept inside the house by an electrical storm or by someone's playing with electricity outside my house or by another person's threat to electrocute me if I leave the house. So the question is when the probabilities of electric shock are equal in the three situations, isn't one equally coerced in all three? What is crucial in the first and second scenarios is that it is my own will that keeps me indoors whereas in the threat situation it is the other person's will that is operative.[11] It is this intentional attempt to direct your will to a course of action rather than the operation of your own will that makes the threat coercive and this does not apply in the other situations. In this respect there is a clear echo of Hayek's account of coercion. There is a link between this and his account of coercion in *Anarchy, State and Utopia* when he says that 'Whether a person's actions are voluntary depends on what it is that limits his alternatives. If the facts of nature do so, then the actions are voluntary.'[12] So coercion has to do with individually identifiable human action in limiting alternatives and, Nozick argues, whether this makes one's resulting action non-voluntary depends upon 'whether the others had the *right* to act as they did'.[13] Coercion is not a sheer physical fact as it would be under the system of pure negative liberty discussed earlier but is rather logically linked to the idea of a right. So, for example, in Hayek's two cases discussed earlier – the well in the oasis example and the employer insisting upon a stringent employment contract in a situation of scarcity in regard to work – the question as to whether these actions are coercive or not would depend for Nozick on whether the well owner and the employer were within their rights in acting as they did. If they were, then their actions cannot be regarded as coercive. So for an act of coercion to occur it must be the result of the action of a human agent and must violate the rights of the coerced person, or to put the point the other way round what matters is whether the person performing the 'coercive' act had a right to act as he or she did.

In this section of *Anarchy, State and Utopia* Nozick recognized that the environment of choice available to a person may well be shaped by the behaviour of others and may severely constrain the choices available to a person, but the crucial issue still is whether this environment has been shaped by others acting entirely within their rights. His example here is instructive.[14] The example cashes out in terms of Hayek's employment example in the following way. Person Z is faced with working or starving – that is his environment of choice and these are his only options. Assume that the environment is shaped by the choices and actions of persons A through to Y, then, if in exercising their choices, they acted voluntarily and within their rights, then Z is not coerced. So capitalism in this sense is not coercive. It contrasts categorically with the position of the highwayman who threatens 'your money or your life' because the highwayman is not acting within his rights in making this threat even though the environment of choice, work or starve; your money or your life, may appear to be remarkably similar.

Therefore, given that for Nozick it seems to be a necessary and sufficient condition for justice in transfer that it should be a voluntary transfer his account of the difference between forced and free exchange is linked to the idea of acting within one's rights and in so doing not infringing the rights of others. His approach to the monopoly on the well in the desert is different because in this context we see that for Nozick his interpretation of the Lockean proviso still applies at the transfer and not just the acquisition level of his theory of justice and entitlement. Nozick argues that once it is clear that someone's ownership 'runs foul of the Lockean proviso', then there are stringent limits on what he may do with his property. Therefore, he argues

> a person may not appropriate the only water hole in a desert and charge what he will. Nor may he charge what he will if he possesses one, and unfortunately it happens that all the water holes in the desert dry up, except for his. This unfortunate circumstance, admittedly no fault of his, brings into operation the Lockean proviso and limits his property rights.[15]

So, the well owner charging an exorbitant rate does act coercively because he is not acting within his rights because those rights are only legitimate in the first place by the operation of the proviso. Hence, in Nozick's view the constraint on the well owner's behaviour does not follow from an attempt to restrict his rights in order to maximize the social good – a point which would be profoundly contrary to Nozick's overall position as we have seen it develop. Rather the restrictions on the rights of the well owner arise out of 'considerations internal to the theory of property itself, to its theory of acquisition and appropriation (which) provide the means for handling such cases'. Therefore, there is, in Nozick's view, no balancing act taking place between individual rights and the social good, or between the rights of individuals. Rather the rights of the well owner are being constrained by the Lockean conditions on property ownership which persist in transfer as well as in acquisition.

It is important not to overstate the position Nozick is taking here. The operation of the Lockean proviso is in fact quite limited. It is operative in the well in the desert example because there is no other possibility of appropriation. It applies only in such a situation of catastrophe or in a desert island situation where for proviso types of reason I cannot order a castaway off my island. It has to do with this lack of possibility of additional appropriation by the disadvantaged person. It does not turn, as it does for Hayek,[16] on the necessity of the good in question – that is to say whether or not it meets basic needs. In the case of a medical researcher who synthesizes a new compound which will save lives and who wishes to charge an exorbitant price for his drug it would not be right to think of this as coercive behaviour because the resources which the chemist used are still available to others to utilize and thus does not infringe the Lockean proviso. The drug may be life saving but that does not mean that the person who cannot afford to pay for the drug at the price specified by the chemist is coerced because the chemist is acting within his rights and the Lockean proviso has not been violated.

It is important to see that for Nozick the derivation of a right to property is not consequential upon some other right such as a right to life which is regarded as more basic. The right to property follows from the whole structure of side constraints and voluntary action subject to the Lockean proviso when it applies. The reason why the right to property does not arise from the right to life is important, as we shall see in Chapter 6. His argument which is deployed against Ayn Rand is as follows: Rand argues that the right to property follows from the right to life because one needs physical things in order to live. However, Nozick cannot in consistency accept this argument because what I need to live may be justly owned by someone else and that person may (subject to the Lockean proviso) be acting entirely within their rights in denying it to me. So at the most Nozick argues the right to life would be 'a right to have or to strive for whatever one needs to live' – to have if one can acquire the things justly or strive to have – perhaps by appealing to the good will of the person who already owns them that he or she may choose to allocate them to you. Hence, a right to life cannot be a right to the means of life if these are owned by others. Indeed in Nozick's view one needs a theory of property before one can understand correctly the nature and scope of the right to life and therefore, he concludes, 'the right to life cannot provide the foundation for a theory of property rights'.[17]

This concludes the exposition of Nozick's theory of rights and in particular his attempt to link his account of rights and coercion and the ways in which these in turn provide strong normative underpinnings of the free market economy. I want now to look at the rights-based theory of Murray Rothbard because again we see how a libertarian thinker, in this case, links together an account of rights and coercion and indeed argues for the privacy of property rights.

Rothbard grounds his account of rights in a natural law doctrine,[18] but it is not one which is defended as opposed to exemplified very much in his work. In so far as he wants to see this natural law doctrine as justifiable by secular reason as much as by religious faith, it has to be said that he provides a very thin account of a secular natural law theory as compared with, for example, the work of John Finnis in *Natural Law and Natural Rights.* Nevertheless, it is worth pointing out that Rothbard's natural law theory is central to his critique of Hayek. He argues that Hayek's theory of individual rights does not stem from some basic moral theory or from some independent non-governmental social arrangement or independent moral source, but rights are rather creatures of government. They flow from government. The rule of law creates rights whereas for Rothbard it should be quite the other way round. This point is central to his essay 'Natural Law versus Positive Law' in *The Ethics of Liberty.* So, for the moment I shall not delve into this doctrine which forms the backdrop to Rothbard's theory of rights and property. Instead what I want to concentrate on in his view is that all rights are in fact property rights and that this is the only way of giving the idea of a right a precise scope and content. This argument is set out in his essay 'Human Rights as Property Rights' which constitutes chapter 15 of *The Ethics of Liberty.* His argument is clear and uncompromising. He states that

> not only are there no human rights which are not also property rights, but the former rights lose their absoluteness and clarity and become fuzzy and vulnerable when property rights are not used as the standard.[19]

Why is this so? Take a right such as freedom of speech. In Rothbard's view taken just as a general right this is inexact and fuzzy and will lead to all sorts of contradictions and complications if taken as just this general right. What we need to know is precisely where this freedom of speech is going to be exercised. I may, of course, exercise it within the confines of my own property; I may also exercise it on your property if I have contracted with you to do so or if you have otherwise given the permission to do so. There is no such thing as a general right to freedom of speech. There can only be a right linked to a property right whether in your own property or in property which you have contracted for this purpose.[20]

In Rothbard's view this approach has two interrelated advantages. First of all it makes the right much more exact: we can pinpoint the property right which is a necessary condition of exercising the right such as freedom of speech. There can be no general right which goes beyond this property right – so we know the nature, scope, and the limit of the right. It also allows us to deal more clearly with cases where it is argued that rights need to be abridged by considerations of public policy. Take Rothbard's own example of shouting 'fire' falsely in a theatre. He points out that it was argued, for example, by Justice Oliver Wendell Holmes that no one has a right to shout fire in a theatre and this was because of public utility – inciting panic among the theatre-goers. Such an approach implies that so-called basic rights could always be overridden by considerations of utility. In Rothbard's view, the restriction on the freedom of someone to shout fire in a theatre does not flow from considerations of utility but from an examination of the property rights involved. The person shouting 'fire' is going to be either a patron or the theatre owner. If the owner shouts 'fire' falsely, then he is infringing the property rights represented in the tickets of those who had booked for the performance. If it is a member of the audience, then the property rights of other members of the audience are infringed in the same way as before *and* the property right of the theatre owner is infringed because the patron is disrupting the conditions of his being present on the theatre owner's premises. Therefore, no utilitarian or policy-related consideration applies. It is purely a matter of determining the property rights and their infringement.[21]

In Rothbard's view this will enable us to deal with alleged conflicts between rights and rationing in relation to rights. He takes the claim of Bertrand de Jouvenal who argued in respect of a general right to freedom of speech that there is an endemic chairman's problem about how to allocate time and opportunity between various holders of the right to free speech who might otherwise wish to speak simultaneously! In this conflict between right holders, it is necessary to ration access to what the right pertains to: space, access to a microphone, or whatever. In Rothbard's view, such conflicts could be resolved perfectly easily in one of the two ways, both of which involve property rights. The problem arises because the right is perceived to be costless and in these circumstances access is not limited by cost or by price. If, however, space to speak was allocated by price, that is to say by coming to own property in a particular time slice of the resource, then the allocation problem would be solved and also demand which at zero price is unlimited, would have a limit. Equally the resource could be allocated perfectly justly by the person who owned it. In the same way as the owner, of say, a newspaper decides which letters to publish, similarly the owner of any other communications resource can make similar decisions. The person who writes the letter or who wishes to be on air has no right to the resource. He may request or petition the property owner, but the right to freedom of speech does not guarantee some sort of equal right to space or time in the media. As Rothbard argues: 'Only when the right to freedom of speech is treated simply as a subdivision of property right does it become valid, workable and absolute.'[22] It is also worth bearing in mind in this discussion that this is also the way in which Rothbard would address the question of discretion in relation to the rule of law which considerably exercises Hayek. There is no need for such discretion in Rothbard's view once property rights have been fixed. What one then has a right to do is clear in the light of property rights and the exercise of such rights does not and indeed should not be controlled by the use of discretionary power. So obviously on such an approach the nature and scope of property rights becomes quite crucial and in particular whether these rights are subject to any sort of constraint, as they are, for example, in the case of Nozick *via* the admittedly rather minimalist 'Lockean proviso'. This again is crucial for understanding the nature of coercion because A in exercising his or her (property) right to Φ cannot coerce B. He or she cannot coerce B because given the theory of rights as property rights if A is acting within his or her rights, there cannot *qua* property rights be a conflict between A's rights and B's rights as we have seen. Rothbard defines coercion as 'the invasive use of physical violence or the threat thereof against someone else's person or (just) property'. As we have seen, such property rights are clear and palpable and as such, if properly delineated, cannot conflict.

This definition of coercion enables Rothbard to resist both of Hayek's qualifications to his own view of coercion, namely that in conditions of acute unemployment an employer's insistence that an employee may be required to work in ways not specified in a contract is coercive and that the owner of the well in the desert charging an exorbitant price is always acting coercively. Rothbard rejects each of these examples. The employer has a property right in his or her own money and the employee has no right, other than within a voluntary contract between the employer and the employee, about how the employer's resources and property shall be used. So the employer is acting within his property rights in acting as he or she does, the employee has no rights other than those specified in the contract and thus the employer in acting outside of the contract is not acting coercively.

In the case of the well owner the same sort of considerations apply. The owner has not poisoned the other wells or caused them to dry up and, in Rothbard's view, in supplying a vital service albeit at a high price he has a right to refuse services or to charge whatever customers will pay. 'The owner of the oasis is responsible only for the existence of his own actions and his own property; he is not accountable for the existence of the desert or for the fact that other wells have dried up.'[23]

So in neither of the examples is the employer or the well owner acting coercively. Nozick of course, as we have seen, does think that the well owner (although not the employer) is acting coercively because of the operation in this specific case of the Lockean proviso. So does Rothbard not think that there is any constraint on the acquisition and the subsequent use of property, particularly in situations of catastrophe such as the oasis case exemplify?

The answer to the question is given by Rothbard's account of homesteading which is a principle which relates to Nozick's account of justice in acquisition. Homesteading (an idea based upon nineteenth century American practice of acquiring land in the West) creates property rights through the self-ownership of the individual and the ability to cultivate and transform the land. Up to this point it parallels Nozick's argument and is essentially Lockean. However, there is a major difference in that Rothbard rejects the Lockean proviso both in Locke's own terms and in Nozick's reformulation of it. This is very important because as we have seen Nozick uses that proviso to show that it has implications (in the oasis example) for current utilization of property and for a significant additional element to his account of coercion. In Rothbard's view there is no case for such a general proviso. There is indeed a case for arguing that there are natural constraints on acquisition since the justification of acquisition relies on self-ownership, the ownership of labour, and the ownership of what is transformed by labour. So original acquisition has to involve some use of land. On these grounds he argues against the Columbus syndrome – of laying title to vast tracts of land on which one cannot bring one's labour to bear. This restriction cannot, however, be reduced to a formula. Obviously in a modern society justice in acquisition is of less direct relevance since all land is now owned, and changes of ownership occur through transfer, bequest, and other such procedures. However, as we have seen in the case of Nozick, the Lockean proviso still has present salience in catastrophic situations like the oasis. Rothbard rejects the proviso and also believes that his doctrine of absolute property rights can also deal perfectly consistently with situations of catastrophe.

Rothbard makes short work of the proviso with a direct critique of Nozick. He points out that Nozick interprets the proviso to mean that none may appropriate land if the remaining population who might desire land are made worse off. Who, Rothbard asks, is to determine if they are worse off or not? And he goes on to claim that on this model a Lockean proviso would outlaw all private ownership of land since everyone could be made worse off. Even if we could figure out who is worse off, this is a risk that everyone faces in an uncertain world. We now live with the consequences of those initial and now completely exercised forms of initial acquisition. Others will have acquired these titles through voluntary transfer – bequest and contract typically. So the rest of us, if we desire access to those legitimately owned resources, have to pay a market price for them. If the owner refuses to sell or to rent, that is their privilege in a free society. This is true whether or not I own the only resource which is an essential supply. Since there is no proviso, there is no coercion on my part. As Rothbard puts the point clearly; Locke could nod once in a while![24]

So, how does Rothbard's theory of property rights fit a situation of catastrophe? He takes the example of too many people for a lifeboat. Given that he is an adherent to a natural law, natural right, or property right type of moral and political doctrine he has to take the view that there is an objective answer to this problem. In Rothbard's view, the crucial question is 'who owns the lifeboat?' If there is an undisputed owner – let's say a shipping company – and if there are rules that have been laid down in advance about the use of the boats and which are known by potential users, then these rules should prevail. To refuse a place in a lifeboat to someone not permitted by the rules to a place is not an act of coercion. The company operative acting on behalf of the clear owner of the property is working within his or her rights to deny such a place. The drowning individual has no right to a place on the boat any more than anyone else has an unconditional right to someone else's property.

In the case of an unowned lifeboat or where there were no rules announced by a now dead owner about the use of his property, then the homesteading principle comes into play, namely the boat is owned by whoever can get to it first. Suppose if the lifeboat accommodates eight people, those eight people become the 'owners' of the boat. If they repel others trying to get onboard they are acting within their rights as property owners and are not acting coercively; if, however, they are thrown out of the boat by the others and they drown in the sea then these people are acting aggressively, coercively, and without right on their side. So it is certainly the case that Rothbard's theory is a much more thorough going account than Nozick's constrained theory, however minimally, as it is by his adherence to a version of the Lockean proviso. What Nozick and Rothbard share in common is a negative view of rights. To have a right is to secure a space free from interference and invasion. Rights are not positive rights to resources because such 'rights' would involve enacting and coming to possess the resources of others. There is no common pot of things to which such rights could be rights asserted. The 'common pot' already has entitlements built into it through the very processes by which it has been produced. Positive rights can come to exist only by voluntary agreement and contract. If I agree to pay for your education and we have a contract to that effect, then you have a right to receive those resources. Outside of these sorts of arrangements there can be no positive rights. This whole approach is summed up clearly, uncompromisingly, and trenchantly by Rothbard when he argues in *The Ethics of Liberty*:

> [T]he very concept of rights is a negative one, demarcating the areas of a person's actions that no man may property interfere with. No man can therefore have a 'right' to compel someone to do a positive act, for in that case the compulsion violates the right of person or property of the individual being coerced. . . . As a corollary, this means that in a free society, no man may be saddled with the legal obligation to do anything for another, since that would invade the former's rights; the only legal obligation one man has to another is to respect the other man's rights.[25]

We need now to analyse the neo-liberal insistence on the negative nature of rights more fully. As we shall see while there are various aspects to the critique of positive rights, the essential unifying theme of this critique is that of scarcity.

It is argued that negative rights are the only rights that can give rise to categorical and compossible duties. There are two aspects to their claim. The first is that my duty in respect of your negative rights is to abstain or to forbear from action. I have a duty not to kill you in respect of your right to life; not to remove your property in respect of your right to property; not assault you in respect of your right to physical integrity; and so on. These duties are clear and categorical. It is absolutely clear when they are being fulfilled and when they are not. This, it is said, contrasts with duties attached to positive rights. How extensive is the duty to provide education, health, social security, and so on? Delimiting these duties – as they must be – has given rise to great controversy and this is not the case with categorical duties in respect of negative rights. It is clear when negative categorical duties are being fulfilled and when they are not.

Secondly the rights and the duties can be categorical because they do not require resources. The right to life is a right not to be killed; the corresponding duty is a duty not to kill. Neither the right nor the duty confers resources and it can therefore be categorical and not subject to political and legal interpretation and controversy.

It also follows that the rights are compossible in the sense that they can be simultaneously claimed by all right holders and the duties can simultaneously be fulfilled by those with the corresponding duties. This again follows from the fact that neither the rights nor the duties imply resources, scarcity, and rationing. The rationing of resources to meet positive rights undermines their status as rights since any such rationing would be utilitarian in nature and it would be paradoxical to have a utilitarian calculus of rights and duties.

It is also argued that the negative nature of rights and duties solves the problem of who is it that has the duty to respect rights. It can be argued by critics of positive rights that it is not clear who has the duty to meet the claims to social goods embodied in such rights. Is it a horizontal right in respect of each citizen to every other citizen or is it a vertical right between the individual and the state? On the negative view of rights it can be taken to be both. Both each individual and the government can be held under the same duty to respect negative rights whereas who holds the duty in respect of positive rights is very unclear.

Underlying all these features is the link between positive rights and resources. Given that there is always a scarcity of resources and given that the claims embodied in positive rights are open-ended and subject to no clear limit, then neither positive rights nor duties can be regarded as categorical and compossible. This claimed defect is crucial to the rule of law in the neo-liberal view. If rights are negative and do not imply claims to resources, then they can be secured on an equal basis to all right holders; if duties are clear, categorical, and, as forms of forbearance, costless, then those duties can apply equally across society. If negative rights and duties are compossible, then they can be claimed simultaneously by right holders and respected by those with the duties without raising any significant issues for the universality and equality of the rule of law.

It is also worth drawing out a final element in the critique as positive rights to resources, namely the intrinsic link between such rights, claims, and social justice. If rights to resources are to be secured by the state to individuals, then this is bound to raise questions about distributive or social justice. What is a fair or a just share of such scarce resources? These are issues of social justice which from the neo-liberal perspective are, as we have seen, a mirage. If rights are to be compatible with the universality and equality at the heart of the idea of the rule of law, then they must be construed in a negative manner. In the case of Nozick freedom within the rule of law depends crucially upon the law recognizing rights since it is on the structure of legitimate rights that coercion rests and since freedom is the absence of coercion there is a logical connexion between freedom and rights.

NOTES

1. Nagel, T. (1982). 'Libertarianism Without Foundations' in Jeffrey Paul (ed.), *Reading Nozick: Essays on Anarchy, State and Utopia.* Oxford: Blackwell.
2. Nozick, R. (1974). *Anarchy, State and Utopia.* Oxford: Blackwell, p. 33.
3. Nozick, R. *Anarchy, State and Utopia*, p. 31.
4. Nozick, R. *Anarchy, State and Utopia*, p. 49.
5. Nozick, R. *Anarchy, State and Utopia*, p. 32.
6. Nozick, R. *Anarchy, State and Utopia*, pp. 32–3.
7. Nozick, R. *Anarchy, State and Utopia*, pp. 178–82.
8. Nozick, R. *Anarchy, State and Utopia*, p. 151.
9. Nozick, R. *Anarchy, State and Utopia*, p. 151.
10. Nozick, R. *Anarchy, State and Utopia*, p. 252.
11. Nozick, R. (1981). *Philosophical Explanations.* Cambridge, MA: Harvard University Press, p. 49.
12. Nozick, R. *Anarchy, State and Utopia.* See also Rothbard, M. (2002). *The Ethics of Liberty.* New York: New York University Press.
13. Nozick, R. *Anarchy, State and Utopia.* See also Rothbard, M. *The Ethics of Liberty*, p. 262.
14. Nozick, R. *Anarchy, State and Utopia.* See also Rothbard, M. *The Ethics of Liberty*, p. 263.
15. Nozick, R. *Anarchy, State and Utopia.* See also Rothbard, M. *The Ethics of Liberty*, p. 180.

16. Nozick, R. *Anarchy, State and Utopia*. See also Rothbard, M. *The Ethics of Liberty*, p. 181.
17. Nozick, R. *Anarchy, State and Utopia*. See also Rothbard, M. *The Ethics of Liberty*, p. 179.
18. Rothbard, M. *The Ethics of Liberty*,
19. Rothbard, M. *The Ethics of Liberty*, p. 113.
20. Rothbard, M. *The Ethics of Liberty*, p. 114.
21. Rothbard, M. *The Ethics of Liberty*, p. 116.
22. Rothbard, M. *The Ethics of Liberty*, p. 221.
23. Rothbard, M. *The Ethics of Liberty*, p. 245.
24. Rothbard, M. *The Ethics of Liberty*, p. 100.
25. Rothbard, M. *The Ethics of Liberty*.

6

The Welfare State and the Politics of Social Justice

Some of the rather abstract issues that I have discussed so far have an intimate link to the neo-liberal critique of the welfare state. Some of these – to do with justice and rights for example – have already been discussed at length. I shall avoid further elaboration of these themes in this chapter except where it seems necessary to shed light on a specific aspect of the neo-liberal critique of the welfare state. To this end I shall begin the discussion with reference to issues of freedom and social justice and look at their relevance to the critique of the modern welfare state.

It seems plain, as a matter of history, that a positive rather than a wholly negative view of freedom played a part in providing a moral justification for the welfare state. This broadening of the concept of freedom also marked in Britain, at least, a move away from the classical or vernacular of the late nineteenth century: 'Old' liberalism in favour of a more interventionist, more social 'New' Liberalism. T. H. Green was the crucial intellectual figure in respect of broadening the idea of liberty, and politicians such as Haldane and Asquith utilized these ideas in their attempt to 'modernize' liberalism particularly under the influence of the great extension of the franchise in the latter part of the nineteenth century which necessitated the Liberal Party becoming more attuned to the idea that laissez-faire capitalism had to be moderated in favour of a greater concern with welfare and social justice.[1]

Neo-liberal thinkers have certainly been well aware of these developments and the role which a more extensive conception of liberty played in this change. So, for example, in *The Constitution of Liberty*, Hayek makes it clear that from his perspective a move away from negative freedom to an idea of freedom as power and ability could very easily and indeed did naturally form the basis of a moral case for the redistribution of income and wealth and therefore a more extensive state in the name of liberty.[2] If liberty is not just to be understood as freedom from coercion but has to involve powers, capacities, and resources, then clearly the idea of equal liberty has to involve some commitment to greater equality of resources and welfare. As we saw in Chapter 3, neo-liberals have deployed many arguments against this historically important shift in the understanding of the nature of freedom. The arguments discussed at length elsewhere are summarized as follows:

1. There is a categorical difference between being free to do *X* and being able to do *X* or having the power to do *X*. No one is able to do or has the power to do all that he or she is negatively free to do. This shows us that the domain secured by negative liberty is not coextensive with the domain of so-called positive freedom or freedom as power. Therefore, a defence of the organization of resources in the interests of extending freedom is wrong. Poverty is not a restriction on liberty.
2. Infringements of liberty have to be intentional and yet the poverty which positive libertarians regard as a restriction on freedom is not usually the result of specific intentions. It is an unintended consequence of free market exchange and since this consequence was not intended it cannot be coercive. Negative liberty allied to methodological individualism means that there can be no meaningful account of structural coercion or social coercion.
3. As we have seen, many contributors to the neo-liberal outlook argue that labour contracts, however harsh and against the background of prevailing conditions, cannot be regarded as coercive, nor can the behaviour of an employer insisting on extra work outside the contract, when the alternative for the worker is severe deprivation. So there is no case in terms of freedom for a welfare state to secure some kind of base line below which an individual could be regarded as being unfree and therefore that any contracts signed in that situation would be coercive. The neo-liberal, to be consistent, has to reject a base line approach grounded in the theory of freedom because that would then mean that there is a clear link between freedom and specific resources.
4. Finally, linking freedom with power, ability, or resources will mean that we would have to abandon the idea of equal liberty. It is perfectly possible to envisage equal freedom when this is understood as negative freedom since such liberties imply duties of cost free forbearance and can thus be equally claimed by all. This is not the case with liberty understood as access to resources. This has implications for the universality of the rule of law. Equal negative freedom can be achieved through universality and equally applicable general rules which also, because of the objective nature of coercion, do not require discrimination or discretion in their application; whereas in the case of liberty understood as implying resources, because people's needs and abilities are different it will be impossible to devise laws which can allocate resources in accordance with the rule of law. It follows from this that for the neo-liberal the welfare state is not compatible with the rule of law when the argument stated earlier is linked to other aspects of welfare provision, as we shall see later.

A parallel critique has been deployed in respect of social justice. Social democratic justifications of the welfare state have usually envisaged the welfare state as an instrument of social justice and as a means of achieving a more egalitarian society. This has been broadly true of twentieth-century social democrats in Britain and Europe and, to a much more limited extent of the Democratic Party in the United States in the period from Roosevelt to Clinton. The view of equality adapted by social democrats has ranged from greater equality of opportunity to be secured by investment in education and skills for the worst off to enable them to compete on a more equal footing with the better endowed, to greater equality of outcome by means of interventions to correct and/or compensate for disadvantageous market outcomes.

Certainly, social democrats typically are concerned about relative positions in society and not just with baselines or absolute positions. The classical case here was argued by C. A. R. Crosland in *The Future of Socialism* and in *Social Democracy in Europe*.[3] The contrast between the position and neo-liberalism is very stark. For Crosland the fiscal benefits of economic growth should be used (*a*) to maintain the *absolute* position of the better off (because otherwise they would not give electoral support for socially just politics) and (*b*) to improve the *relative* position of the worst off members of society.

As we shall see as the argument progresses the neo-liberal takes the opposite view. Therefore what is central here is that the welfare state including state funding and, until more recently, state provision of welfare in a broad sense including education, health service, and social benefits was to be pursued in the interests of social justice from a social democratic perspective. As we have seen, however, the neo-liberal provides a critique of social justice focusing on the following main points which were more fully discussed earlier:

1. Injustice, like coercion, has to be the result of individual intentional action. The outcomes of market exchanges are not intentional. They are rather the unintended consequences of market exchanges. There is no 'maldistribution' of income and wealth to be rectified because there was no 'distribution' in the first place. Therefore, we bear no collective responsibility to be discharged by government for the outcomes of markets. For particular individuals such outcomes may be unfortunate, but they are not injustices to be rectified by collective action.
2. Even if we thought that appeals to social justice had some kind of moral merit they would in fact at the best be politically inert and at the worst freedom threatening. It is inert because we cannot in fact agree on the criteria for social justice: whether it should be merit, need, equality, entitlement, or contribution. Equally, we could not agree on any ranking of these criteria. Nor could we agree on whether all goods should be distributed according to the same criterion or whether there should be different criteria applied to different sorts of goods such as health and education. On the neo-liberal view it is best to leave such choices to the market where individuals with their own subjective values can in fact decide for themselves what something, some service, or some good is worth to them.
3. The argument of Nozick and others that distributive justice assumes some unallocated social pot or fund that has come into existence as the result of economic activity but without entitlements built into it. This is false on a strong view of property rights and entitlement.

4. Social justice and the welfare state to which it gives rise assumes falsely, certainly at the libertarian end of neo-liberal thought, that there is a positive obligation to help others that arises out of the general relationship between persons rather than the morally correct view that it arises out of explicit contract between one person and another. The tax regime necessary to sustain a welfare state implies this generalized positive obligation, whereas in fact there is no such obligation in the view of many neo-liberals.
5. There are other aspects of the critique of a social democratic approach to social justice which I have yet to discuss in this book particularly in relation to equality and to needs, but before moving on to them we also need to recall the critique of social rights and entitlements. Basically at a conceptual level the critique was based upon the following points:
   i) Rights exist to protect liberty. Liberty is negative liberty – to be free from coercion. Thus, rights and laws protecting rights are about preventing coercion and securing duties of forbearance so that coercion does not occur. 'Social rights' are not genuine because they seek to protect a false understanding of freedom; a positive understanding implies command over resources.
   ii) Social rights like social justice generally imply that there is an unallocated social pot or fund to which rights can be allocated whereas in fact such a fund comes into existence with legitimate allocation of entitlement built into it or to be more precise, there is no such fund once those entitlements are taken into account.
   iii) Social rights cannot be made subject to the rule of law because of scarcity. Access to limited resources cannot be made a matter of justiciable rights. In addition because people's needs and their abilities to transform goods differ, goods cannot be distributed in accordance with the rule of law so discretion will be central to such a system and such discretion will not be effectively made accountable.

So, taken together arguments in favour of negative liberty, against the meaningfulness of social justice and social rights is a formidable attack on the normative foundations of the social democratic welfare state. Such a critique, however, does not stop here and we need to consider further aspects of the critique of greater equality as a political ideal, at the critique of the idea of needs, at the implications of the welfare state for bureaucracy, and its implications for interest group politics.

As I have already said, the welfare state has been seen by social democrats as an instrument of greater social justice understood as greater social equality. So we need to look in detail at the neo-liberal critique of equality. I shall start with equality of opportunity. For the neo-liberal there is a strong case for pursuing a narrow view of equality of opportunity. This is partly for moral reasons, and partly for efficiency. What is meant by equality of opportunity in this perspective is the removal of intentionally erected barriers to prevent individuals from doing or trying to do something that they would like to do. As such, these types of restrictions on opportunity can be regarded as coercive and as limiting freedom and since they are intentional restrictions on action, they can also be regarded as unjust if those imposing such restrictions are not acting within their rights. As we shall see, this latter point is more complicated than it seems. For the moment however, we can see that there is a moral case for equality of opportunity as non-discrimination.

There are also arguments of efficiency and consequentialist nature to be found in favour of this account of equal opportunity. The argument here is that there can be no a priori reason for debarring people from jobs in the market economy on the grounds of gender, race, and religion because we have no evidence that people with the discriminated-against qualities are not able to do the job. In an efficient market economy it will make sense for the person who is regarded as the best person to do the job to be appointed to it. This is not so for moral reasons but because it is in the interest of the firm to have the best person appointed. There can be no a priori reason for debarring people on the grounds that they exemplify some particular set of characteristics. On this view it is claimed that the market economy is inherently non-discriminatory.

Competitive markets will, therefore, provide strong reasons of self-interest for non-discrimination and for the narrow view of equality of opportunity.

Such a view of equality of opportunity whether defended on moral grounds to do with the neo-liberal account of freedom and coercion or on the grounds of market self-interest is also compatible with the rule of law. This is because any such anti-discrimination rules, if indeed such rules are needed, would be rules which require forbearance from action – to abstain from discrimination. Such forms of abstinence or forbearance can be entirely general, costless, and are not directed to securing a particular benefit for any particular individual and as such are compatible with the rule of law.

This is not the case from a neo-liberal perspective in regard to those forms of equality of opportunity which go beyond non-discrimination and seek to use state action and the tax system to improve the position of the less-advantaged members of society by investing differentially higher levels of resources in their education, skills, and social environment in order to improve their human and social capital so that they can compete more effectively in the market economy. In the view of economic liberals such an approach cannot be consistent with the rule of law and must be discriminatory and subject to discretionary judgement by welfare officials. This is so for several reasons: First of all, there is a high degree of subjectivity about basic or generic needs which such a positive account of equality of opportunity would have to take into account – an argument which will be subjected to much more analysis later. Secondly, the capacities of people to utilize the same set of goods will differ enormously. Some will be more able to exploit a particular good secured to them by a welfare state; some will be less able. If we want to secure equality of opportunity, then there would have to be some attempts to create a more differentiated system to meet different capacities. Finally, there is the question of desert or merit. If the disadvantaged starting point is the result of circumstances outside of one's control, then that is one thing;

if it is the result of one's own poor choice, then that is another. Any attempt at compensatory justice will have to take account of such factors not least if it is to command political support. However, to take this into account is going to involve first of all precisely the difficulties involved with distributive criteria which the neo-liberal had identified in relation to social justice, but also and additionally, because such judgements about who deserves what will not be objective there is going to be a lot of scope for administrative discretion to separate the deserving from the undeserving and this is going to be incompatible with the rule of law. Hence, in the view of the neo-liberal, any positive theory of equality of opportunity which goes beyond non-discrimination is not compatible with the pre-requisites of the rule of law.

In any case for mid-twentieth-century social democrats equality of opportunity was 'not enough'[4] to use Crosland's words. It was not enough in two respects: First of all it is about a fair competition to become unequal. The aim of equality of opportunity is to equip people with the appropriate skills and resources so that they can compete in the market and this competition will have profoundly inegalitarian outcomes. Most social democrats of this period entertained what Nozick called 'end state' or patterned principles of social justice of an egalitarian nature. This patterned view of greater equality of outcome or greater equality of welfare was to be achieved partly through the welfare state which it was thought would diminish social inequality, and partly by economic management and intervention and a tax regime to try to secure a closer approximation to the preferred egalitarian pattern.

The other reason why equality of opportunity was not enough for a thinker like Crosland is that such an approach would concentrate only on some aspects of the human personality, namely those which it was thought would be most appropriate for greater success in the market. Thus, it led to a neglect of other very important aspects of human nature and sought to nourish a narrower market-driven view. This latter approach is not directly relevant at this point to the neo-liberal argument and will be taken up when later on in the book I discuss the issue of markets and commodification.

In what I have already described as the mid-twentieth-century view of equality I have been careful to say that such egalitarians believed in greater equality of outcome, not in strict or absolute equality in such terms. Indeed from Tawney through to Crosland one can find defences of necessary inequalities.[5] In Crosland, for example, such inequalities were to be justified not because an individual *deserved* some differentially high reward; rather inequality was justified in terms of a 'rent of ability' – that is to say what turns out to be necessary to mobilize a talent the exercise of which is valuable to the community as a whole.[6] As Crosland himself argues[7] such an approach developed by him in *The Future of Socialism* in 1956 is very close to Rawls' ideas about 'democratic equality' and 'the difference principle' set out in *A Theory of Justice* in 1972. So for the social democrats there were justified inequalities, but they did need to be justified. They could not, as they would be for the neo-liberal, be regarded as acceptable just because they arose naturally out of free exchange. The voluntariness of the exchange which leads to inequality does not mean that such an inequality is justified.

This social democratic approach was a practical political doctrine as well as a philosophical one, and an important aspect of it as a political doctrine requiring a strategy to secure electoral support for it reveals its clear contradistinction from neo-liberalism. In order to pursue an egalitarian strategy in Crosland's view it was necessary to secure the support of the better-off middle classes and induce them to vote for such a strategy. This meant for Crosland that one could not expect such support if an egalitarian strategy was going to make such people worse off in real or absolute terms.[7] Therefore the way to success for an egalitarian strategy was to maintain the absolute position of the better off while improving the relative position of the worst off. This could not be done by direct transfers since that would undermine the absolute position of the better off, thus, the solution was to be found in continuing and incremental economic growth so that the fiscal dividends of such growth could be used by government to improve the relative position of the worst off while maintaining the absolute position of the better off. The neo-liberal on the contrary is concerned only with the absolute position of the worst off, not their relative position, nor with the degree of inequality. In the view of the neo-liberal a free market and the trickle down or echelon advance of such a market is much more likely to improve the absolute position of the worst off. It seems fairly clear from the general thrust of the book so far why this should be so and why the concern should be with absolute position rather than with inequality.

First of all, of course, there are the Nozick-inspired criticisms of a patterned principle of social justice which we have already considered in detail. Allied to this is a critique of the role of the state in seeking to pursue patterned principles. This raises three issues. The first is the competence of the state to secure such outcomes even assuming that they were to be regarded as morally desirable. The neo-liberal argues very strongly for the recognition of government failure in much the same way as twentieth-century social democrats argued about market failure. So, for example, the neo-liberal might argue that if we are to take seriously the argument that entrepreneurship and other talents valuable to the community must be allowed to secure their reward by means of the rent of ability how exactly could government determine which types of action should be allowed to meet the rent of ability criteria? Some of these points will re-emerge in Chapter 7 (on the institutional critique of the politics of social justice).

Secondly, there is the more moralized argument that liberty upsets patterns and therefore whatever the other defects may or may not be patterned principles are undesirable because maintaining the pattern undermines individual liberty to exchange, to bequeath, and to give – all actions which can disrupt some sort of end state or patterned view of social justice.

Finally, it is argued that such a role for the state is incompatible with the idea of the rule of law because again it consists in trying to secure to individuals a particular outcome and indeed a differential outcome, and the tax regime for a social democratic state seeking to secure a particular patterned end state would be unlikely to satisfy the requirements of the rule of law. This again is revealed in the case of rent of ability. The tax regime would have to be able to distinguish between differential resources going to those with socially valued talents and where that is not the case. Thus, tax rules are going to have to be highly differentiating and be incompatible with the rule of law.

I do want, however, to come back to two aspects of the political strategy relating to social democratic egalitarianism which the neo-liberal will find difficult. The first is to do with growth which in the view of someone like Crosland is a *sine qua non* of such a strategy. In the view of the neo-liberal, incentives are crucial to economic growth. This means that the incentives available to the entrepreneur in particular, as the agent of dynamism and growth, will be particularly important. So, from a neo-liberal perspective, equality may be the enemy of the very growth which social democrats rely upon to achieve their aims. It may be, of course, that the rewards of the entrepreneur might be covered by Crosland's rent of ability argument for justified inequalities, but then the neo-liberal might well reply that if the social democrat is prepared to reward the entrepreneur as well as others whose talents are important for the rest of the community what is left of the egalitarian vision endorsed by the social democrat?

The second problem with the political strategy is that the welfare state turns out in any case not to be a very effective instrument for securing greater equality even assuming that it was desirable. The argument here has been put not only by neo-liberals, but also by social democrats such as Julian Le Grand in *The Strategy of Equality*.[8] In the view of such commentators the welfare state including health, education, and higher education may secure the support of the better endowed but it does this at the cost in practice of giving such groups greater benefits – not intentionally – but because of the fact that the better endowed are going to be better at playing the complex bureaucratic systems that the welfare state actually spawns. Therefore, a strategy which sought to diminish inequality may do little or nothing to improve the situation and could even make it worse in certain areas such as higher education unless even more draconian action is taken by the state. From the neo-liberal standpoint, this strategy is also morally flawed because in so far as the welfare state creates dependency (see below) a middle-class welfare state spreads this unreasonable dependency more pervasively across society and creates very strong vested interests among the most articulate groups in society who may well use their position to resist reform since they will turn out to be worse off following reforms.

The final element of the moral critique of the welfare state and social justice has to do with the role of needs. It would be very difficult to provide an account of the normative basis of the welfare state without referring to needs. Indeed, some have argued that it is the division between needs on the one hand and wants and preferences on the other that makes the difference between the welfare state and the market. The welfare state exists to meet needs; the market to satisfy wants and preferences. So, what is the neo-liberal approach to the idea that it is a responsibility of the state to meet needs? There are in fact many facets to this critique as well as many ambiguities in the neo-liberal approach.

One of the ambiguities here lies in the fact that some significant neo-liberals such as Buchanan and Mises[9] adopt a subjectivist view of values. On this basis the idea of needs is quite difficult to accept. It is difficult because needs are always related to ends, goals, or purposes. I need *X* in order to Φ. In one sense the need is objective. It is true that I need the object in order to Φ; in another respect the relationship is value-laden in that the question arises: Is Φing a valuable goal or purpose to pursue? So, it may be objectively true that I need insulin in order to be healthy (as a diabetic); it is also true that the burglar needs a jemmy to pursue his goals. Relative to the goal, the need may indeed be objective, but whether the need is legitimate depends crucially upon the end, goal, or purpose for which the good in question is needed and whether that end or goal is regarded as good. So, given the neo-liberals' general subjectivism about values, it might be thought that all needs are relative to subjectively endorsed values.[10] There would be no reason to think that people generally will agree in their subjective valuation of ends to the extent that they could arrive at a set of human needs entailed by such common ends. We cannot expect to arrive at a set of common objective needs unless we assume that there are common objective human ends and the thrust of neo-liberal subjectivism goes against precisely that assumption.

It should, however, be noticed in passing though that not all economists who have contributed to the development of neo-liberal ideas share this sort of subjectivism in relation to needs. A central figure who does not is Carl Menger in his *Principles of Economics* in which he assumes a doctrine about objective human needs.[11] Menger operates with an idea of 'imaginary goods' which links very closely to his idea of needs in the following way: a useful good or thing for Menger is a good which is capable of satisfying human needs and this relationship between needs and such a good is a matter of objective fact. Indeed in Menger's view the relationship is a causal relation which can be known. So the provision of good X causes the need A to be satisfied. However, the fact that this is an objective relationship means for Menger that one can in fact be mistaken about it and in respect of both sides of the relationship: the nature of the need and the good to satisfy it. I may have needs that I am unaware of – but they can be ascribed to me on an objective basis, equally I ascribe to myself needs that objectively are not in fact needs; in respect of the good concerned I may be mistaken in thinking that the good stands in the causal relationship of satisfying needs. In Menger's view we become clearer about our needs and about what will satisfy them as civilization progresses. It is part of the role of government to educate people about needs and the causal relations they stand in to goods. All of this would be quite difficult to understand on a wholly subjectivist basis. One aspect of Menger's argument that might alarm neo-liberals is that if needs are objective they can be ascribed to people independently of their own avowals. This might well then be the basis for empowering state officials to ascribe needs and the means of satisfying them to people independently of their own avowals. Overall, Menger's argument sits very badly with subjectivism because it implies that there is a place for the state in relation to needs.[12] Many neo-liberals would want to dispute any claim that need has anything to do with justice or social justice.[13] If we recognize needs even as an objective set of states following Menger, it does not follow that this recognition has anything to do with justice. This point is made by H. B. Acton in *The Morals of Markets* when he argues as follows:

> [The Liberal] argues that in a humane and wealthy society the poorest should not be left to suffer from illness and exposure and forced to remain without education in the basic skills. To help those in distress, he holds, and to respond to the call of humanity, is a moral demand that no one can reasonably question, but this response is concerned with the relieving of suffering not with achieving justice. The first does not necessarily lead in an egalitarian direction whereas the second tends to do so. If the poor or the casualties of life are helped because it is *unjust* that they should remain as they are, then the way is opened for saying that it is unjust that some people should be less well off than others. But if the help given to them is on humanitarian grounds, then there is no presumption in favour of continuing the process of redistribution beyond the point at which distress is relieved.[14]

This passage is full of complexities which lead neo-liberals in different directions. According to Acton the claim of need is a claim about humanity rather than justice and the natural way of reading his argument is that this humanitarian help is given by the state supported by the tax system. This presupposes that there is a positive duty of humanitarian aid which can be coerced. That is to say that Acton is distinguishing his position from someone like Nozick who would agree that we could easily, as reasonable people, recognize need when we see it while arguing that the appropriate response to this is individual charity or beneficence or altruism – not collective action by the state. After all people in need do not have a right to have their needs met because the resources to meet those needs are the property of others. They may, of course, voluntarily choose to dispose of their property to the needy but should not be coerced into it by the state. So, there is quite a difference of approach here between the neo-liberal and the more libertarian argument. Acton also is clearly reflecting Hayek's view set out in *The Constitution of Liberty* that we can distinguish clearly between a minimum standard of provision – presumably to meet needs – although Hayek does not put the point this way, and a socially just form of provision. The former, in Hayek's view, is defensible while the latter is not. We shall consider this point further when we come later to the critique of the neo-liberal position on this point but it has to be said at this stage that neither Acton nor Hayek has given any very clear reason for thinking that an obligation to meet needs exists and that this obligation should be discharged through collective mechanisms.

There are other aspects to the critique of a need's view of distribution to be found in the writings of neo-liberals. The first of these is the idea that needs are incommensurable and as such we have no principle available for determining primacy between incommensurable needs. This is a specific or more applied version of Hayek's general strictures about the indeterminate nature of social justice. His more general argument is that we have no way of determining overall criteria such as distribution according to merit or need. Here the argument is more specific, namely that even if we could agree that resources should be distributed according to need there are still non-rationally determinable choices to be made between incommensurable needs and we lack the normative resources to make such determinations. This in turn has two baleful results.

The first is that if we see needs as underpinning social and economic rights then those rights will not be compossible because the rights will embody claims about incommensurable needs. Thus, the neo-liberal argument about needs adds to the case against social and economic rights.

The second issue is that if needs are incommensurable but are nevertheless the basis of claims and perhaps claims expressed as rights, then officials charged with running a welfare system to meet needs will have to act with discretionary power. It has to be discretionary and not governed by rules because we cannot write determinate sets of rules to govern the allocation of incommensurable resources. Thus, on this view a needs-oriented view of distribution – central to the social democratic welfare state – embodies at its heart discretionary power which cannot be made subject to the rule of law.

This argument will be evaluated in more detail in Chapter 13 which seeks to assess the overall plausibility of the neo-liberal case against the welfare state, but it is just worth pointing out at this stage that both Hayek and Acton are in favour of a safety net form of welfare provision so long as it is clearly distinguished from a commitment to social justice. So how is this minimum safety net to be set if not with reference to some account of basic needs? If this is the case, how is it to be determined? The above-mentioned argument would seem to apply to such views as much as to the social democratic approach. Obviously, the criterion would not apply to thinkers such as Nozick and Rothbard who do not accept the case for safety net provision.

The second additional argument against needs-based allocation is the claim that needs, including basic needs, are not in fact satiable. If they are not in principle satiable and yet there is a policy commitment to meet them, then that commitment becomes totally open ended. This open-ended commitment to satisfy insatiable needs is assumed against a background of scarcity. Given that, officials charged with meeting needs will again have to act in arbitrary and discretionary ways – allocating scarce resource between incommensurable types of needs which cannot finally be satisfied.[15] If these needs are to be made a matter of collective or state responsibility outside of the market, then demand for the resources to meet such open-ended needs is infinite. This again strengthens the case for not seeing such needs as rights in the neo-liberal view. If they are rights, and if needs are insatiable, then it is not possible to produce a coherent account of the duty corresponding to these rights. The needs are insatiable and the demand for their satisfaction is unlimited, hence the corresponding collective duty is also unlimited. This contrasts squarely on the neo-liberal view, with the limited, categorical duties which correlate with negative rights. It also follows that the insatiability of needs and the rights associated with needs are not compatible with the idea of the rule of law.

The final point about needs, which picks up a point from an earlier chapter, is the Nozickian one that there is no reason why needs should be the basis of collective provision and no reason why we should think that there should be a general obligation to meet such needs. So, for example, why should medical needs be regarded as a basis for such an obligation and barbering needs not? If the internal goal, to use Bernard Williams' phrase,[16] of medical care is meeting medical need then why does this give rise to a collective obligation whereas the job of the barber, on a similar basis, might be thought to meet barbering needs but we do not think that there is a similar collective obligation. Why not? The obvious answer would be to point out that medical needs are more important, they are part of a set of basic or generic goods that people need to have before they can act autonomously and pursue other goods. Whatever the merits of this argument Nozick would then resist it by saying that this does not consider the position of the service providers or the entitlements of those whose resources would be coercively utilized by the state to meet such needs.

Again though, this view cuts across the neo-liberal view as found in Acton and Hayek who do recognize an obligation to meet basic needs in effect even if they do not put the point in this way. Therefore, Nozick's position is as much an argument against that position as it is against the social democratic approach.

In order to complete this exposition of the neo-liberal case against the welfare state we need to look finally at arguments about dependency. The claim that the social democratic welfare state creates dependency is a view that neo-liberals share with both libertarians and neo-conservatives, although the prescriptions in each case differ fundamentally.

The discussion of dependency has become quite a contested political issue and my aim here will be to outline the normative basis of the neo-liberal idea of dependency. This normative critique engages claims about freedom and autonomy, the rule of law, and bureaucratic discretion and power. Because I want to try to keep the discussion rigorous it might be as well to start with a definition of dependence which I take from Alan Gewirth's book *The Community of Rights*.[17] Gewirth proposes the following definition of dependence which seems to me to be satisfactory:

> For A to be dependent on B for commodity X means that B, or B's activity, is a necessary condition of A's having X. This involves that there is no source other than B from which A can receive X.
>
> If A is dependent on B for X then B has a certain degree of power over A in relation to X.

On the face of it dependence in this sense might be thought to apply in the context of the welfare state and its officials – the B in the above formula. If A needs *X* where *X* is a benefit like social security or a good like health care and B is the only supplier available because A cannot afford to buy *X* in the market, or is in a communist state where there is no private market in these goods, then according to the definition B has power over A in respect of *X* and A is dependent on B for *X*.

So what is wrong with dependency from a neo-liberal view since it is part of the human condition that we are mutually dependent on one another for all sorts of things – not least in markets? Is not the employee dependent on the employer, for example? What *is* wrong with dependency thus understood for the neo-liberal is that it limits freedom and autonomy. Of necessity it increases the discretionary power of officials; it makes the dependent person's life less predictable and because of that makes such a person less able to carry through what Hayek has previously called 'a coherent plan of life'. Finally, the power which B exercises in this relationship is not compatible with the rule of law. These features will be discussed in turn.

First of all I want to look at the neo-liberal claim that dependency in a welfare state is very different from the mutual dependence which may be regarded as characteristic of markets. In the circumstances in which A is placed (i.e. unable to meet his or her needs out of his or her own resources in the market) B is in effect the sole monopoly supplier of *X* which A needs. This is the key, so it is argued, to the difference between the welfare situation and the market. During the period of employment the employee is dependent on the employer for his or her wages but the employer is not the monopoly provider of wages. The employee may choose to change his or her employer if he or she is dissatisfied with the terms and conditions of his or her employment and even if he or she has to make a disadvantageous choice in respect of a subsequent employment contract that is not a restriction on liberty in the general neo-liberal understanding of these things. Similarly, the employer is not dependent on the employee so long as there is a pool of labour available with the appropriate skills. Therefore while employment relations, when they are operative, may involve relations of mutual dependence they are different from welfare dependency because this takes place in a monopolistic situation in which the costs of exit, unlike in a typical labour market in a dynamic economy, may range from being very high to catastrophic since it is basic needs that we are talking about.[18]

Of course, monopolies may occur in markets, and we have looked more than once at the example of the monopoly supplier of water in the desert, but neo-liberals look for a legal regime which will be hostile to monopoly. However, where they do occur Hayek, for example, argues that the monopoly supplier should be required to 'treat all customers alike, i.e. to insist that his prices be the same for all and to prohibit discrimination on his part'. So if such a way of dealing with customers is a way of dealing with dependency in relation to a monopoly in the private sector, why can the same principle not be used to at least mitigate the degree of dependency in the welfare state?

The answer to this question for the neo-liberal is that it cannot in fact be done. As we have seen, it is central to the neo-liberal case against the welfare state that there is a large degree of ineliminable discretion at work in the welfare state. The reason for this claim has already been stated and will not be repeated, but basically it is due to the complexity of the goods being provided, their incommensurability, and the fact that there will not be agreement on distributive criteria that makes a welfare state monopoly very different from a private monopoly. A private monopoly is typically providing some relatively simple type of good not a multifaceted and insatiable good like health or education and because of this a private monopoly could, in principle, be regulated in terms of impartiality and treating like cases in like manner, an outcome which cannot be achieved for the more complex, insatiable, and incommensurable goods of welfare.

The second issue in relation to dependency has to do with liberty and autonomy. If the goal of the neo-liberal is a free society in which people will be able to act as autonomous agents, then dependency in the way defined earlier is a threat to liberty. It is crucial to the exercise of freedom that one operates in an environment of predictable rules – a point made particularly strongly by Hayek – and one in which such rules are applied and interpreted in a predictable manner. The link with autonomy comes into the equation by means of, for example, Hayek's commitment to a 'coherent plan of life' but such a plan would be impossible without a stable, rule-governed environment. This, however, is impossible, so it is argued, in a relationship of dependency. It is also part of this argument that a predictable and rule-governed environment is necessary for the utilitization of the limited, dispersed, and fragmented forms of knowledge that people have. Given limited knowledge, life would be chaotic without such a rule-governed framework. In the view of the neo-liberal critic of dependency in relation to welfare, these conditions do not hold for the reasons already given: the rules governing the distribution of welfare goods cannot in their interpretation and application by officials have the appropriate degree of predictability about them.

There is rather a different approach at the libertarian end of the neo-liberal spectrum. Rather than a focus on predictability, the argument here is that a person can only be free and autonomous if he or she controls the general rules of his or her behaviour – that he or she is the author of his or her own ends in life and the rules, principles, and maxims which will enable these ends to be realized. In a situation of welfare dependency as defined earlier this set of conditions for autonomous life will not be satisfied because what Hayek called the 'data' of one's own actions will in fact be in the power of another person, namely the welfare official.

So, taken together, these arguments constitute the normative neo-liberal case in respect of welfare dependency. Associated with it, however, is a more practical policy-related case but one which, nevertheless, implicitly presupposes the normative case that I have outlined. The argument here is that dependency has a baleful effect upon *character* and that this in turn intensifies the problems of poverty that the welfare state was designed to cure. Poverty from this point of view is not just lack of resources – it is also a matter of character and attitude and in the view of some neo-liberal critics of the welfare state as people grow more reliant on the welfare state and their entitlements from it they lose their sense of initiative, the work ethic is weakened, and people lose their sense of obligation to their family in the sense of supporting it by their own efforts and to the wider community on which they become parasitical. A crucial document in the formulation of this view was *The New Consensus on Family and Welfare* published by the American Enterprise Institute. Its claim was unambiguous:

> [S]ome observers have come to see existing welfare policy as toxic; they believe that it is damaging to the very poor it intends to help. Even if welfare policy has not caused the widespread behavioural dependency that has now become so highly visible, at the very least existing public policies have done little to remedy the situation.[19]

The effect of welfare is to separate clients from the world of work and a distancing from the values which are a necessary part of such a world of work: order, self-discipline, and positive relationships to others. Welfare dependency undermines these essential forms of human and social skills which are necessary to live an autonomous life. It also generates a destructive culture of complaint in that the welfare recipient does not have an incentive to look to his or her own character and skills for the remedy for his or her poverty; rather there is every incentive to rail against the state for not getting what one believes is one's due. So on this view public welfare has a deleterious effect on character. But there are radically different approaches to its solution from those who take this kind of view. There is an approach exemplified by Lawrence Mead in his book *Beyond Entitlement* which argues that benefits must become conditional on the discharge of obligations.[20] What is wrong with the post-war welfare system is that it is too oriented to rights and entitlements. This attitude needs to be displaced by one which stresses obligations and to make benefits more and more dependent on discharging these obligations particularly in regard to work. This will mean workfare and learnfare schemes funded by the state to link the benefits system much more to the world of work, and the benefits for character formation that will arise from that. Such arguments are, however, very difficult for the neo-liberal to accept, even if agreeing with Mead's diagnosis, because it is a prescription for a larger role for government and its agencies rather than just dispensing benefits. If the neo-liberal is worried about the competence of government, the unintended consequences of collective action, the power, and discretion of officials, then all of these would increase enormously under the type of modern welfare state envisaged by Mead and it would be very difficult to see how this approach could be made compatible with neo-liberal assumptions about the rule of law.

The other alternative policy prescription arising out of the dependency diagnosis of the problem was proposed by Charles Murray in *In Pursuit of Happiness and Good Government* in which he argues in a more libertarian mode for the dismantling of most of the benefits available from the welfare state.[21] To remove the welfare safety net would force recipients onto resources given by family, friends, church, charities, and such bodies and persons are much more able than the state to influence the character and motivation of the poor. No doubt the experience of people forced back into these sorts of circumstances will be very variable but because they are private persons and institutions, would not need to be concerned about issues to do with impartiality, justice, and the rule of law.

The problem for the neo-liberals, Hayek or Acton, is that they do think that a welfare safety net is justified and possibly not even a very limited one – remember Hayek's talk about it increasing in a wealthy society.[22] However, if the arguments developed by Mead and Murray have salience for the neo-liberal position, then even these limited safety net views of the welfare state – and in the case of Hayek not so limited – would also involve the problems of dependency. However, it is not clear how the neo-liberal would deal with these problems without embracing an extension of the role of government and inherently discretionary power with Mead, or abandoning the idea of a welfare minimum and moving in this respect at least much closer to the position of Murray and Nozick. I shall return to this point when I come to the evaluation of the overall critique of the normative basis of the welfare state.

NOTES

1. For this theme, see references in Chapter 3, note 4.
2. Hayek, F. A. (1960). *The Constitution of Liberty.* London: Routledge and Kegan Paul, pp. 16–17.
3. Crosland, C. A. R. (1956). *The Future of Socialism.* London: J. Cape; (1972). *Social Democracy in Europe.* London: Fabian Society.
4. Crosland, C. A. R. (1956). *The Future of Socialism.* London: J. Cape, chapter 10.
5. Carter, M. (2003). T. H. *Green and the Development of Ethical Socialism.* Exeter: Imprint Academic, chapter 6.
6. Crosland, C. A. R. (1974). *Socialism Now.* London: J. Cape, p. 15; See also Plant, R. (1981). 'Democratic Socialism and Equality', in D. Leonard and D. Lipsey (eds.), *The Socialist Agenda, Crosland's Legacy.* London: J. Cape.
7. Crosland, C. A. R. *Social Democracy in Europe,* p. 145.
8. Le Grand, J. (1982). *The Strategy of Equality,* London: Allen and Unwin.
9. Mises, L. von. (1996). *Human Action,* op. cit., pp. 94–6.
10. Mises, L. von. *Human Action,* New York: Foundation for Economic Education. p. 96.
11. Menger, C. (1994). *The Principles of Economics.* Grove City, PA: Libertarian Press; see also, Caldwell, B. (2004). *Hayek's Challenge: An Intellectual Biography of F. A. Hayek.* Chicago, IL: Chicago University Press, chapter 1; Campagnolo, G. (2008). *Carl Menger entre Aristote et Hayek, Aux sources de l'economie moderne.* Paris: CNRS; and Ebenstein, A. (2003). *Hayek's Journey.* Basingstoke: Palgrave, chapter 2.
12. See Campagnolo, C. *Carl Menger.* There are clear links between the quasi-Aristotelianism of Menger as set out clearly in the above books and current neo-Aristotelian writers such as Martha Nussbaum.
13. See Mises' critique of a separate category of needs in *Human Action,* pp. 95–6.
14. Acton, H. B. (1993). *The Morals of Markets,* ed. D. Gordon and J. Shearmur Indianapolis, IL: The Liberty Fund, pp. 99–100.
15. There is an interesting example of the practical application of this argument in Hillary Rodham's now Clinton's 'Children Under the Law', in *Harvard Educational Review,* (1973), 43(4): 487–514, at p. 496 when writing as a lawyer working for the Children's Defense Fund, she argues that 'How would a "right to be wanted" be defined and enforced? The necessarily broad and vague enforcement guidelines could recreate the hazard of the current laws, requiring the state to make broad discretionary judgements about the quality of a child's life'. I am indebted to Rothbard, M. (2002). New York: New York University Press, *The Ethics of Liberty,* p. 107 for the source of this quotation.
16. Williams, B. (1962). 'The Idea of Equality' in P. Laslett and W. G. Runciman (eds.), *Philosophy, Politics and Society,* Series 2. Oxford: Blackwell.
17. Gewirth, A. (1996). *The Community of Rights.* Chicago, IL: Chicago University Press, p. 118.
18. Hayek, F. A. *The Constitution of Liberty,* p. 137.
19. American Enterprise Institute (1987). *A Community of Self Reliance: The New Consensus on Family and Welfare.* Milwaukee, WI: American Enterprise Institute, p. xiv.
20. Mead, L. (1986). *Beyond Entitlement: The Social Obligations of Citizenship.* New York: Free Press.
21. Murray, C. (1988). *In Pursuit of Happiness and Good Government.* New York: Simon and Schuster.
22. Hayek, F. A. *The Constitution of Liberty,* p. 257ff.

7

Social Justice and the Welfare State: Institutional Problems

In this chapter I want to concentrate on various aspects of the institutional critique of the welfare state developed by neo-liberal thinkers. I shall look at three things: the critique of the 'public service ethic'; the critique of interest group politics which, it is argued, the welfare state encourages; and the role of the voluntary and charitable sectors within welfare states which, in the view of neo-liberals, lend themselves to being corrupted by such states.

The idea of a public service ethic has been historically very important to the social democratic state. Given that within such a state a range of significant goods and services are not distributed by the market, and therefore not subject to market incentives or constraints, it has seemed to be important to argue that there is a particular ethic ethos animating the public sector which energizes the delivery of services but equally constrains the exploitation of such non-marketed services by the producers. What makes the service provider act in the interests of the clients of such services is the public service ethos or ethic.

This idea goes back quite a long way and it is important to have an understanding of its history and how it is thought to differ both from a business ethic or ethos and also a voluntary sector set of motivations and constraints.

The idea of a public service ethic has for a long time dominated thinking about the motivation, character, and moral importance of the public sector within the political community. Initially in Britain the idea was applied to the civil service and the administration of the Empire, but as the public sector has grown, it has been applied to the character of administration in the spheres of health, education, and social services. During the nineteenth century the role of the state expanded considerably as Professor Greenleaf has made clear in his magisterial *The British Political Tradition*.[1] Quoting from Professor MacDonagh's classic article 'The Nineteenth Century Revolution in Government', Greenleaf endorses the view that 'a new sort of state was being born'.[2] Allied to this growth in government went some serious thinking about the moral basis of government and those who worked in its service. As a substantive feature of thinking about the public sector the idea of a public service ethic had its roots in the late nineteenth century when influential university dons such as B. Jowett, E. Caird, T. H. Green, A. Toynbee, and subsequently R. H. Tawney and W. Temple saw the role of the university as that of training young men in the ideals of citizenship and the service of the common good. They would enter the service of the state believing the state to be a body with moral purposes, articulating a sense of the common and public good which they would then pursue in a disinterested way. In turn these ideas were rooted in Plato and in Hegel whose works exercised enormous influence on the intellectual life of this period. In Plato's *Republic* the Guardians pursue the public good without that pursuit being contaminated by private interests. Hegel too in *The Philosophy of Right* published in Berlin in the 1820s wrote about the civil service as the universal class – that is to say the class who found in pursuing the public interest its own self-interest.[3] Public service was an exercise of civic virtue and that virtue consisted in the pursuit of the common good.

Allied to this was the idea of professionalism. As has been made clear in a number of studies on nineteenth-century ideas about professions, members of professions saw themselves as gentlemen, not only in the sense of social status but as being bound together by common professional ties, common experiences, particularly at school and university, and by common norms. This led to the formation of a gentlemanly class which differentiated itself from the aristocracy on the one hand and those who worked in trade on the other. They were bound together by the ideas of profession and service both of which produced 'fine and governing qualities' in Matthew Arnold's phrase. These ideas were particularly influential at the time because it was an era of civil service reform. Recruitment to the public service was made competitive rather than being based upon nomination and purchase of office and this required assumptions to be made about what public servants needed to know – the kinds of education and qualifications they needed to have and also, just as importantly, the values that they would follow. So there was a need to provide a normative basis for modern public administration. It was also a time of questioning about the nature and scope of the Empire and, in this, issues of justice and fair administration played an important role. Hence, normative questions in public administration could not be side-stepped.

The issue of knowledge also was crucial in an important way because the growth of public administration based upon knowledge, professionalism, and expertise raised deep questions about trust. If medically qualified people were making demands for more public involvement in health issues, then there was clearly a question as to how far public officials with this expertise could in fact be trusted. This point was in fact made with great insight when the Permanent Secretary to the Treasury in 1871 R. W. Lingen said: 'I do not know who is to check the assertions of experts when the government has once undertaken a class of duties which none but such persons understand.'[4] While this was particularly so in the field of public health, the point could be generalized over a range of fields in public administration. The obvious solution to Lingen's dilemma, which we shall explore in modern contexts later, is that such people have to be trusted as professionals bound by an ethical code or ethos, and that they are gentlemen who are seeking to do the public good and not recommending schemes which will mean their own enrichment.

Of course, the scope of the state has been transformed out of all recognition since that time, but appeals to a public service ethic and ethos are still very salient politically. Central questions are, therefore, whether the idea of a public service ethic and ethos makes sense and if it does, can it be applied as an explanatory tool across the public sector given the growth in size and complexity of that sector? Also salient is the question of how far a public sector ethos and ethic does require, as these earlier thinkers believed, a sense of the common good if not for the state as a whole then for a particular area of the public sector. On this view a public service ethic has to be based upon a shared view of a common good to be pursued, which goes beyond the particular desires and interests of those employed in the sector so that they have a shared and clear sense of common purpose which can both have a motivating force and also act as a constraint on sectional and self-interested behaviour on the part of those employed in the public sector.

To help facilitate the analysis I shall try to set out in as clear a way as I can those features of the public sector which have been taken as central. At this stage in the argument I shall treat these features in a largely uncritical manner. Critical analysis will be reserved for later when I discuss the critique of the public service ethic from the neo-liberal public choice school. The marks of the public service ethic are usually taken to incorporate the following:

Motivation Individuals do not enter the public service out of concern for self-interest or personal utility maximization. They may derive satisfaction from what they are doing but that is to be seen in terms of service rather than utility maximization. The assumption here is that there is a common good or purpose within the service or organization to be pursued and that this will either constrain or displace sectional interest.

Professionalism This has clear links to motivation. Sometimes the motivational point can be put in terms of vocation – that those in the public service have a vocation to serve the public. In so doing they are guided by professional values which emphasize service. Professionalism also has a link to knowledge in that the administrator or the provider or services in the public sector has access to knowledge which may not be widely shared and indeed in the case of the law or medicine may be esoteric. There is a need, therefore, to ensure that this knowledge which can be used to meet social needs in law, medicine, education, etc. is to be used for the public good rather than primarily for private benefit.

Trust This in turn is linked to the issue of trust which is in many ways the most difficult and complex issue with many different dimensions. It is however, extremely important in an account of the public sector ethic and indeed it is arguable that there can be no such ethic as it is conventionally understood without a central place for trust. Trust is essential in each of the following ways:

1. Trust between citizens in the sense that the public sector embodies a degree of political agreement to provide certain sorts of services funded in a compulsory way via the tax system. Hence, those who administer, manage, and deliver services have to be trusted to do so and to reflect in their behaviour the values which the organization was set up to serve. One complexity here is that institutions will often embody compromises between certain values. Take for

example universities: they have duties to advance research and scholarship; to teach undergraduates; to ensure greater access from all sections of society; to protect minority disciplines as part of the Western tradition of knowledge, and no doubt other purposes too. They also have a general requirement to secure efficiency in the expenditure of public money. So trust between citizens and organization requires that those involved in the organization are sensitive to a wide range of purposes and not to favour one at the expense of the rest. Trust between citizens is also reflected in the sense that institutions should behave impartially and with equity and that they should provide universally to those who fall into the appropriate group whose needs are to be catered for by the institution.

2. Related to this is also the issue of trust between government and citizens. Citizens have charged government with delivering services the nature and scope of which have been agreed politically. Given that public sector institutions have this necessary relation with the state and with politics, if citizens are to trust public sector institutions they must be seen to be delivering, in relation to the public, purposes for which they were set up and not diverted to put other interests before the needs of the citizens they are supposed to serve. This requires a strong ethical stance within the organization so that they do not become captured by special interest groups whether of producers or consumers.
3. Equally there are issues of trust between government and the public sector. This requires that government can rely on the public sector to deliver services in an efficient and equitable way but also that these forms of delivery will be subject to constant review and change wherever necessary so that they serve the needs of citizens rather than such organizations becoming havens of entrenched producer interests.
4. There will also have to be trust between people who work in the public sector. A little more will be said about this in the context of judgement later. There will have to be shared values within a complex organization to make it work properly; there will also have to be trust in professional competence and integrity. A very central issue is whether such trust can in fact be sustained if the internal arrangements of a public sector organization are made subject to competitive pressures, for example, through internal market reforms or performance-related pay.
5. Finally, there will also have to be trust between the public sector on the one hand and possible future partners in either the private or the voluntary sectors and others if partnerships and PFI arrangements are to work. I have discussed below the extent to which the conventionally understood public service ethic relates to the normative framework of both business and the voluntary sector. At this point, however, it is worth making this point: If it is assumed that the market sector and the voluntary sector operate with very different and possibly incommensurable normative assumptions, then it is difficult to see how

cooperation will work without the public sector ethic being transformed out of all recognition. If, however, there are similarities or common features, then this can be the basis for common understanding and dialogue about further cooperation.

6. It is also argued sometimes that the nature of the goods provided in the public sector leads to important questions about trust. The obvious example here is that of medical care. The arguments here would be first of all that typically there is a large asymmetry of information and expertise between doctor and patient such that the doctor who has to make a profit from his patients to provide his salary is in a position to exploit the relative ignorance of the patient and oversupply medical help relative to need. Sometimes it is also argued that the effect of the good supplied are irreversible or at best difficult to reverse – again medical care or poor education come to mind – and thus there has to be a very high degree of trust between producer and consumer and that this should not be contaminated by financial considerations.

Impartiality This is often seen as the first virtue of public administration and bureaucracy. The central issue here is the rule of law which it is argued has to apply directly to public organizations that serve public purposes and are underpinned by public finance. Although, as we shall see later, issues around impartiality and the rule of law are really quite complex, nevertheless, it can be argued at this stage that rules are central to the administration and delivery of public services and rules have to be enforced in an impartial and disinterested way.

Judgement It might seem odd on the face of it to turn from impartiality to judgement but this is an important issue that ties together issues about trust, impartiality, and professionalism. However much we want to emphasize the idea of impartiality and the rule of law in the delivery of public services, it is, I think, the case that the role of judgement is ineliminable. This is not a new point and indeed has been understood since the time that Aristotle wrote the *Nicomachean Ethics*. However detailed a rule or a law is, there is always going to be a gap between that rule and its application in particular cases or indeed to which cases it should apply. This gap has to be filled by the exercise of judgement. Usually in the context of the public services this judgement cannot be guided by one dominant value – as it might be, for example, in business in terms of efficiency. Given, therefore, that there will be a limit on what might be called calculative judgement in terms of the issues facing decision in the public sector, there has to be both *vertical* and *horizontal* trust within a public sector body in terms of the judgement exercised. That is to say in terms of vertical trust, the consumers of the service have to have confidence in the way that judgement is exercised particularly given that they may be disadvantaged by it in a particular case. In terms of *horizontal* trust there has to be confidence on the part of others who work in the organization that judgement will be exercised appropriately since these other people may have to deal with the consequences of the exercise of judgement. The delivery of health care to an individual within a medical practice in a hospital is a crucial example of this. Part of what will make the exercise of judgement appropriate is that in many cases where professional competence is involved it will be exercised in a way informed by professional standards and professional codes. Equally, part of it will be that the judgement is exercised in terms of the values that characterize and inform the organization and its wider public purposes. Finally, it will be a judgement made, as far as possible, on impartial grounds discounting any interests and prejudices of the individual exercising the judgement.

It is important to recognize that neo-liberals are rather critical about the role of judgement in the public sector or rather what they would call discretion and we shall look at the arguments here later. It is worth pointing out at this juncture that the role of judgement as I have outlined it should be compared with what Oakeshott and Hayek said about the difference between adjudication in a nomocratic legal order and the exercise of managerial discretion within a telocratic enterprise and the superiority of the former compared with the latter, at least in the case of public institutions.

Some of these values and principles, it might be claimed, differentiate the public sector from both the world of business and the voluntary sector.

It is distinguished from the world of business because in a business it is argued that people do act in order to maximize their utilities both as producers and consumers. They are concerned with the needs of the firm and the consumer, not with some general idea of the common good and the public interest. Equally, the dominant relationship in the market is that of contract within which self-interested individuals bargain together to arrive at as mutually advantageous agreement as they can. Similarly, the world of business does not have to be linked to the principle of impartiality. Apart from providing rules-governing contract and specifying property rights the rule of law does not directly affect individual business transactions except in these procedural ways. As I pointed out earlier, the idea of equity seemed to be an essential feature of public institutions in a way that does not apply to business. No doubt in business once a contract has been concluded it has to be administered and followed through in an impartial way but the requirement of impartiality is much more restrictive. The fact that I, as a businessman, have concluded a contract with person X does not at all entail that I should conclude a similar contract with person Y who is in all respects in an identical situation to person X. Discretion, choice, personal feeling, experience, etc. all have an appropriate place in the world of business. This also means that issues of trust are far more circumscribed. No doubt the parties to a contract have to trust one another. Buyers and sellers in everyday transactions have to have a degree of trust for these to take place efficiently. There may also be a need for a generalized degree of trust in market institutions like contracts and the right to property. Nevertheless, relations of trust are more circumscribed than in the context of large-scale delivery in the public sector. Indeed, as we shall see later there are some arguments that certain types of goods such as medical care should only be provided in the public sector just because the degree of trust to enable the private sector to work efficiently without heavy regulation is not in fact present. Finally, it can be argued that the purposes of business are more limited and determinable. That is to say a firm sells a product of a specific sort, and the buyer wants to buy a product of a specific type. In the public sector, however, the types of goods to be delivered are complex and in some sense abstract, for example, good health, good education, therapy, and knowledge. This implies a greater degree of complexity in the nature of the product and a degree of trust that the suppliers will act ethically in the delivery of less determinable outcomes than a business with its much more limited set of goods. These differences also give us the reasons why the world of business is able to keep the rule of law in the sense of public law at bay. The spheres of public sector delivery of services and the business sale of services are fundamentally different and public law does not impinge upon the private sector – a feature which neo-liberals welcome. In Chapter 13 we shall look at some of the emerging pressures in modern society which are likely to undermine these distinctions and the role of public law, not the least of which will be contracting with private sector organizations to deliver publicly funded services.

The public sector can also be differentiated from the voluntary sector on this view of the central features of a public service ethic although not in all respects. Those who *volunteer* in the charitable sector are clearly not motivated by utility maximization unless utility is made trivial as meaning whatever gives you a sense of satisfaction. There is rather some kind of altruistic behaviour oriented towards the achievement of some common rather than private value and it can be seen as an exercise of civic virtue. Nevertheless, in other ways, the voluntary sector can be seen as rather different from the public sector. First of all, most voluntary and charitable activity is devoted to a specific sector of need: the homeless, drug addicts, youth work, or whatever. Benevolence and altruism are of necessity discretionary because of scarcity of time and resources. The fact that I choose to give money to a particular charity or spend my time helping people in particular circumstances does not mean that I am committed through some principle of justice or impartiality to giving similar sums to similar charities or spending more of my time with similar groups. I have to have the ability to choose how I shall spend my time and to whom I shall give my money. It also follows from this quite crucially that the recipients of benevolence do not have a right to those resources whereas in the public sector there is very often a statutory right to the service or the goods provided. This is also true at the organizational level in the sense that a charity does not have to be impartial in relation to the sorts of people in the kinds of needs which it is trying to relieve. So, for example, it is possible to have charities for the homeless in particular geographical areas or perhaps those who profess a particular religious faith; since they are not part of the state they have the right to privilege one group before another and not be neutral between conceptions of the good. Given that there are rights or entitlements to many public sector goods, it follows that citizens in general have to have confidence in the impartiality of the administration and provision of these resources and also in the predictability of the provision. In the voluntary side of the voluntary sector (excluding for the moment not-for-profit organizations in the third sector) this degree of predictability cannot be present just because of limitations of time, resources, and the centrality of choice and discretion. In addition, the purposes of the voluntary organization are usually prescribed with a great deal of specificity, not least to protect the trustees in the exercise of their voluntary duties. However, as I have already said, this is often not the case with organizations in the public sector. Therefore, given that recipients of voluntary services cannot have a right to them, that their purposes are prescribed, and that the role of impartiality has a much more limited role in the voluntary sector, it seems to follow that trust has less of a general role to play in the voluntary sector than it does in the public sector. This might appear counter-intuitive since many commentators have written about the importance of the voluntary sector in enhancing trust and social capital generally in modern societies. I have no wish to deny that the voluntary sector is important in creating trust in some dimensions particularly in the sense popularized by Robert Puttnam,[5] that is to say in terms of interaction between citizens. This is however somewhat different from the dimensions of trust I distinguished earlier. These aspects of trust do not apply so clearly to the voluntary sector as they do to the public sector.

Finally, there is also the question of expertise and professionalism. As we saw earlier these are essential aspects of the public service ethic and give rise to issues about trust and ethical constraints on the use of expertise. Again, excluding not-for-profit organizations, the role of professional expertise is less obvious in the context of voluntary organizations – at least those that do depend a great deal on volunteers. There is no doubt an issue for the voluntary sector about the extent to which professionalization has taken a hold there and how this can be constrained by values specific to the voluntary sector. Nevertheless, it seems to remain true that the role that expertise plays in the voluntary sector is much less by comparison with the public sector.

I want now to look at the rather different perspective on the public service ethic developed by neo-liberal critique. This has been very indebted to the public choice school of economics, particularly thinkers such as Buchanan, Tullock, and Niskanen[6] and for inspiration to a previous generation, Friedrich von Hayek and Ludwig von Mises. The fundamental point of the public choice school is the denial that there can be an ethic of public service because that ethic assumes that in the public sector motivation differs from the dominant motives in the private sector of business, industry, and the market. In their book, *The Calculus of Consent*, published in 1962, Buchanan and Tullock reject the idea of what might be called different 'ethical realms' governed by different forms of motivations. People in the public sector act out of the same motives as those engaged in the market, namely rational self-interest. At the root of the public choice approach is the idea that the best explanation of bureaucratic behaviour and bureaucratic growth in modern society is not the assumption of a disinterested service ethic, but it is rather the rationally self-interested behaviour. They also take the more metaphysical view that there are simply no such things as social objectives, national goals, or social welfare functions to provide public goals for which public servants can work.

It is these ideas, according to the public choice theorists' approach to the understanding of particular bureaucracies, which can explain:

1. the increasing salaries of bureaucrats;
2. the increasing budgets of bureaux;
3. the increasing sphere of responsibilities of bureaux, etc.; and
4. the overall growth of bureaucracies.

The reason for these features for a public choice thinker like Niskanen lies in an understanding of the motivation and the behaviour of the bureaucrat in the public sector and service delivery. He argues that the following are possible goals of the bureaucrat: salary, perquisites of office, public reputation, power, patronage, output of the bureau, ease of making changes, and ease in managing the bureau. These goals all form part of the utility function of the bureaucrat that he or she – like everyone else – seeks to maximize. Apart from the last two goals on his list, Niskanen argues that they are all linked positively to the size and the budget of the bureau. So utility maximization on the part of the bureaucrat is intimately linked to increasing the size of the bureau, its budget, and the size of its responsibility since that is clearly linked to budget and thus to personal utility maximization. In the process the social democratic welfare state plays a critical role. The reason for this is as follows.

First of all, the social democratic state operates under the influence of ideas like social justice and equality has created more branches of government, dealing with social needs and social disadvantages. This has its effects in terms of rational self-interest. The reasons for this are easy to see. The realm of need to which the social democratic state is supposed to respond is vague, indeterminate, abstract in some respects, and complex in terms of the values to which meeting needs should be sensitive: equity, inclusion, justice, and the like. It can be bid up by pressure groups making claims for either enhanced needs or enhanced resources to meet existing needs. It is in the interests of those in health and social service departments, for example, to accept or even collude with this inexorable expansion of need since meeting new needs will expand the size of the bureau, the budget, the status, and the salary of the bureaucrats, all of which are a matter of personal utility maximization. The transformation of perceived needs into rights to be satisfied by government which was central to the political practice of post-war social democratic welfare states has exacerbated this process as has the support for it by those professionals whose interests are indirectly served by it.

The welfare state is not pervaded by an illusory public service which motivates providers and constrains them to meet the needs of their clients or customers outside a market setting. Rather the welfare state is a site for utility maximization.

So the public choice theorist wants to assimilate bureaucratic behaviour to market behaviour in terms of motivation, but of course, for the public choice thinker, while bureaucratic behaviour may be like market behaviour in terms of motivation, it does not take place in a market setting – that is to say, a setting in which there is a prospect of bankruptcy, a threat which concentrates self-interested behaviour in the market on the needs of the customer without which bankruptcy is likely to ensue. Thus, part of the solution to the problem of bureaucracy in the social democratic state for the public choice theorist is to situate this self-interested behaviour in a market or quasi-market context – a point to which I shall return to later.

Overall, therefore, the public choice view takes seriously and works through the consequences of David Hume's dictum that so far as public officials are concerned 'every man must be supposed to be a Knave'.[7] We should not, and indeed cannot, in his view rely on ethical ideals such as honour and civic virtue for security and trust in terms of political and public provision. Thus, for the neo-liberal thinker instead of trying to shore up a cultural approach to the public sector – seeking to enhance and entrench the idea of a public service ethic – we would be much better off devising institutional mechanisms for constraining self-interested behaviour within institutions.

This neo-liberal view of the public service ethic has achieved some political salience, a point put very well by Nigel Lawson, the Chancellor of the Exchequer in Mrs Thatcher's second Government, when he argued in his lecture *The New Conservatism*:

> We are all imperfect – even the most high-minded civil servant. Academic work is still in its infancy on the economics of bureaucracy, but it is already clear that it promises to be a fruitful field. The Civil Servants and Middle Class welfare administrators are far from selfless Platonic guardians of popular mythology.[8]

In the view of the neo-liberal critics, these features of rationally self-interested behaviour amongst bureaucrats are fed, or have been fed, by what might be called the 'social democratic state' and in particular the growth of bureaucracy in the welfare state. Similar sentiments to those expressed by Nigel Lawson can be found in Nicholas Ridley's 'Introduction' to Niskanen's *Bureaucracy: Servant or Master*, published by the Institute for Economic Affairs. Ridley called it 'a paper of devastating importance'.[9] If the public service ethic does not act as a constraint on producers in the public sector, how is their behaviour to be controlled and be made accountable within a welfare state structure, or does that structure have to be abandoned? The problem of accountability is considerably exacerbated by the role of discretion within large welfare bureaucracies and, as we have already had reason to note in earlier chapters, this too is related to a welfare state based upon social justice rather than minimal safety net provision.

The social democratic state enhances the role of discretion for bureaucrats which again increases their power. The reason for this is quite deep but equally straightforward and is a central plank of Hayek's critique of the social democratic state. A state should embody the rule of law and that law should be impartial in its application. Ideally, the rule of law should be restricted to proscribing actions which lead one citizen to infringe the negative liberty of another. Such rules are essentially about prohibitions on action. In a welfare state, however, the state seeks to secure to individuals access to or possession of certain sorts of real resources such as health, education, the services of social workers, etc. On the neo-liberal view, it is not possible to write rules of law which secure to individuals such resources in a universal and impartial way because of the fact of scarcity. Because of scarcity, the health professional manager, the teacher or head teacher, the social worker or his or her manager will have to act in arbitrary and discretionary ways in the allocation of resources which, in turn, is in the interest of the manager or the provider since discretion or the exercise of judgement is one way in which an individual can rationally find satisfaction through having a sense of autonomy and, as such, is in the individual public sector official's interest. What the public service ethic position would regard as an essential feature of judgement and trust, the neo-liberal theorist regards as arbitrary power.

So can this power be monitored, controlled, or made accountable within the social democratic welfare state? The neo-liberal answer is 'no'. First of all the role of utility maximization in the motivation and the behaviour of bureaucrats mean that it cannot be made properly subject to democratic accountability which would be the social democrats' preferred solution. The answer of the left to the problem of unaccountable power has been to argue for rendering it accountable through more extensive democracy and by the decentralization of state-provided services that they can become more accountable at a local level. There have been proposals for the development of local citizen's juries and panels and the like to try to engage local citizens in fixing the priorities that decentralized bureaucracies should have, and holding bureaucracies to account in terms of those priorities. So the left's solution to the problem of bureaucratic power is the extension of what might be called democratic citizenship which will have to be more extensive and more participatory. It is important to notice that these proposals share something in common with the neo-liberal, namely a distrust of bureaucratic power and an unwillingness to accept the degree of trust in a public service which would have to be in place for such a service ethic to be a guiding precept for the legitimacy of bureaucracy.

However, the idea that bureaucratic power can be made accountable through democratic means has to face two formidable challenges from the neo-liberal.

1. There is a strong asymmetry in motivation between the democratic representative and the deployer of bureaucratic power. The bureaucrat has every incentive in terms of preserving discretion, autonomy, and freedom of action to keep the detail of what he/she is doing out of the hands of the democratic representative to whom he/she is supposed to be accountable. The motivation of the representative to make the bureaucrat accountable is by no means as strong and it is held that the asymmetry will mean that the democratic model is unlikely to work.
2. There is also an asymmetry of knowledge (usually) between the representative and the bureaucrat. Usually, the representative will be a layperson without specialized knowledge of the details of the bureaucrats' work. This in particular is true in relation to professionally delivered services, for example, in health, education, and welfare. The expertise available to the professional is much greater than that available to the typical representative and thus the ability of the representative to keep the bureaucratically delivered,

> expert-based service, accountable to public priorities may be limited. It is also difficult for democratic representatives to use one layer of bureaucracy to keep in check a lower layer of bureaucracy when each layer shares common expertise and common experience. So, for example, the Conservative Government in the United Kingdom fundamentally changed the schools' inspectorate for precisely this reason: the then school inspectorate were usually ex-teachers and, as such, had more in common in terms of expertise and experience with the teachers and therefore that this attempt to limit the scope of one set of professionals with another higher order set to avoid the problem of asymmetry in knowledge is broadly bound to fail on this view.

So, the rational, utility-maximizing behaviour of the bureaucrat makes it very difficult to see that these political, non-market forms of monitoring and accountability can work. So the question then becomes much more whether or not there can be market-type solutions to these problems which could still operate within a publicly funded welfare state which sought to achieve social justice. Of course, the problem is well known in the market sector. The separation of ownership by shareholders and control by managers raises similar questions about the monitoring relationship between the shareholders and the managers of an enterprise. It is argued by neo-liberal thinkers, however, that while the maximization of sales and the growth of the firm is the central objective of both managers and shareholders, this can only be done in a market by being attentive to the needs of customers under a constraint of takeover or ultimately bankruptcy. The situation in the public services is different. There is no clear risk of bankruptcy if the public's needs are not satisfied; the service is usually a monopoly service; and the good to be maximized such as health or education is complex, unlike consumer goods, and different goods under the same generic name such as health may be in tension with one another or even incommensurable. So the problems of monitoring and accountability in the public services are more acute in the view of neo-liberals than they are in the private market. Suggestions, particularly from Niskanen, for improving the effectiveness of monitoring would include:

1. The introduction of competition between bureaucracies and service providers. This would enable us to see which providers meet needs more efficiently than others. To be effective, however, this would need to allow the possibility of bankruptcy to occur so that the underperforming bureaucracy or services providers could go out of business. This could prove very difficult particularly with schools and hospitals. If a service provider X in area A creams off a good many of the clients in area B because X is thought to be a better provider than Y, then this may lead to problems of those who cannot move from area B to A to access the better services. This is a problem for the social democratic welfare state because of considerations of social justice and equality of access. Therefore, again in the view of the neo-liberals, social democratic beliefs undermine the effective management of public provision.

2. It is also argued by Niskanen and others that given the rational maximizing motivation of bureaucrats which drives the expansion of services, then one way to deal with the problem would be to incentivize the bureaucrats to make cost savings and to reduce the budget. To do this it might be necessary to give the bureaucrat a share of the savings. The problem with this, however, is that it might be perfectly possible for the bureaucrat to create artificial savings given his or her greater knowledge of the service and the more restricted knowledge of the public officials and politicians who would sanction the rewards for savings. In addition, to judge whether savings were in fact real or artificial, it would be necessary to specify an identifiable output. This raises again the question of complexity and coherence of the bundle of goods provided by the public services and whether or not they are commensurable with one another.

Hence, the neo-liberal critique of the social democratic state applies not just at the level of values and principles like social justice, but also to the bureaucratic institutions which are held to be necessary for the achievement of the socialism of social democracy and, as we have seen the issue of the rule of law is important to this.

I have presented the problems as applying particularly to the social democratic state committed to the idea of the welfare state being an instrument of social justice. From the public choice perspective there is little doubt that social justice complicates matters, particularly in relation to equality of access, but, nevertheless, for those neo-liberals such as Hayek and Acton who believe that there is a collective obligation to provide for a social minimum, the problems raised by the public choice critique apply in more or less the same way to any set of state-provided services, not just those seen as an instrument of social justice. It is not at all clear that to insist that welfare provision is of a minimalist, safety net variety avoids all the problems the public choice theorists have identified. No doubt under the Hayek–Acton proposals the welfare state would be smaller, but those charged with running it would no doubt have the same motivations as those ascribed to bureaucrats by neo-liberals and public choice theorists – with the same consequences.

The alternative approach would be to take the libertarian line of Nozick, Rothbard, and Murray and dismantle the welfare state altogether and reject the argument that it embodies a morally compelling obligation about positive help. In that case, welfare goods would become like other goods to be traded in a market and for those who could not take part in such exchanges, they would have to be regarded as suffering from misfortune or bad luck which engages impulses of charity and benevolence rather than injustice which engages collective requirements of rectification.

This is not, however, the route which most neo-liberals have taken, so it does seem that the neo-liberals or public choice critique of the public service ethic they have adopted applies to their own more minimalist welfare state as well.

It would, of course, be wrong to assume that the acquisition of goods can only occur through the market or by government. There are a large number of voluntary organizations in civil society which have as their goal the meeting of needs and many of these pre-date the state. So what is the neo-liberal view of what is variously called the voluntary sector, the third sector, or the independent sector?

The first thing about participation in the work of charities, churches, and other voluntary sector organizations is that it is an exercise of individual liberty and therefore the existence of such sectors is welcomed by neo-liberal thinkers. In the view of neo-liberals such bodies may have great advantages over the state when it comes to meeting needs. It may be that citizens do see the necessity of providing certain goods collectively – for example, the safety net form of welfare provision which Hayek endorses, but in the view of neo-liberals while there might be a case for publicly financing such provision there is no reason at all why the state should be a *monopoly provider* of the services to meet those needs, or indeed a provider of services as opposed to *finance* at all. This is a point made strongly by Hayek in *Law, Legislation and Liberty, Vol. 3: The Political Order of a Free People.*[10] He recognizes that there are public or collective goods both in the pure economists' sense which will be discussed later and also need for public or collective action to address negative externalities of market behaviour. Therefore while government may have to act in such areas, it can act as a *funder* not as a *supplier* of whatever service or good is needed.

In undertaking the calculation about the appropriate suppliers of such services, government could take into account clearly straightforward types of costs and benefits, but some of the benefits of the voluntary or independent sector suppliers may be very salient but quite difficult to quantify. It is frequently held that supply from the voluntary sector has many advantages over the government as supplier.

First of all, it is argued that the voluntary sector has a capacity for innovation and working in new ways which publicly funded bureaucracies staffed by civil servants or state employees do not have.

It is argued that if the government funds a range of voluntary sector organizations to undertake the provision of what might loosely be called public goods, there will be competition between such organizations to secure sector-funding contracts and this competition will, in turn, constrain or reduce costs compared with the state sector given the neo-liberal or public choice view of the role of bureaucracies discussed earlier.

This competition for government funding will also lead to the creation of social entrepreneurs who will act in this sector much as entrepreneurs act in the market – matching resources to demands in new and innovative ways.

Most of the organizations in the voluntary sectors bidding for such contracts will be not- for -profit – that is to say surpluses are not distributed to shareholders or private owners but are ploughed back into the organization to enable it to operate more effectively and add greater value to their operation. This not-for-profit dimension both improves efficiency compared with governmental organizations since it does involve greater financial discipline; but equally it does constrain self-interested behaviour since there is no profit for private consumption – other than paying for the costs of the organization that have to be covered.

It is also argued by supporters of this approach that the voluntary sector acting as the deliverer of services adds to the richness of civil society – a key element in a free society; the voluntary sector is trusted more than the welfare bureaucracies and might therefore be able to engage with parts of the population that government-employed welfare professionals cannot. This is particularly important in that the mainstream neo-liberal approach is in favour of a minimalist welfare state which will be dealing with groups of people lacking the ability and skills to operate effectively in the market. The very marginalization of these groups may mean that voluntary sector providers, neighbourhood groups, churches, and the like will be able to reach such citizens in ways that may be impossible for agents of the state whether national or local.

Since there would have to be judgements made about who is the best provider between the various competing groups bidding for government funding, it is worth dwelling for a moment on the nature of the 'value' that can be attributed to the voluntary sector because this shows something practical about the nature of value from a neo-liberal perspective. Neo-liberal economics have a conception of value which can be attributed to not-for-profit organizations in a way that is not true, for example, of Adam Smith. In *The Wealth of Nations*, Smith draws a clear distinction between productive and unproductive labour. Productive labour increases the output of material goods and thus wealth and value, whereas unproductive labour goes into providing services.

> The labour of some of the most respectable order in society is, little more than that of menial servants, unproductive of any value, and does not fix or realise itself in any permanent object or vendible commodity.[11]

Among the respectable orders Smith goes on to include 'the whole army and navy – churchman, lawyers, physicians, men of letters of all kinds' as well as 'players, buffoons, musicians, opera singers, opera dancers etc'. Given such a view of the nature of value it might be thought to be difficult to engage in the type of calculation necessary for government as a basis for choice between one provider and another. Since the not-for-profit sector does not make goods for sale in the market, normal economic analysis based upon profit maximization cannot be applied to them. This however, is definitely not the approach of neo-liberals. They reject this objectivized and materialist theory of value in favour as we have seen of a conception of value as anything which is valued from a subjective point of view and which is often striven after by an individual in pursuit of the value he or she has placed upon it. Mises could hardly be clearer on this point which is highly salient for an understanding of the voluntary or not-for-profit sector since, on a standard view of rationality that links it to the pursuit of individual utility understood as material gain, it is more or less unfathomable why someone would operate in that sector. This is what Mises says in *Epistemological Problems in Economics:*

> Because the classical economists were able to explain away the action of businessmen and were helpless in the face of everything that went beyond it, their thinking was oriented towards bookkeeping, the supreme expression of the rationality of the businessmen (but not that of the consumer). Whatever cannot

> be entered into the businessmens' account, they were unable to accommodate in their theory. This explains several of their ideas – for example their position in regard to personal services. The performance of a service which caused the increase in value that could be explained in the ledger of the businessman had to appear to them as unproductive. Only thus can it be explained why they regarded the attainment of the greater monetary profit possible as the goal of economic action. Because of the difficulties occasioned by the paradox of value, they were unable to find a bridge from the realization which they owed to utilitarianism, that the goal of action is an increase of pleasure and a decrease in pain, to the theory of value and price. Therefore they were unable to comprehend any change in well being that cannot be valued in money and the account books of the businessman.[12]

So a sector of society which looks almost irrational can look entirely rational from what, as we saw in Chapter 2, Mises called a 'praxeological standpoint'. Prices and monetary values represent subjective forms of valuation not the outcomes of only 'productive' labour.

Therefore, following Mises' view, the neo-liberal would need to distinguish between two sorts of voluntary organizations: not-for-profit organizations and non-profit organizations. This is a very important distinction. A not-for-profit organization will price and buy and sell what is necessary to secure its goals. The point is however that the profit made is not owned by shareholders, entrepreneurs, or other individuals, it is rather reinvested in the organization. In this sense not-for-profit organisations are like a normal firm at least in the sense that they face and pay market prices for their inputs and charge market prices for their outputs. They, therefore, calculate in a normal way and a Buchanan style of the comparative advantage of one sort of delivery compared to another can be done.

A non-profit organization is much more like the traditional community-based voluntary group. They may of course lease or buy inputs at market prices – the rental of a church of community hall; out-of-pocket expenses for volunteers; leaflets; information; and publicity campaigns – but they do not price their products or outcomes. This does not mean that there is no rational way of determining whether outcomes are good or bad, but some of these processes will be qualitative rather than quantitative. Again, Mises is instructive on this point:

> Economic calculation cannot comprehend things which are not sold and bought against money. These are things which are not for sale and for those whose acquisition sacrifices other than money and money's worth must be expended. He who wants to train himself for great achievements must employ many means, some of which may require expenditure of money. But the essential things to be devoted to such an endeavour are not purchasable. Honour, virtue, glory as well as vigour, health, and life itself play a role in action both as means and as ends, but they do not enter into economic calculation.
>
> These are things which cannot at all be evaluated in terms of money; there are other things which can be appraised in money only with regard to a fraction

of the value assigned to them. The appraisal of an old building must disregard its artistic and historical eminence so far as these qualities are not a source of proceeds in money goods. What touches a man's heart only and does not induce other people to make sacrifices for its attainment remains outside the pale of economic calculations.

However, all this does not in the least impair the usefulness of economic calculation. Those things which do not enter into the items of accountancy and calculation are either ends or goods of the first order. No calculation is required to acknowledge them fully and make due allowance to them. All that acting man needs in order to make his choice is to contrast them with the total amount of costs their acquisition or preservation requires. Let us assume that a town council has to decide between two water supply projects. One of them implies the demolition of a historical landmark, while the other at the cost of an increase in money expenditure spares this landmark. The fact that the feelings which recommend the conservation of the monument cannot be estimated in a sum of money does not in any way impede the councilmen's decision. The values that are not reflected in any monetary exchange ratio are, on the contrary, by this very fact lifted into a particular position which makes the decision rather easier. No complaint is less justified than the lamentation that the computation methods of the market do not comprehend things which are not vendible. Moral and aesthetic values do not suffer any damage on account of this fact.[13]

The point in the second paragraph is very important here. Some of the value to be found in the voluntary sector has to do with rather intangible things like trust, a sphere of freedom, strengthening social ties, etc. Mises is arguing that these have enormous value but they cannot be represented in monetary values. What matters in respect of value for the economist Mises is whether I can fulfil a subjectively valued plan (on which, in the case of a voluntary organizations I cooperate with others with similar plans). It is possible for them to decide whether one course of action is better than another in relation to overall value even though because of a substantial lack of market values inside the organization it will not be possible to make this judgement on the basis of calculation. This does not mean for Mises that it has to be inefficient. It will all depend on whether the value is served or how this can be determined in ways that do not require calculation.

I now want to consider the final aspect of this non-institutional critique of the social democratic welfare state and discuss the neo-liberal claim that a distributive state creates a destructive form of interest group competition. The core idea which is subjected to considerable elaboration in neo-liberal writing is again focused on social justice. If the state is to pursue social justice in the absence of clear and rule-governed criteria of distribution – a situation which Hayek regards as being endemic – then it is perfectly natural to think that interest groups will arise to press for what they regard as being their just entitlement from the state. This is because on the one hand government is pursuing a distributive ideal – 'social justice' which, because it is being pursued in an ethical vacuum, since we cannot agree a criterion of just distribution and will become, in effect, a fig leaf for special pleading for benefits whether in terms of goods, services, tax breaks, or legal concessions by interest groups which claim their 'just' share of social goods. This is a very destructive form of interest group pressure, particularly for the worst-off members of society whom policies of social justice are assumed to help since the natural political development would be for coalition of the strongest groups to act in concert in order to extract from government their perceived entitlements. This is likely to leave the worst-off members of society outside this arena of the greatest benefit distribution. These interest group-based distributional conflicts cannot be resolved by government through an appeal to political principle since it is precisely the lack of principle that has caused the problem in the first place. This is a very important area of debate and discussion and can be made subject to a very great deal of elaboration. The neo-liberal approach to interest groups and their relation to questions of distributive justice challenge a fairly general post-Second World War assumption on the part of political scientists that interest groups are in fact a vital component of a democratic society. They were seen, particularly in the aftermath of war, to be an essential defence against the emergence of totalitarian regimes. These sorts of thinkers usually known as 'pluralist' were particularly concerned about two things.[14] The first is a rejection of individually based participatory democracy as naive and as inappropriate for modern, complex, large-scale societies. They saw direct participatory democracy as applicable, if at all, to small-scale societies such as the Greek *polis* or the Swiss canton. In their view, democratic politics is not about direct participation but rather about the accommodation of a wide range of interest groups none of which has a degree of power to countervail the rest. Government is not able to function properly unless it pays regard to the interest groups in the activities of which the major interests of society were to be represented. At the same time as interest groups constrain the power of government no single interest group can outweigh all others and it is in the competition between interest groups that, as Robert Dahl has argued, democracy resides.[15] Interest groups and their impact on politics and policy displace the idea of individual participatory democracy. At the same time, however, they have an important impact on individuals whose range of interests is represented by such groups. For example, they can play an educative role, creating a sense of group or corporate identity; they mediate between the isolated individual and the state and as such they play an important role in fostering social cohesion. This leads to the second important feature of interest group or pluralist theories. Totalitarian dictatorships have often been thought to have derived their support from individuals, who in modern, large-scale, mass societies feel isolated and alone. Belonging to a political movement with a strong message, particularly those relating to national or ethical identity, can seem appealing to isolated anonymous individuals in a mass society.[16] So interest groups are central both to democracy and giving people a sense of identity and these are less susceptible to the appeal of atavistic forms of totalitarian belief.

This rather benign picture of interest groups is rejected by many neo-liberals. They would take the view that it is one thing to endorse group identities and group endeavours as part of a vibrant civil society in a free state – churches, voluntary groups, charities, community and citizen organizations, unions and clubs, etc., it is, however, quite another to argue that such groups should have a political agenda of their own, particularly when this agenda is linked to the illegitimate distributive function of the state from a neo-liberal point of view. A rich variety of interest groups in a state in which government is involved in a limited set of activities providing public goods and a welfare safety net is one thing; but when interest groups play a central role in a state with an agenda of distributive justice what is a benign feature of a free society becomes corrupted by that agenda and complicit in the social ills to which it leads. The demands of interest groups for the resources to meet the interests which they represent will be insatiable because the demands are for goods: education, health, welfare, legislative concessions, tax breaks, and the like all of which, albeit in different ways, are open-ended. Furthermore, the demands of different groups may well be incompatible with one another so that given intrinsic limitations on public expenditure an increase in resources is likely to be at the cost of some other groups in society. Hence, there takes place an intense rivalry between groups and they will be engaged in a zero-sum game. Samuel Brittan has given a very good account of these processes in his book *The Economic Consequences of Democracy*:

> Each party to the bargain is likely to be given some concession which is only mildly damaging to the rest of the community. One group may receive an injection of public money to finance a wage increase unavailable in the market; another large section will receive rent controls and subsidies; and another large group 'mortgage concessions' leading to overinvestment in dwellings. But the harm done by the sum of these restrictive practices and special deals is very far from mind. Each of us suffers from the concession to special groups to which we do not belong. We would all be better off in the not so long term if we could achieve the only horse trading worth doing, i.e. an agreement by every group to its special privileges on the understanding that other groups did the same.[17]

Once such concessions have been granted by the government, they are very difficult to withdraw. A state which confined its activities to a range of public goods narrowly defined and a minimal form of safety net welfare provision would provide a much more limited environment for the growth of interest groups and the pressure that they can exert.

The problem is further exacerbated in the view of many neo-liberal critics if government operates in an environment within which the role and limits of government are not antecedently fixed. Without such constitutional limitations it becomes very difficult for parties in competition for votes to allow themselves to be outbid in terms of the services and concessions to be given to interest groups and citizens more generally.

In the view of critics such as Hayek the growth of interest group politics living in a symbiotic relationship with the growth of government was a central institutional factor in stagflation in the 1970s. The combination of high unemployment and high inflation, against all the assumptions of Keynesian economics, was attributed to the influence of interest group pressures on the supply-side of the economy.

The argument here is very indebted to public choice theorists. In their view interest group pressures mean that governments allocate resources not in terms of principle or widespread moral agreement in society, because this is not available for reasons which were discussed earlier, but in response to the political power and clout of interest groups. This is the point made in a discursive way by Brittan in the quotation given above, but in the view of the public choice theorists this poses central problems for democracy. The reasoning here is as follows: The gains made by interest groups or 'distributive coalitions', as Mancur Olson calls them, are highly concentrated on the members of such groups, and the possibility of obtaining such concessions helps to mobilize support for such interest groups and to account for the political pressures which they are able to exert. However, the costs of such concessions are widely dispersed in society among taxpayers and voters. The gains are palpable and immediate; the costs are dispersed and marginal. The costs of each concession to the dispersed and fragmented citizenry are small, and the gains to the interest groups are large and immediate. Hence, it is very difficult to mobilize citizens against interest groups which are so concentrated. However, although the costs to each taxpayer for each interest group concession are small, the aggregate costs are very large, particularly because they inhibit economic growth, innovation, and change. Interest groups become entrenched over time and indeed can come to exist in a symbiotic relationship with governmental agencies when these are the agents of resource allocation and subsidy. We can take two frequently cited examples. In the United States it is argued that the Interstate Transport Commission, far from being a neutral regulatory agency acting in the public interest, has in fact become the spokesman for the American railroads; in Britain it was argued that the Ministry of Agriculture had become the representative of farming interests. If this point is conjoined with the same theorists' approach to bureaucracy which we discussed earlier, it can be seen to be a powerful analytical theory. If an interest group increases its resources to its members by a price rise, a subsidy, or a tax concession, then this will not only increase the resources available to that group, but it will also produce inefficiency and rigidity for two reasons. In the first place it will encourage further resources into the area where the concession has been gained and, since the concession has been made for political rather than market reasons, this will result in further inefficiencies. Secondly, again because the interest group concessions have been made for political rather than market reasons, they will prove difficult to withdraw in the light of changing economic circumstances.

Mancur Olson argues in *The Rise and Decline of Nations*[18] that interest group politics of this sort produces social rigidities which affect the supply-side of the economy and which produce stagnation. He applies this analysis to the pattern of economic development in some Organisation for Economic Co-operation and Development (OECD) countries and argues that one element in the superior economic performance of Germany and Japan, compared with Britain and some regions in the United States, is the result of the fact that defeat in the Second World War broke down interest group rigidities in such countries. It has often been argued that the war was, paradoxically, beneficial to Germany and Japan because industrial regeneration, when it occurred, meant that they re-equipped with the latest technology. Olson argues that while this may be true, the breakdown of interest group rigidities was also very important.

The solution to the problem is seen by neo-liberals as twofold. The first is, as Brittan argues, to induce interest groups simultaneously to give up special interests. This is a Hobbesian problem for which there is no clear solution. It is obviously easier after a war when rigidities have broken down, but it is difficult to achieve in normal conditions. Indeed, David Stockman's (President Reagan's Budget Director) *The Triumph of Politics*[19] is a plaintive account of how someone who thought that it was possible to do so received a political education from Congress. The second issue is for government. It is not surprising, therefore, that a good deal of the work of the public choice theorists has been in the area of trying to think up new constitutional restraints on government to limit its power in this field which stimulates the creation and sustaining of interest groups. Neo-liberal critics argue that the very extension of the role of government has in fact weakened it. In order to mobilize legitimacy and consent, government has to appease major interest groups which are not constrained by either long-term considerations or a concern for the public good. Because government has extended its responsibilities, interest groups have moved in on these broader responsibilities in a competitive way, leading to economically dangerous levels of public spending.

The neo-liberal argues that the government in extending its responsibilities has become enmeshed in open-ended commitments which are electorally important in the fields of welfare, social security, health, and education. Indeed, government seems to have a widely assumed responsibility to take care of a range of unforeseen consequences, even in the wholly private sector. The only solution is to try to narrow the framework of government and the sphere of its responsibilities. Limiting the role of government can in fact increase its authority.

It would be a mistake to leave the analysis of this long chapter without including in the argument about groups in a social democratic state the role of unions. Given that the neo-liberal wants to place the protection of individual freedom at the centre of the neo-liberal vision, then it might be thought they should look favourably on unions – given the assumption that joining a union is a form of free action. In addition, it might be thought that free trade unions are an important aspect of a rich and variegated civil society which is very important for the culture of a democratic society. Indeed, in the 1980s many neo-liberals supported unions in Eastern Europe, particularly in Poland, because they were in fact able to challenge the extensive and arbitrary powers of tyrannical governments. In most respects, however, neo-liberals have a negative view of the role and status of unions as they have developed in Western societies since the nineteenth century in that they organize to secure economic and social benefits, legal privileges, and immunities from the distributive state, and thereby distort prices which are arrived at ideally by free exchange on the neo-liberal understanding of freedom.[20]

Secondly, unions share the other feature of groups in a distributive state: that in the absence of clear criteria for the allocation of goods and services or benefits and burdens unions which exist to represent the interests of their members will have very strong incentives to combine with other unions whose interests are similar to use that combined power to extract concessions from government and private sector employers on pain of strike action. In the neo-liberal view, these coalitions of powerful groups will work to improve the interests of those who belong to such strong organizations against the weaker and more dispersed interests in society – particularly the poor and the vulnerable.

However, in the neo-liberal view unions are able to go much further than this because they are not just organized interests but rather coercively organized interests through the institution of the closed shop or compulsory membership. As Mancur Olson explains, the free market economy itself provides considerable incentive to the formation of larger unions with more power, and when that is allied with compulsory membership, which he regards as the essence of unionism, then these powers increase enormously. The argument about the role of the market in reaction to the increasing size of unions is stated very clearly by Olson. He argues that the market may work against any organization that is active in only part of the market and therefore there is an incentive for unions to extend their scope; unions have an incentive to seek to ensure that a firm supplying a particular kind of good in the market will pay the union rate; if many unions compete in a particular market, the employers will be able to deal with them more in their interests through recruiting strike breakers either from other unions or from the non-unionized; and finally the political power of large unions is greater than that of small unions.[21] Overall, there is a logic at work which means that unions will increase in size particularly with the closed shop and legal immunities. Therefore, one can understand in terms of market economics and incentives why large unions came into being; but unlike other groups they are not *voluntary* organizations because they have compulsory memberships and in very many occupations membership of a union is a necessary condition of employment.

The reason for the closed shop can also be fully understood on the kinds of motivational grounds of rational self-interest espoused by neo-liberals. Given rational self-interest, the case for the closed shop closely parallels the argument about public goods and the need for taxation to provide those goods because of the freerider problem and the non-divisibility of the goods to be secured. Unions provide collective goods for the members – wage rates of a particular level and[22] terms and conditions of work which, it is claimed, would not be on offer were it not for the union. There are collective goods for those working in the firm and these exist only because of the power of the union. Also, the goods are indivisible just because they exist only as the result of collective action. If non-union labour is to be allowed into the firm, usually the union sets rates of pay that would apply to that individual as well as other terms and conditions. Given that such collective goods exist because of the power of the union and given that the ultimate power of the union rests on the threat of strike, then there are clear possibilities for freeriding in the absence of a closed shop. As an individual I have an incentive to work and not forego my income during a strike because I shall still share benefits in terms of wages and conditions shared by the strike action when it is over because the collective goods are indivisible. Given this individual incentive there will be no strike, no ultimate power for the union, and no collective goods to share in. Hence, the closed shop is absolutely essential to motivation even on the neo-liberals' own assumptions about rational self-interest and collective action.

Nevertheless, most neo-liberals regard closed-shop unions as wholly undesirable. The first reason is that the closed shop is coercive on its own understanding of coercion. While they may accept Olson's account of the role of the closed shop they reject the nature of the coercion involved, even though it is regarded as intrinsic to the achievement of the collective goods which are the aim of the union. This in turn leads to the neo-liberal arguing that these collective goods supposedly achieved by unions, and which provides the rationale for the closed shop, are in fact illusory certainly if looked at from the standpoint of workers as a whole. In Hayek's view, for example, if the myth that compulsory unions produce collective goods for workers could be exploded, then the case for legally condoning the degree of coercion increased in the closed shop would fall away.

The argument here has two parts. The first is a very general point which I have discussed at length earlier. It is just not the case, from a neo-liberal point of view, to think that the free market capitalist system exploits or coerces workers to the extent that it needs the closed shop-based collective action of unions to fight against. While it is true, as we have seen, that Hayek accepts that in the case of a monopoly supply of an essential good or in a situation in which an employer imposes additional duties on workers in a situation of high unemployment coercion may indeed occur, but even in his view such circumstances are rare and unlikely to be a feature of a properly functioning capitalist economy.[23] Other neo-liberal thinkers would not go even as far as this and would deny that labour contracts are ever coercive and, if they ever are, would not justify the degree of coercion exercised by unions. Therefore, on this view, unions are not needed to counteract coercion and exploitation in the economic market. Nor do they produce other collective goods which in the view of the neo-liberal could be produced just as effectively and non-coercively by the market. The focus of this argument is about *real* wages. One of the collective goods that the unions argue that they produce and which justifies the closed shop is rising real wages in unionized firms. This is a complex argument and has several strands to it.[24]

One argument is that even if it were true that union A in industry X raised real wages in that industry, and similar action by other unions in other industries did the same, nevertheless this would be against the interest of workers as a whole. The reason for this in the neo-liberals' argument that real wage increases negotiated by unions which would be in excess of what would be produced in a free market can only occur by limiting the *supply* of labour.[25] Therefore, such negotiations and outcomes may well be in the interests of those who are currently employed but will work against others – whether those who get employment at lower wages or are not employed at all. How does this work? The argument is that if union A negotiates a rate in industry X, then the union will possess a good deal of power to have produced this result. The exercise of this power is most likely to mean that in this industry none will be employed for less than that rate. This is the key factor from the employers' point of view: The employer will only agree to that rate when sure that the union can keep out others whom the employer might have employed at a lower rate. The union's capacity to do this depends upon the power of the closed shop. Therefore, if real rates of pay are increased by the exercise of union power this is based on the limitation of supply and this is against the interests of the workers as a whole. The aggregate effect of this is that in the long run unions cannot push up real rates of pay for those wanting to work above the level that would be established by a free market. But again for the neo-liberal this shows the iniquity of the closed shop and the way in which unions and for that matter other groups, as we saw earlier, act in a way that is against a common interest. The union can secure support for the closed shop because it can produce benefits for a small group, not for workers as a whole.[26]

The second argument is wholly empirical. It is the claim that real wages have often, or usually, risen at a faster level when unions are weak rather than strong and that there are rises in particular trades and industries when labour has not been unionized.[27]

On the neo-liberal view the need is to break down the idea that real wages can be increased for the benefit of working people as a whole by unions operating a closed shop. This is what sustains the coercive power of unions. Once this illusion is pierced, then the case for closed-shop union collapses. Of course, there is no objection on the part of neo-liberals to non-compulsory unions. They can provide collective benefits and services to their members as only a kind of voluntary organization can, but the crucial difference is the role of coercion. Without that unions like other voluntary organizations may well play a significant role in a vibrant civil society.

All of these arguments about interest groups, unions, and the organization of economy have been brought together in a very neat set of propositions propounded by Mancur Olson in the book *The Rise and Decline of Nations: Economic Growth, Stagflation and Social Remedies*, although the detailed argument in favour of these propositions is set out more fully in *The Logic of Collective Action*. I shall conclude this chapter by setting out the most important of Olson's propositions. They are as follows:

1. There will be no countries that attain symmetrical organization of all groups with a common interest and thereby attain optimal outcomes through comprehensive bargaining.
2. On balance, special interest organizations and coalitions reduce efficiency and aggregate income in the societies in which they operate and make political life more divisive.

3. Distributional coalitions make decisions more slowly than the individuals and firms of which they are comprised and tend to have crowded agendas and bargaining tables, and more often fix prices than quantities.
4. Distributional coalitions slow down a society's capacity to adopt new technologies and reallocate resources in response to changing conditions, and thereby reduce the rate of economic growth.
5. Distributional coalitions, once big enough to succeed, are exclusive and seek to limit the diversity of incomes and values of their membership.
6. The accumulation of distributional coalitions increases the complexity of regulation, the role of government, and the complexity of understandings and changes in the direction of social evolution.

The argument, as assimilated by the neo-liberal, is that the social democratic state logically encourages the formation of such groups since it has a distributive agenda but without agreed distributive criteria. The neo-liberal state on the contrary without such a distributive agenda is committed to a more objective and drastically less expansive form of safety net welfare provision can escape from the baleful effects of distributional coalitions. The move to a neo-liberal state does, however, mean the necessity of law to remove legal immunities from trade unions in respect of the effects of their actions and legislation to reduce their coercive powers.

NOTES

1. Greenleaf, W. H. (1983). *The British Political Tradition, Vol. 1: The Rise of Collectivism.* London: Methuen, chapter 4.
2. Greenleaf, W. H. *The British Political Tradition, Vol. 1: The Rise of Collectivism,* chapter 4, p. 224.
3. Hegel, G. W. F. *The Philosophy of Right,* trans. T. M. Knox. Oxford: The Clarendon Press, paragraph 289ff.
4. Greenleaf, W. H. *The British Political Tradition, Vol. 1,* p. 242.
5. Puttnam, R. (2000). *Bowling Alone.* New York: Simon and Schuster.
6. See Buchanan, J. and Tullock, G. (1962). *The Calculus of Consent.* Ann Arbor, MI: University of Michigan; Niskanen, W. (1973). *Bureaucracy: Servant or Master?* London: Institute of Economic Affairs; Niskanen, W. (1971). *Bureaucracy and Representative Government.* Chicago, IL: Aldine-Atherton.
7. Hume, D. (1875). 'On the Independency of Parliament' in *Essays, Moral, Political and Literary,* Vol. 1, ed. T. H. Green and T. H. Gross. London: Longmans, pp. 117–18. For a modern take on this theme, see Le Grand, J. (2003). *Motivation, Agency and Public Policy: Of Knights and Knaves, Pawns and Queens.* Oxford: Oxford University Press.
8. Lawson, N. (2000). *The New Conservatism.* London: Centre for Policy Studies.
9. Ridley, N. in Niskanen, W., *Bureaucracy; Servant or Master.*
10. Hayek F. A. (1979). *Law, Legislation and Liberty, Vol. 3: The Political Order of a Free People.* London: Routledge and Kegan Paul, p. 43ff.

11. Smith, A. (1998). *An Inquiry into the Causes of the Wealth of Nations.* Indianapolis, IN: The Liberty Fund.
12. Mises, L. von (1990). *Epistemological Problems in Economics.* New York: Foundation for Economic Education, Indianapolis, IN: The Liberty Fund.
13. Mises, L. von (1996). *Human Action,* pp. 214–16.
14. Parry, G. B. (1969). *Political Elites.* London: Allen & Unwin, provides a good overview of the strengths and weaknesses of pluralism.
15. The *locus classicus* is Dahl, R. (1961). *Who Governs?* New Haven, CT: Yale University Press. For a strong restatement, see also Dahl, R. (1982). *Dilemmas of Pluralist Democracies.* New Haven, CT: Yale University Press.
16. See Kornhauser, W. (1959). *The Politics of Mass Society.* Glencoe, IL: The Free Press.
17. Brittan, S. (1977). *The Economic Consequences of Democracy.* London: Temple Smith, p. 76. See also Brittan, S. (1983). 'Hayek, Freedom and Interest Groups' in *The Role and Limits of Government.* London: Temple Smith, pp. 48–79.
18. Olson, M. (1982). *The Rise and Decline of Nations, Economic Growth, Stagflation and Social Rigidities.* New Haven, CT: Yale University Press.
19. Stockman, D. (1985). *The Triumph of Politics: The Crisis in American Government and How It Affects the World.* New York: Coronet.
20. Hayek, F. A. (1960). *The Constitution of Liberty.* London: Routledge and Kegan Paul, p. 267.
21. Olson, M. *The Rise and Decline of Nations,* chapters 2 and 3.
22. Olson, M. *The Rise and Decline of Nations,* chapters 2 and 3.
23. See Chapter 3 of this volume.
24. Hayek, F. A. *The Constitution of Liberty.*
25. Hayek, F. A. *The Constitution of Liberty,* p. 270.
26. Hayek, F. A. *The Constitution of Liberty,* p. 270.
27. Hayek, F. A. *The Constitution of Liberty,* p. 271.

8

Government and Markets

The aim of this chapter is to focus on the neo-liberal understanding of the nature of markets and their relationship to the role of government. This will clearly draw upon and presuppose many of the themes we have looked at so far – the nature of freedom and coercion, social justice, rights, group interests, etc. However, there are other issues which are equally important to the nature of markets from an economic liberal point of view, so, as well as drawing upon arguments already considered, we shall also break new ground in looking at the nature, scope, and legitimacy of markets as the neo-liberal sees them.

I want to begin this discussion by looking at economic planning since the issues at stake here not only draw upon what has gone before, but also raise new aspects of the neo-liberal outlook on a range of very important matters. Some of the most salient and enduring of neo-liberal writings have been focused on the question of economic planning – for example, Mises' volume on *Socialism*[1] and Hayek's historically significant *The Road to Serfdom*.[2] Hence, understanding the arguments against economic planning will in fact reveal a very great deal about some central tenets of neo-liberal economic thought.

Centralized economic planning has often been thought to be basic to the socialist project of securing a socially just society. After all, a free market left to itself cannot be guaranteed to secure a just distribution of resources to meet the needs of all, to provide for the realization of rights, and to ensure that individual's capacities are developed. On the socialist view these ends can be achieved only by planning the economy both in terms of production – to make sure that the 'right' goods are produced to meet human needs; and in terms of distribution – so that the outcomes of markets embody some patterned principle of social justice such as Marx's distribution 'from each according to his ability to each according to his needs' as set out in the *Critique of the Gotha Program* or just to achieve greater social and economic equality without having a commitment to a principle as definite as Marx's. Planning, to secure the aim of a patterned or end state principle of distributive justice, embodies all sorts of requirements and assumptions. It assumes first of all, of course, that such an end state is desirable and achievable and, as we have seen in detail in earlier chapters, for the neo-liberal this is not the case – at least its desirability is not. I want, however, to concentrate on the question of *achievability* because the neo-liberal critique of the practicability of socialist planning is very important. Some of these arguments are empirical, some are more a matter of logic and the theory of knowledge, and also some are more or less to do with morality.

Let us take the moral argument first since it is prefigured in what has gone before. Mises argues that the socialist planner has to be able to answer the question: What should be produced in the economy? This in turn depends upon what the aims of socialism are and these will depend upon an end state or patterned principle of justice – let us say distribution according to need. However, if such a goal is to guide the planning process, it will have to become rich, thick, and detailed. Now, as we have seen, it is part of the neo-liberal critique of social justice that it can embody none of these features which are essential factors if planning is to work. The ideas of social justice are contestable and vague. It might, of course, be argued that this is not true about basic human needs. There is a degree of objectivity about them; they can be fixed by some psychological or biological account of human nature which can establish that they are independent of subjective preferences. Therefore, in spite of whatever else is wrong with ideas of social justice, we could plan to meet human needs so objectively defined. An account of objective needs will provide the planner with a prospectus of what has to be produced by the economy to meet such needs and this approach will not be contaminated by the subjectivity which is so central, on the economic liberal view, to the defects of social justice more broadly.

In the neo-liberal view, the objectivity of basic needs is delusive. It is as delusive as claims about the objectivity of merit or desert. There are several reasons for this. First, even if it was possible (as Menger clearly thought it was) to establish a schedule of basic needs, there would be problems of priority amongst them – what priority should health needs have, for example, over education and security? This problem of prioritizing needs cannot be solved by scrutinizing further the nature of the need. It is rather a moral question to which there is more than one answer and these answers are formulated from a wholly subjective perspective.

The second problem is that such needs are open-ended in that the need for health, education, and welfare have no *natural* stopping point and the decision as to where in fact to stop is a subjective one and so again a plan to mobilize the economy to meet objective needs meets this subjectivist argument deployed by the neo-liberal.

There is also the argument that needs do not exhaust the range of human striving – there are wants, preferences, and desires too – desires for goods which do not just meet basic needs. So any economic plan in a developed economy will have to find a place for the production of consumer goods. But what is the relationship between the imperative to meet needs and the imperative to allow preferences to be satisfied? When do we stop meeting needs and move to production to meet consumer preferences? Given the open-endedness of needs, there is no answer to this question. In the market individuals can decide these questions for themselves, but in a planned economy they are decided by bureaucrats. This, however, is as much a subjective judgement as the personal one by an individual in the market, but there is a very big difference in that the bureaucrat is empowered to make this subjective decision on behalf of all citizens. There is no objective answer to the question, so it has to be done by bureaucratic *fiat*.

It might, of course, be objected at this point that the picture being painted neglects the possible role of democracy in the formulation of the plan. On this view, all the questions about the lack of objectivity and the role of subjective judgement can in fact be dealt with by democratic deliberation and majority voting. So the balance, for example, between meeting needs and producing consumer goods certainly would not be settled by some set of rational or objective criteria but that does not mean that the answer has to be privately subjective as a consumer in a market, it can rather be settled by democratic agreement. We shall delay examining this argument further until later in the book but the idea of a democratic input into planning has to be kept on the agenda at this stage of the argument as a possible answer to the critique of a needs-based view of planning.

The second element of what can be seen as the broad moral case against planning is that it is inconsistent with neo-liberal ideas about the rule of law. As we have seen, for the neo-liberal, the rule of law cannot be reconciled with the idea of using the law to produce particular outcomes or to facilitate particular goods and goals such as need satisfaction. Law cannot be used to allocate specific resources to particular individuals which would have to happen in relation to the highly individualized nature of needs. While A and B may have a need for health and education, their situations may be sufficiently different that the same bundle of goods for each would not meet their respective needs on an equal basis. Yet in a planned economy and society the whole of law and public administration under the law would be suffused by the telocratic or goal-directed considerations and as such is incompatible with what the liberal regards as a compelling view of the nature of the rule of law. A further point not unconnected with this is that the whole of the neo-liberal critique of bureaucracy would also kick in at this point. We have already looked at this critique so I shall not repeat it. It is, however, important at this juncture in the argument because on the neo-liberal view the subjectivity of judgements about needs which we have reviewed would very considerably empower the bureaucracy in a planned economy and of necessity entrench discretion at the very heart of that power precisely because rules of law cannot be written to control and guide bureaucrats in the making of inherently subjective decisions. This is not malfeasance on the part of the bureaucrats; it is rather endemic in the position of the bureaucrat in a planned economy.

Two final aspects of the moral critique of planning are worth elucidating. The first is that a planned economy both is and has to be indifferent to the differences between persons. Take the case of needs to illustrate this. If there can be a list of objective needs for human beings, they are going to be highly generic and abstract in the view of the neo-liberal critic – like a need for health or a need for education. The fact remains, however, that we are individuals and our circumstances differ. So, even our basic needs have a personal or individual dimension to them. This becomes even more the case when questions about the balance or the trade-off between needs and preferences become important. Nozick puts this point well in *Anarchy, State and Utopia.* Among other things Nozick believes that people in their diversity would disagree about is whether the society in which they live would be one of 'greater material luxury or austerity with basic needs satisfied'. There is not sufficient commonality of purpose and value across the lives of diverse individuals on which to base a planned economy in pursuit of a patterned or end state set of distributive principles.

Whatever else may turn out to be important about this response, it does not, of itself, deal with the final element of the moral critique that I want to mention, namely individual liberty in a planned society or economy. We have already looked at this, but it is nevertheless important briefly to restate the argument in the different context. A planned society means the imposition of a particular plan in the service of certain values on society and this has severe implications for personal liberty even if those values and the plan supporting them were secured by majority vote. I may disagree with the values and with the plan – but would its imposition on me be coercive and a restriction of liberty? It is very clear from a neo-liberal view of both freedom and coercion that it would be. On the strict view of coercion as distinguished and discussed earlier in the book where A requires B not to do *X* which he would otherwise do; or where A prevents B from doing *Y* which he would otherwise do, then a planned economy would be coercive since, in order to preserve the plan and protect the patterned values that the plan facilitates, all sorts of economic activities which A might want to do (like leave his goods to his children) may be banned and all sorts of things he would otherwise not do – such as working in a particular way to satisfy the needs of the others, may well be required. On the more complex view of coercion favoured by Hayek, for example, a planned economy would also be coercive. Recall that his view of coercion involves coercion occurring when the 'data' or components of one's actions are determined by another. In a planned society the authorities would typically own and allocate resources and this would fall within Hayek's account of coercion. Secondly, coercion occurs when I have to follow the ends of others and not my own. In the situation that I am describing this would occur. In none of these cases of coercion would the fact that the values and the plan had been subject to democratic endorsement make any difference to the fact of coercion. Therefore this concludes the moral case against the planned economy. It draws upon and applies to rather particular circumstances, including earlier arguments about the nature of freedom, coercion, and social justice.

The aforementioned argument applies to the potential for the coercion of individuals in a planned economy; there is, however, also a serious risk of coercion of groups and thereby the incompatibility of a planned economy with political pluralism under which groups of people – most obviously unions – seek to advance their interests through political and economic means. As we have seen in the earlier discussion of the role of interest groups, the neo-liberals have a rather negative attitude towards the role of interest groups and unions in economic affairs, but nevertheless it remains true to say that a planned economy appears to be incompatible with political pluralism and unions because the aims of a union are to improve the terms, conditions, and wages of *its* members and in doing so would, if successful, disrupt the allegedly rational economic plan that the government was seeking to implement in pursuit of some patterned or end state principle of economic justice and distribution. For the economic liberal there is a harsh paradox at the heart of the planned economy. On the one hand, for the neo-liberal, it is the distributive state *par excellence* and, as such, as we have seen, is likely to bring into existence interest groups and unions to claim from such a distributive state what, from their point of view, they regard as their just deserts while at the same time the planning system necessary to maintain the patterned principle of justice, whatever it is, will in fact run counter to the legitimacy of such groups organizing their interests. Again, for the neo-liberal, the answer is for the state to disavow a concern with distributive justice altogether, then there will be no need for planning and no need to be hostile to political pluralism while at the same time removing the legal protections for what neo-liberals see as coercive forms of union organizations.

So, we have looked at the moral case against planning which is also by implication an argument in favour of free markets. At the same time, however, it has been a central tenet of neo-liberalism that socialist planning is, in any case, impossible whatever its moral defects. These arguments which have been central to thinkers such as Hayek and Mises are actually very profound and not only apply against socialist planning but also take us deep into some of the most fundamental arguments for the market economy. The first set of arguments is actually about the nature of knowledge and what would have to be the case about knowledge for socialist planning to work. The planning would have to be about consumption and production: consumption to meet the needs identified in the plan or to meet the balance between goods to satisfy need and goods to satisfy wants or preferences; and production in terms of the processes needed to produce these types of goods along with the recognition that there may be many alternative ways of producing a given set of goods, and presumably the planned way will be to produce such goods in the most effective way possible. Hence, the knowledge requirements of the plan would be very substantial to do with ends (consumption, needs, or preferences) and means (production and efficiency) – all of this to be carried out in the absence of market prices. In the view of the neo-liberal these demands on the nature of knowledge are completely unsustainable. There are several interconnected reasons for this.

The first is that knowledge is fragmented and dispersed between people. This is an argument ultimately derived from Burke's *Reflections on the Revolution in France* – that it is not possible to have some kind of single, synoptic, and comprehensive understanding of society just because of the dispersal of human knowledge. Practical knowledge which is, after all, what we are talking about in planning and economics is highly particularized. In a market the mechanism is attuned to this fact – indeed it would be truer to say that it embodies it. In a market, as opposed to a planned order, Hayek says:

> Into the determination of the prices and wages there will enter the effects of particular information processed by every one of the participants in the market process – a sum of facts which in their totality cannot be known to the scientific observer, or to any single brain. It is indeed the source of the superiority of the

> market order, and the reason why, when it is not suppressed by the powers of government, it regularly displaces other types of order, that in the resulting allocation of resources none of the knowledge of particular facts will be utilised which exists only dispersed among uncounted persons, that any one person can possess.[3]

This is, as he recognizes in the same passage, a central part of the case against planning as well as a positive case for markets. A planned society would make demands on social science and economics which are impossible to meet because of this dispersed and individualized nature of knowledge with the effect as he says: '[W]e, the observing scientists, can thus never know all the determinants of such an order, and in consequence also cannot know at which particular structure of prices and wages demand would everywhere equal supply.'[4] Knowing this is central to the coherence of the argument for planning, but in point of fact, it cannot be known.

The problem, however, goes deeper than this because not only is the knowledge at stake widely dispersed, it is also in many respects not propositional or in a straightforward way 'factual' at all. If, as Hayek himself says, in the passage quoted earlier we are talking about information and facts – albeit dispersed information and facts – the advocate of planning might well argue that the problem about the central coordination of information from dispersed sources is only a practical difficulty and not a fatal difficulty of principle. The defender of planning might argue that while, following Hayek, he or she is prepared to acknowledge the complexities posed by the dispersal of knowledge, nevertheless they may well be capable of being overcome by the use of computers. After all if people are able, online, to communicate the relevant facts about their needs and preferences, then these could be collated by a central computer and a rational plan constructed on the basis of material so collected. It is, however, central to the neo-liberal argument against planning and in favour of markets that this cannot in fact be done because of a further argument about the nature of knowledge.

The neo-liberals argue that the nature of the knowledge utilized by individuals in making the economic choices that they do is often a matter of habit and practical experience – of 'knowing *how* rather than knowing *that*' in Gilbert Ryle's felicitous terminology.[5] It is practical knowledge not propositional knowledge. It is rooted in the experience of everyday life, not in the understanding of a set of propositions and, indeed, cannot be represented in a series of propositions. When I go to the supermarket I shop efficiently, but in shopping, I rely on experience and habit – upon a range of tacit knowledge, to use Polanyi's phrase. I do not contemplate sets of facts and propositions before making purchases. Rather, I rely on my previous experience. When I drive a car I equally rely on habit and tacit knowledge to drive efficiently and effectively. I do not 'drive by the book'. On the assumption that this is true (and there is more to the argument that we have yet to uncover) it follows that the planner's answer to the dispersed nature of knowledge will not work because knowledge is not just dispersed and fragmented, it is also practical, tacit, and habitual. Put differently, it is not propositional and factual. Computers only deal in propositional knowledge, so it might be argued and, if they do, then in fact it would still not be possible to process the material for a rational plan by computer since the knowledge is tacit rather than propositional. It is, however, precisely the sort of knowledge that can be utilized in markets as my example of supermarket shopping shows. I draw upon my experience, my tacit knowledge, or I act according to habit and disposition in placing value on A rather than B amongst the goods and ranking C higher than D.

Now, it might be possible for the defender of planning to come back on this and make the following argument: I can accept that knowledge is dispersed and individualized, I can accept that it is also tacit and habitual rather than propositional. Nevertheless, it might well be possible to abstract from habitual behaviour a pattern or a set of rules which are embodied in that behaviour and which an expert system might well be able to mimic, copy, and utilize and this could still allow a computer-based form of planning to take place. What is necessary is to make the rules governing the utilization of tacit or habitual knowledge *explicit*. If this can be done, then the argument about planning becomes a practical one about what computers and expert systems can do, rather than an argument against planning on grounds of epistemological principles.

This response, however, takes us deeper into the neo-liberal approach to knowledge, habits, and rules. If all knowledge is at its basis practical, tacit, or implicit, a matter of habit rather than ratiocination, of skills and not the contemplation of truth, then it is not basically propositional in form. However, habits as such will create regularities in behaviour which eventually will or at least may assume the status of rules. If there is technology that could mimic rule following behaviour, then it is at least theoretically possible that planning might work and its impossibility is not shown by this epistemological argument. It is vital to remember when looking at this complex argument that at least part of what is at stake here is whether the price mechanism of the market can in fact be replaced by a planned system of prices and wages to meet demand and stimulate supply.

In fact, Hayek argues that it is not possible to articulate and make explicit many of the rules by which we proceed in thought and action. This is the central theme of his book *The Sensory Order*[6] and he clearly sees his argument in that book as having major negative implications for any theory of economic planning although it is a book that was published well before the advent of computers. Nevertheless, its argument is highly relevant to the case that if some modern computing packages are able to mimic rules of thought and action it will still be possible to rescue the case for central planning. In Hayek's view it is impossible to extrapolate the rules that could conceivably make it possible. A central version of this argument is as follows:

> So far our argument has rested solely on the incontestable assumption that we are not in fact able to specify all the rules that govern our perceptions and actions. We still have to consider the question of whether we should ever be in a position discursively to describe all (or at least any one we like) of the rules or whether mental activity must always be specified by some rules which we are in principle not able to specify. If it should turn out that it is basically impossible to state or communicate all the rules which govern our actions including our communications and explicit statements this would imply an inherent

> limitation of our possible explicit knowledge and, in particular the possibility of ever fully explaining a mind of the complexity of our own.[7]

It is important to recognize that for Hayek this is not just an empirical claim about the nature of knowledge, but a philosophical or metaphysical one which in the same book he relates to the highly significant work of Cantor on set theory in mathematics and to Gödel's theorem about incompleteness in proof. He says on these points that our inability fully to articulate the rules by which we act

> would follow from what I understand to be Georg Cantor's theorem in the theory of sets according to which in any system of classification there are always more classes than things classified which presumably implies that no system of classes can contain itself.[8]

In the case of Gödel he argues that

> it would thus appear that Gödel's theorem is but a special case of a more general principle applying to all conscious and particularly all rational processes, namely the principle that among their determinants there must always be some rules which cannot be stated or even be conscious.[9]

Much the same points were also made by Michael Polanyi in his book *Personal Knowledge*[10] in which he talks not only about tacit knowledge but also about ineffable knowledge and the inexplicability of knowledge, and he on this point also refers to Gödel and to the work of the mathematician and philosopher A. N. Whitehead. The work of Gödel is particularly important in this context because there is today very considerable interest in his thought in relation to the nature of human consciousness and also on the limitations of computers in replicating the workings of such consciousness.[11] If not all the rules governing rational processes can be fully specified, then given a computer has to work on transparent data there has to be a question of whether a computer can in fact replicate consciousness and if that is so, this is a further reason for thinking that it would not be possible to plan an economy by means of a computer because of the centrality of tacit or unspecified knowledge to the nature of consciousness and rational action which in turn is central to economic efficiency in everyday life.

These are some very big issues. For the moment; however, I want to stay focused on the critique of economic planning which is part and parcel of the arguments in favour of a free society and the market economy. We shall leave rules and tacit knowledge at this stage and move on to the claimed impossibility of economic calculations in a planned economy where the central arguments are set out by Mises rather than Hayek. Two things are essential for the proper understanding of this debate. The first is to understand why prices are absolutely essential to any efficient economic system. The second is to understand how defenders of the planned economy have both recognized the need for prices or a functional substitute for them and their failure to produce an explanation as to how calculation would work in a planned economy. Therefore, the first question is: Why is pricing essential? If the aim of a planned economy is to produce goods to meet the patterned principles of justice – say distribution according to need, then there will, of necessity, have to be a way of remodelling productive resources to produce such consumption goods. It is, however, a fact that complex and productive economies – and after all, socialism in the twentieth century has been proposed as the appropriate form of organization for such an economy – that consumption of goods, even those directed to meeting needs, can in fact be produced in a variety of ways, using a variety of raw materials. This is to be done efficiently even with a single good like building a house (Mises' own example). This particular concern with efficient production of this one good will in Mises' view requires some consideration of at least the following:

1. The plan of the architect which will involve the use of a large number of different commodities which will enable an estimation of the physical and chemical properties of such products.
2. The physical productivity of machines, tools procedures, labour, etc.
3. He will have to determine how, when, where, and at what level of consumption mechanical power should be used on all the raw materials and the commodities concerned.
4. The location of these components has to be taken into account along with transport, etc.[12]

All of this seems to be uncontroversially true about the alternative choices available in the process of production to build a single house to meet a single human need for shelter. So, how do we make rational choices between the utilization of different resources to secure the common end of building a house and how much more can this be with a heterogeneous set of ends: houses versus hospitals or roads versus schools, etc.? The only way of arriving at a rational procedure for settling this type of issue is by economic calculation – by arriving at some schedule of prices and costs so that the values involved in these diverse and seemingly incommensurable materials can be put in a clear relationship with one another. In a free market prices are arrived at as the result of the value that individuals, each from his or her own subjective point of view, place upon goods, services, machinery, labour, etc. This process is itself complex and we shall return to it later. However, the challenge laid down by Mises for the socialist who believes in planning is how is it possible to carry out economic calculation in the absence of market prices in a planned economy?

In Mises' view there are six possible answers to this question to be gleaned from the writings of defenders of the planned economy. They are as follows:

1. Calculation by barter;
2. Developing the Marxian labour theory of value into a method of calculation;
3. A utilitarian approach where what is calculated is utility rather than price;
4. Calculation by the use of *quasi* markets;
5. Calculation by means of complex differential equations; and
6. 'Calculation' by, or more precisely a substitution of, trial and error for calculation.

The first of these alternatives called 'calculation in kind' (*Naturalrechnung*) was developed by Otto von Neurath in his book *Durch die Kriegswirtschaft zur Naturalwirtschaft*. This book was based on Neurath's experiences as head of the socialization bureau of the Munich Socialist Republic which emerged for a very short period in the chaos surrounding the end of the First World War. Neurath's views attracted the interest and severe criticism of Max Weber in *Wirtschaft und Gesellschaft*. In a judgement endorsed by Mises, Weber argues that *Naturalrechnung*, central to barter, was impossible and there was no way at all of avoiding money and money accounting.[13] Therefore, although Neurath believed that the administrative economy, a fully planned economy, would inevitably be a barter system that could establish non-monetary equivalences between bartered products, no one actually followed Neurath's line after Weber's thorough critique.

The second alternative is to seek to build upon the labour theory of value and in order to make this argument Mises cites Engels in *Anti-Dühring*, where he says the following:

> As soon as society has taken possession of the means of production and applies them to direct social production, the labour of welfare, however different its specific use may be, will immediately become direct social labour. The amount of social labour inherent in any product does not require to be ascertained in any roundabout way: everyday experience will show how much of it on the average is necessary. Society can easily reckon how many hours of labour inhere in a steam engine, in a hecto litre of wheat of the last harvest, in a hundred square metres of cloth of a certain quality. Of course society will have to find out how much work is required for the manufacture of every article of consumption. It will have to base its plans on a consideration of the means of production at its disposal – and of course, the labour force falls into this category. The utility of the different objects of consumption weighed against one another and against the labour necessary for their production will finally determine the plan. The people will decide everything quite easily without the intervention of the much vaunted value.[14]

This is the *locus classicus* of the claim that the labour theory of value can provide the basis for economic calculation in a planned economy. Mises argues against this, but his argument is not in this context directed against the labour theory of value as such but rather against the thesis that it can form the basis of economic calculation. This does not mean that Mises thought the labour theory of value is correct, but rather that even if true it cannot provide a basis for economic calculation. So, what are Mises' reasons for this? There are two broad reasons why the labour theory of value must fail the calculation test.

The first has to do with what Marx understood by socially necessary labour time. It clearly involves the natural conditions of production as well as the human element of labour and, indeed, would be very implausible if it did not. So, for example, if the demand for a commodity increases and less favourable natural conditions have to be exploited to produce the commodity, then the average socially necessary labour time will increase. Conversely, if favourable natural conditions of production can be found, then the necessary social labour time will decrease. Marx sets out this case very clearly in Volume 1 of *Das Kapital.* However, Mises argues that this is not enough for economic calculation because the computation of changes in marginal labour costs, as set out earlier, takes account of natural conditions in so far as labour costs are concerned. Most importantly in Mises' view, it leaves the 'consumption of material factors of production entirely out of account'. He then gives the following example of the intractable problem that arises from that:

> Suppose the socially necessary labour time for producing two commodities P and Q is ten hours, and that a production of a unit of both P and Q requires materials A, one unit of which is produced by one hour of socially necessary labour, and that the production of P involves 2 units of A and eight hours of labour and of Q one unit of A and nine hours of labour. In a calculation based on labour time both P and Q are equivalent, but in a calculation based on value P must be worth more than Q.[15]

Therefore 'value' as opposed to labour time does return and cannot be eliminated by the computation of labour time. The underlying reason for what has gone wrong here is that 'the surplus by which the value of *P* exceeds that of *Q*, this material substratum, is furnished by nature without the help of man'. Mises regards this as being the central fault in Marx's argument in *Das Kapital* on this point.

The second argument is based upon the homogeneous view of the nature of labour that the labour theory of value is reputed to take. Mises argues that for Marx all labour is after all nothing more than the 'productive expenditure of human brain, muscles, nerves, hands' as Marx explains in Volume 1 of *Das Kapital.*

This approach has a rather dramatic effect in that Marx has to see skilled labour as only intensified or multiplied simple labour so that a small quantity of skilled labour equals a longer quantity of simple labour. Therefore Marx concludes by saying that 'a commodity may be the product of highly skilled labour, but its value equates it to the product of simple labour and represents only a certain quantity of simple labour'. The labour theory of value and, indeed, its possible role in economic calculation, requires this reductionist view of labour down to a set of sheer simple physical movements. Mises agrees with Böhm-Bawerk's judgement on this argument set out in his *Kapital und Kapitalzins*[16] namely that it is a 'masterpiece of outstanding naivety'. It is, however, a necessary form of naivety because the only possible way in which labour could be used in economic calculation is that labour should provide a common denominator of value in all different circumstances and in a way that excludes the ascription of value by a consumer. If it is to be a common denominator, then clearly labour in its various aspects cannot ever be heterogeneous never mind incommensurable in form. However, a common denominator view of labour belies experience in Mises' view because we are all aware that 'differences in capability and skill' result in different qualities of the goods and services provided, and then qualitative differences cannot be reduced to quantitative differences in labour.

It might, of course, be argued by the Marxist that this argument proceeds too quickly because in an exchange of relationship there can be substitute relationship between a commodity based on simple labour and one based on skilled labour which shows up in wage rates. On this approach, labour is still homogeneous and value is still independent of the consumer. However, as Mises argues, this is to put the cart before the horse in that this substituting relationship takes place *via* the market exchange. So Mises argues that

> Calculations based on labour cost rather than on monetary values would have to establish a purely arbitrary relation by which to resolve skilled into simple labour and this would make them useless as a instrument of the economic organisation of the resources.[17]

This then brings us to the third possibility. That economic calculation could be done on utilitarian grounds by taking utility as the common denominator rather than labour, and maximizing utility as the economic imperative. It has to be said that Mises does not devote much time to this approach and indeed does not fully develop the counter argument. It is, however, fairly easy to figure out what the counter argument would in fact be. First of all, the whole idea of seeking a common denominator of value, whether it is labour or utility, is in Mises' view fundamentally mistaken because the important fact about value is its diversity, its heterogeneity, and its subjectivity – being in the eye of the valuer, the consumer, not in some kind of essential inner quality of the commodity. 'Market prices are not expressive of an equivalence, but of a divergence in the valuation of the two exchanging parties.'[18] This indeed for Mises is the message of utilitarianism if it is properly understood. He makes this point clear in chapter 7 of *Human Action*. We do not, he argues, seek to measure utility as some quality inherent in an object or a good, nor is there just one scale for the ranking of utility. Rather the individual ranks things in terms of his own satisfaction. 'The satisfaction derived from food and that derived from a work of art are, in acting man's judgement, a more urgent or a less urgent need; valuation and action place them in one scale of what is more intensively desired and what is less.' For an 'acting man' (Mises' term) there exists primarily nothing but various degrees of relevance and urgency with regard to his own well-being. This means that, properly understood, utilitarianism is not some sort of objectivized alternative to subjective value but is rather a form of such value which is embodied is the price mechanism of a free market rather than a planned economy.

The next alternative considered by Mises is that the calculation problem could be resolved by the establishment of what he calls an 'artificial' or *quasi* market. The idea here is that it is possible to have socialist institutions, the common ownership of the means of production, and the pursuit of an end-state principle of distributive justice while at the same time within such a society markets, prices, and competition. Mises quite reasonably spends some time in *Human Action* pointing out that if socialists feel themselves driven to accept markets, the price mechanism, competition, and consumer-ascribed value, then this does show the degree of retreat there has been from the idea of a planned economy without any of these things. So the issue for Mises is whether it is possible to understand how market mechanisms could in fact work within a socialist society – and his answer is a very clear 'no'!

The key to the argument, at least at Mises' time, is the role of management. In a capitalist society, particularly one in which there has been a growing separation of ownership and management, the role of the manager is to manage the business in the interest of shareholders. The manager does not manage on his own account or at his own risk. He is accountable to the shareholders whose assets he is charged with maximizing. Hence, in a capitalist society he will use the price system of both materials and wages to devise ways of producing whatever the product of the business is in as cheap and efficient way as possible to maximize shareholders' value. In a socialist society, it is argued, this can continue with society at large taking the place of the shareholder. The only difference will consist in the fact that the fruits of his endeavours will enrich the whole society and not just the shareholders.

There are many problems with this approach from Mises' point of view. First of all, the population at large to whom the manager would be accountable on this view does not have a single overriding interest in the way shareholders of a company do. There will be more divergent ends in society at large and therefore the drivers of managerial decision-making will be similarly diverse. Secondly, companies are dynamic entities: They expand, they contract, they take over other companies, they are taken over in turn, they innovate and discard existing products, and they buy and sell shares and bonds. This much wider range of company activity is just not recognized in the model that we are considering. In addition and fundamentally for Mises there is a fundamental difference between management and entrepreneurship. The latter is fundamental to innovation, to discovering new markets, creating new goods, and these are essential to the market. Yet, it is not at all clear whether there could be a role for the entrepreneur in the model that we are considering. In contrast to an entrepreneurial economy, a situation in which the fortunes of a company is in the hands of managers responsible to the people at large is very likely to mean that the manager will adopt risk-averse strategies and 'lowest common denominator' approaches to management. The fundamental flaw in managerial market socialism for Mises is that '[t]he capitalist system is not a managerial system; it is an entrepreneurial system'.

What Mises is arguing at this point though is that there cannot be a market without the capitalist system, including entrepreneurship, commodity trading, futures markets, speculators, and investors. On this view the market is a 'thick' institution. It is not some kind of neutral mechanism which can be made compatible with different sorts of social orders. It is sometimes said that the market and capitalism are separate things: the market an institution of exchange; capitalism a framework of ownership – with the implication that a market can exist without capitalism and capitalist forms of ownership. Mises denies this.

I now want to discuss a rather different issue but it is one that engages government and markets, which is the theme of this chapter. It is frequently argued that a nomocratic government providing the framework only for a market order within which rational economic persons will seek to maximize their utilities actually is missing an absolutely central point. It is argued that in a nomocratic market order we still have to have some kind of orientation towards a sense of the common good and common purpose and that this is completely indispensable. The common good in question is the set of conditions which provide the basis for the market order. These might be thought to include things like trust, promise-keeping, and being prepared to take a long-term view as a constraint on rational maximizing behaviour. Let me take two examples of what the critic has in mind here. Dahl, for example, postulates that while neo-liberals argue very strongly for the control and preferably the elimination of monopoly, they do not address the question as to why a rational utility-maximizing businessman should not seek monopoly for his firm if he has the chance.[19] After all it is in that individual's interest. The fact that monopoly is anti-competitive and against the basic principles of the market, including the crucial role of prices which emerge through acts of free exchange between competing individuals and firms, will not as such mean anything to the rational utility maximizer unless that person has in some sense internalized an idea of something in the market sphere which is comparable to the idea of civic virtue in the sphere of citizenship. I will seek monopoly unless I see my behaviour as being constrained by some sense of what is essential to the market order as such – not just my self-interest within it. Equally, if we look at the idea of a contract which is absolutely essential to the market order, it might be said that the same point holds true, if it is in my interest to evade, avoid, or renege on my contractual obligations when I think it will maximize my utility by doing so. Again I need to have internalized the moral and practical importance of contract in the economic order within which my utility maximization can occur. Equally as Durkheim famously said, 'not everything in the contract is contractual' meaning by that a contract draws upon the virtue of trust and promise-keeping. On this view it seems that it is centrally important to ensure the cultivation of a set of what might be called 'economic virtues': those that are essential for the economy to work properly. What is important from the critic's point of view is to challenge the neo-liberal to reconcile these virtues first of all with the power of the model of the economic agent as a rational utility maximizer and secondly with their own view that moral values are subjective. These are not, as it were, incidental aspects of the neo-liberal outlook but are central as, for example, their critique of social justice shows in the case of values or the centrality of rational utility maximization shows in relation to the critique of bureaucracy and the ethic of public service. If economic virtues are essential to our understanding of how economic life proceeds, then we have to be able to understand how these virtues can be rendered from the rational utility maximizing and morally subjectivist point of view. There is a further complication too in that critics will argue that what I have called the 'economic virtues' are in fact embedded in and underpinned by a traditional moral inheritance derived from the Judaeo-Christian tradition which the development of capitalism has in fact undermined consistently over the past few centuries displacing this tradition by individualism and subjectivism. This is a central theme in Karl Polanyi's *The Great Transformation*[20] and in more contemporary terms in Francis Fukuyama's *Trust: The Social Virtues and the Creation of Prosperity*.[21] In *The Communist Manifesto* Marx famously wrote that in capitalism 'all that is solid melts into air', the point in the present context is that in so far as it undermines and displaces traditional values and understandings then capitalism may well be undermining the moral order on which it itself depends and which it cannot replenish or recreate. This argument is sometimes put in terms of the idea of social capital.

The idea here is that for the economy to work properly we have to look far wider than the idea of individual utility maximization within a nomocratic state and consider the whole range of values that secure compliance with social norms which are indispensable for the operation of markets. It will not do, in the view of critics, for the neo-liberal to argue that in fact if these values are indispensable for market operations, then they can just be enforced by the laws of a nomocratic order. So, for example, there can be heavy penalties for non-compliance with contracts and there can be rigorous anti-monopoly legislation with equally vigorous enforcement of it. In the view of critics this response is not sufficient in two respects. The first is that legal regulation of what might otherwise be produced by a normative order constraining behaviour will in fact be much more costly than such normative constraints. This is, however, a rather contingent argument. The deeper point is that legal systems to have legitimacy must be based upon some degree of shared morality and moral conceptions. Legal systems and the markets which they regulate cannot exist in a moral vacuum but the legal framework of a nomocratic order has to reflect shared moral beliefs. On this view of the matter there can be no way in which the question of shared norms or social capital can be avoided and we are still left with the question of what the neo-liberal can make of these given their individualist and subjectivist assumptions. The central question is: If shared norms are necessary how do we arrive at collective or social norms from a wholly subjectivist point of view?

Before considering possible answers to that question, however, we need to look at neo-liberal responses which cast a great deal of doubt on two claims set out in the aforementioned critique. The first is a rejection of the claim that at least in some respects social capital is essential to markets; the second is the idea that markets can in fact create their own relevant forms of social capital. The first claim is to be found in *Rescuing Social Capital from Social Democracy* by John Meadowcroft and Mark Pennington.[22] They argue two important points. The first is that if we look at the ideal neo-liberal order, namely a free market and a nomocratic state, then in fact the amount of social capital needed is very different from what would be the case under a more extensive state with a much wider and deeper agenda. They point out that social capital can be of two rather different sorts. The first is *bonding* social capital that is to say a set of shared norms that define or constitute a particular social practice. Such practices may be of all sorts: voluntary organizations, churches, unions, interest groups, and so on. They are bound together by a shared ethos and by shared norms. This ethos and these norms bind the group together into a group with common values. Nevertheless, such groups may not in fact be compatible with one another and that will apply also to their values. Indeed, some of the values which bind some groups together may be anathema to other groups. Cultural and ethnically based values may well be significant forms of bonding social capital but these values may be rejected by other parts of society, and thus the pursuit of bonding or binding social capital may in fact be socially disruptive and at the least we need to have some sort of yardstick by which to judge bonding social capital and we cannot just assume that a set of collectively accepted norms is *ipso facto* a good thing. In any case, as we have seen neo-liberals have a very sceptical view of the role of bonding groups when they have economic interests at stake and the sort of social capital which binds them together may well be inimical to other normative aspects of the market order as we saw in the context of the critique of interest groups and unions. In the view of these thinkers what is necessary for the capitalist order to work is *bridging* social capital which will be thin compared with the thick bonding and potentially divisive social capital. This thin social capital will be that set of normative agreements that will support the nomocratic state and the market order. To that extent we are back where we started since the point that critics make is that neo-liberals cannot even explain this thin bridging capital on their own terms. One point made by Meadowcroft and Pennington is that if the critics' views were to be accepted, then in a sense they add up to a counsel of despair in that if social norms even of a bridging sort are in fact dependent on an inherited moral tradition which is becoming more and more diluted, then what could strengthen or replace this sort of outworn moral framework? It is easy here to appeal to ideas like moral authority (an appeal likely on the political Right) or community (an appeal more likely on the political Left) but the pathway from these to strengthening bridging social capital is shrouded in obscurity and in any case the communitarian response is most likely in fact, if it works at all, to strengthen bonding as opposed to bridging social capital or abstract normative structures. On the Meadowcroft/Pennington view the argument about social capital is conservative – attempting to preserve a moral order which is eroding and which may well in its turn not have strengthened the thin social capital which markets and nomocratic states need but may well have rather strengthened social divisions instead.

They argue that in any case it is false to think that markets cannot create social capital through normal market activity and in this context they point to things like creating brand loyalty, the ways in which brands can create a kind a standard for a product, the way that this can be extended over a broader area by franchising and similar sorts of things, the use of guarantees for products, and so forth. In these contexts we do not need to appeal to some kind of antecedent moral order. Rather, relevant levels of social capital can be provided by the market itself. We should not bother too much about grand theories of social capital but concentrate on how market mechanisms can themselves generate loyalty and trust. This in turn could have an effect outside that particular product or area of the market. We could take the example of how a neo-liberal government might fund a basic form of welfare provision which could then be provided by private companies or voluntary organizations competing in a market for government contracts. They would have every incentive to develop standards of trustworthiness and compliance with contracts in order to continue in business. Therefore, from this point of view once we concentrate on the thin social capital required by a neo-liberal order we can see that it can in fact be supplied by the market.

Even if the neo-liberal believed that the larger issue raised, for example, by Dahl and Polanyi was worth considering, then at least some of them would have what they would see as answers to the question. Certainly, this would apply to Hayek and

Buchanan. In Hayek's view, while it is true that values are subjective, nevertheless they do emerge through a process of evolution and will persist in subsequent social contexts if they in fact perform a useful or indispensable function. These values cannot be given some kind of metaphysical justification, but even if they grew and developed in a particular context – for example the Judaeo-Christian tradition – if they have proved to be useful in social and economic evolution, then they will still have a kind of functional place even if they cannot be given a rational grounding and even if the moral tradition of which they were initially a part has become eroded. In this sense they are like some of the enduring principles of the common law. The social context in which a principle was initially enunciated may well have disappeared but the principle has remained because it has been found to be useful or indispensable in quite other contexts. As we saw in Chapter 2, Buchanan is very dismissive of Hayek's position on what might be called moral evolution. Nevertheless, he has what he would see as an answer to the critic through his principle of unanimity. For Buchanan, morality is wholly subjective and one cannot in the name of social capital or the shared norms required for market behaviour legitimately just seek to impose such norms. Either these norms have to be seen as agreed at the constitutional level of government and the rules in that context, as we saw, can only be agreed on a unanimous basis or they emerge via the productive part, that is to say post-constitutional part of the state. Agreements on specific things, if constitutionally sanctioned, can be concluded on a less than unanimous basis. The point, however, is that there is a mechanism here within a neo-liberal and wholly subjectivist standpoint for the agreement on such norms. Indeed, in many ways the arrival at such bridging norms supporting the nomocratic order is rather like the production of public goods. Public goods can be produced in the productive state by less than unanimous agreement if there is a constitutional agreement so to do; the same could happen with agreed social norms. It might be said by the critic that this just puts the problem of collective norms further down the track, but there is still the same question at the constitutional level. How from a subjectivist point of view do we in fact arrive at an agreement even with the principle of unanimity? Buchanan's answer to this question as we saw in Chapter 2 was with reference to the need to escape the defects of anarchy. These are the answers to the critic at the moment but I shall return to this issue in Part II of the book.

In Chapter 9, I shall now turn to a range of more detailed and in a sense more practical aspects of the role of the state in relation to the economy from the neo-liberal perspective.

NOTES

1. Mises, L. von. (1981). *Socialism.* Indianapolis, In: The Liberty Fund.
2. Hayek, F. A. (1944). *The Road to Serfdom.* London: Routledge and Kegan Paul.
3. Hayek, F. A. (1978). *New Studies in Philosophy, Politics, Economics and the History of Ideas.* London: Routledge and Kegan Paul, p. 27.

4. Hayek, F. A. (1978). *New Studies in Philosophy*, p. 27.
5. Ryle, G. (1949). *The Concept of Mind*. London: Hutchinson, chapter 2.
6. Hayek, F. A. (1952). *The Sensory Order, An Enquiry into the Foundations of Theoretical Psychology*. London: Routledge and Kegan Paul.
7. Hayek, F. A. (1967). *Studies in Philosophy, Politics and Economics*. London: Routledge and Kegan Paul, p. 60.
8. Hayek, F. A. (1967). *Studies in Philosophy, Politics and Economics*, p. 61.
9. Hayek, F. A. (1967). *Studies in Philosophy*, p. 62.
10. Polanyi, M. (1958). *Personal Knowledge*. London: Routledge and Kegan Paul, chapter 5.
11. Hofstadter, D. R. (1980). *Gödel, Escher, Bach: An Eternal Golden Braid*. London: Penguin. For a brilliant feat of explication, see Findlay, J. N. (1962). 'Goedelian Sentences, A Non Numerical Approach', in his *Language, Mind and Value*. London: Allen & Unwin, chapter 3.
12. Mises, L. von (1996). *Human Action*. New York: Foundation for Economic Education. p. 698.
13. Weber, M. (1978). *Economy and Society*. Los Angeles, CA: University of California Press, p. 104.
14. Engels, F. (1962). *Anti-Dühring*. London: Lawrence & Wishart, p. 229ff.
15. Mises, L. von, *Socialism*, p. 115.
16. Böhm-Bawerk, E. (1914). *Kapital und Kapitalzins*, Vol. 1. Innsbruck, p. 531.
17. Mises, L. von, *Socialism*, p. 116.
18. Mises, L. von, *Human Action*, p. 703.
19. Dahl, R. (1982). *Dilemmas of Pluralist Democracies*. New Haven, CT: Yale University Press.
20. Polanyi, K. (1944). *The Great Transformation*. Boston, MA: Beacon Press.
21. Fukuyama, F. (1995). *Trust: The Social Virtues and the Creation of Prosperity*. New York: The Free Press.
22. Meadowcroft, J. and Pennington, M. (2007). *Rescuing Social Capital from Social Democracy*. London: Institute of Economic Affairs.

9

Government, Money, and Taxation

In this chapter we shall look more directly at the neo-liberal view of the role of government in relation to taxation and money. These issues too are, I shall argue, central to the neo-liberal ideal of the rule of law. It might be thought that these lie outside the rule of law – surely, it might be argued, monetary policy and tax policies are precisely *policies* and, as such, they should not be brought into the constitutional architecture of a liberal state. That should rest on basic rights and liberties, not on constitutionalizing monetary and tax policies. No doubt in the case of taxation, policies are embodied in laws and codes and many of these will embody the qualities of the rule of law: non-arbitrariness, public accessibility, non-contradictoriness, and non-discrimination. Indeed, in his writings on such themes James Buchanan, for example, has emphasized the ways in which tax laws do indeed embody such central principles of the rule of law. But, it might be argued, the rule of law should not impinge upon the setting of tax rates – that is a matter of policy. Many neo-liberals disagree with this. They believe that there should be constitutional rules and institutions which both constrain governments in the exercise of tax-raising powers and in terms of their role in determining the money supply. It is very important to see why these two aspects which are often thought of as essential to politics should be brought within the rule of law and indeed the constitutional structure in the view of many neo-liberals. On the face of it, there seem to be very strong arguments from a neo-liberal perspective for not doing any such thing. The questions of what the level of money circulating in the economy ought to be and how much tax ought to be taken out of the economy seem to be straightforwardly normative; that is to say questions of value. Yet, as we have seen, many neo-liberals regard values as inherently matters of subjective preference and judgement. Indeed, James Buchanan, a fervent defender of a monetary and fiscal constitution, also takes it as axiomatic that values are subjective. Given this view, should not the level of taxation and the rate of growth of the money supply be regarded as matters of subjective choice expressed through the ballot box or in some other way not elevated beyond choice into a basic constitutional rule? Indeed, in some respects, Hayek at one stage shared this view, at least as far as the money supply was concerned, because he argued that rather than subjecting the supply of money to a national constitutional rule, money should be denationalized – leaving it to the individual to decide in what currency debts would be paid and freeing banks and other financial institutions to create their own currencies. In this way, in his view and in a version of Gresham's law, good money would in fact drive out bad, and through choice and competition with value being located in individual preference for a currency, a virtuous level of money supply would be arrived at by a spontaneous process. The alternative, namely a constitutional rule, requires some kind of collective agreement in a situation of radical subjectivism. Therefore, what could be the basis of that judgement in relation to both the money supply and the tax system? One core claim is that neo-liberal doctrines about the tax system and the money supply are in some sense fundamental truths which should be recognized by constitutional rules and not be made subject to policy choices. So, for example, as we saw in Chapter 2, Mises sees his monetary theory as setting out a set of what can be seen as synthetic a priori truths, although he was not hung up on the precise epistemological terminology for what he was arguing. These truths are contained, as he sees it, in the concept of money and they cannot be challenged. If this is correct, then there might well be a case for saying that the quantity of money theory should be put into a constitution beyond the reach of political judgement and policy choice. If, however, it turned out to be the case that such an epistemological theory about the nature of money is not sustainable, then there is no case for constitutionalizing a contested conception of monetary theory. Before confronting this question directly, we need to understand something of the neo-liberal approach to monetary policy, supply-side economics, and the basis of taxation.

Crucial in this respect has been the critique of Keynes and Keynesianism. This critique is at the heart of Buchanan's defence of the fiscal-monetary constitution as it is also at the centre of Hayek's case for the denationalization of money. Both policies would have the effect of moving fiscal and monetary policy out of the hands of elected representatives and to see why they thought that this drastic approach was necessary we need to understand the critique of Keynes and the Keynesian social democratic state in relation to both money supply and taxation. This will be done in two parts. First of all, I shall outline the basis of economic doctrines characteristic of neo-liberalism particularly monetarism and supply-side theories, exploring the ways in which these differ from the interventionist Keynesian approach to the post-war world. Second, I shall look at the free-market critique of the role of government as it has grown up in relation to Keynesian economic doctrines and political practices. The aim is to produce a clear account of the economic basis of neo-liberalism. The analysis of neo-liberal economic doctrines requires a brief study of the essentials of three economic positions: monetarism, supply-side theories, and Keynesianism. The debates over these doctrines, carried out in the context of claims for the efficiency of the market as opposed to government as the allocator of values and resources, are at the heart of the revival of free-market, neo-liberal ideas.

I shall discuss monetarism first. Monetarist theories have to be considered in light of the prevailing Keynesian orthodoxy because it was Keynesianism in both academic and political terms which monetarist doctrines rejected.

After the experiences of the 1930s, when both Britain and the United States had endured a major recession and very high levels of unemployment, it was natural that governments should cast around for new mechanisms for securing full employment and a more predictable economic environment. The fate of the Conservative Party in losing the 1945 general election had convinced majority opinion on the Right that governments could no longer survive by a passive acceptance of the levels of employment thrown up by the free operation of the market. The legitimacy of government itself was at stake in relation to employment, and Keynesian theories provided a basis for arguing that government had definite positive responsibilities in this area and also that it had the competence to act in relation to the economy in light of these responsibilities, and the tools with which to intervene in a positive way in the economy. These assumptions produced a profound change in the conception of the role of government on the Right, a view which was already accepted by and congenial to those on the Left.

In his *General Theory of Employment, Interest and Money*, Keynes said: '[T]he ultimate object of our analysis is to discover what determines the volume of employment.'[1] Keynes rejected the view that full employment can be either maintained or restored after a slump by the market mechanism on its own. Levels of employment, at least in the short run, are determined by output. When output in a firm is running at a high level, then that firm will have an incentive to employ more workers. In its turn output is determined by effective demand, which is demand backed by money and resources. Effective demand has two features: individual consumption and investment by firms. In Keynes' view economic recession and consequent unemployment such as was experienced in the 1930s is the result of a deficiency in demand. Not enough goods are being bought and sold, and there is not sufficient investment. In its turn this is subject to a multiplier effect so that, for example, a lack of demand for heavy industrial goods will create a consequential decline in demand for other goods and services in the economy. In so far as the economy is left to its own devices, free of government intervention, this depression in demand will intensify in a downward spiral until such time as a demand for the goods which initiated the multiplier effect picks up. Keynes rejected this passive laissez-faire approach. Government, in his view, should seek to expand demand in both its consumption and investment aspects and stimulate it by a variety of means which are directly under the control of the central government. It could use its (that is to say, the taxpayers') resources to increase investment to break the downward spiral of demand, engage in programmes of public works, lower interest rates by the use of the central bank, lower taxes, give subsidies, and increase its own spending. It could, therefore, increase demand by pumping money into the economy and do this at least in the short term by running a budget deficit. Deficit financing was contrary to orthodoxy in both Britain and the United States at least until the period of the New Deal in the 1930s.

Government could also seek to redistribute income as a way of increasing demand, because money redistributed to the worst-off members of society would be likely to be spent rather than saved, and thus demand for goods and services would be increased.

Therefore, macroeconomic management was to become a central function of government. With this would come a change in the role and extent of government, but, perhaps more importantly, a change in public perceptions about what government could do, what it is capable of doing, and what its responsibilities are. Keynes was very clear about these when he wrote in the *General Theory*: '[T]he central controls necessary to secure full employment will . . . involve a large extension of the traditional functions of government.'[2] This change would extend the proper role of government far beyond what was seen in the classical liberal tradition are being its legitimate function. As we have seen the neo-liberal case is that the role of government should be restricted to external defence, the provision of a framework of law and order to prevent mutual coercion, and the provision of certain public goods which would not be supplied by the market. Keynes' economic theories are predicated on a rejection of the classical liberal view of the efficiency of markets, together with a very limited role for government. Keynes rejected this view and argued on the contrary for a role and a competence in central government which free market neo-liberals reject.

Keynes was not a believer in economic planning in the direct sense of government's having detailed policies about prices and wages and setting precise targets for industry to fulfil. Rather, he assumed that demand management and the fiscal and monetary policies outlined earlier would be sufficient. Nevertheless, a more direct approach to planning was a natural political consequence of Keynes' ideas and here it has seemed to many that the experience of war was crucial. From the wartime experience it did seem as though government was able to play an effective role in the more direct management of the economy in terms of prices and incomes, if not in the setting of targets for industrial performance. The experience of the New Deal in the United States, and even of Gosplan in the Soviet Union, led to a significant change in attitudes towards the role of government vis-à-vis the economy.[3] It seemed to many that there clearly were ways in which the experiences of the 1930s could be avoided in the post-war world. The intellectual power of Keynesian ideas and the experience of the war which seemed to confirm the competence of government were crucial in marginalizing the intellectual case for economic liberalism and laissez-faire, and the theory of limited government which went with these views.

The political impact of these ideas could be seen most clearly in the 1944 White Paper, *Full Employment in a Free Society*. This White Paper was the outcome of a very long period of gestation and discussion in which Keynesian ideas were very important, and James Meade, a subsequent Nobel Laureate in Economics, a follower of Keynes, and at the time a member of the War Cabinet's Economic Section, seems to have played a pivotal role. The main thrust of the argument can be seen in a paper considered by the Committee on Reconstruction which argued as follows:

> Government should not be negative or interfere unnecessarily with the growth of business organisation, or seek merely to get back to 19th century *laissez-faire*, but rather to promote, by positive action, an increasing volume of employment and consumption.

Unemployment was seen as the central issue after the experience of the inter-war years and the capacity to deal with it seemed to be central to the legitimacy of government. The wartime coalition of Conservative and Labour ministers accepted this assumption and with it embraced, at least, in part Keynesian techniques for dealing with it and the role of the state which these implied. The White Paper embodies this commitment in the following way:

> The government accept as one of their primary aims and responsibilities the maintenance of a high and stable level of employment after the war. Total expenditure on goods and services must be prevented from falling to a level where general unemployment appears.

The contrast with pre-war assumptions about the role, limits, responsibilities, and competence of government could hardly be greater. The rise of neo-liberalism in the past generation is a direct challenge to these post-war assumptions. As Keith Middlemas says in his magisterial book of this period, *Power, Competition and the State*: 'There is little here that was not still at issue, forty muddled years later.'[4]

By the 1970s it appeared the Keynesian policies had run into the sand. Particularly after the rises in the oil price in the early 1970s, Western economies were faced with stagnation which did not seem responsive to Keynesian remedies. In place of the demand-led view of the way out of unemployment both academic monetarists such as Milton Friedman and political monetarists in Britain such as Sir Keith Joseph, Mrs Thatcher, Sir Geoffrey Howe, Nigel Lawson, Leon Brittan, and Nicholas Ridley, argued that inflation, at least in the longer term, is the central cause of unemployment and that inflation is largely a monetary phenomenon, which is precisely the result of governments adopting Keynesian assumptions that it was possible for governments to spend their way out of recession. The very techniques whereby government sought to secure full employment were themselves inflationary. They might well bring respite in the short term, but they actually exacerbated the problem in the longer run. Each time demand is expanded by deficit financing, a greater stimulus is required to produce smaller and smaller improvements in the rate of unemployment. The monetarist view is that the techniques which government uses (demand management and deficit financing) are actually inflationary and that these inflationary pressures would destroy the very levels of employment which they were in fact designed to protect.

This analysis seemed to many to be borne out by the simple fact that by the mid-1970s inflation was running at 25 per cent per annum, and that unemployment was rising inexorably. In the view of monetarists the causes of unemployment are many and specific such as wage levels, productivity, immobility of labour, unwillingness to take the type of jobs going at realistic wages and the profitability of industry, and world trade. These are all crucial factors in the causation of unemployment. To seek to cure these with the general formula of expanding demand and deficit financing may work in the short term, but, precisely because of these specific blockages in the system, shortages will emerge in the market, prices of domestically produced goods will rise, as will the level of imports and very soon the 'stop' phase of the stop-go cycle will be reached. In this sense, state spending is the central cause of unemployment in that raising the level of aggregate demand requires the state to spend more.

Before moving on directly to the monetarist thesis we need to address one puzzle in the neo-liberal position. Given that on their view the control of inflation is the primary purpose of monetary policy and this is a central role for a neo-liberal state, does this not turn a neo-liberal state into a telocratic state? After all, it might be argued that the control of inflation might be thought to be a policy aim in the same way as, for example, the maximization of welfare might be thought to be a central policy goal for social democrats. Then why is the latter objectionably telocratic for the neo-liberal, while the former is not. The answer from the neo-liberal, whether plausible or not, is simple. The control of inflation is about the *framework* within which freedom is to be exercised. As we saw earlier freedom requires a predictable and secure framework of rules on which an individual can rely in making the choices that he or she makes. The securing of a stable currency is part of this framework in much the same way as a framework of law securing mutual non-coercion is. Given that there is in the view of at least a neo-liberal like Mises a non-contestable synthetic a priori set of truths underlying the mechanism for supporting a stable currency, then there is every reason for regarding the control of inflation as a central part of the nomocratic framework of a liberal society rather than one of a number of competing policy objectives of such a society.

So what in non-technical terms is the specifically *monetarist* element in the monetarist thesis?

This book is not the place for the explanation in detail of complex economic arguments that constitute a separate field of study. Nevertheless, it is very important to try to identify the 'core' features of monetarist doctrine because, as we shall see, monetarism *by itself* does not yield the full range of neo-liberal thinking on the social democratic welfare state with which this book has been concerned, and we have to look at other aspects of the financial and economic critique of a social democratic state as well as the narrow doctrine of the quantity theory of money. This is actually rather an important point because if monetarism does not take us all the way to a neo-liberal state, then what are the other elements that will and how far can they be claimed to be incontestable synthetic a priori truths about the fundamental basis of political and economic life, which in turn because of this status could be made part of a fiscal and monetary constitution?

The 'core' thesis of monetarism is based upon the quantity of money theory that, in the long run, the main determinant of monetary demand or the total level of spending, and thus the main influence upon the gross domestic product (GDP), is the quantity of money circulating in the economy. This can be expressed in the following equation:

$$MV=PQ$$

where, M is the quantity of money in the economy; V is the average velocity with which this money circulates; P is the price of this output; Q is the output produced by the economy.

This is the thesis of the quantity theory of money. PQ is the nominal domestic product measured in cash terms. This must equal the amount of money in the economy multiplied by the velocity of its circulation. Since velocity is assumed to be nearly constant, it follows that the quantity of money equals the GDP at current prices. Hence, changes in the money supply will change GDP (at current prices). It is also part of the monetarist thesis that there is a clear definition of money compared with other financial assets, and that this can be controlled by central banks and monetary authorities. Hence, the relationship between money supply and GDP can be made predictable and stable. For Mises, as I have already said, this is not a hypothesis which has to be subjected to a process of potential falsification, but is rather a necessary truth given the nature of money. It is this claim which can in principle sustain the idea of a monetary constitution, that is to say one which would embody a constitutional rule controlling the growth of the money supply and insulating it against political pressures and judgements.

Given the relationship between the quantity of money and GDP at current prices (*PQ*) in the equation, the crucial question then becomes whether an increase in the money supply causes a rise in the *P*(rice) or *Q*(uantity of goods) part of the equation. Will the real resources generated by the economy increase, or will there simply be a rise in the price level for these real resources? It is central to monetarism that an increase in the quantity of money causes a rise in prices rather than in real output. The monetarist view is that a market economy, free of government intervention, runs at the full utilization of resources and maximum output. It follows that any increase in the supply of money divorced from increases in real output will push up prices and hence be inflationary. Any regime which seeks to reduce or eliminate inflation will seek to expand the money supply *only* in line with increase in real output. Any increase over and above estimated real output will merely add to the *P* side of the equation and hence be inflationary. Clearly, monetarism puts a major obligation on government in relation to the *MV* part of the equation for, as Samuel Brittan says:

> The government and the central bank are all the time influencing total spending (MV). When they determine the size of public sector deficits and the way they are financed, when they act to influence interest rates or the ability of banks to lend, and sometimes too when they intervene in the foreign exchange market.[5]

Three immediate policy issues flow from this:

1. A government should seek a neutral supply of money based upon feasible assumptions about the real growth rate in the economy.
2. Inflation, which is regarded as the long-term cause of unemployment, should be the main target of general economic policy. Since inflation is caused by increasing the money supply, both the problem and its solution lie with government. However, this requires that the government should try to stick rigidly to its monetary targets and not be seduced into a general reflation of the economy by panic over what in its view should be short-term rises in unemployment and decline in output.
3. The government and monetary authorities have to have a measure of money which was both clearly definable and within the power of government to control. Broadly speaking, there are three possible definitions in the British

> context: (*a*) Sterling M1 which consists of notes and coin in public circulation plus sterling current accounts in the private sector of the UK economy; (*b*) Sterling M3 which consists of M1 plus UK residents' deposit accounts and saving accounts; and (*c*) Sterling M2 which is basically the same as M3, less bank deposits held for investment purposes. Sterling M3 was the chosen monetary indicator, although in 1980 there was a good deal of pressure to adapt the tighter definition embodied in M1.

In view of some commentators, such as Samuel Brittan, the indicator chosen was actually less important than the need to stick to it once it was chosen. The whole aim is to provide a binding and inescapable monetary discipline such as had been imposed by the Gold Standard or fixed exchange rates. These policy provisions provide the general basis for the monetarist element in neo-liberal theories and its counter-revolution to the Keynesian model of government-economy relations. It is clear, however, that monetarism can only be a necessary condition of the free-market neo-liberal policy, because it would still be possible to reduce government deficits and the public-sector borrowing requirements by raising taxes. To look at the other conditions which would make the whole package constitute a set of necessary and sufficient conditions for the free-market neo-liberal strategy, we must consider their supply-side proposals and, equally important, their critique of the institutional structures and expectations which the post-war Keynesian world has engendered.

As we have seen, monetarism as a technical doctrine, as opposed to its use in everyday political debate, has very little to say about the level of public spending in itself. It is more a theory about how it should be financed, together with a vigorous critique of the Keynesian view about its financing. The Keynesian view was that public spending has a function in increasing demand and expanding employment and that this could be achieved by deficit financing or by printing money, the latter being just another way of stating the former. The monetarist rejects this. Either the level of public spending has to be cut in order to reduce, or ideally eliminate, deficit financing, or taxation has to be raised in order to wholly finance the chosen level of public spending. Other arguments have to be deployed in order to show that the latter course will have bad consequences for the economy and that the preferred solution is to attack the level of public spending by reducing state spending as far as possible on public services or limiting it, so that as a result of economic growth public spending will decline as a percentage of GDP. Market-based neo-liberals have been in the forefront of this argument, both at the levels of theory and practice.

The argument has tended to fall into two parts. The distinction is somewhat artificial but does show something about the strategy of the neo-liberal counter-revolution. The first is a set of economic arguments to show the deleterious effect of public spending on the private market sector and the baleful consequences that would follow from trying to finance excessive public expenditure out of taxation. The second is more institutional than economic. Neo-liberals are concerned to attack some of the assumptions which lie behind ever-increasing public expenditure: that it is necessary to secure greater equality between citizens; to secure greater economic freedom for citizens to secure greater social justice; together with false assumptions about the capacity of government. Some of the negative consequences of high levels of public expenditure are social effects such as an increase in bureaucracy and discretionary power, and a destructive sort of interest-group competition in politics which has a deleterious effect upon the legitimacy of government.

The free-market neo-liberal emphasis is, in a sense, the counterpart in terms of a theory of institutions to monetarism as a more technical doctrine in economics. In this section, we shall explore the main features of this doctrine and consider the ways in which free-market ideas have been incorporated into a broader doctrine of conservative capitalism. Samuel Brittan is quite right when he argues that

> [b]ehind the smokescreen of the monetarist controversy, therefore lies a much more serious argument between rival views of human society . . . which was papered over by several decades of good fortune and money illusion.[6]

It is vital to bring together this institutional debate with the more technical economic debate. In Britain Sir Keith Joseph was quite right when he said in the title of his famous pamphlet that 'Monetarism Is Not Enough'. In this chapter therefore it is important to try to identify the exact nature of these additional economic arguments which, when combined with strict monetarism, would yield the economic side of the critique of state expenditure.

Broadly speaking, these arguments concern the role of taxation and the role of public expenditure coupled with supply-side suggestions about how to improve the labour market. These suggestions, when combined with strict control of the money supply, were to lead to a longer-term improvement in employment prospects than any degree of Keynesian demand management.

In Britain the response to the decline of Keynesianism was monetarism, whereas in the United States supply-side theories became intellectually dominant in the 1980s. Such theories were developed by Laffer and Wanniski and were taken up and made politically salient by David Stockman who became President Reagan's Budget Director, by Congressman Jack Kemp, and, of course, by President Reagan himself. As we shall see, supply-side theories in some respects complement monetarist assumptions about the nature of the capitalist economy and the nature of human motivation in the economic sphere. In the discussion of monetarism we quoted from Samuel Brittan's perceptive comment that behind the technical issues of monetarism lay a whole view about the nature of human society and its desirable form. The same is true of the supply-side theories, and David Stockman, in particular, waxes very eloquent on this point when he says in *The Triumph of Politics*:

> Its vision of the good society rested on the strength and productive potential of free men in free markets. It sought to encourage the unfettered production of capitalist wealth and the expansion of private welfare that automatically attends it.[7]

On this view, left to its own devices, free of government intervention and the pressure group politics, and pork-barrelling which necessarily accompany it, the free-market economy will produce more and more wealth and resources. The free market is a source of dynamism and innovation but it does depend upon individuals using their own skills and knowledge. If it can mobilize those skills, then the economy will be dynamic, and the supply of goods will increase, and there will be sustained economic growth which will benefit all sections of society including the worst off. Monetarists had been particularly concerned with the ways in which the inflationary consequences following from the adoption of Keynesian techniques actually damaged the economy and led to unemployment. Supply-siders, however, were more concerned with the effect of taxation on individual incentives and thus on economic performance, and this in turn meant that they had a direct concern with public expenditure by the central government.

It is central to the supply-side view that people work best when they have the economic incentive to do so, when they can keep more of what they earn. The poor will benefit more from a general increase in economic growth which would be the result of increasing incentives to individuals than they would under any other alternative which would seek to redistribute resources through state policy.

The solution to the problem of poverty lies in the trickle-down effect (about which more later) whereby the poor will benefit most by the increase in the supply of goods in the economy, which will trickle down to the poor eventually, rather than through a politically led redirection and redistribution of resources which will have negative incentive effects.

Clearly, this emphasis on the necessity for incentives immediately implies the supply-sider's concern with tax levels, and it is on this point that the academic arguments of Laffer and Wanniski come into play. Such views are cited by Buchanan in favour of a fiscal constitution.[8] In their view, cuts in taxes and tax rates will have a positive effect on work incentives and this will increase the supply of goods in the economy which will, on the argument adumbrated earlier, be to the benefit of the poor as much as the rich. In the view of supply-siders taxation may come to be at a level at which it is having a marked disincentive effect on the economy. People will work harder only if they are able to keep what they earn; otherwise they will find other things to do with their time. Only by releasing the inventive energies of individuals would wealth be created.

Laffer and Wanniski had argued that there is a clear link and subsequent trade-off between taxation and productivity and that the central problem in tax policy is to identify that level of taxation at which both productivity and tax revenue will be maximized. It is possible for government to set tax levels so high that revenues are actually less than they would be under a lower tax and more productive regime compared to a tax regime under which the same levels of revenue could be raised by a lower level of taxation on a more productive economy. This point is echoed by Buchanan.[9] It is important to note though that Buchanan is not arguing that taxes can be considered to be too high since that can only be judged against a subjective normative standard. What can be determined by the work of someone like Laffer is whether the tax system and its rates are optimal for the level of revenue required to meet whatever normative standard is in play. Obviously, the argument depends crucially upon how convincing the theory of motivation is behind the argument about the link between productivity and incentives. As it stands, supply-side theory does not of itself imply a need to cut public expenditure because the argument turns upon the idea that cutting taxes will so increase revenue from increased production that existing levels of public expenditure could be maintained. The supply-side view needs much more to turn it into a critique of public expenditure per se. It is only when it is combined with arguments about various baleful economic and political effects of high levels of public expenditure, and the corresponding growth in the role of the state, that it turns into an argument for limited government and reduced expenditure. It is the combination of the technical economic arguments, both from monetarism and supply-side theory, into a powerful practical doctrine in political economy.

Although tax levels were the central issue for supply-siders, there are other aspects of their arguments which are important for their view about how the supply side of the economy could be made to work better. These are particularly concerned with the regulation of the economy by government. Supply-siders argue that such regulation acts as a brake on economic performance and, in order to increase the supply of goods in the economy, should be rescinded. The argument is that instead of firms spending money in meeting these unproductive regulations, they would be able to invest in new products, new plants, and thereby increase economic growth and employment.

In addition, a central aspect of the critique of public expenditure has been the 'crowding-out thesis', namely that public expenditure, whether on welfare or state-owned industry, crowds out the private sector. This argument usually contains two strands: physical crowding out and financial crowding out. The physical crowding-out thesis is fairly straightforward, namely that the growth of the non-market sector of the economy produces a higher tax burden for the market sector; and, given supply-side assumptions, discussed earlier, about the impact of taxation on individual's incentives to productivity and firms' investment, this crowding out will lead to lower productivity and lower investment. Hence, it is imperative that public expenditure should be reduced in order to free resources for the private sector in the way of incentives to both productivity and investment. In its turn the reduction of public expenditure will depend upon reducing government-funded services in the field of welfare and, to be effective, this will require not just arbitrary cuts but a full-scale attack on the intellectual case for the welfare state. It will also depend crucially upon withdrawing from state ownership of industry in Britain; limiting and ideally abandoning the place of subsidy for industry in government policy; and limiting the regulatory role for government discussed earlier. This gave the role of the privatization programme in Britain one of its central justifications and with the redirection in public expenditure could go on reduced tax rate.

There is also financial crowding out which has been described by Sir Alan Walters in the following way:

> Financial crowding out occurs when the government issues a bond to finance expenditure and that gilt edged security is substituted for an industrial debenture in the portfolio of the private sector. Government borrows money hitherto borrowed by private industry (or persons) and the private sector will have that much less to spend.[10]

Given the finite amounts of money available in the market, the need to finance government expenditure and the nature of the security which it can offer will drive out investment in the private sector (i.e. the wealth-producing sector). The additional demand for credit by government will also drive up interest rates which will again have a deleterious effect on private-sector borrowing, given the rates of return which financial investors will demand.

This argument runs directly counter to many of the assumptions about public expenditure made during the period of Keynesian ascendancy, namely that appropriate expenditure could increase the supply of goods and services, increase economic growth, and act as a stimulus to the private sector. These assumptions still lie behind ideas on the Left for a public-sector-led reflation and expansion of economic activity. These arguments are rejected by the proponents of neo-liberalism because of the supply-side argument which we discussed earlier. In Walters' view:

> [S]uch public expenditures merely increase costs of either labour or capital, this being dissipated in inefficiency or increased rents to unionised labour or capital owners.[11]

The reasons for this lie deep in the capitalist critique of nationalized industry. Walters himself argues, drawing from empirical studies, that the efficiency of resource use is usually lower in those industries than in the private sector and indeed involves a negative rate of return in many cases. He takes the example of public and private provision of bus services in cities and nationalized versus private airlines to support his case and draws from his evidence the conclusion reached by David Friedman in *The Machinery of Freedom* that 'public provision doubles the cost'.[12] The Keynesian argument that public expenditure in industry can increase supply is, in his view, flawed because of the inefficiency of such industry, its low levels of productivity, and the rate of return. Hence, on this view of crowding out because of high levels of public expenditure there could be no prospect of public-sector-led growth.

From what has been outlined we can now see why the neo-liberal is tempted to the view that a fiscal and monetary constitution is necessary. Inflation and unemployment are great evils but in the neo-liberal view unemployment flows from inflation and can only be tackled by dealing with inflation which in turn requires a control of the money supply that is not dictated by short-term political interest and an interest rate policy which will ensure low inflation and appropriate responses to inflationary pressures. These appropriate responses may be deflected again by short-term political considerations. The public choice account of political behaviour – as fundamentally utility maximizing, the role of interest group politics, the entrenched interests of bureaucracies which inhibit change and adjustment, the role of distributive justice, and a redistributive agenda have all played a central role in creating a political context in which both monetary policy and fiscal policy are disastrously influenced by short-term political considerations or the achievement of false political goals such as the social democrats' goal of greater social justice. All of these require that political institutions should be constrained in the range of what they can do and that they should be bound in advance by constitutional rules that can protect them from coalitions of interest groups seeking to exert pressure in pursuit of rent-seeking objectives. This sort of case relies on the economic and political science evidence in respect of the relationship between inflation and unemployment in the one case and interest group and rent-seeking behaviour in the other. If the goal is the lowest achievable rate of unemployment, then this cannot be pursued as a direct aim of policy but rather will follow from appropriate anti-inflationary fiscal and monetary policies. It has to be said, given earlier neo-liberal views about the non-instrumental role of law, that this looks to be a pretty telological account of law – that is to say the rule of law as supporting the pursuit of certain sorts of goals and values. Even if the values such as a high level of employment are thought of as universal, the rules in question are still not purposeless.

There are other aspects to the justification of constitutionalizing fiscal and monetary policy too. The first has to do with something, as we saw earlier, that Hayek particularly emphasized, namely the importance in the context of liberty of a predictable framework within which one could act on the information that one has at hand and the resources that one has available. It is argued by those in favour of the constitutional route in economics that a well-formed fiscal-monetary constitution will in fact provide such a framework of stability. So, for example, a low-inflation economy locked in by guaranteed fiscal and monetary measures will enable businesses to invest, savers to save without worrying that their savings will be radically eroded by inflation, and those on fixed incomes to enjoy them at a relatively low eroding level. Again the critic might argue that whatever the merits of analysis, this hardly makes the rule of law non-instrumental but rather utilitarian in a broad sense. I think that there can be only two answers to this forthcoming from the neo-liberal. The first is just to argue that since freedom is a universal value and aspiration and since social and economic predictability is a central aspect of freedom then while the rule of law may indeed be telocratic, nevertheless its *telos* is a universal one. This would be a parallel claim to the one made earlier, although with a greater degree of generality. The alternative view would be to take the line proposed by Michael Oakeshott which we noted in Chapter 1, namely that security, peace, and the like were not somehow ends or goals of a nomocratic order but were, in some sense, rather to be seen as constitutive of such an order. On this basis then a nomocratic order, the rule of law, and predictability would stand as an interconnected whole rather than the rule of law somehow securing the goal of predictability.

Given this context of constitutionalizing fiscal and monetary policy and the strictures on public spending, what role do neo-liberals see for government expenditure? There is no settled answer to the question which would be affirmed by all neo-liberals, but broadly the answer falls into three parts: the provision of public goods in the technical economists' sense; the rectification of market failure; and provision for some basic level of welfare expenditure. Neo-liberals are not anarchists or libertarians. They do believe that there is a case for public expenditure but emphatically not in pursuit of some overall collective moral aims such as social justice, redistribution, or the common good – or any other such notion.

This is the important point in respect of public goods. The idea of a public good in the neo-liberal view has to be distinguished from any idea of a common good in a normative sense as an overall aim for society. Rather a public good is identified normatively as a good which people want but which is not likely to be provided by the market. The reason for this is that the good requires cooperative production but there is either no mechanism or only a very costly mechanism for excluding non-contributors from the benefit of the good. Such goods will not be provided by the market because there is no way of preventing freeriders from benefiting from the good. Hence, every individual will have an incentive to freeride and the good will not in the end be produced. The purest kind of examples might be clean air and nuclear deterrence. No mechanism can exclude those who do not wish to contribute to the cost of securing clean air from enjoying its benefits – but because it is impossible to exclude people from the benefit there is an incentive to freeride and the good will not be produced through free action. The same is true of nuclear deterrence. These sorts of goods can only be produced by governments utilizing the law and the tax system – the framework of coercion. Indeed, a neo-liberal such as James Buchanan also regards basic constitutional law as a public good. Other sorts of public good may in fact be less pure examples. Both roads and public parks are frequently regarded as public goods but this categorization can alter, and indeed is changing in the case of roads with changes in technology. With new computer technology it is relatively easy to exclude from the roads those who will not pay to use them. Hence, some roads as public goods have been turned into semi-private goods by road charging, congestion charging, motorway tolls, etc. A generation ago this would have been very costly and inefficient because the technology was not available. Now it is and the perception of the road network may well change over time making it seem more like the railways in the United Kingdom.

Hayek discusses at some length the issue of public goods and coercion.[13] He argues that there are indeed genuine collective or public goods and that they will not be supplied by voluntary effort in support of some sense of common interest or common purpose. He accepts that in small groups it may be possible to galvanize people into collective action behind a common purpose but this will not happen in large-scale settings. The reason is clear: in a large-scale setting the individual will have an incentive to freeride on the efforts of others since he or she will judge that his or her contribution will make no difference. Here, coercion has to be used to produce such goods. The individual would agree to this compulsion if it is clearly limited to the production of the good and if it is applied to all equally – according that is to the rule of law. Hayek recognizes, however, that there is a difference between the exercise of coercive power to prevent one person infringing the freedom of another and the exercise of coercion to require him or her to make a contribution – particularly if the person does not want the good in question – nuclear deterrence would be a good real-world example. Hayek argues though, that the situation should be seen as an exchange. 'So long as each may expect to get from this common pool of services which are worth more to him than what he is made to contribute', it will be in his or her interest to submit to the coercion. He argues that it may well be impossible to measure these variables but that consent to the provision of public goods will be likely to be secured if 'each should feel that in the aggregate all the collective goods which are supplied to him are worth at least as much as the contribution he is required to make'.[14] This in turn might well mean that the performance of bureaucracies providing public goods has to be clearly monitored for internally motivated growth and the use of discretionary power given the public choice critique of public bureaucracies. In his book *The Demand and Supply of Public Goods* Buchanan echoes these points but with a rather different twist. He takes the view that a state will always be providing a mix of public goods and that a citizen will consent to them even if his or her access to one or another of them is physically limited because he or she will see a benefit in aggregate from the mix.[15]

Hayek's argument at this point is very interesting and it raises a question about the coherence of the position of the neo-liberal in endorsing a case for public goods while being critical of the ideal of social justice. The problem is this: public goods are produced by coercion following a vote in favour of the production of such goods, but what is unclear is what the terms of access to such goods are. The goods cover everyone in society, whether they have voted for them or not, but what do we mean by coverage here? Take a typical example of a public good – say a fire station, which is Buchanan's chosen example. A fire station is a physically located public good and some people who live closer to it may well expect to be able to derive greater benefit compared with someone who lives at a distance. So what do we mean in this kind of context by saying that a public good is available to all citizens equally since this is essentially what underpins the rationality of tax sharing for the good, it underpins the legitimacy of coercion, and, as applying to all equally it also embodies the principle of the rule of law? Does availability to all mean equal access to a fire station, or does it mean equal consumption of the good which the fire station or any other public good provides, or does it mean an equal or a fair fraction of the services of the fire station? There are two things to notice about such questions which are unavoidable once the case for collective or public goods has been accepted. This issue is discussed by Buchanan. His point is that it cannot in fact be equality of consumption, even if one could get over the conceptual problems as to what in fact constitutes 'the same quantity of a public good' it would be impossible to define equal shares in a physically located public good just because of factors like distance from the good in question. The equality in question is not of consumption but rather equal availability of the good and a procedure for ensuring that. Hence to put Buchanan's point in a rather different way which links it to social and economic rights, we might say that from his viewpoint there cannot be a substantial right to a share in such a good even though one has contributed equally to its funding. At the most the right is to a fair procedure first of all in determining the location of the good and then to access to it – but not consumption of it.[16] I shall return to this issue in Chapter 12 when in the case of police forces I argue that the situation is more complicated than Buchanan thinks that it is. An important point to be made, however, is that such questions seem very much like questions of social or distributive justice – what should be the principle of allocation? Hayek argues that a public good should be pitched at a level so that a person has at least as much and preferably more benefit than his contribution cost. Again though, we need to have an account of benefit: Is it access or actual consumption? And why should his own principle of allocation – the benefit exceeds the cost – be accepted? These are surely questions of distributive justice and political deliberation which on the whole he wishes to exclude from the spheres of economic exchange. Additionally, if an individual has paid equally for the production of a public good as is presupposed by the argument about the legitimacy of coercion in this context and compatibility with the rule of law, then it might be argued that he or she has a right to an appropriate share in that good however that is to be defined. This, however, raises the thorny issue for neo-liberals that at the heart of the argument about public goods are questions of rights and social justice which will not go away. These are intensely political questions – for example, the location of a fire station could have a big effect on whether or not there is or can be equality of access to the facility. If there is one fire station and two fires simultaneously then the Fire Chief will have to use his discretion about the deployment of resources – he cannot divide them equally because to do so to respect equality of consumption might mean that both houses burn down – yet discretion is regarded as arbitrary power which should be severely limited. We shall return to these issues in Chapter 12 when we look critically at the neo-liberal view of rights.

Difficult questions for the neo-liberal, however, do not just arise in terms of the allocation of public goods but also apply to the pre-production stage of a public good. How does a proposal for the coercive funding of a public good get onto the agenda of politics. Clearly, neo-liberals believe that it is reasonable for the state to facilitate the production of public goods through the use of coercion, but how does a specific proposal get to this stage in the first place? One very likely response is that such proposals reach the political agenda through the use of interest group pressures of precisely the sort of which they are, as we have seen, so critical. So, for example, a proposal to move to a clean air environment would in any country almost certainly be put on the political agenda by interest groups and would almost certainly be opposed by other interest groups – coal miners' unions, for example.

Interest groups are also likely to arise in respect of proposals to privatize an already-existing public good because technological changes have made this possible. It is possible to think that lighthouses will change their category if the proximity of a ship to land or underwater rocks could be established by a mechanism like GPS positioning which is essentially a private service available to subscribers only. So while the definition of a public good may be fixed and while some public goods look pretty secure, it has to be accepted that some conventional public goods can be turned into private goods because of changes in technology. However, many neo-liberal theorists support the provision of public goods while, at the same time seeking ways to privatize them since they are still subject to the critique of public expenditure set out earlier and the organizational provision of the goods by public officials will also be subject to the public choice critique of bureaucratic utility maximization and unaccountable discretion discussed earlier. Such proposals for either privatization or retention as public goods are going to draw into being interest groups on one side or the other of this argument. What seems obvious is that once the case for public goods has been accepted by the neo-liberal, then what are seen as the bad effects of distributive politics and interest group competition cannot be banished from politics but are endemic.

It is also true though that some thinkers whose work has been influential on neo-liberals are much more sceptical of the need for government action in relation to public good. Here, the work of Murray Rothbard and in a different way James Buchanan is significant. Rothbard is highly sceptical of the concept of public goods. If a good is genuinely collective it would be like the air where its consumption is non-rivalrous. Any consumption of the good does not adversely affect you. But it is precisely in areas such as these where the question of provision and allocation does not arise. Goods like police forces or defence, however, are not in Rothbard's view collective goods because consumption may be rivalrous: a police force cannot in fact protect all equally; nor can a system of national defence. If we all cannot be allocated access to such goods on an equal and compossible basis, then they do not fit the standard definition of public or collective goods. Individuals who may not be protected by the police, for example, would not see the provision of the good as a good exchange for a coerced contribution and might prefer some private solution such as a security firm contracted to the person and his or her family or firm in exchange for a specified contribution. As we have seen, Hayek and Buchanan take a different view of this and the issue is unresolved by neo-liberals.

The second general heading under which public provision and government expenditure can be justified in neo-liberal terms is market failure and the negative externalities of market operations. Each of these embodies complexities in terms of a coherent account of neo-liberal ideas.

Let us turn to negative externalities first. Negative externalities occur when an individual, group, or firm operating in a market in pursuit of a legal goal, that is, the exchange of legal commodities cause 'bads' or negative externalities to fall upon other individuals and groups without their consent. There is a big question here about what is the appropriate role for government. Should it be to compensate for such externalities? Should it be to regulate such activities to seek to prevent the occurrence of such externalities? Or should it be to provide an effective framework of civil and tort law so that individuals should be able to pursue compensation claims through the courts? It will be obvious that as far as possible the neo-liberal approach would favour the latter alternative. The reasons for this are clear enough in the light of arguments hitherto. In the case of government compensation the argument would be that it is an illegitimate use of the taxpayers' money to compensate for private 'bads' caused by identifiable agents whether individual or corporate. In the case of negative externalities caused by agents who, in specific circumstances, cannot be identified – for example, when my car was damaged during the night by a lorry which did not stop – the answer is then not the state. It might be argued that the state has a central role not by providing compensation but rather regulation. While neo-liberals do not reject particular examples of regulation when there seems to be little alternative, they are in general opposed to it as the general basis set out earlier: it can act as a brake on economic dynamism; it will always involve unaccountable discretion by bureaucrats; it will create bureaucratic vested interests in seeking to refine, embellish, and gold plate regulations; it may well lead to large-scale unintended consequences which might be very difficult to correct given this growth of vested interest; there is always the possibility of regulators 'going native' either favouring the business or industry regulated over those on whom negative externalities are visited or on the other hand favouring this group over the causer of the negative externalities. In addition, it might be argued that externalities (positive and negative) are endemic functions of economic activity and exchange. It would be impossible, as well as highly undesirable, for government to seek to regulate all such externalities. This being so, there would have to be some government or collective view of which negative externalities on which 'bads' are to be regulated by the state. This would then turn into a normative question and a claim that the liberal state should regulate some 'bads' but not others could be seen as problematic. Given that regulatory rules are part of the rule of law in a liberal state – laws which would for example empower regulators to impose fines on businesses – then the fact that these rules exist to secure a prescribed goal or end which has been preferred to some other goal or end means that such laws or rules cannot be seen as non-instrumental and nomocratic.

Finally, the other aspect of state expenditure to which I want to draw attention as being of particular importance to the neo-liberal case is welfare expenditure. At one end of the neo-liberal scale as represented by Robert Nozick there is a very clear position on this. The state has no duty, no responsibility to meet the welfare needs of the population. Indeed, in seeking to do so, it would in fact infringe the most basic rights of its citizens, the protection of which provides the fundamental and perhaps only rationale for the state. The state infringes these rights via a tax system which seeks to remove property that is to say pre-tax money from those who legitimately own it to transfer to others to meet their needs. These actions infringe in the most basic way the rights of ownership and there is no way of making a tax-financed welfare state compatible with full rights of ownership. Most neo-liberals do not go as far as this. Certainly, Hayek accepts that there is a case for a basic level of welfare provision for those who cannot either temporarily or permanently earn a living in the market and that this commitment may well reasonably grow in line with the growth in the prosperity of the society.[17] It has to be said, however, that Hayek's views on the welfare state are very underdeveloped in terms of being incorporated into the coherent picture of the neo-liberal state that he has given us and I have taken up this point in more detail elsewhere. In the case of Buchanan the picture is rather different in that on the one hand he does not want to impose his own views on others. Recall that he is a moral subjectivist and does not believe in the role of the philosopher king. Therefore, he cannot say in advance of negotiations by people deploying their own subjectivist points of view whether or not a welfare state should be set up. All that he could reasonably say is that at the constitutional level of the state one has to proceed by unanimity, in the productive or policy-oriented side of the state one can proceed on a less than unanimous basis but only if the procedure is sanctioned by the constitution. So while Buchanan thinks that he can set out a procedure for decision-making that is consistent with subjectivism what he cannot do is to say in advance what conclusions would be arrived at under the procedure. However, going back to an earlier discussion, if Buchanan believes that there should be a fiscal and monetary constitution, then the existence of such a set of arrangements would have severe constraining effects on any welfare state proposals since such a state would have implications not directly on the money supply but it would have indirect impacts for reasons set out earlier and, in addition, the tax basis of a welfare state would have quite a profound impact on the fiscal constitution. So, depending on what unanimity yielded in the way of rules at the constitutional level, this could have the effect of ruling out the provision of a welfare state at the productive or policy level of the state.

NOTES

1. Keynes, J. M. (1973). *The General Theory of Employment, Interest and Money.* London: Macmillan, p. 89.
2. Keynes, J. M. *General Theory of Employment*, p. 89.
3. For a very good account of the influence of these events on the development of left-wing economic thought in the United Kingdom, see Durbin, E. (1985). *New Jerusalems: The Labour Party and the Economics of Democratic Socialism.* London: Routledge and Kegan Paul.
4. Middlemas, K. (1986). *Power, Competition and the State*, Vol. 1. London: Macmillan, p. 87.
5. Brittan, S. (1983). *The Role and Limits of Government.* London: Temple Smith, p. 135.
6. Brittan, S. *The Role and Limits of Government*, p. 256.
7. Stockman, D. (1985). *The Triumph of Politics.* New York: Coronet, p. 9.
8. Buchanan, J. and Brennan, G. (1999). *The Reason of Rules.* Indianapolis, IN: The Liberty Fund.
9. Buchanan, J. and Brennan, G. *The Reason of Rules.* p. 95.
10. Walters, A. (1986). *Britain's Economic Renaissance.* p. 41.
11. Walters, A. (1986). *Britain's Economic Renaissance*, p. 36.
12. Friedman, D. (1978). *The Machinery of Freedom.* New Rochelle, NY Arlington House, p. 116.

13. Hayek, F. A. (1979). *Law, Legislation and Liberty, Vol. 3: The Political Order of a Free People.* London: Routledge and Kegan Paul, p. 43.
14. Hayek, F. A. *Law, Legislation and Liberty, Vol 3.*, p. 45.
15. Buchanan, J. (1999). *The Demand and Supply of Public Goods.* Indianapolis, IN: The Liberty Fund, p. 152.
16. Buchanan, J. *The Demand and Supply of Public Goods*, p. 52.
17. Hayek, F. A. (1960). *The Constitution of Liberty.* London: Routledge and Kegan Paul, p. 257.

Part II

Neo-liberal Principles: A Critical Perspective

10

Freedom and Coercion: An Alternative Account

I now want to turn to an analysis of the ideas of freedom and coercion first of all. Freedom for Hayek is the absence of coercion and the prevention of coercion by one private individual by another is through the threat of coercion by the state *through* the law. Hence, for Hayek freedom is a product of law.

At this stage of the discussion I want to concentrate most on the idea of coercion and the thrust of my analysis will be that Hayek does not employ a coherent account of coercion and hence of freedom. A clear and convincing account of coercion is vital if Hayek's account of freedom and his vision of a free society are to have purchase.

I shall start the analysis by looking at negative liberty. Hayek claims to be defending negative liberty and it is useful to have before us what has sometimes been called the 'pure' theory of negative liberty or in the view of its detractors, 'crude' negative liberty. On this view coercion is a matter of the coercer A making it *impossible* for B to do *X* which is what he or she wants to do; or to refrain from doing *Y* which he or she does not want to do.

On the face of it at least, this view has a number of advantages. The most obvious one is to understand coercion to be a matter of objective fact. Whether A makes it physically impossible for B to act is an *empirical* issue. It raises no normative considerations. Laws directed at preventing coercion would therefore have a wholly factual objective that is, removing the intentional coercion involved in one person making it impossible for another person to act. We would have a clear answer to the question of whether B is free to do *X* or whether A is coercing him since impossibility is a physical state of affairs. This would mean that the question of freedom and coercion would not be involved in subjective judgement as to whether B *feels* coerced or made unfree by A in respect of doing *X*. Whether he or she is coerced or not is a matter of fact, not to be interpreted against an understanding of what B's beliefs and desires happen to be.

In terms of an account of the rule of law such an account of coercion has a lot to recommend it because it would mean that in one sense of the word, law by preventing coercion, would not be arbitrary. It would be concerned with coercion as impossibility rather than with psychological judgements, which could vary from person to person. However, most infringements of liberty in commonsensical understandings of the term do not occur when someone has made it literally impossible for me to do something but, rather have made it very costly for me to do it by attaching some kind of sanction to my preferred course of action.

While this may be so, the relaxation of the idea of coercion in this respect is costly to neo-liberal views on the relationship between freedom and the rule of law. If, for example, we were to abandon this pure idea of negative liberty of freedom as unpreventedness and argue for the view that threats are coercive, then it is difficult to see how the objectivity of the idea of coercion and thus an objectively determinate sphere of freedom can be preserved. The reason for this is straightforward. To regard a threat as coercive seems to imply some reference to individual psychology and an individual's own scale of values. To take a fanciful example, if I say to an ardent religious believer 'unless you stop doing *X* I will destroy this religious object which is sacred to you', then, set against that believer's framework of values, this is undoubtedly a threat. If I am an ardent atheist, the promise to break and destroy the religious object unless I comply and stop doing *X* will not be a threat. So while it may seem eminently plausible to move from a strict account of coercion as impossibility to the idea that threats are coercive, this move is at the cost of making the idea of coercion much less determinate compared with the case of impossibility. This, in turn, would have some effect on the scope of law which is there to prevent coercion. If, however, coercion depends on psychological states and beliefs, then the scope of law might be thought to be less determinate unless we thought that there were beliefs, interests, desires, or needs which all rational persons share such that to threaten these would always be coercive and the reason for that would depend on these 'facts' of philosophical anthropology rather than the variable beliefs of individuals. It is clear that Hayek does in fact think this as we saw in Chapter 3. He talks about the beliefs and values of the average person in the context of coercion and he also argued that coercion takes place when certain things valued by such a person are threatened, for example, his or her life, valued possessions, his or her nearest and dearest.[1] So from this point of view a broader conception of negative liberty to include threats (not to mention offers) might maintain the objectivity of the idea of coercion by means of reference to such a theory of human nature and human goods. This would pose great difficulties for a Hayekian conception of coercion which is supposed to be separate from an account of human goals as is law as a whole in a nomocratic system.

Even on the pure theory of negative liberty A's act of coercion in rendering it impossible for B to do *X* has to be seen as intentional. There might be all sorts of things which prevent B from doing *X*: he may be physically incapable of doing *X*; *X* may be a practical impossibility; there may be physical constraints to do with time and place which prevent him or her doing *X*, etc. Equally some of A's actions may unintentionally eliminate options for B and make it impossible for B to pursue them. For example, if I have bought the last copy of *Le Monde* from that newspaper seller, then B cannot buy that paper from that seller. But these are not coercive circumstances unless the outcome of preventing B doing *X* had been intended. Those forms of impossibility, which do not depend on human agency, would not be forms of coercion. Coercion, on the pure theory, comes in through human agency and intention. This, however, is not as clear as it might seem as we shall see in Chapter 11. There are a lot of questions about intention: the proximity of the coercer to the coerced person; intention versus foreseeability; acts and omissions; and the relationship between moral responsibility for coercion and causal responsibility. These questions are raised by Hayek's own treatment of these issues and will be considered shortly. All that needs to be pointed out at the moment is that even the pure theory of negative liberty contains very complex issues which become even more salient in a theory such as Hayek's which, it will be seen, does not defend such a pure theory of negative liberty.

There is one final point worth making about the pure theory of negative liberty and that is the idea of impossibility which is at the heart of this position's account of coercion. It could be argued that the seeming objectivity of coercion as impossibility is delusive in the sense that what makes it *impossible* for B to do *X* or to abstain from doing *Y* could just as easily depend on an account of B's psychology and his or her abilities or capacities as was the case with *threats*. Persons B and C, with rather different capacities and beliefs, may well have a different view about whether A has or has not made it impossible for each to do *X* or to abstain from doing *Y*. Indeed Hayek comes close to recognizing this.[2] If this is so, then it is not clear that there can be an account of intentionally imposed impossibility which is wholly factual. This raises the question mentioned earlier about whether a general, rather than person-specific view of capacities, powers, needs, etc. has to be presupposed to have a coherent account of impossibility. That is to say that there are certain types of general human goods and capacities the withholding or infringement of which will always count as A making it impossible for B and C to do *X*. This would seem to be the only way to move the issue away from subjectivity, but in so doing it goes way beyond the literally demoralized view of liberty for which most neo-liberals argue.

So, given the problem with what might be called the 'pure theory' of negative liberty, how does Hayek's own theory stand in relation to different conceptions of negative liberty? This is a question of broad salience since all neo-liberals, as far as I am aware, adopt a negative view of liberty. It seems clear that Hayek adopts a much looser view of coercion than the advocate of pure negative liberty. His account of coercion incorporates the depiction of coercion as impossibility, but in his view it involves a wider set of constraints. Recall that he defines freedom as a state in which 'a man is not subject to coercion by the arbitrary will of another or others'.[3] Let us put on one side the issue of arbitrariness of the will for the moment and concentrate on coercion.

As we saw in Chapter 3, Hayek clearly wants to distinguish between coercion and direct, inescapable, physical force when he argues that a person subject to coercion still retains the capacity for choice in those circumstances. So physical force and violence which would be the paradigm case of coercion for the defender of pure negative liberty are certainly restrictions of freedom for Hayek, but have to be distinguished from coercion. The reason being that coercion is about action rather than just physical movements. If I have no choice, I do not act. The man who signs with a gun held to his head is not acting as per his will; he is more like a robot rather than an agent. There seems to be some running together of these points about coercion and action when he argues that 'coercion is the control of the essential data of an individual's action by another'.[4] But what does he mean here by 'essential data'? It must mean the actions' constituent parts and these include bodily movements since all actions are constituted out of such bodily data. Even the action of remaining stationary so as not to alert a burglar depends for its performance on the physical state of the body. So if bodily data are essential data of actions, and if coercion involves the control of bodily movements, it then becomes very difficult to see what is the difference between coercion in this sense and the forcing of bodily movements of the type that Hayek wanted to distinguish from coercion in the passage previously cited.

Now, it could be that the essential data of an individual's action has to be interpreted much more broadly than I have suggested but Hayek does not say. All he does say is to speak about 'certain facts not being deliberately shaped by another', but what these facts are is left vague and indeterminate.

In his account of freedom and coercion outlined earlier Hayek wanted to distinguish personal freedom or individual liberty from political freedom on the one hand and what he called 'inner' freedom on the other. However, I doubt very much whether Hayek can in fact give an account of coercion without a logical link to inner freedom from which he wishes to distinguish individual liberty. By inner freedom Hayek means the capacity that a person has to follow purposes of 'his own considered will, by his reason or lasting convictions' and not to act on momentary impulse or circumstance. In terms of inner freedom my own weakness of character, my own lack of foresight, my own obsessions and neuroses may impede my liberty to achieve the goals that I want to achieve. For Hayek, however, this has nothing to do with personal or individual freedom understood as the absence of coercion and the possession of an assured private sphere. The problem here is recognized by Hayek, however, but this recognition is not properly incorporated into his account of coercion. The problem is this. If coercion goes beyond physical impossibility, then it is perfectly feasible to think that there will be an irremediable subjective element to the perception of coercion. As Hayek says:

> [T]he same conditions which to some constitute coercion will be to others merely ordinary difficulties which have to be overcome, depending on the strength of will of the people involved. To that extent 'inner freedom' and 'freedom' is the sense of absence of coercion will together determine how much use a person can make of his knowledge of opportunities.[5]

But he continues after this quotation to say that nevertheless freedom as the absence of coercion should still be clearly distinguished from inner freedom. Certainly as the quotation makes clear inner freedom does not have a place as part of the definition of freedom. At the most it is about what we are capable of doing within an uncoerced space, which is defined independently of inner freedom. However, having made the point as he has in the passage quoted, this claim is barely credible. His link between the reaction to coercion and a person's inner freedom is not incidental and is repeated, for example, at page 138 of *The Constitution of Liberty.* Here he contrasts the case of a person who is not deterred from his goals by the threat of assassination and someone who is so deterred by a mere inconvenience.

The difficulty here is that if coercion is a matter of individual perception, related to what Hayek calls 'inner strength', then the idea of coercion and the idea of freedom, since that is the absence of coercion, lose the objectivity which they seemed to have under pure negative liberty. If the state is to use the threat of coercion to prevent coercion between private individuals, then this claim becomes problematic and inexact if coercion is essentially perceptual and evaluative. In the view of some philosophers, it is of vital importance to distinguish between 'being free' (objective fact) and 'feeling free' (perceived and evaluated situation). Indeed, it is arguable that this distinction between feeling free and being free is essential to the idea of the rule of law. The law applies to all to prevent coercion, but if what is regarded as coercion depends on subjective perception, then this is put into jeopardy. Secondly, the law is supposed to be general and indifferent to the values of specific individuals but if coercion involves an individual's perception of how his or her values are threatened in a particular situation, as the example of a threat to a sacred object shows, then how can the law stand aside from such specific purposes?

Hayek's solution to the problem as set out briefly in *The Constitution of Liberty* is to claim that he is taking into account coercion in respect of what he calls 'the normal, average person' and in his view this means that coercion will be seen in terms of threat of bodily harm to oneself or those dear to one; or damage to a valuable or cherished possession. That is to say there are certain sorts of goods in human life threats against which are to be regarded as coercive. However, this list appears rather perfunctory and underdetermined. It could be subject to a very great deal of interpretation. A 'cherished possession' might refer to material goods only or it might include a belief and a value system. Certainly the list could be added to with some degree of plausibility – so, for example, it might quite reasonably include some reference to an individual's needs such that if he or she were to be threatened in respect of the satisfaction of those needs, the individual might well regard this as coercive. The point is partly that Hayek's list is far from being plausibly exhaustive, partly that this means that it may be indeterminate and controversial – which would then affect the objectivity of the related concepts of freedom and coercion. We might also take the argument a bit further by utilizing an example which Hayek himself gives in *The Constitution of Liberty.* I suggested that needs could plausibly be added to Hayek's list of what the normal average person would regard as valuable. Now for reasons that will be more fully discussed in Chapter 11 most neo-liberals are very suspicious of the concept of needs, believing that it produces an inexact and open-ended basis for building up ideas of entitlements and rights to the satisfaction of needs. However, in *The Constitution of Liberty* Hayek himself produces an argument in the context of coercion which could easily be extended to show that even in Hayek's own terms needs have a part to play in the list of what might be thought of as the informal average man's basic interests – interference with which would be coercive. The argument is available on page 136. This is the case considered in Chapter 3 of the monopolist in the desert oasis who owns the only spring. If the monopolist required people to pay an extortionate price to secure a supply of water from him in order to survive, then this, for Hayek, would be a clear case of coercion. The reason being that water is, to use Hayek's terms 'an essential commodity'. One way of understanding an 'essential commodity' would be that water is a basic need and therefore withholding that 'indispensable supply' to meet such a need would be coercive. It would not be coercive if the monopolist were the only supplier of beads, let us say, at the oasis. The coercion turns partly on the monopoly being the only supplier, and partly on the fact that he is frustrating the satisfaction of a basic need. Indeed, taking our guide from this example and using Hayek's own language about coercion being the control of the data of an individual's actions, it would be possible to argue that the satisfaction of basic needs is an essential datum for any action whatsoever. If the withholding of supply to meet such needs by those capable of supplying such goods can be coercive, then the satisfaction of them may be seen as part of freedom given Hayek's own views of the link between freedom and coercion. This, as we shall see later, would take us some way from the normal approach of neo-liberals.[6] So, for example, given Hayek's own emphasis on the nature of freedom involving following a coherent plan of life (or what we might reasonably call autonomy) why does not freedom involve access to these resources which are the necessary data to that achievement? In fact, Hayek himself argues at page 136 that I am indeed coerced by someone who refuses me goods and services 'which are crucial to my existence or the preservation of what I most value'. Hayek, as we have seen, has argued that pursuing a coherent plan of life is crucial to what it is to be a thinking and valuing human, and as such it could certainly be argued that the satisfaction of needs is essential to freedom. This would, however, turn Hayek's theory from a negative to a positive theory of freedom.

Given that the idea of coercion and its absence is supposed to provide the legal basis for a private assured domain, it seems that his account of coercion so far is too inexact to perform this function. This point can be taken further by looking at further aspects of Hayek's account of coercion. As we have seen, for Hayek coercion has to be compatible with choice. The problem with coercion is that the ends for which I act are in the hands of another and I act according to this evil to avoid a greater evil. As we saw earlier, Hayek rejected the view that freedom involves the possession of a particular range of options, but as we have seen the argument developing he has come to accept that there is in fact a link between freedom and particular sorts of options. Certain types of goods are more significant than others in human life and being unable to choose those goods is implicitly for Hayek a restriction of liberty. There are two aspects of this. First of all, as we have seen, Hayek regards certain sorts of goods to be indispensable for human life and for the pursuit of a coherent plan of life and to be a thinking and valuing person. Hence, these goods are always going to be highly significant for freedom. Secondly, the goods which are essential to freedom for a particular individual are going to be those which are central to his or her rational and coherent plan of life.

So it does seem – contrary to what Hayek had claimed earlier – that the types of options and the number of options open to us in relation to those goods does have a bearing on the nature of liberty. This aspect of Hayek's work on freedom also moves Hayek even further away from a purely negative account of freedom. This is so for several reasons.

First of all on the purely or strictly negative view of liberty, freedom does not entail the possession of any set of goods – it means just the absence of coercion. Negative freedom is not usually thought to involve any particular assumptions about human nature and in particular does not involve a view about human flourishing and the goods necessary for that. Whereas Hayek's theory has had recourse to the beliefs and values of normal or average people and to their views about basic goods. His theory also involves a degree of perfectionism in the sense that for Hayek a free society will lead to the development of the capacity to follow a coherent plan of life. One could point to three further arguments which drastically undermine the Hayekian case that the range of options open to an individual has nothing to do with the nature of freedom and coercion. The first is in terms of Hayek's own argument about whether the offer of an employment contract at a low wage in a depression is coercive or not. Hayek argues that it is not because there are other options for employment open to the individual. Hence it is the existence of that range of options which impacts upon the individual and means that he is not coerced. Given that the existence of a particular range of options is central to the identification of coercion or its absence, it is difficult to see how Hayek can maintain his view that the range of options from which an individual may choose has nothing to do with the essential nature of freedom. The second argument has been put forward by neo-liberal critics of Hayek's view about the relationship between coercion and the rule of law. In Hayek's view it is the generality of law, its universality, and the fact that it does not prescribe specific ends to be pursued – in fact its nomocratic nature – which means that the law is not coercive. However, it would be perfectly possible as Rothbard points out to have a wholly general law that applied to all that prevented foreign travel to everyone in a society.[7] In Hayekian terms we would have to say that such a law is not coercive. This is not credible. What makes the law coercive is that it denies an important human good. The conclusion here would be that we cannot make sense of coercion without some conception of important or central human goods. Rothbard believes that such goods are underpinned by a natural law doctrine. Hayek, as we saw in the earlier example, in fact implicitly recognizes such a recognition of basic goods but beyond referring to the views of the normal average person he has done nothing to incorporate this view into his own account of negative liberty. This point then links up to the well-known argument of Charles Taylor's in his essay 'What's Wrong with Negative Liberty?[8] In that essay he points out that if negative liberty is separated from an account of important human goods, then it becomes very implausible. The reason is that a judgement about whether society A is freer than society B would be more or less impossible to make and yet this kind of judgement is quite important to neo-liberalism as a political movement. The reason is this. In the absence of an account of human goods the infringement of which is coercive the question as to whether one society is freer than another has to be answered on *quantitative* grounds – namely how many rules are there preventing action in society A compared with society B? It cannot be a judgement of the significance of the acts prevented because that would presuppose a view of the good. This would have the paradoxical result that a very underdeveloped society without say laws relating to financial services or to transport would almost certainly have fewer rules than another society even if the few rules that it had restricted political rights, freedom of speech, foreign travel, etc. Taylor uses the argument to compare Albania under the communists with Western societies. It would be incredible to think that because Albania was relatively underdeveloped and would have fewer laws, then it was a freer society than say the United Kingdom. What matters is the goods that we are able to pursue in an unrestricted way. It is a *qualitative* question as to whether society A is freer than society B, not a *quantitative* one. The issue here though is absolutely fundamental and it has to do with goods and abilities. That is to say we think society A is freer than society B because of the goods that we are able to pursue. It has, however, been central to a neo-liberal account of negative freedom that freedom and coercion have to be separated from goods and abilities as indeed is required by a nomocratic conception of law. This is, however, impossible.

These moves away from pure negative liberty are very important for the general coherence and distinctiveness of neo-liberalism. The first reason is that in respect of freedom the ideal of the neo-liberal is equal freedom. It can make sense in respect of pure negative liberty to attain this because all potentially and actual coercive acts by private individuals will be constrained equally by the legal system, the main purpose of which is to threaten or to use coercion to prevent coercion. Therefore, on a strictly negative view of liberty the law can secure equal liberty in the sense of freedom from coercion when coercion is understood in the context of the pure theory of negative liberty. However, this view has to become much more complex than that in the specific case we are looking at and it may well have to involve possession of certain sorts of goods (to meet at least basic needs) and the capabilities (in so far as they can be developed) to pursue such goods if coercion is to be avoided. There is, however, a genuine difficulty here about how far it would be possible to secure to individuals what might reasonably be regarded as *the basic goods of agency* – to allow an individual to be able to follow a coherent plan of life. This is an issue that will be postponed until later when we discuss social justice and rights in Chapters 11 and 12. Suffice it to say at the moment though that for the neo-liberal there is a big difference between securing a set of rules applicable equally which would secure mutual forbearance from coercion on the one hand and securing to individuals a set of basic goods of action which are required for agency and action. The first secures forbearance which is abstaining from action and is therefore costless; the second involves securing resources to individuals and involves substantial costs.

The second problem for the coherence of the neo-liberal project is the idea of universalizability in respect of an account of the rule of law. If the rule of law implies universalizability, then again it is easier to see how this could be done in respect of securing a set of forbearances and forms of inaction rather than a set of goods as conditions of action and agency.

The same point could be made about the idea that the rule of law in a free society should not set or imply particular goals. It should be neutral between them. It should also not discriminate between one person and another. However, it is then difficult to see how two conditions could be met if the law in a free society was supposed to secure to individuals the basic goods of action. There would be potentially, at least, a specific purpose at stake here; secondly if we were to ensure that people had some kind of rough equality in respect of these goods it might be necessary to adjust the bundle of goods between individuals and deal with them unequally in respect of their differential needs and their capacities to utilize those goods. These points are being made as markers in the argument so far and will be pursued in much more detail in Chapter 12 on rights. However, we have already seen in the previous paragraph that it is very difficult to make sense of the idea of universalizability without presupposing some conception of important human goods. So from a neo-liberal perspective the idea that we have to move away from the pure theory of negative liberty for all the reasons cited earlier, many of which are represented in Hayek's own arguments, is fraught with difficulties for the coherence of the neo-liberal conceptual framework largely because they are likely to imply a concern with social justice and positive rights to resources.

There is, nevertheless, a final point to be made at this juncture and it has to do with the question of what is so bad about coercion, or wherein lies the evil of coercion? as Hayek puts it. Hayek has a strong answer to this question because he says quite clearly that

> coercion is evil precisely because it thus eliminates an individual as a thinking and valued person and makes him a bare tool in the achievement of the ends of another.[9]

He had previously defined coercion as 'such control of the environment or circumstances of a person by another that, in order to avoid greater evil he is forced to act not according to a coherent plan of his own but to serve the ends of another'.[10]

Given that coercion prevents the following of a coherent plan of life it would seem reasonably natural therefore in today's idiom to argue that coercion is wrong because it restricts autonomy. Freedom as the absence of coercion (negative liberty in Hayek's version of it) is valuable because it facilitates autonomy. The question then arises as to whether Hayek has given sufficient specification of what the good of autonomy consists in and what it requires for its development.

He is, of course, clear that it requires a private sphere of non-interference, but it is his account of the relationship between autonomy and material goods on which I want to focus. We have already seen that for Hayek an autonomous life in terms of its negative liberty aspect means that very great importance is attached to the preservation of life and loved ones and cherished or valuable aspects and attachments. Interference with these is coercive. We have also seen in the oasis well example that there are goods essential to my existence the lack of access to which may, if another agent is involved in denying that access, threaten my freedom. I have suggested that a critique of Hayek, wanting to transform and develop his work, could well build upon these points.

There are problems, however, and Hayek himself has a very limited view about the goods which together with the absence of coercion would lead to an autonomous life. First of all, as we saw earlier while he stated that property was an essential condition for a coherent plan of life, the protection of the private sphere – in short for autonomy.[11] He quickly moved away from that and argued that the circumstances of the modern world meant the ownership of property was not essential given the role of the law of contract. I can, using that law, rent at least some of the resources necessary for my autonomy. I do not need directly to own them if I can rent them in the market. So while he presumably sticks to the idea that 'property is an essential condition for the prevention of coercion' because we are 'rarely in a position to carry out a coherent plan of action unless we are certain of our exclusive control of some material objects'.[12] But his argument is that the circumstances of the modern world this can be achieved without direct ownership, but rather through market exchange and contract. He says that the network of rights secured by contract is as much an essential part of the security of a private sphere and thus as contributing to autonomy as is private property.

A major issue needs to be raised at this point. Let us grant Hayek's point about the importance of the role of contract and the market and that these can in fact play the sort of role that property can. What I want to concentrate on at the moment is how an autonomous agent can become a player in the market and a party to the contract. It seems obvious that in order to do these things some set of material goods needs to be in place (even to rent the other goods necessary for autonomy). If contracts are made between people who are vastly different in power and the ownership of material goods, can the concluding of such a contract be regarded itself as a form of coercion? This point has played a very considerable role in the history of liberal thought, as well it might, because it is a central issue for the moral basis of the capitalist economy. Within the liberal tradition the classical liberals argued that such contracts were not coercive, whereas social or 'New' Liberals like the Oxford philosopher T. H. Green argued that they may in fact be coercive.[13] So what are we to make of this?

As we saw earlier in a rather different context Hayek certainly regards the behaviour of a monopolist well owner in an oasis as behaving coercively if he enforced a contract requiring the community to do whatever he wanted for the supply of this 'essential commodity'. However, in Hayek's view the coercion is the result of the coming together of two things: monopoly and an indispensable supply of an essential good. Monopoly on its own is not coercive as he argues at this point – even though the monopolists' demands may be unpleasant, they are not of themselves coercive. So what makes the monopolist behaviour coercive is the monopoly over the supply of the essential good which bears out the point made earlier that Hayek's account of freedom and coercion does imply a positive view of at least a set of basic goods.

Where, however, there is no monopoly in other sorts of goods, such as paid work, the terms of an employment contract, even if very disadvantageous or painful to me, are not coercive because there are other suppliers of work with whom an individual could sign a contract. Where there is more than one source of work, a particular employment contract – when there are other options open to me – cannot be coercive. (It is worth noting at this point that this rather runs against his argument cited earlier that the range of options open to me has nothing to do with liberty.) 'So long as he (the employer) can remove only one opportunity among many to earn a living, he cannot coerce, though he may cause pain.'[14]

The key thing here is that there are other options open to me, which may of course be equally unfavourable, so the contract is not coercive nor is the behaviour of the employer in refusing to negotiate a more favourable contract. So coercion or the lack of it will crucially depend on the assessment of the number of options open. Hayek expresses confidence that significant numbers of employment options will still be open in a competitive market economy for this not to be a problem.

The argument would be more cogent on Hayek's own terms if it had been linked to the idea of basic goods discussed earlier. If my basic needs are to be met (as a basic condition of autonomy), then this would improve my position in relation to contracts because the employer could not in effect act in such a way as to remove from me all capacity to secure 'essential commodities' but he does not say this, he just accepts that the employer will not be acting coercively so long as there are other potential employers around (or he could also be looking to lower the rate of pay to the employee). What matters for Hayek is the fact of choice and not the standards between which his choice will be made. Nevertheless, this does seem quite a long way from the claims that

1. Private property is an essential condition of freedom.
2. The sphere of contract and market provides an equally satisfactory substitute for private ownership in the modern world.

The sphere of contract is important for a full understanding of Hayek's theory of freedom for a further reason. He has argued, as we saw earlier, that coercion has to be intentional and obviously contracting is an intentional act between the parties, so it is a potential area for coercion. This is why the action of the oasis monopolist is coercive whereas if the spring had just dried up as a result of natural processes the settler on the oasis would still be deprived of water and would be unable to drink it since it is unavailable but would not be coerced.

The case which Hayek makes in relation to contracts and coercion is rather startling in its simplicity. He argues that outside of the oasis type of case, the withholding of a benefit from me by the intentional action of another is not coercive. The fact that A has withheld this benefit from B – such as an offer of employment – has changed the context in which I exercise my autonomy; it may have reduced the options open to me to 'distressingly few'; nevertheless this action does not coerce me, even though I have to act under 'great pressure'. He goes on to say:

> Even if the threat of starvation to me and perhaps to my family impels me to accept a distasteful job at a very low wage, even if I am 'at the mercy' of the only man willing to employ me, I am not coerced by him or anyone else.[15]

Why is this so? There are two reasons: the fact that even though my plans and my capacity to follow a coherent plan will now be truncated and will take on a 'makeshift character', it is still 'my own and not some other will that guides my action'. He then goes on to say:

> [S]o long as the act (of withholding the benefit) has placed me in my predicament is not aimed at making me do or not do specific things, so long as the intent of the act that harms me is not to make me serve another ends, its effect on my freedom is not different from that of any natural certainty – a fire or a flood that destroys my house, or an accident that harms my health.[16]

Coercion is a threat or an action or the action itself which replaces my own ends by another's. So it is not coercive to make an offer of employment on very disadvantageous terms to me which I am compelled to accept to avoid starvation – in the case cited by Hayek. Such an approach implies that *threats* are coercive and *offers* are not. It also implies that there is a clear and categorical distinction to be drawn between threats and offers – even offers which in the extreme case cited by Hayek can hardly be refused. There is, however, a very considerable literature about the basis of such a distinction, and the implication of that literature is that, at the very least, Hayek's argument here needs to be made much more sophisticated before we can assume that there is such a clear distinction between coercive threats and uncoercive offers, however poor my position would be in accepting what is the only offer available to me in Hayek's own example.

One reason why defenders of pure negative liberty want to argue that offers cannot be coercive is that it would make the idea of coercion too subjective. What might be seen by person A in situation *X* to be a very onerous and therefore potentially coercive offer may be seen by B in situation *Y* in a different light. Of course, such defenders of pure negative liberty take the same view of threats. Steiner puts the point with his usual clarity:

> Interventions of an offering or a threatening kind effect changes in an individual's relative desires to do certain actions. But neither the making of threats nor that of offers constitutes a diminution of personal liberty.[17]

Because of the link between threats, offers, and desires, to assume that either or both could infringe liberty is to make liberty wholly subjective and to confuse 'being free' with 'feeling free'. However, it is not open to Hayek to use this argument in relation to the non-coerciveness of offers since he has already argued that coercion is to be seen largely in terms of threats and that the perception of the threat is a matter of the perspective provided by 'inner freedom'. This includes the desires and beliefs which normal or average people have which include the preservation of life, loved ones, and valuable or cherished objects. So in order to argue that the offer made in the example he gives, set against the background of potential starvation for the agent and his or her family, is not coercive he has to distinguish between threats and offers on other grounds.

His argument is partly to do with ends or goals and purposes and partly to do with intention. A coercive threat is such because the threat is to displace my own will, my own purposes, or my own values as the controlling force in my life and to replace it by the will of another. As the result of a coercive threat I shall not be able to act on a coherent plan of life. An offer in Hayek's view is not coercive – as long as the intent of the offer is 'not to make me serve another person's ends'. This is quite ambiguous as any offer by A to B is going to invite B to perform some service to A and thus will in *that respect* serve A's ends. Presumably Hayek means that an offer is coercive when a substantial portion of B's purposes are replaced by A's and that A's ends then dominate B's There is, of course, then a question of how far any offer does or does not do this and how that is to be determined – so reducing the question of whether an offer is coercive or not to a highly subjective perception of how extensively the terms of the offer will affect B's own goals and coherent plan of life – in other words affect his autonomy.

As we saw earlier Hayek does implicitly link liberty with essential goods in his oasis example. Therefore, given the example of his which we are currently examining talks about avoiding starvation through concluding a harsh contract, why doesn't he regard such a contract as coercive? After all it is the potential absence of a necessary good, namely food – he or she is facing starvation – that leads the individual to conclude the contract. His answer to this brings into play the central role of intention in his account of coercion. In the oasis case the well owner is intent on denying the supply of a necessary good except on extortionate grounds and it is this fact together with the fact that water from the well is a necessary good, that makes it a case of coercion. The present example – one concerned with a necessary good, the absence of starvation – is one in which the absence of food is not the result of the behaviour and intention of the person offering the contract. In the oasis case the situation caused by the absence of the good would be an intentional act; in the present case it would not. Therefore, the situation we are considering would be coercive only if the poverty of the individual was caused by the intentional action of another and that is not the case in Hayek's example. So we can say that while Hayek, in the oasis example, recognizes a link between liberty and an essential good or a basic need, the lack of such a good is only a form of coercion if the lack of the good is caused by intentional action. The starving man may not be able to fend for himself but that is just a form of inability rather than unfreedom, unless someone else has put him in this situation as the result of intentional action.

There are two issues at stake here. One is the link between coercion and intention and the second is the relationship between being free and being able to do or not to do something. We shall spend more time on the issue of intention in Chapter 11 on social justice and the role of markets. At this stage in the argument I just want to indicate without very much analysis the dimensions of the issues which are quite critical to the coherence of economic liberalism and its difference from social liberalism and social democracy. The question at stake is whether and in what way poverty can be regarded as coercive and thus a form of unfreedom. In Hayek's view it can, if it is caused intentionally by another. The obvious case would be when I am robbed of my wages or my house or my land by the intentional actions of another. These actions are coercive in that they infringe my negative freedom and I am made poor by them. However, if my poverty is caused by non-intentional forces such as famine or harvest failure caused by the weather etc., then my subsequent poverty makes me unable to do things, but is not coercive or a form of unfreedom – remember inability is not the same as unfreedom. So in a free society with a very large role for the market, would the poverty which some would experience as the result of market exchanges be a form of coercion and unfreedom? For Hayek the answer to this question is 'no' because while it is true that in a market millions of people buy and sell they do this intentionally, nevertheless the overall, aggregate outcomes of all this economic activity is not intended by anyone. The distribution of income and wealth that arises as the aggregate outcome of market exchange and the place of the poor in that distribution is not an intentional result or outcome. Therefore poverty that is not caused as part of the deliberate intention of another is not unfreedom and it does not mean that the poverty of the poor person acts as a form of coercion upon him when, for example, he may conclude (for him) a tough employment contract.

This position raises some serious questions about the role of intention in distribution and the relationship, for example, between intention and foreseeability; intention and acts and omission; and the way in which human agency can be identified in complex processes. However, these questions are more at home in Chapter 11 on social justice and will be postponed until then.

I now want to move to the second issue at stake in the debate – that is to say the relation between freedom and ability or power. There is a sharp political issue here to which Hayek draws our attention. If freedom is understood in terms of ability, power, wealth, or opportunity, then the character of a free society will depend upon whether all members of such a society have equal access to power and wealth and thus to have broadly similar abilities. If freedom is understood entirely negatively as the absence of intentional coercion, then it is perfectly possible to secure equal liberty and the means to do this is through the rule of law. General, universal, and predictable laws preventing mutual non-coercion can protect each individual equally. This is not the case if freedom is understood positively as the possession of ability, power, wealth, and opportunity. Any rules or laws seeking to secure such things to individuals will have to operate in a highly discriminatory way. Amartya Sen, for example, has pointed out that the ability and capability of people to transform power, wealth, and opportunity will differ quite fundamentally.[18] Given this fact, equal liberty if it were to include ability or power would for Hayek become an illusion since we cannot secure equality in respect of ability, power, and opportunity. So, here is the political rub, but what is the philosophical basis for the distinction between freedom on the one hand and power and ability on the other?

The answer goes like this. No person is able to do or has the power to do all that he is negatively free to do. If I am free from coercion, then a whole range of action (and inaction) is open to me. Nevertheless, it is not possible for an individual however able or powerful or rich to do more than a small number of the indefinitely large number of things that such an individual is free to do. Given that no one is able to do all that he or she is free to do, power, ability, and freedom must be different things. This argument is made better by Murray Rothbard than by Hayek when he argues:

> Each man's power, then, is always necessarily limited by the facts of the human condition, by the nature of man and his world; but it is one of the glories of man's condition that each person *can* be absolutely free, even in a world of complex interaction and exchange.[19]

So, Rothbard argues, that while a man's power of action is limited, because it is always limited by nature, these limitations are not a curtailment of liberty.

What are we to make of this argument? One has to accept, I think that the account is partly correct, but fails to do justice to the great complexity of the relationship between freedom and power or ability.

First of all, let us look at the value of liberty as understood by the neo-liberal. Why is it valuable to be free from coercion? Hayek gives us two answers to this question. One is the instrumental one – that if we are free from coercion, we shall be able to make the best use of our share of dispersed fragmented knowledge in the situations in which we find ourselves. Freedom facilitates our ability to utilize knowledge. The second reason seems to be less instrumental. If we are free from coercion, then we are able to pursue our coherent plan of life and in so doing utilize the knowledge and experiences gained through the previous instrumental justification of freedom. Each of these reasons for finding freedom valuable involves an idea of what we are *able* to do if we are free from coercion. So the value of liberty in human life is linked indissolubly to the idea of what being free will *enable* us to do. If the value of freedom involves the idea of what being free enables us to do, is it possible to regard freedom and ability as categorically different? There is an argument here based upon a Wittgensteinian theory of meaning that the circumstances in which a concept is acquired become *criteria* for the use of such a concept. If we learn why liberty is valuable to us by considering what we are able to do when we are free, then we cannot detach the idea of liberty from that of ability.[20]

Now, of course, it might be said that an argument about the *value* of freedom is quite different from an account of what *constitutes* freedom. For Hayek, however, things are not as simple as that. First of all, it has to be recognized that Hayek completely neglects to focus on the role that ability or power play in his account of why freedom is valuable, but beyond this it is arguable that Hayek believes there to be a necessary or a logical link between freedom and ability in terms of the *nature* and not just the *value* of liberty. If this is so, then it would not in fact be possible to establish a categorical distinction between freedom and ability or power. So what is the argument? On the pure theory of negative liberty discussed earlier which, as we saw Hayek – mistakenly in Rothbard's opinion – rejected, it was perfectly possible to produce a non-moralized account of freedom. This was possible for two reasons.

Firstly, the account of coercion is purely physically identified and does not, as we say, involve any reference to the desires or the scale of values adopted by the person coerced.

Secondly, freedom is not understood in terms of whether or not I desire to do an action that I am free to do. I am still free in relation to X whether or not I have any desire or interest in doing X. These two aspects of pure negative liberty mean that such a conception can, in a literal sense, be regarded as *demoralized.*

This is not the case with Hayek's conception and it is arguable that his moralized notion of liberty involves an account of ability and also basic desires and needs.

This seems clear enough in the case of his account of coercion. Freedom is the absence of coercion and this logically depends upon the characterization of coercion. For Hayek though coercion means that an individual is not able to do various things such as follow a coherent plan of his or her own, or is only able to do this at greater cost than prevailed before the coercive act. It is, therefore, not the case for Hayek that he can give an account of freedom which distinguishes it clearly from ability and power. To this can be added the point made in the monopoly in the oasis example discussed earlier that Hayek has to assume some account of general goods which include basic needs, values, and desires to explain his account of coercion and thus of liberty.

What we need to do here is to say that instead of claiming that freedom and ability or power are categorically different we should rather focus on the nature of their interrelationship, and in doing this we can bring back into the picture Hayek's own views about the role of intention. If we say that A is disabled from doing *Y* we need to know the source and cause of this disability before determining whether it is a sheer inability and not a restriction on freedom or a disability that is caused by the intentional action of another. If my aim is to play my cello tonight in a string quartet and you have stolen it, then I am no longer able to play my music and this is a restriction on liberty caused by your action. If however, I am prevented from playing in the quartet because I lack the musical ability and the lack is not the result of intentional action, then it is a sheer disability rather than a restriction on liberty. As I have already said some of these issues about intention will be discussed further in Chapter 11 on social justice.

For the moment, however, the point can be made that we need a more subtle understanding of the relationship between freedom and ability or power than Hayek and Rothbard have provided. One way of putting this point would be to say that for the question of the liberty of A to do *X* to become relevant, there has to be a generalized ability of people to do *X*. It makes no sense to ask whether or not we are free to jump from Oxford to New York since there is no such generalized ability to do this. Once there is a generalized ability to do *X*, then the question of whether A is free or unfree to do *X* will become relevant and the answer will depend on whether or not A is coerced, and if so, his or her ability to do *X* will be intentionally restricted by that coercion, then A will be unfree to do *X*. Hence a generalized ability to do *X* is a necessary condition of determining whether A is free or unfree to do *X*. If a generalized ability is a necessary condition of determining freedom in relation to *X*, then freedom and ability cannot be categorically different.[21]

If these points are valid, however, then Hayek's thought can be taken in a much more social democratic direction. As we have already seen in relation to the oasis example basic needs are critical to autonomy and the ability to act autonomously. If there is a generalized ability to follow a coherent plan of life (central to Hayek's account of liberty), then we have to enquire into whether the inability of person A to do this is the result of intentional action or not. The question of whether and how goods relating to those abilities are to be distributed will depend crucially on arguments from neo-liberals against the idea of social or distributive justice, which will be discussed in Chapter 11. What seems clear though is that they cannot be blocked by arguments about the categorical distinction between freedom, ability, and power.

Freedom is essential to the neo-liberal ideal of the rule of law. I hope that I have given strong reasons that the issue of what constitutes freedom and coercion is much more complex than neo-liberals are prepared to acknowledge.

NOTES

1. Hayek, F. A. (1960). *The Constitution of Liberty*. London: Routledge and Kegan Paul, p. 138.
2. Hayek, F. A. *The Constitution of Liberty*, p. 138.
3. Hayek, F. A. *The Constitution of Liberty*, p. 12.
4. Hayek, F. A. *The Constitution of Liberty*, p. 139.
5. Hayek, F. A. *The Constitution of Liberty*, p. 15.
6. As Murray Rothbard trenchantly points out in *The Ethics of Liberty* (2002), New York: New York University Press, chapter 28.
7. Rothbard, M. *The Ethics of Liberty*, p. 228.
8. Taylor, C. (1985). 'What's Wrong with Negative Liberty?', in *Philosophical Papers, Vol. 2: Philosophy and Human Values*, Cambridge: Cambridge University Press, chapter 8.
9. Hayek, F. A. *The Constitution of Liberty*, p. 21.
10. Hayek, F. A. *The Constitution of Liberty*, p. 21.
11. Hayek, F. A. *The Constitution of Liberty*, p. 140.
12. Hayek, F. A. *The Constitution of Liberty*, p. 140.
13. Green, T. H. (1888). 'Liberal Legislation and Freedom of Contract', in *T. H. Green Collected Works, Vol. 3*, ed. L. Nettleship. London: Longmans, p. 365ff.
14. Hayek, F. A. *The Constitution of Liberty*, p. 136.
15. Hayek, F. A. *The Constitution of Liberty*, p. 137.
16. Hayek, F. A. *The Constitution of Liberty*, p. 137.

17. Steiner, H. (1974). 'Individual Liberty', *Proceedings of the Aristotelian Society.*
18. Sen, A. (1999). *Development as Freedom.* Oxford: Oxford University Press.
19. Rothbard, M. *The Ethics of Liberty*, p. 42.
20. See S. N. Hampshire (1960). *Feeling and Expression.* London: H. K. Lewis for University College London, p. 18.
21. This sort of argument is called by philosophers a transcendental argument. On this point see Strawson, P. F. (2008). *Scepticism and Naturalism.* London: Routledge and Kegan Paul, p. 16ff.

11

Social Justice and Neo-liberalism: A Critique

We now need to turn to a proper analysis of the neo-liberal critique of social justice. This is of great importance firstly because it goes to the heart of their views about the role of the state in a modern society; and secondly because it involves a number of large claims about the market and the role of individuals and collective responsibility. In many ways the issue of social justice and its ramifications for freedom, rights, the role of government, and the market is the central fault line between neo-liberalism and social democracy.

We shall however begin by looking at the relationship between freedom and social justice. It will be recalled from Chapters 3 and 10 that Hayek wanted to resist the idea that there is any kind of analytical connection between freedom and ability because as he saw very clearly this would lead, and did lead historically, to a justification of social or distributive justice in terms of liberty. If liberty equals ability and if someone lacks the means to be able to do something, thus making him or her unfree to do it, then there is a case in terms of equal liberty for a redistribution of resources and the provision of goods to increase that individual's liberty. As we have seen however, the neo-liberal approach to the understanding of the relationship between freedom and ability lacks subtlety and neo-liberals have not established the claim that there is a categorical difference between being free and being able to do something. In addition, in Hayek's case (and for this he is criticized by other liberal thinkers) he does argue in the well in the oasis example that certain kinds of action when an individual does not have the resources to meet his or her needs can be coercive which does mean therefore that having the resources to meet such needs impinges critically upon liberty. If there are a set of generic, or in Rawlsian terms, primary goods, these goods are necessary to pursue any other sorts of goods and which among other things meet basic needs, and if such goods are essential to not only the exercise of freedom, but to the nature of freedom since not to have them renders one liable to coercion (i.e. the opposite of freedom), then in a society with a commitment to equal liberty there are going to be questions about the distribution of such goods – or about social justice. However, even if one did not want to go so far as to claim that such generic goods are essential to liberty as opposed to being crucial in its exercise, it still follows that there is an indissoluble link between liberty and social justice.

Neo-liberals have, however, wanted to blunt the claims of social justice by arguing that injustice can arise only out of intentional human action, and that while individual market transactions are obviously intentional, the aggregate outcomes of markets are not. So, if in the so-called distribution of resources in a market someone is left without generic or primary goods, this is not injustice because it is not the result of anyone's intention. Therefore, it is argued while the state has a duty to secure justice, this should be understood as securing the conditions of mutual non-coercion and not as some kind of collective responsibility for the provision of basic goods since their absence is not a failure of justice.

The first thing to note about this argument is that in light of the earlier point about freedom and resources, and how the lack of the latter can be a cause of coercion, even a commitment to law and justice as being concerned with mutual non-coercion can in fact lead naturally to a concern with the distribution of generic or primary goods.

This is crucially important for the issue of social justice and the rule of law. Law for neo-liberals should be concerned with mutual non-coercion and should not prescribe particular ends. However, to recognize the relationship between freedom and primary or generic goods does not necessarily breach such a principle of the rule of law. The law could confer access to generic goods without its prescribing particular ends since these are the goods necessary for the pursuit of any end. After all, Hayek himself argues that coercion occurs when one cannot follow a coherent plan of life because the 'data' of a previous action is under the control of another. The law's job is to prevent this, but it does it in the service of autonomy – following a coherent plan of life. This is a general end so it does not contravene the principle of the rule of law. All that I am suggesting is that if we accept that certain goods are essential for autonomy, then they will be compatible with the rule of law in the crucial respects: They will be essential for mutual non-coercion and will not be end- or goal- or purpose-specific; other than in facilitating autonomy.

It is, however, the argument about intention and markets on which I want to concentrate. The argument, used to resist the idea that there can be collective responsibility for outcomes when these outcomes are unintended. In this sense they are like the weather – naturalistic sorts of happenings about which questions about justice are inappropriate. Let us accept first of all that market outcomes are not intended. Nevertheless, they can in broad terms be *foreseeable* and *predictable.* If they are foreseeable, then it is perfectly legitimate to argue that we can be morally responsible for the foreseeable, if unintended, consequences of action. This is certainly so in relation to individual action. If it were not so, then there would be no crime of manslaughter. In manslaughter the death of the individual is not intended, but is foreseeable as a consequence of the sequence of actions or omissions involved or could have been regarded as foreseeable by a reasonable person. Therefore, if market outcomes are foreseeable, even if unintended, there can be collective moral responsibility for the consequences, and thus it is perfectly possible to criticize the outcomes in terms of their injustice. They may, like the weather, be predictable in that misfortunes are likely to fall the heaviest on those least able to bear such burdens. Those groups in society which are best equipped with resources, economic knowledge, and entrepreneurial skills are still liable to be the groups most likely to benefit from impersonal forces of the market. The impersonal market does not distribute its benefits and burdens in a wholly random way.[1] Such outcomes may be unintended, but if they are foreseeable, then there can be space for collective moral concern and responsibility for their outcomes.

However, we need to address the question of whether or not market outcomes are foreseeable. Neo-liberal thinkers tend to deny this claim, and Hayek constantly writes that the outcomes of markets are neither intended nor foreseen. However, it is not at all clear that this is a coherent position. After all, the economic liberals have been arguing for the past thirty years that extending markets into new areas would produce all sorts of benefits: increased supply, lower prices, greater efficiency, and the like compared with the public sector. Therefore, it could hardly be said that in a *macro* sense market outcomes are in principle unforeseeable since market liberals have been trading on the claimed likely outcomes to justify the extension of markets.

In addition, there is a point made by Amartya Sen in *Development as Freedom*, when he argues that it is impossible to understand how the market economy would be able to operate if people did not have some sense of the predictability of outcomes. As he argues in explicitly criticizing Hayek:

> It is not so much that some causal consequences are unintended, but that causal analysis can make the effects reasonably predictable. Indeed, the butcher may predict that exchanging meat for money not only benefits him, but also the consumer (the buyer of the meat), so that the relationship can be expected to work on both sides and is thus sustainable. An unintended consequence may not be unpredictable, and much depends on this fact. Indeed, the confidence of each party in the continuation of such market relations rests specifically on such predictions being made or being implicitly assumed.[2]

Therefore, for these two reasons it is probably not a coherent view and certainly not a view that can help to secure the sustainability of the market economy to believe that market outcomes are unforeseeable and unpredictable.

So given that this general principle is true, what kinds of predictions about the market economy are most salient for the idea of social justice? It is my view that those who enter the market with the fewest skills and the least resources will in fact end up with least at the outcome stage. There is a vast amount of evidence to justify this claim and this does seem to be a foreseeable outcome of the market, generalizing on the empirical evidence that we have.[3] So if these outcomes are foreseeable, then it is perfectly legitimate to argue that there is collective responsibility for this and that the results are unjust. This is particularly the case if generic or primary goods are subject to market forces and individuals are disabled in their access to them.

Of course, there still leaves a very large and controversial question unanswered: What should be done to rectify the injustice and in particular whether there should be redistribution at the outcome stage which would have to be based upon some notion of equality of result, or whether the rectification should come at the input stage when people enter the market in terms of enhancing their skills, knowledge, and capabilities? We shall discuss this question when we turn more specifically to the discussion of equality. An important issue for the moment is that all the evidence supports the view that in the round those who enter the market with least will leave it with least and that the foreseeability of this when there are things that could be done to rectify the position makes it a social injustice.

It is worth remarking in passing that some market liberals such as Michael Novak reject this argument, claiming that it is only if a specific outcome is foreseeable for an identified individual that this claim would have merit.[4] This objection is linked to the thesis of methodological individualism espoused by some market liberals. This is the thesis that statements about social wholes, whether they are about markets, groups, or classes, have to be resolvable into sets of statements about the behaviour of individuals. Only individuals and their behaviour can be observed; social entities cannot and therefore, to be meaningful, talk about such entities must be capable of being translated into statements about individuals. Leaving aside this controversial metaphysical theory, those who espouse it must accept that it undermines their very own case for the extension of markets. For example, the market liberal does not justify a freer market in the private-rented sector by considering its outcome on each separate individual in that sector, but rather justifies it by the claimed beneficial effect on the generality of tenants who remain wholly anonymous in the claim. If such a macro argument is legitimate in the case of arguments for the extension of markets, it is perfectly legitimate to use similar types of claims in relation to the outcomes of markets and thus the scope of responsibility that we have for the market sector and the consequences of the responsibility for justice and injustice.

It is also doubtful in any case whether we should accept the foundational neo-liberal argument here on which everything else turns, namely that justice and injustice depend upon intentional action. On this view, natural processes which are unintended cannot cause injustice. Therefore a child blown into a pond by the wind has suffered misfortune not injustice. The effects of drought are unfortunate but not injustices. The responses that are called for in each case are acts of charity and compassion not collectively inspired responses to injustice since no injustice has been caused because these are natural and unintended processes. Such acts of charity and compassion are inherently discretionary. Those who are beneficiaries of such acts are lucky and they do not have a right to the performance of such an act. Similarly, if market outcomes are not intended, they cannot produce injustice. If there is poverty as the result of the operation of the market, then that too is a matter for charity and benevolence and not for collective action by the state. The poor person does not have a right to have his or her position remedied.

However, things are not as simple as that. This is so for two reasons.

First of all it can be argued that justice and injustice are logically related to our response to a situation, not just how a situation arose (i.e. whether or not it was the result of intentional action). This point is well made by Sen who argues:

> Why should our concern stop at only protecting negative freedoms rather than be involved in what people actually do. Should one be under an obligation to save the person who has been pushed into the river but not the person who has fallen in?[5]

We do not in general believe that how a situation arose and whether or not it was the result of an impersonal and unintended process removes the issue of justice from the situation. If the situation, even if caused by an impersonal force, can in fact be remedied at no comparable cost to those doing the remedying, and if the situation has a clear negative impact on a generic good – like the good of life itself, in the example given – then not to undertake the remedy would be a failure of justice. Therefore, to take another example, someone is born with a genetic defect which is the result of a random and impersonal process, the effect of this genetic defect is an impairment in the capacity for personal development, and there is a remedy available for this defect. Surely we would argue that what was at stake here is an issue of justice rather than charity, and we would not regard the issue of justice as being irrelevant just because the situation had arisen through an impersonal and unintended process.

Additionally, part of the process of civilization has been the assumption of responsibility by human beings for what were previously regarded as natural phenomena. This point will become very important in the future with greater human control over disease and the sources of disease, for example, in our genetic make-up. These will no longer be regarded just as natural misfortunes if we are able to do something about them whether in terms of prevention or cure. If diseases, and particularly genetic diseases, are to be regarded as natural and unintended and thus not giving rise to injustices, although we might be able to prevent them or cure them, this would put issues to do with their prevention and cure outside the boundaries of social justice and collective responsibility but this is an absurd claim as it stands. Hence as Stuart Hampshire writes:

> The ground for hope is the thought that the sphere of political action may be gradually extended as more of the great evils, such as starvation and poverty are moved from the column headed 'natural misfortunes' into the column headed 'political failures'. This has regularly happened in the past.[6]

This final point is very important because it is part of the further political critique of the idea of social justice that it leads to all sorts of unsustainable demands upon collective political action and involves financial costs which are by their nature out of control. We shall address this point more directly in the next section.

It might be argued, as indeed it has been argued by Jeremy Shearmur,[7] that at least in the case of Hayek a good deal of this case has in fact been conceded. In *The Constitution of Liberty* Hayek argues in favour of the collective provision and financing of a set of basic goods. I will refer to two passages which I shall quote at length since they are of capital importance. The first passage is from *Law, Legislation and Liberty: The Mirage of Social Justice*:

> There is no reason why in a free society government should not assure all protection against severe deprivation in the form of an assured minimum income or a floor below which nobody need to descend. To enter into such an insurance against extreme misfortune may be in the interests of us all; or it might be felt to be a clear moral duty of all to assist, within the organised community, those who cannot help themselves. Such a uniform minimum income provided outside the market to all those who, for any reason, are unable to earn in the market an adequate maintenance, this need not lead to a restriction of freedom or a conflict with the rule of law.[8]

and

> All modern governments have made provision for the indigent, unfortunate and disabled and have concerned themselves with health and the dissemination of knowledge. There is no reason why the volume of these pure public services should not increase with the general growth of wealth. There are common ends that can only be satisfied by collective action and which can be thus provided for without restricting individual liberty. It can hardly be denied that, as all grow richer, the minimum subsistence which the community has always provided for those who cannot look after themselves, and which can be provided outside the market, will continually rise and that government may usefully, and without doing any harm, assist or even lead in such endeavours.[9]

These passages raise interesting questions for a neo-liberal, particularly since Hayek does not himself offer much by way of a moral or theoretical justification in favour of these positions. First of all, given that these are to be non-market, collectively provided resources directed at particular people – those who cannot look after themselves – how are the laws conferring such benefits on those individuals to be written if, as Hayek claims in the first passage quoted, such a proposal does not compromise the rule of law. How are we to distinguish between the type of provision Hayek endorses and regards as being compatible with the rule of law and programmes and policies inspired by social justice which he regards as outside the rule of law and, indeed, incompatible with it? Second, how are the administrative rules governing the allocation of such resources to be interpreted by bureaucrats, and in particular how are they going to be able to distinguish in non-arbitrary ways between those who can help themselves in the market and those who cannot or have not? Surely Hayek's own position here gives at least as much discretionary power to administrators and managers of services as any regime of social justice and what makes the former compatible with the rule of law and the latter not? Why should this scheme be financed out of presumably compulsory taxation or insurance (recall he calls it a public good) if the appropriate response to those in need is altruism, charity, and benevolence – all of which are discretionary virtues and indeed are destroyed by compulsion, rather than by an appeal to justice which as what he calls a common end could underpin collective and compulsory provision. Also we need to know, but we are not told, why uniquely such a form of provision is compatible with freedom on Hayek's understanding of it, whereas schemes inspired by social justice involve limitations on freedom. The other philosophical incoherence in Hayek's position is that how something has come about is supposed to be central to moral responsibility as we saw earlier. However, in the first passage cited Hayek regards meeting the needs of the worst off as a moral duty without any explanation of how the lack of assets, capacities, or abilities which have put the worst off in this position have in fact come about. Hayek is here detaching his idea of a collective moral duty, a positive duty, compulsorily enforced from any account at all of how it has come about that those to whom he believes the duty is held are in the position they are in.

It is also worth pointing out that he completely fails to take into account the views of what might be called rights-based neo-liberalism, particularly those based on property rights. If the position of the worst off is not unjust because it did not come about by one individual intentionally depriving another of crucial resources by an act of injustice such as fraud or deception, why should the property rights of the rest of society be attached in order to provide a collective fund for the worst off?

It seems that Hayek still wants to argue that his approach to collective provision can be clearly differentiated from one inspired by social justice. He argues that there is all the difference in the world between a form of government action to provide a safety net for the less well off and an attempt by government to arrange people's relative position in terms of a preferred principle of social justice. But is this argument convincing?

The reasons to think otherwise include the following:

Part of the critique of social justice was that the criteria of distribution are controversial and contestable. Yet in his endorsement of the social safety net, it is not at all clear that Hayek can escape his and other neo-liberals' views about the contestability of values. In Hayek's depiction of the social safety net, contestable values enter in the situation in number of ways.

1. As Hayek sees it, the role of the safety net is to protect the position of those who lack ability or who cannot make a living in the market. So it does seem that some conception of merit or desert must play a role here – namely that those in this situation deserve the protection of the safety net. It also seems quite likely that the judgement as to who are in a position to receive the benefit of a safety net is bound to involve judgements about deservingness. There would surely have to be a differentiation between those genuinely unable to earn subsistence in the market and those who would prefer to receive the benefit (however low) and not work even though they were able to do so. It is very difficult to see that issues of desert are avoidable. It cannot be resolved by means of a minimum income (which Hayek floats in the first passage quoted)

because as the literature on basic income amply reveals, there are profound questions about desert and entitlement. Should a basic income be paid to all on an unconditional basis including to those who could work but prefer to freeride? My point is not to try to resolve the problem one way or the other but rather to point out that it seems inevitable that unless the safety net applied to all as an unconditional basis, it will have to make an appeal to ideas about desert. Given that Hayek and many neo-liberals see the contestability of ideas about desert as fatal to the coherence of social justice, they cannot consistently argue that in the safety net case these contestable issues do not arise. The neo-liberal cannot argue that these problems can be dealt with by political means: deliberation, political judgement, majority voting, etc., because these processes could also be invoked to deal with the problem in the context of social justice.

2. Value issues also enter in relation to needs. Again it has been a typical argument of economic liberals that 'needs', like desert, are contestable. Take the passage cited from John Gray in Chapter 4 as a good example of this. However, in *The Constitution of Liberty*, Hayek talks about 'common needs that can be satisfied only collective action and which can be thus provided for without infringing individual liberty'. My point here is not that Hayek thinks that there is this link between liberty and the satisfaction of common needs, so much as the fact that Hayek is seemingly invoking some idea of an objective or at least intersubjectively argued conception of need. Such a conception seems to be absolutely crucial for Hayek's attempt to distinguish between a safety net and social justice. If there are a set of basic needs which can in principle be satiated, then this might allow a distinction to be drawn between a limited level of provision to meet such needs and a concern with social justice which in Hayek's view is focused on relative positions.

However, this is a very difficult position to maintain for the following reasons:

(i) Common needs are not in fact all that easy to identify at least in terms of what is required to satisfy them. Food, shelter, and education – all of which might quite plausibly be regarded as common needs – are all inextricably linked to norms when it comes to be question of what level of satisfaction is required as being adequate to meet such needs. There are also common needs which seem plausibly to be genuine needs but can hardly be satisfied by collective provision. We all have a need for love and for sexual gratification but these cannot (in the case of love) or ought not (in the case of sexual gratification) be met by collective provision. Then normative questions arise in respect of what will satisfy basic needs and how, if at all, they can be satisfied by collective action. If such norms are invoked by Hayek because he believes that they are a set of norms shared across society, then this is rather at odds with his own subjectivism and also with his rejection of such a degree of social, moral, or political consensus in the critique of social justice.

(ii) Now it may be that Hayek believes that needs are both obvious and straightforwardly satiable, but if he does believe this he does seem to be at odds with a good deal of neo-liberal thought. Neo-liberals both political and in academic arguments have tended to take the view that needs are open-ended and therefore the claims of need can always be 'bid up' because there is no obvious stopping point. This seems obviously to be the case in respect of health and education. This point about the open-endedness of needs can be linked with another neo-liberal theme already discussed, namely the public choice explanation of the growth of public bureaucracies. On this view, briefly put, the argument is that public bureaucrats are utility maximizers like everyone else whether in the market or the public sector. Utility maximization leads to an increase in the size, responsibilities, and therefore, very likely, the salaries of bureaucrats. One way in which the scope and responsibilities of a welfare bureaucracy would be increased would be by seeking to bid up the scope of needs that their bureaucracy is set up to satisfy. Therefore, the open-endedness of needs plus the utility maximizing tendencies of officials could well lead to a situation in which needs could come to be seen as insatiable and public responsibility and resources essentially without a limit. I doubt very much whether Hayek sees needs as easily satiable because in the passages quoted earlier he endorses the view that as a society grows richer, so could the resources being put into common needs increase. Why would such a real increase be necessary if needs were satiable?

Hayek does not deal with the difficult issue identified by some neo-liberal or libertarian thinkers, namely why should needs be in some kind of special moral category such that the recognition of the need confers duties on others, which is not the case with plain wants or preferences? We expect people to pay to meet the wants or preferences so why not needs? Or is it as once stated by a neo-liberal economist: 'A need is a want that you are not prepared to pay for.' The issue is: Why does need play the role that it does in the justification of collective provision usually without having to pay for it? Again, an appeal could be made to building a social consensus on such matters. That would hardly work for a thinker such as Hayek since social consensus is debarred as a consideration for those whose political preference is for social justice rather than a much more limited, needs-based conception of the role of the state. Why consensus can be thought to be available in the latter case but not in the former is both unexplained and indeed implausible.

Why should needs play a role in distribution as they clearly do for Hayek as a way of identifying a social minimum? We need to know why some needs are more important than others, and why they are so important they can place other members of society under an obligation to pay taxes to meet them. After all, Nozick's argument is that when things get produced in the economy, they have producers' entitlements built into them. Yet given that Hayek is arguing for collective provision, which might always increase with the wealth of society to meet basic needs, he is, in the view of a thinker like Nozick, neglecting this fundamental point about entitlement. For Nozick, the entitlement cannot be overridden by an appeal to the interests of society. In some respects, of course, this position reflects something of Hayek's own view about the nature of appeals to society. Recall the passage quoted earlier in which he rails against treating the society as a kind of deity to which we complain when our sense of our socially or economically just deserts is disappointed. Yet, from a Nozickian perspective, Hayek is himself implicitly appealing to the interests of society to justify constraining its members and their entitlements in such a way as to provide resources for those who cannot secure their own position in the market. This would seem to be inconsistent with his rejection of such an appeal in respect of social justice. While Hayek, like Nozick, is a methodological individualist he does not, like Nozick, use his individualism to provide the basis of a set of inviolable rights and side constraints on behaviour. While his appeal to society to justify basic welfare provision may infringe his own strict views about the meaning of the word 'society' – his approach to this issue reveals a much more utilitarian approach to these questions than is to be found in Nozick.

Nevertheless, it still remains for the critic of neo-liberalism to make the case for meeting needs given that Hayek has not done this and given Nozick's argument to the contrary. Such an approach would have to explain the centrality of the idea of needs and the moral grounding that it gives to the idea of collective responsibility to meet such needs and issues of social justice involved in the allocation of such resources.

The centrality of need can be established, it seems to me, in Hayek's own terms. He wants to see a free society in which each individual is able to follow a coherent plan of life and the control of what he calls the 'basic data' of action by another is coercion. So, coercion is the infringement of the capacity to follow such a coherent plan of life. However, as we saw earlier, the lack of certain set of essential goods, when these are denied by the intentional actions of others, is coercive since such goods are necessary for such a form of autonomous life. As we have seen, however, intentional restriction of access to such goods is not the only way coercion can occur as the result of human actions. If such a result is foreseeable, whether or not it is intentional, then in so far as this is the result of human action in the market, it is coercive. So there is a case for arguing that the goods relating to those generic needs necessary for living an autonomous life gives such goods their central moral importance. The lack of such goods either through intentional or foreseeable action gives rise to a claim that there is a collective duty to meet such needs and ensure that they are satisfied. Therefore, it seems perfectly possible to produce a case for collective responsibility to supply the generic goods of agency which would include the satisfaction of generic sorts of needs. As we saw in the discussion of Hayek, there is bound to be controversy about the level at which needs and other generic goods should be met. However, short of the libertarian position in which the state has no positive duties at all, this is going to be an endemic problem and it certainly is central to a position like Hayek's as we have seen. The neo-liberal, however, is hampered in the response that can be made to this because of the neo-liberal downgrading of the importance of democratic politics as opposed to markets. The obvious answer to this problem is that there has to be democratic debate against a recognition of the background of scarcity in order, if possible, to arrive at a reasonable consensus as to the level of provision and if such consensus cannot be attained, then the level has to be fixed by majority vote.

Before we leave the point about the moral importance of the idea of social justice it is perhaps worth noting that in the second volume of Hayek's masterwork *Law, Legislation and Liberty*, which is interestingly subtitled *The Mirage of Social Justice*, he argues very openly that despite his own view that social justice is an empty concept it may nevertheless be that markets will depend on the false belief, as he sees it, that market outcomes are distributed according to just principles. Indeed a market may be unsustainable and its legitimacy undermined if it is seen in all its Hayekian bleakness uninformed by moral principle except in terms of process. This is what Hayek says:

> [I]t is therefore a real dilemma to what extent we ought to encourage in the young the belief that when they really try they will succeed, or should we rather emphasise that inevitably some unworthy will succeed and some worthy fail . . . and whether without such erroneous beliefs the large numbers will tolerate actual differences in rewards which will be based only partly on achievement and partly on mere chance.[10]

As Hayek points out a good deal of the history of economic theorizing about the market has rested on the assumption that it rewards desert and is thus socially just according to a desert-based view of social justice. Hayek's emphasis on the unintended and random consequences of markets shatters this link between virtue and the market. Can the market sustain its legitimacy if it is seen so much to be the site of chance and luck? Amongst theorists of capitalism Hayek is not alone in such fears. They are shared for example by Irving Kristol in his influential essay 'When Virtue Loses All Her Loveliness'.[11]

This is very important point. If it is right to argue that the case for legitimacy and, indeed, the extension of markets has to depend on their foreseeable and predictable consequences, and if Sen is right in arguing that the whole basis of economic exchange involves some degree of reciprocity based upon predictability and foreseeability, and if Hayek is right in thinking that a false belief in social justice may be central to the legitimacy of the market economy – a belief that is rendered false because of the unintended and unforeseen nature of market transactions – then it is difficult to believe that the neo-liberal position has any force in terms of arguing for the legitimacy of markets since that legitimacy and sustainability depends on exactly the aspects of social morality that Hayek denies! This, of course, is not to deny the centrality and vital importance of markets. It does mean, however, that the theories such as Hayek's and those of economic liberals in general cannot provide convincing account of the *moral* basis of the market economy. We have to recognize that markets are human creations and that they are embedded in different cultures and different moral practices. They are not amoral or demoralized technical devices. Once they are seen in this way, then it is perfectly possible to develop the moral space for thinking about our collective responsibility in respect of the market order whether in terms of freedom or of social justice. The market is not part of nature, it is part of the human order and as such is alterable. As Stuart Hampshire argues, this has been a central insight of the social democratic or socialist tradition when he argues that '[t]he essence of socialism as a moral and political theory, discernible in all its many varieties, is the commitment to political agency far beyond the domain recognised in earlier centuries and in other political philosophies'.[12] Freedom, the capacity for agency, resources, opportunities, social justice, and the market are, despite the best efforts of neo-liberals, inextricably intertwined.

It has been a theme of this book that the issue of social justice is the major dividing line between the neo-liberals and social democrats and there is a clear way of fixing this point by referring to the work of C. A. R Crosland, a paradigmatic twentieth-century social democrat, and contrasting it with that of an opponent of social justice such as Hayek. In his Fabian Tract, *Social Democracy in Europe*,[13] Crosland argued that the social democrat is committed to improving the relative position of the worst-off members of society by utilizing the fiscal dividends of economic growth to achieve this. At the same time it was necessary to secure the absolute position, or the real incomes, of the better off by using the same dividends. This was partly an issue of political principle: if the absolute position of the better off were to be maintained and the relative position of the worst off were to be improved, then there would be an improvement in equality because the relative position of the poor would be improved vis-à-vis the rich. It was also a matter of political strategy in that in order to mobilize a political majority for improving the position of the worst off in society the absolute position of the better off had to be protected otherwise they would not vote for egalitarian measures. The neo-liberal position is the reverse of this both in terms of principle and in terms of strategy. In the neo-liberal view what matters to the worst-off members of society is not their *relative* but rather their *absolute* position. What matters to the poor person is whether he or she is better off in real terms this year than he or she was last year, not whether the gap between the worst off and the rest of society has increased. It is absolute improvements and not a concern with relative positions that matters in the view of the neo-liberal. It is the view of the neo-liberal that the absolute or real position of the worst off will in fact be improved by the trickle-down or echelon advance effect of the market. At the same time, it is important to allow inequality to increase, that is to say allowing the incomes and resources at the top of the income scale to grow for two reasons: the first is because the economy needs incentives as part of the necessary conditions for the economic dynamism that will increase trickle-down effects; secondly because of freedom as non-coercion – if someone is capable of earning more in non-coercive ways in the market there is no reason to stop that person from doing so. In the neo-liberal view, the Croslandite strategy is fundamentally flawed because the fiscal dividends of growth will not materialize without incentives higher up the income scale. So without growing inequality as a result of this there will be a smaller pot for distribution. Therefore not only is social democracy flawed in terms of principle, but also as a strategy because the economic growth on which it rests will not in fact be created as a direct negative consequence of this egalitarian strategy. In addition, the social democratic position is to improve the relative position of the worst off and maintain the absolute position of the better off; whereas the neo-liberal position is just the reverse, to secure the absolute position of the worst off and improve the relative position of the better off. Each strategy implies a different role for the state: in the social democratic view the state utilizing tax receipts either spends that money directly on the worst off or invests it in public expenditure on the assumption that public services differentially improve the position of the worst off; for the neo-liberal, the state has no direct role in this context: the market will both improve the absolute position of the worst off through the trickle-down effect and will also improve the relative position of the better off. The state has a role only in terms of removing those intentionally imposed restrictions on recruitment to positions higher up the income scale.

The social democrat will, however, first of all want to argue that trickle-down effects are not in fact going to be sufficient on their own to play even the limited role assigned to them by the neo-liberal. People have to be able to take advantage of trickle-down effects. They cannot just be passive recipients; otherwise those benefits will pass them by and not have the effect of improving their real or absolute position. In order to be able to take advantage of trickle-down effects, people have to have the capabilities to do so. In the neo-liberal view all that needs to happen is that the economy is growing and that there are no imposed restrictions on individuals' freedom to engage in economic activity. There is no positive duty of the state beyond that. If, however, the social democratic position is right, and people have to be capable of taking advantage of trickle-down effects, then it will follow that a neo-liberal government assigning special importance to trickle-down effects as the way of improving the absolute position of the less well off will have to be concerned with capabilities. These capabilities are first of all individual ones: the level of skill, education, health, and so forth to be able to take advantage of these effects – what are these days called 'employability skills', without which advantage cannot be taken of such effects. Therefore, even in the neo-liberal view there is a strong case for investment in employability skills to improve the capabilities of the worst off. At the same time, the social democrat will also argue that human capital and such skills cannot grow on a purely individual level, but are likely to be impeded in their development by poor neighbourhoods and communities in which work skills, for example, have been lost over time and there are peer group pressures operating against individual self-improvement. Therefore, in terms of capacity-building for individuals there is a case also for investment in social capital to increase the receptivity of communities to trickle-down effects when and where they occur. This cannot just be left to the removal of restrictions on freedom, but requires a positive commitment by government to invest in both individuals and communities. This, in turn, raises a range of questions about distributive or social justice. First of all if there can be a legitimate positive duty on government to do this?

Then there are bound to be questions about the fairness and justice of different allocations. The neo-liberal can only resist these by arguing that trickle-down effects are not the concern of government beyond securing equal liberty to take advantage of them. If, however, as a strategy to improve the absolute position of the worst off does indeed require investment in social and human capital, then distributive questions will move to the centre of the agenda even on the neo-liberal conception of that agenda. Secondly, the pursuit of such an agenda of strengthening capabilities is likely to presuppose a commitment to an account of generic goods, which, as I have suggested intermittently during this book, are as essential to neo-liberalism as much as they are to social democracy. That is to say government in pursuing investment in both human and social capital is going to have to be guided by an account on what are the generic skills and generic capabilities which are essential to enable people to take advantage of trickle-down effects. Finally, there is the need to consider the impact on relative positions of a more active and positive role for government in investing in individuals and communities to enable them to take advantage of trickle-down effects. Obviously, such investment is going to take taxpayers' money to produce anticipated advantages for the worst off both individually and in terms of the communities of which they are a part. This process, which would have to be ongoing and intergenerational if it is to work effectively, is in fact going to have some impact on the structure of inequality of society. So the reasoning is this: taking advantage of trickle-down effects requires the capacity to do so both individually and at the community level – not just the absence of coercion. The financing of the development of these capabilities is actually likely to have some impact on income at the upper end of the scale, while in fact, even though not intentionally, improving the relative position of the worst off. Therefore, the effect is that if neo-liberals agree that there is need to improve the capacity to take advantage of trickle-down effects, then there is no clear difference both in policy and outcome between the neo-liberal and the social democratic approach. The neo-liberal can only preserve the purity of the distinction between itself and social democracy by rejecting the idea that trickle-down effects have to be facilitated.

Sometimes this is called 'empowering people' – that is empowering them to take advantage of these effects – and I now want to turn to some issues about power and ability. It is sometimes said that markets are empowering and what is meant by this is that the trickle-down effect means that people have resources this year which they did not have the year before. They have more income and more goods and they can do more than they used to do. Is this properly called 'empowerment' or would we better calling it 'enablement'? This question is not just about semantics because the answer will have quite profound implications for our view about the role of the state and about inequality. Let us accept the argument just deployed that people have to be capable of taking advantage of trickle-down effects and that this implies investing in both human and social capital. Would this be best described as empowerment? In order to answer that question we need to think carefully about the nature of power. First of all, we need to draw a distinction between power *over* and power *to*. Power *over* occurs in a situation in which A can get B to do *X* which he would not otherwise do; power *to* occurs when B is able to do something which he wants to do or joins with A in doing something that they both want to do and can only be achieved conjointly. Let us concentrate on power over for the moment. It is arguable that power in the sense of power over is a positional good.[14] That is to say it is a good which cannot be distributed more widely at the same level of value and if it is distributed equally it disappears altogether. Take as the paradigm case of a positional good my standing on tiptoe better to see a procession that is passing. If I am the only person to do this then I get an advantage, but if more people standing in front of me do this, then my advantage declines rapidly and if everyone stands on tiptoe then my advantage disappears altogether. Power *over* is a positional good in this sort of sense.[15] I may be able to increase my power over you but only at your cost. If the power in this sense between us is equalized, then it disappears altogether. So, what has this to do with whether or not markets empower people? Markets cannot increase the supply of positional goods at the same level of value. It can increase the supply of consumer goods like electric fires because the fact that I acquire a 1 kW electric fire does not interfere with or reduce the value of your electric fire to you – you still derive a 1 kW benefit from it. Markets can increase consumer goods at the same level of value but not positional goods. Of course, some goods may be consumer goods but also be goods with positional qualities. Therefore, no doubt when electric fires were first invented, they were a status symbol when few people had them. As they become more widely distributed the status or positional effect of the good declines and is eventually eliminated even though its value as a consumer good – that is to say capable of generating 1 kW of heat – is retained however widely it is distributed. It follows from this that if power over is a positional good which declines in value the more people have it and disappears when it is distributed equally, then in a strict logical sense markets cannot be empowering because they cannot increase the supply and distribution of positional goods at the same level of value. If this is right, then it follows that power in the sense of power over is not something that can be addressed by markets nor can the maldistribution of power in this sense be addressed by markets. The question of who legitimately exercises power over whom has to be a political and not a market question. Clearly it is quite closely linked to issues about coercion that we discussed in Chapter 10 and not only that it involves questions of justice because we cannot just take the present distribution of power as a given and see any attempt to change it as matters for the market rather than government. So the question of who exercises power over whom, and the corollary of who is in a position to coerce whom, becomes very important and it has to be a distributive question because the power of A over B can only be changed by increasing B's power over A. That is to say the issue the distribution of power over is a zero-sum game. B, in the simplified example given, can only win if A loses. There is no way of dealing with this question through markets. Given the connection between power and coercion this is very important for the neo-liberal since they want to achieve a free society in which individuals are free from coercion – part of which is the exercise of power over another – but there has to be a political and not a market answer as to who legitimately exercises power over other persons. The answer to this question will engage with a whole set of issues that neo-liberals have sought to sidestep in favour of markets.

What is the situation in respect of power *to*? In this context to claim that the market is empowering can make more sense in that if it increases the supply of goods and income then an individual may well have more power to do things than he or she had previously. This still, however, takes us back to the issue of the capacity to take advantage of trickle-down effects so that increasing the power of A to do *X* may well imply improving A's capacity as part of the enabling process and this itself will not be an intrinsic part of the market. Therefore, in the context of power to we might say that having the individual power to may well work through markets but only if that individual has capabilities of a generic sort that he or she has not had to rely on the market both to fund and produce. It would certainly be true to claim that taking advantage of trickle-down effects will enable A to do *X* which he or she was not able to do before but as I have suggested the situation in respect of power is more complicated.

This is particularly true if we look at power *to* as it applies to more than one person which may turn out not to be capable of being exercised in markets at all. What I have in mind here is something like a situation in which power in the sense of power to can be increased by collaborative and cooperative action. It may be that one person is relatively powerless to do *X*, but in cooperation with others becomes capable of doing that. In this sense power to is not a positional good because its scope can be increased without lowering its value. On the contrary, in fact, its value may be vastly increased. This sort of power is very difficult if not impossible to exercise in a market because the market rather runs against the idea of cooperative and strategic action. Individuals make their preferences and choices in markets and rarely if ever do this in cooperation within the market. We have to be careful here because it is, of course, possible for consumers to follow a cooperatively agreed policy within the market once they enter it, for example a policy of not buying fruit from South Africa during the apartheid years. The neo-liberal may well argue that this was an effective and cooperative strategic action within the market and was a clear exercise of power to – in this case to contribute to effecting change in that country. It is of course true that people were in fact able to do this but it was a policy agreed outside the market and then acted on within the market. The question the neo-liberal has to answer in the context of the claim that the market empowers people is whether individuals as consumers without having pre-market agreement on a policy could as consumers, without such agreement, have come to such a strategic policy as consumers within a market?

There is a link between power to and power over in the following way. It is arguable that most of the political challenges to power *over* come as the result of cooperative power *to*. Take for example community organization in a community where a local authority or a housing corporation owns the houses and rents them to members of the community. If the owners behave in an over-powerful or coercive way towards those who rent property, then we might say that A (the owner or owners) exercise power over D–Z taken as individuals. As individuals they may have little ability to challenge this exercise of power. If, however, they cooperate they may well increase their power to influence the policy of the owners. At the extreme this may well involve a rent strike which as an action taken by one individual would be unlikely to undermine the power of A but if D–Z cooperate in this, then A is likely to modify or moderate policy. In this sense power *to*, which can be increased, may challenge the legitimacy of power *over* which cannot be increased but only redistributed. These sorts of considerations would also provide the rationale in terms of power which could provide the basis of the response to the neo-liberal critique of both interest groups and unions. The basic point though is that questions of power cannot really be resolved within markets. Rather, markets reflect quite a lot of the distribution of power within society which can be challenged at the political or social level but is difficult and sometimes impossible to challenge within markets.

NOTES

1. See Plant, R. (1984). *Equality, Markets and the State.* London: Fabian Society.
2. Sen, A. (1999). *Development as Freedom.* Oxford: Oxford University Press, p. 357.
3. For a sophisticated approach to this issue see: Marshall, G., Swift, A., and Roberts, S. (1997). *Against the Odds: Social Class and Social Justice in Industrial Societies.* Oxford: The Clarendon Press.
4. In a conversation with the present author at the Institute of Economic Affairs.
5. Sen, A. (1985). 'Rights and Capabilities', in T. Honderich (ed.), *Morality and Objectivity*, London: Routledge and Kegan Paul, p. 137.
6. Hampshire, S. N. (1999). *Justice Is Conflict.* London: Duckworth, p. 48.
7. Shearmur, J. (1996). *Hayek and After: Hayekian Liberalism as a Research Programme.* London: Routledge and Kegan Paul.
8. Hayek, F. A. (1976). *Law, Legislation and Liberty, Vol. 2: The Mirage of Social Justice.* London: Routledge and Kegan Paul. p. 87.
9. Hayek, F. A. (1960). *The Constitution of Liberty.* London: Routledge and Kegan Paul. p. 259.
10. Hayek, F. A. *Law, Legislation and Liberty, Vol. 2: The Mirage of Social Justice*, p. 74.
11. Kristol, I. (1970). 'When Virtue Loses All Her Loveliness', *The Public Interest*, No. 21.
12. Hampshire, S. N. *Justice Is Conflict*, p. 80.
13. Crosland, C. A. R. (1972). *Social Democracy in Europe.* London: Fabian Society.
14. See Hirsch, F. (1977). *The Social Limits to Growth.* London: Routledge and Kegan Paul.
15. I owe this point to a conversation many years ago with John Gray.

12

Neo-liberal Rights: A Wider Perspective

In this chapter we shall focus on the critique of neo-liberal views of rights. This is a very important issue, particularly in terms of understanding the difference between neo-liberalism and social democracy in respect of the rule of law. As we saw in Chapter 5, for many neo-liberals it is in fact a set of negative rights protecting negative liberty that is essential for a *Rechtsstaat.* Equally, many social democrats have argued that there can be legitimate social and economic rights or welfare rights the recognition and legal protection of which would make for a socially more just society and would make the welfare state compatible with the rule of law. On their view, a *sozialer Rechtsstaat* is a feasible political ideal; for the neo-liberal it is a contradiction in terms since there is no way that economic rights can be seen as genuine rights. Clearly the ideas of rights and the rule of law are closely linked and therefore this issue at stake between the neo-liberal and the social democrat is crucial.

I shall consider the issues in that order starting with the argument that positive rights are not genuine rights. So my approach now will be more like an immanent critique – taking standard arguments against social and economic rights and showing either that they are not plausible or that they demonstrate too much from the point of view of their protagonists since these arguments, if they were to be regarded as plausible, would actually undermine what the protagonists of this position would regard as genuine rights, namely civil and political rights.

I want to argue that it is possible to explore some of the characteristics of rights as they are generally conceived, features which, in the view of critics, entail that social and economic rights, including rights to income, cannot be regarded as genuine rights. I shall not seek to develop a general theory of rights because of limitations of space. Rather I shall consider the arguments under the following headings:

1. Rights and liberty
2. Rights, scarcity, and obligation
3. Rights and social justice
4. Rights, needs, and agency.

It is often argued that there is a close connection between rights and liberty, that rights exist and, indeed, are justified because they protect liberty. On the general point, Jules Coleman[1] argues that '[r]ights demarcate a realm of liberty or control. Rights are secured or protected liberties'. Similar points are to be found in Steiner in his essay 'Working Rights',[2] in which he says that rights are 'normative allocations of freedom'. Therefore, if this is a general feature of rights, then a great deal turns on the nature of liberty to be protected. This leads immediately into one of the arguments about the legitimacy or otherwise of social and economic rights. It is argued by many defenders of negative liberty that if rights are to protect negative liberty, then they cannot include social and economic rights. The argument here is that to be free is not to be coerced, that is not to be compelled to do something that one would not otherwise do or compelled to abstain from doing what one would otherwise do. Rights protect people from unjustified coercion and are therefore to be seen as central to the protection of liberty. On this view liberty has to be understood as negative freedom: freedom from compulsion, coercion, interference, the use of force, physical assault, and so forth. Rights protect a domain of freedom and this freedom is classical negative freedom. That is to say rights do not exist to protect so-called positive freedom – the freedom to do things and the associated abilities, capabilities, resources, and opportunities which such freedom would entail. Rights do not protect such sorts of freedom in the view of the critic because such freedoms are essentially misconceived. As we saw in Chapter 3 it is argued by neo-liberals that there has to be a sharp distinction between freedom as freedom from coercion on the one hand, and ability and capability on the other. To be free to do *X* is not the same thing as the ability to do *X*. No one is able to do all that he or she is free to do. I am free to do an indefinitely large number of things, namely those things which I am not prevented from doing by the actions of others and no one is able to do all the actions that a person is not prevented from doing. Thus, the concepts of freedom and ability have to be seen as categorically different. It follows, therefore, that rights which protect liberty have to be distinguished clearly and categorically from the *soi-disant* rights to resources and opportunities which would enhance abilities and capabilities. These are not genuine freedoms and indeed are, at the most, contingent conditions for making genuine freedoms and rights (i.e. negative liberties and negative rights) effective. Rights like liberty are negative. They are forms of protection from interference and coercion. They are not positive, implying rights to resources and opportunities. Social and economic rights including, for example, a right to a basic income would, on this view, not be regarded as genuine or basic rights, but rather as disputable contingent conditions for the exercise of genuine rights. They are matters of public policy rather than constitutional rights.

It does seem, therefore, that a defence of the idea of social and economic rights would have to undertake one or two strategies. The first, to be considered later in the chapter, would be to argue that while rights may well be forms of protection for negative types of liberty they are not exclusively founded on such a set of considerations and that there is a strong case for basing rights on, for example, *needs and abilities* as well as on *liberty*. The second, alternative, approach is to argue that in fact the concept of freedom used by those who argue against social rights is defective and that there is a compelling alternative view of freedom to the strictly negative view propounded by such critics. It is to this approach that I turn first.

The argument of the critic depends upon the view that freedom and ability are categorically distinct, and that this categorical difference blocks any account of positive freedom in terms of ability, capability, resources, and opportunities. These are reasons to doubt this.

In his essay 'Rethinking the Theory of Legal Rights',[3] Coleman argues that in the classical liberal view, the right is the liberty, not the value (i.e. utility) to anyone of having or exercising that liberty. So we must draw a sharp distinction between liberty and the value of liberty. At the best, social and economic rights secure the value of liberty and not liberty itself. The protection of liberty can be constitutionalized in terms of rights; the conditions for the exercise of rights – for example, health, education, and welfare – are matters of policy not constitutional arrangements. The first thing to notice is that such an approach makes the idea of the value of freedom to human beings difficult to explain. Why should I want to be free from coercion? Surely the answer will be that if I am free from coercion, then I shall be able to live a life shaped by my own intentions, goals, and purposes. That is why freedom is valuable to me. However, if the value of freedom is explained in terms of what I am able to do with it, then it becomes quite difficult to maintain that freedom and ability are totally separable (see Chapter 10 for the details of this argument).

This point can be made much tighter. Freedom in the sense of non-coercion is of no value to a stone or a blade of grass. The fact that they are left alone and not interfered with does not mean that this absence of interference is of any value to these things or indeed, that it makes sense to say that they are free. Freedom applies to human beings because they are able to make choices and entertain goals – that is to say to act as *agents*. If this capacity or set of capacities among humans is not just a matter of explaining why freedom is valuable to human beings but also why the category of freedom intelligibly *applies* to them, then it can hardly be claimed that freedom can be understood in the absence of a characterization of the capacity for choice and agency. This point embodies a strong claim, that is freedom can only be made intelligible in terms of a conception of human agency and that in turn such a conception of agency cannot be formulated without reference to human abilities, needs, and capacities. Hence, it cannot be argued that freedom can be defined independently of some account of a basic capacity or capability amongst human beings, namely the capacity for choice and agency. Thus, it follows not only that the value of freedom has to be explained with respect to what freedom enables us to – to live a life shaped by our own goals – but also that freedom is only *meaningful* as a concept if it is linked to some account of choice and agency. This in turn means that the concept of freedom has to be embedded in a normative framework since such a conception of agency, its needs, and capacities is itself going to be a moral one. Obviously this argument is a long way from justifying social and economic rights, but it does have the merit of undermining the idea that freedom and ability are two radically different things, a claim that has been invoked, for example, by Hayek in *The Constitution of Liberty*, to reject any kind of link between liberty and resources. If rights protect freedom and freedom has to be understood in terms of choice and agency, then rights have to protect these capacities. It is through unpacking our understanding of these capacities that we will come to the argument that there can indeed be genuine social rights.

This point can be backed up in other ways too. As we saw in Chapter 10 another way of illustrating the centrality of human agency to an account of liberty, is to argue that a generalized ability to do *X* is a necessary condition of determining whether or not A is free or unfree to do *X*. It is only because there is a general ability to sign cheques or to fly on aircraft that it makes sense to ask whether A is or is not free to undertake these actions. Hence, not only are agency and choice conditions of the meaningfulness of freedom, but also particular examples of generalized human capacities are conditions of determining whether an individual is free or not in respect of exercising those capacities. Again, therefore, it is not possible to maintain a sharp distinction between freedom and ability, capacity, or agency which a strict account of negative freedom and a strict account of negative rights presupposes. If it can be shown that a resource such as income is a generic condition for the exercise of such agency, if this agency is a necessary condition for the intelligibility of the ascription of freedom, and if rights are there to protect such freedom, then a right to such a resource could be seen as a genuine right on this view. It is important to reiterate the point at stake here. It is not that resources are ways of making rights effective or turning nominal rights into effective rights, but rather that such rights are genuine rights on their own terms, and not in terms of being instrumental to the achievement of other (negative) rights.

As we saw in Chapter 11 this point can be further reinforced by taking into account an argument from Charles Taylor. He argues that if the purist account of negative freedom is correct, then the answer to the question of whether country X is freer than country Y will be a purely quantitative one – turning upon the number of rules there are preventing or requiring action in these two different societies. This would then lead to the unbelievable judgement that, given fewer rules, Hoxha's Albania was freer than the United Kingdom. The answer for the proponent of strict negative liberty has to be *quantitative* because otherwise we would be weighting rules not purely in terms of their pure preventing or requiring characteristics but in terms of the types of things which the rules prevented or required. Given that the negative libertarian cannot do this without self-contradiction he or she has to be prepared for a quantitative outcome in terms of judgements about how free two societies are which will produce results that are very difficult to believe. The appropriate point here is that what made the United Kingdom a freer country than Albania is that people were able to do things like emigrate and criticize the government which are regarded as valuable human capacities (and freedoms). What makes these freedoms valuable, and more valuable than others, is that there are certain basic or generic capacities for agency which we regard as being valuable and these freedoms protect these capacities. We have to have a qualitative view of human freedom and not just a quantitative one. This means that rights which protect freedom will have to be linked to ideas about basic and valuable human capacities. It also means that freedom cannot be understood only negatively, but that there are also centrally important positive aspects to liberty and thus to rights as mechanisms for the protection of freedom.

These issues can be brought to bear more directly upon the issue of regarding income, let us say, as a basic social right in the following way, utilizing an argument from G. A. Cohen.[4] Even if we take a wholly negative view of liberty, it is still the case that the lack of money explicitly becomes a restriction on negative liberty. Take the following two cases. In a totalitarian country there is a law restricting travel for various groups of people. If I am in one of those groups, then that is a restriction on my freedom and this restriction is in the form of a law prohibiting travel. That this sort of example constitutes a restriction on freedom seems to be completely uncontroversial. Take, however, another society in which having a valid ticket to travel depends upon having the resources to pay for it. If I turn up at the airport without a ticket (i.e. not having the money to purchase it), I shall be prevented from flying; it will be the law that prevents me from flying, and I will have committed an offence if I fly without the purchased ticket. Now defenders of negative liberty have argued that the lack of resources is not a restriction on liberty. Such restrictions arise out of the intentional acts of others: individuals, groups, and the state. However, the example given shows that it is not possible to distinguish clearly in this sort of case between a legal restriction on my choice, namely to travel, and a resource restriction since not having the resources will in fact mean that I fall within a legal restriction which prevents flying if I do not have a valid ticket.

As the example shows, it is impossible to separate the issues of liberty from issues of resources. The question of whether people should have a specific set of resources is, of course, a different matter, but having a right to resources cannot be ruled out on a priori grounds in terms of a logical analysis of the concept of liberty because, as the Cohen example shows, even a pure theory of negative liberty implies a resource dimension. If rights are to be seen as ways in which liberty is protected, and if no account of liberty that neglects resources and neglects the capacity for agency is available, then rights imply resources – those resources that will secure the capacity for agency.

The final point that I want to discuss under the heading of liberty is that of choice and the range of choice. I argued earlier that it was not possible to explain the nature of freedom without linking it to an account of choice and agency. However, it has to be said that defenders of a strict form of negative liberty do not accept one obvious consequence of this, namely that the more choices you have, the freer you are. On their view, neither the range nor the quality of choice has anything to do with freedom. It is clear why neo-liberals would want to defend this position because to link freedom to the exercise of choice and to the range and character of choice would make negative liberty into positive liberty – concerned with whether individuals had trivial or non-trivial choices that they could make, whether one person had a wider range of options than another for example. This would entrench at the heart of the concept of liberty a moral and qualitative feature which many defenders of pure negative liberty wish to reject because on their view it would mean that such moral or qualitative judgements would be subjective and moralized and thus cause problems for their idea of a nomocratic rule of law. This position, however, is not very plausible. If liberty is linked to the range of choices open to a person, and if, as the Cohen argument showed, the lack of money can be seen as (and possibly justified) restriction on freedom, then a right to resources which could secure an adequate range of choice could be seen as essential to freedom and this as a genuine right.

I now want to turn to a second set of issues which are frequently raised by critics of the idea of positive social and economic rights. These issues are concerned with the interlinking questions of scarcity and obligation. My aim is not to show that these are not real and genuine questions – indeed they are – but rather to argue that the ways in which critics of social rights deploy these arguments is in danger of cutting the ground from under civil and political rights too.

Let me set out in a programmatic way what the critic's argument is. Genuine rights (in the critic's view), namely civil and political rights, are fundamental ways of protecting negative liberty. Negative liberty is to be free from coercion and interference. Hence, the duties that correspond to negative rights are clear and categorical. They are to abstain from interference, for example, from coercion, compulsion, assault, rape, etc. Since the duties corresponding to such rights are duties to abstain and to forbear from action it follows that they do not involve resources. Since they do not involve resources and involve not doing anything, then they are always capable of being performed. They are duties that can always be performed simultaneously in relation to right holders. I can simultaneously perform the duty of not interfering with everyone who has the right not to be interfered with. The duties are in this sense *perfect* duties – they are not subject to constraints and are compossible in that the duties can be performed simultaneously towards all right holders. They are also clear and categorical in the sense that it is clear what performing the duty means – namely to abstain from action. One has a clear sense of the nature and the limits of duty.

Contrast this with *soi-disant* social rights according to the critic. Positive social rights intrinsically raise questions about scarcity and resources. Because, in respect of at least some sorts of social rights, resources will be in relatively short supply, there will be a need to ration the resources which each individual is entitled to claim under the right. Thus, such rights cannot be realized simultaneously nor can the duties be discharged simultaneously unlike duties in respect of negative rights. The duties and the rights cannot be clear and categorical because it is not clear what would be regarded as fulfilling a social right such as a right to health care. The duties will be subject to political negotiation rather than being completely definite as they are in respect of negative rights. Because of the indeterminacy of the right, both rights and duties will be in a constant process of dispute, negotiation, and adjudication, unlike negative rights where it is clear where and when coercion, interference, assault, etc. has taken place. I will use an extended quotation from Charles Fried to illustrate the point. Fried argues first of all that '[r]ights are categorical moral entities such that violation of a right is always wrong'. He then goes on to make the following case:

> A positive right is a claim to something – a share of a material good or to some particular good like the attention of a lawyer or a doctor, or perhaps to a result like health or enlightenment – while a negative right is a right that something not be done to one, that some particular imposition be withheld. Positive rights are always to scarce goods and consequently scarcity implies a limit to the claim. Negative rights, however, the rights not to be interfered with in forbidden ways do not appear to have such natural, such inevitable limitations. If I am let alone, the commodity I obtain does not appear of its nature to be a scarce or limited one. How can we run out of not harming each other, not lying to each other, leaving each other alone?[5]

and

> It is logically possible to treat negative rights as categorical entities. It is logically possible to respect any number of negative rights without necessarily landing in an impossible and contradictory situation.... Positive rights, by contrast, cannot as a logical matter be treated as categorical entities because of the scarcity limitation.[6]

Hence, there cannot be genuine right to resources because positive social rights run up against scarcity constraints and are therefore not categorical moral entities like negative rights. This sharp contrast between negative and positive rights is not just a philosopher's device but was, for example, used in the *Maher v. Roe* case in the US Supreme Court in 1977 and in Judge Richard Posner's judgment in *Jackson v. City of Joliet.* All of these arguments go to show, for the neo-liberal, that positive rights cannot be made compatible with the idea of the rule of law on their understanding of it.

The critic's point about the indeterminacy of a positive right and its corresponding duties can be sharpened up a bit by looking at both further conceptual and empirical implications of the recognition of positive social and economic rights. The conceptual point is that a right to resources would inevitably bring into play issues concerned with social justice and fairness. If there are positive rights to scarce resources, then there has to be a way of distributing such scarce resources according to defensible criteria of social justice. There would have to be a way of determining a right to a fair share of such scarce resources and this will require allocative norms rather than the idea of categorical forbearances, as in the case of the duties correlating to negative rights. The provision of resources to meet positive rights cannot be left to the vagaries of the market within which ideas of just distribution and fairness in terms of outcomes do not operate. If rights are rights, then they must involve some framework of provision for their claims and this is going to give rise to questions about distributive justice and fairness. However, in the view of the critic, this is a further fatal defect in the whole programme of social rights because the idea of social justice is fraught with indeterminacy. If social justice is at all meaningful, and some critics such as Hayek deny that it is, then what justice requires can only be resolved through political processes and therefore the claims of right are put at risk through these processes. Hence, in the view of the critic there is a clear line to be drawn between genuine and categorical rights and *soi-disant* rights to resources.

A great deal in these arguments can be doubted, and where the points that are made are valid I shall argue that, if they are fatal to positive rights to resources, they are also fatal to negative rights too. Although usually theories of negative liberty underpin theories of negative rights, let us put on one side my criticisms of negative liberty and look at the current arguments on their own merits.

The central issue, as Fried suggests, is one of scarcity because it is scarcity that must change the nature of the obligations from a clear and categorical claim to non-interference to a politically mediated set of obligations about a fair or just allocation of resources. There is a fairly obvious answer to this point and it has been made frequently, but in order to undermine the critic's claim it has to be made more sophisticated.

The rather straightforward version of the argument is that as a matter of fact the protection of negative rights such as the right to be free from assault or interference involves the police, the courts, imprisonment, and other things such as street lighting and security measures in at risk areas and so forth. So it is argued a negative right does imply the commitment of resources in much the same way as positive rights, and that this will inevitably mean that questions of distributive politics will arise as well as making the distinction between the negative and positive rights seem less clear cut or perhaps completely undermined. This is a good argument in itself and has been very effectively deployed by Stephen Holmes and Cass Sunstein in *The Cost of Rights*.[7] Nevertheless, there is a potential reply from the defender of the distinction. Recall that Fried argued that it was logically possible to treat negative rights as categorical entities. It would be open therefore for the defender of this particular claim to argue that there is in fact still a logical or conceptual difference between negative and positive rights and this might involve two points.

The first would be that while it may be true in the world as we know it that the protection of negative rights may involve the commitment of resources with all of the difficulties attendant on that, nevertheless logically they are distinct. It is possible to imagine a world like Kant's 'kingdom of ends', in which all obligations of forbearance in respect of negative rights are always respected. In that possible world negative rights would not involve anything to do with resources. Whereas in such a possible world positive rights would still, of their very nature, imply claims on resources. Hence, there is a logical difference and this difference of logical type would justify preserving the idea that rights are negative and that positive rights are not genuinely rights.

The second argument would be that resources are, at best, conditions for the protection of negative rights. They are not part of the internal logical nature of negative rights. In the case of positive rights, however, the resources are internally or logically connected to the nature of the claim. (This argument parallels a claim made in respect of negative liberty, that at the most resources are contingent conditions for the realization of negative freedom, whereas, positive liberty is logically linked to resources.) So, the critic could reply to the counter-example of resources being required for the protection of rights that these may be conditions of rights, but they are only contingently related to such rights claims and are therefore not part of their basic internal logical nature.

As far as the first argument about possible worlds is concerned, there are two not very important ad hoc responses that might be made. The first is that if the critic of positive rights wants to posit a possible world in which there is no scarcity of motivation for forbearance (unlike in the real world), then it could equally be open to the defender of positive rights to posit a possible world in which there was an abundance of material goods so that questions of scarcity of goods, and all of the consequences which the critic argues goes with that, would be dissipated.

Secondly, in both cases the issue is scarcity: in the negative rights case of the scarcity of the motivation of forbearance; in the positive rights case, the scarcity of material resources. These can be imagined away by combining Kant's 'kingdom of ends' and the 'garden of Eden' but this seems to show what common sense should already have shown by now, namely that if we lived in a combination of the kingdom of ends and the garden of Eden there would be no need for rights of any sort; and secondly, rights are about what kind of protection individuals can have in a world of scarcity both of *motivation* and *resources.*

There is, however, a deeper response that could be made to the critic's argument. It will not do to regard resources as some detachable condition to negative rights and not as part of their conceptual or logical nature. The reason is this. There is a conceptual connection between the idea of a right and enforceability. This is a point noted by many theorists who otherwise differ about the nature of rights. So Steiner argues that:

> [t]his construal of rights as freedom allocations is sufficient to explain why those duties are uncontroversially seen as enforceable. For, putting the matter as broadly as possible, we can say that to prevent someone's chosen disposition of elements within his or her domain is to diminish that persons allotted freedom: specifically, it makes that person unfree to secure whatever is aimed at in that disposition. A set of rights-creating rules that lacked provision for the enforcement of those duties – could not then consistently be described as doing what it purports to do: namely assigning that discretionary domain to that person. 'No right without a remedy' as the legal maxim says.[8]

If, however, the enforceability of a right is not just a contingent condition for the protection of rights but part of what makes a right a *right*, then it is difficult to argue that there is a fundamental asymmetry between social rights which imply resources and negative rights which do not. Enforceability, which is a condition of a right being a right, or a 'genuine' right, is going to involve costs and those costs are going to involve questions of justice and fairness in the distribution of the resources necessary to enforce rights. So if enforceability is a necessary condition for a right being a right, then all rights necessarily involve the costs of enforcement. It is worth pointing out at this juncture that even Nozick seems to endorse this view although he does not draw out its consequences. In the section on procedural rights from page 96ff, Nozick argues in favour of procedural rights that is to say not just rights as forbearances. So, for example, he argues that 'each person has a right to have his guilt determined by the least dangerous of his known procedures for ascertaining guilt'. Given that there is a right to such a procedure, since a right is clearly a positive right, if this is a genuine entitlement or a right to a fair procedure, then it would be legitimate to compel their performance. So, even for Nozick rights are not just about forbearance but have positive aspects of enforcement.[9]

There is another way in which this argument can be developed. It might be said that we have all sorts of desires, preferences, needs, and interests, only some of which are turned into claims of right. Those that are so turned into rights have to embody two things. The first is that these are basic, vital human interests of one sort or another and not just passing claims or preferences. Secondly, it must make sense to believe that others can be put under an enforceable obligation in respect of those rights. So while a need for love may be a basic human interest, it makes no sense to turn this into a right because there is no way of creating a corresponding enforceable obligation and even if there were, it would actually destroy what the claim is a claim to. If enforceability is an essential feature of rights, including negative rights, then this is, of necessity, going to involve resources in that it is not feasible to think of enforceability as costless. If this is so, then enforceability costs are not, as it were, contingent conditions for the protection of rights but are part of the logical structure of rights' claims. Thus, the arguments about resource allocation and its problems apply to negative rights and enforceability as much as they do to positive rights. These will be subject to political mediation in terms of policy and practical discretion in terms of provision of resources. Policy and politics will determine the level of resources dedicated to the protection of different sorts of rights and there is no philosopher's stone to determine outside such processes what the level of resource should be. This applies to the protection of negative and positive rights. At the level of provision there will have to be discretion and if this is regarded as being fatal to positive rights, it is difficult to see why that is not so in relation to negative rights. Take the following example. A police service is part of the enforcement framework of negative rights in terms of securing compliance with forbearance and non-interference; a hospital service is part of the enforcement aspects of a positive right to health care. In the latter case it is clear that managers and doctors will have to use their professional discretion in terms of their allocation of resources between patients all of whom it is supposed have a right to health care. In view of the critic such discretion in allocation undermines and renders invalid the whole idea of a right in this context. It is certainly a very long way from Charles Fried's idea of a right as a categorical entity. However, if this point is fatal against the idea of a positive right, a similar argument in relation to the police is equally fatal against the negative rights thesis if it is accepted that enforceability is an essential feature of rights and not just a contingent condition of them. In the same way as the doctor has to use discretion to manage resources, so the police chief will have to decide on the basis of professional judgement the level of resources that should be put into the investigation of a particular crime which has involved the breach of someone's negative rights. Therefore, this argument about discretion can prove far too much for the negative rights theorist in that it makes that person's position impossible to sustain if the argument about the incompatibility between rights and discretion is regarded as fatal to the idea of positive rights.

It is worth noting at this juncture, in the particular case of a right to a basic income, that this is a right that given some assumptions is less likely to involve the exercise of discretion than many other rights – whether positive or negative. Once the sum payable as a basic income has been fixed as the result of political decision, then on the assumption that the income is paid to each citizen on an individual and unconditional basis above a certain age, there is no scope for discretion. If the income is made conditional on some forms of participation, for example, caring or working in the voluntary sector, then there will be greater scope for discretion in terms of what is an adequate level of commitment by an individual to the participatory framework which is the gateway to the income. Even in this case, however, the inevitable role of discretion does not militate against the claim that there can be such right since, as we have seen, the connection between rights and resources is an essential one and therefore the problems associated with the exercise of discretion apply across the board. This point was discussed further in Chapter 6. It is also worth saying that, so far as government and the law are concerned, in the provision of welfare it is possible to minimize discretion by state actors by separating the funding of welfare services and providing those services. If the state funds services there is no great degree of discretion required, and if it then contracts with a range of providers from the private sector and the third sector, then no *overall* bureaucratic discretion is involved in the delivery of the service and, at least ideally, beneficiaries of such services can in fact change their provider if the provision does not meet their needs. Hayek himself recognizes that this is a perfectly legitimate move for government, to make and indeed in the United Kingdom it has made it. The main point of principle though is that the government, at least from a social democratic perspective on this issue, is providing resources to meet welfare rights but in so doing it does not have to be in the business of directly providing the services with all the problems of bureaucratic power, discretion, and growth which on the public choice view goes along with that. This completes the discussion of the relationship between rights, scarcity, and obligation. There are genuine and complex problems involved in resolving the problems about the relationship between rights and social justice but I hope that I have argued sufficiently cogently that these are problems for the generality of rights and not just rights to resources including basic income.

It might still be claimed, however, that the argument in relation to scarcity still has not gone through because some issues in relation to breaches of rights and the question of social justice have still not been resolved. It might be argued in the first place that what is a matter of concern in relation to breaches of rights is intention and action. If there is a categorical distinction between negative and positive rights, such that negative rights correlate with strict duties of forbearance, then the infringement of such a right by a duty bearer has to be active and intentional since the right is respected by inaction and forbearance. The critic might claim that there is a very big difference between this sort of case where a right is intentionally breached and the situation in which the resources that would meet an alleged right to such a resource are not forthcoming. This point is well made by Fried when he argues that '[n]egative rights are related to categorical wrongs in the sense that every violation of a negative right is a wrong. But a wrong can only be inflicted intentionally.'[10] Some critics of social justice and economic rights make this point about intention a central plank in their case against both. As we have seen, this is for example a major theme of Hayek. The argument goes as follows: An injustice can only be caused by an intentional act in the same way as for Fried a wrong in relation to a right can only result from an intentional act. So, Hayek argues, this is the underlying reason why we do not regard the consequences of the weather or of the genetic lottery as injustices even though they may cause great suffering. They are not injustices, nor do they infringe the rights of anyone because they are not intended. This argument is then transposed to the operation of free economic markets. In a market, individuals buy and sell on an intentional basis and in this, wrong and injustice can arise between individual parties to transactions. These are dealt with by contract law and other forms of law covering the buying and selling of goods. However, the overall outcomes of markets, and, in particular, the so-called 'distribution' of income and wealth are not intended. They are the aggregate effects of individual acts of intentional buying and selling. The distribution of resources which a market produces at any moment is an unintended consequence of this activity. Because market outcomes are unintended they are not wrongful, nor do they cause injustice and for this reason there is no case for assuming collective responsibility for these outcomes and conferring on individuals social and economic rights to protect against such outcomes. The critic could accept the earlier arguments that social and economic resources are an internal part of human agency, while at the same time arguing on the fact that someone does not have the resources necessary for agency when this deprivation is caused by an impersonal and unintended process, does not constitute either a wrong or an injustice. Therefore, on this view these different circumstances enable us to keep to the distinction between negative and positive rights in terms of the intentionality of the wrong-doing.

This argument may, however, be doubted for the reasons discussed in Chapter 13 and I will not repeat them here except to say that the argument depends on the idea that what matters is the intention from the neo-liberal point of view and not the foreseeability of outcome. In Chapter 11 I argued that if market outcomes are foreseeable, then there can indeed be collective responsibility for them and this claim would apply to rights in the sense that if it is a foreseeable outcome of markets that some people will be left either without or with an impaired set of the generic goods of agency as the result of market outcomes, then this situation can be regarded as unjust and should be rectified by the recognition of rights to such generic goods. The main point for the moment though is to draw the analogy between a reasonably foreseeable, but unintended, infringement of a negative right which would be both wrong and unjust and a similar situation in respect of the position of a disadvantaged group as the result of a reasonably foreseeable but unintended consequence of the aggregate outcomes of market behaviour. If it is reasonably foreseeable that in a market those who enter it with least will in general leave it with least, then there is a case for claiming that there is a wrong and an injustice at work here. On the argument that this is so, then the case sketched out above can be regarded as a way of dealing with the negative right or intentional wrong tie-up which is used to block the idea of social and economic rights.

There is, however, a further argument which needs to be examined at this stage, namely the question about the relationship between the wrongfulness of the infringement of a right and the identification of the individual who is under the duty to respect the right and has committed the wrong. The point here from the perspective of the negative rights theorist is that not only is the duty in respect of the right clear and categorical, namely to abstain from the action proscribed by the right, but also that, since the duties are duties of forbearance, they can be assumed by everyone else without the identification of a duty bearer being a particular problem. Such a theorist would, of course, accept that positive rights and duties can arise out of contract and in that context both the right holder and the right bearer can easily be identified. In the case of social and economic rights, however, it is argued it is not clear who is the duty bearer. Is it an individual so that another individual without the means to meet his social and economic rights has a direct right in respect of the resources of the first individual, and this first individual has a duty of respect of the first individual's rights? This point is made very fairly by Jan Narveson in the course of a critique of social and economic rights:

> But a duty has to be someone's duty. It can't just be no one's in particular. Consequently the thing to do is to make it everyone's duty to do something, even if that something is a matter of seeing that someone else does it.[11]

This would seem to be correct and would follow from the earlier argument about collective responsibility. The strict duty for individuals in the case of social and economic rights would not be that of personal provision of resources for deprived individuals (although there is nothing in this argument to prevent necessarily discretionary acts of altruism and beneficence) but rather a duty to support the tax system, and other aspects of provision for social and economic rights which the entity, usually a state, through which collectively accepted responsibility for market outcomes takes place. This emphatically does not mean that this is another case for drawing a contrast between duties in respect of negative rights and positive rights. Take two examples. Firstly, if the argument set out earlier about the logical link between rights and enforceability is accepted, then the duty in respect of negative rights is not to infringe them but also, and crucially, to support, for example, through the tax system those aspects of enforceability – the police, the courts, and the prisons which are required for enforceability; secondly in the case of some civil rights, for example, due process, this involves the direct provision of a service that is funded by the taxpayer as a way of meeting the duty to respect and enforce the right to due process. In the case of such a negative right, the duty bearer does not have the responsibility of providing due process himself or herself (although they have the negative duty not to interfere with it). Rather the duty is to support the funding and other forms of provision of due process. Therefore, in the case of positive rights to resources, I do not have a positive duty to provide those resources myself (although I have a negative duty not to remove those resources). Rather the duty is to support the funding and other mechanisms to meet such social and economic rights.

So far my argument has been rather negative and opportunistic. I have argued that if there are any rights, there is no good case for denying that positive rights to resources are genuine rights because the denial that such rights embody essential logical features of genuine rights does not carry conviction. In these concluding remarks, I shall sketch the basis of a moral framework within which it would make positive sense to claim that there is a right to basic resources. I shall only sketch this since the argument was worked out in much more detail elsewhere. What I want to show is the link between needs and rights and to do this we need to go back to an argument from the first section of the chapter in relation to liberty. I argued that it is impossible to make sense of the idea of freedom without some conception of the nature of human choice and agency. If agency is essential to an account of freedom, then it seems reasonable to argue that, if there are any general or generic conditions of the exercise of agency, then these will be of particular importance in relation to a full account of the nature of freedom. The basic intuition here is very well articulated by Holmes and Sunstein when they argue: 'No single human actor can single handedly create all the preconditions for his own action.'[12] In this book so far I have argued that indeed there are such general conditions for the exercise of agency, which are well-being and autonomy. Well-being in the sense that basic needs are satisfied in a reasonably predictable way; autonomy in the sense that the capacity for autonomy seems to be what the end result of the exercise of human agency and freedom would be. Let me just say a few words about autonomy first. It might well be argued that autonomy is the main site of negative freedom. Autonomy requires that individuals are free from interference and coercion so that they can live lives shaped by their own purposes. This is what makes negative freedom valuable to us and indeed intelligible. Negative freedom, and the negative rights associated with it, is not to be understood as an end in itself but is rather valuable or instrumental in achieving a broader and more basic good – that of autonomy that is, living a life shaped by one's own aims and goals – the exercise of our capacity for agency. I have already argued that this conception of freedom and rights involves resources and in that respect both the freedom and rights have positive aspects. However, autonomy is something that has to be *developed*. It is an achievement, not some kind of antecedent status, and the development of autonomy creates certain sorts of basic needs which are essential to its realization. These are the needs connected with well-being without which an autonomous character will not be developed. For the capacity for autonomy to exist there has to be a degree of physical integrity and health in so far as this is achievable and alterable by human agency, there has to be an appropriate level of education, and there has to be an appropriate level of security in terms of outcome and social security in that individuals will not develop the capacity for autonomy if the whole of each individual's life is devoted to securing the basic means of subsistence. If this is correct (as a sketch) then autonomy, freedom, and an account of the fulfilment of basic needs has to go together. Negative freedom, freedom from coercion, is a generic condition of agency and autonomy; positive freedom, access to resources and opportunities, and the satisfaction of basic needs are also a generic condition of autonomy.

This gives me the basis for arguing not against a moralized view of freedom and coercion but rather against the limited normative framework within which Nozick embeds these ideas. On the view that I am putting forward, it is not just an illegitimate invasion of negative liberty that is coercion but also that economic and other activities which intentionally or foreseeably dispossess people of these goods of agency, or intentionally or foreseeably withhold them, can equally be regarded as coercive. If both negative liberty and the positive freedom embodied in the basic goods of agency are both essential to autonomy, then any interference in access to such goods is a restriction of freedom.

It might, of course, be disputed that the needs and capabilities which are part of autonomy embody standards that are then subjectively or conventionally set. In the view of the critic, this could limit the objectivity of the view of freedom. I think that this objection fails because it would apply also to a moralized view of negative liberty as well. As can be seen, for example, in Nozick's view of liberty in acquisition, there are lots of conventional or even subjective standards about how far an act of appropriation extends and these uncertainties are present in Rothbard too. They cannot, as it were, be 'read off' the rights concerned.

Thus, there is a good case for seeing social and economic rights as being part of positive freedom for two interrelated reasons.

The first is that social and economic rights, and within these perhaps pre-eminently an income guarantee as a basic income, or some other such approach, will increase autonomy in terms of enhancing an individual's capacity for choice and for living his or her life in his or her own way. As we saw in relation to Cohen's argument in respect of negative liberty, income can increase the choices open to you because the lack of money will mean that you could be legally proscribed from being able to undertake an action. Also as I argued, contrary to the defender of pure negative liberty, the range and quality of choice does have a central bearing on the meaning of liberty.

The second point is that a basic income increases autonomy relative to provision in kind in that in spending the income, the purchases will reveal the preferences of the agent rather than that of government and its agencies and, as I have already argued, it does diminish the possible role of discretion in the provision of resources. This is very important in terms of the rule of law as we have seen throughout this study. One aspect of the argument about social and economic rights has been the charge of paternalism. The emphasis upon a right to income is less paternalistic than provision in kind and less discretionary in operation.

Therefore, if autonomy and agency are central to freedom in that both negative and positive freedom acquire their value and, as I argued earlier, their intelligibility in relation to the idea of a person as a centre of choice and agency, then the generic conditions of agency will determine the content of both negative and positive freedom: Negative freedom defining the forms of unjustified coercion and interference which would limit autonomy; positive freedom defining those sorts of goods which are necessary conditions for the achievement of the capacity for agency and autonomy. I have argued that social and economic rights including a basic income could be seen as in part fulfilment of these conditions of agency.

There is, however, a major problem remaining, namely the specific argument for turning the general conditions of agency into *rights.* I am not going back on my earlier arguments in saying this. I have argued that there is no reason for thinking that social and economic rights cannot be thought of as rights. The argument has, however, been conditional: If there are any rights at all, then positive rights in general are in fact genuine rights in the sense that they share in the general features of rights. This, nevertheless, leaves a central problem untouched. Would it not be perfectly possible for an individual to recognize in his or her own case that the capacity for agency is dependent on a combination of negative and positive freedom, and indeed recognize the same situation in respect of others, namely that their capacity for agency depends also on such negative and positive forms of freedom, without recognizing that this was the basis of a claim to a *right* to these negative and positive forms of freedom and, the corresponding duties of provision.

This is a deep problem in moral and political philosophy and certainly among the thinkers we have been concerned with Rothbard recognizes its force. In the *Ethics of Liberty* he argues that the basic question for any non-theological theory, including his own natural law theory, is: 'Why are such principles felt to be binding or me? How do such universal tendencies in human nature (underpinning natural law) become incorporated into a person's subjective value scale?'[13] Rothbard's answer is itself rather obscure but seems to be based upon the universality of the principles and the fact that 'righteousness' will lead people to identify with and incorporate such principles into their own subjective values. Rothbard adopts this thematic view of right reason – that is reason apprehending the objective good for man and dictating the means to its attainment.[14] However, along with Rothbard's general approach to natural law, this is highly general and does not really either grapple with the detail of getting from his own conception of objective good to the rights he specifies.[15] Nor does he deal with the myriad of objections that can be made to natural law theories.

There are other approaches. As we shall see below, this problem was posed in an interesting way by Kant, but for the moment I want to concentrate on the answer given in the remarkable writings of the philosopher from Chicago, Alan Gewirth, over the past twenty-five years. What we have to get from is a recognition that there are common preconditions of agency, to the idea that these preconditions can be conceived of as rights and thus as matters for collective and governmental concern, which will impose strict duties on all members of society. Gewirth's argument is complicated but crucial and it has to be repeated in full.

First of all there is the recognition, which I have already stressed, of the centrality of agency and action. So when I act, I do so to attain some good for myself – not necessarily a moral good but something which I think is worthwhile. Hence the first step in the argument is:

1. I do *X* for end or purpose *E*.

The second step is

2. *E* is good (for me).

Since the generic goods of agency are necessary for me to value and to seek to attain *E*, then the next step becomes:

3. The generic goods of agency (freedom and well-being) are necessary goods.

Given this, an individual agent has to be committed to the claim that

4. I must have freedom and well-being (i.e. the necessary goods of agency).

The next step is crucial in that Gewirth argues that on the basis of (4) the individual has to accept:

5. I have rights to the basic goods of agency.

Now this is a big step and the reasons for it are as follows. Imagine that having got as far as, (4), the agent rejects (5). It then follows, given the link between rights and obligations, that he gives up any claim that other people should refrain from interfering with his access to the necessary or generic goods of agency. If I do not claim them for myself as rights, then I have no reason for resisting the idea that others can interfere with these goods. Given this, it then follows logically that I regard it as permissible that I do not have access to the basic goods (i.e. because not claiming them as rights for myself means that others have no strict obligation to respect the goods that I need for agency and action). However, this claim contradicts (4), which follows from (1) to (3). Since every agent has to accept (4), because it recognizes the necessary conditions of agency and action, any agent must therefore reject the idea that it is permissible for other agents not to have an obligation to respect my need for the necessary goods. Since this would follow from the denial of (5), any agent must accept (5) and therefore the necessary or generic goods of agency and action have to be accepted as rights.[16]

I regard this as a powerful argument in favour of the idea that the generic goods of agency, both negative and positive, can be justified as rights and if this is coupled with my earlier claims that there are no logical reasons for thinking that social and economic rights are different in principle from civil and political rights, Gewirth's argument can be used to turn my initial hypothetical claim that, if there are rights, social and economic goods can be seen as rights, into a categorical one.

I would, however, just go on to argue the case in two further respects. The first is a point made by Charles Fried, who argues that it would be morally inconceivable to think that individuals should be credited with negative rights, the protection of which may involve colossal costs (an example might be the right of Salman Rushdie not to be killed as the result of the Fatwa) while leaving us totally indifferent to the needs of others (because we reject positive rights) which may be desperate and which we could alleviate at potentially much lower costs. A theory of rights which divided through negative and positive rights producing such counter-intuitive conclusions would not seem very compelling. Even a theorist like Robert Nozick, who has wanted to resist all accounts of positive rights in favour of basic negative rights protecting individual inviolability, has argued that this would not apply in a situation of moral catastrophe.

The second subsidiary argument to that of Gewirth is derived from Kant's argument on this topic in the *Groundwork of the Metaphysic of Morals*, where Kant argues famously as follows where he reflects on four examples of the principle of universalizability which is as we have seen central to the nomocratic, neo-liberal ideal of the rule of law:

> Yet a fourth man is himself flourishing, but sees others with great hardships (and whom he could easily help), and he thinks, 'What does it matter to me? Let every one be as happy as Heaven wills, or as he can make himself: I won't deprive him of anything; I won't even envy him; only I have no wish to contribute to his well being or to his support in distress!' . . . But although it is possible that a universal law of nature could subsist in harmony with this maxim, yet it is impossible to will that such a principle should hold everywhere as a law of nature. For a will which decided in this way would be at variance with itself, since many a situation might arise in which the man would need love and sympathy from others, and in which, by such a law of nature sprung from his own will he would rob himself of all hope of the help that he wants for himself.[17]

Later Kant goes on to argue that humanity could no doubt subsist if everybody contributed nothing to the happiness of others but:

> At the same time refrained from deliberately impairing their happiness. This is, however, merely to agree negatively and not positively with humanity as an end in itself unless everybody endeavours also, so far as in him lies, to further the ends of others. For the ends of a subject who is an end in himself must, if this conception is to have its full effect in me, be also, as far as possible, my end.[18]

One way of putting these arguments is that a combination of strict negative rights to mutual non-interference plus a general duty of benevolence will not do because the duty of benevolence has to be discretionary in its operation and therefore will not secure to individuals on a predictable basis the resources that they need in order to pursue their own goals as ends in themselves. The security of reciprocity which Kant is looking to in this argument could be achieved by treating the basic goods of agency as rights. Therefore, in terms of Kantian arguments about common humanity, there is a case for positive rights including rights to resources or social and economic rights that can be developed. Of course, as the second argument makes clear, humanity could subsist with a regime of negative rights respecting mutual non-interference but if all rights involve resources, as I have argued, then it is highly questionable that a set of purely negative rights with duties understood in terms of a negative idea of respect rather than a positive idea of respect, enforcement, and provision is in fact feasible and thus there is a strong normative case for social and economic rights.

As we saw earlier, Nozick as well as more mainstream neo-liberals adopt the Kantian position here in relation to respect for persons but he and they deny that such a view can yield social and economic rights. So even if my arguments so far have validity, Nozick would still deny that they could be genuine rights since they are rights to a 'social pot' which does not in fact exist because of individual entitlement. This is how he makes the point:

> The major objection to speaking of everyone's having a right *to* various things such as equality of opportunity, life and so on and enforcing this right is that these 'rights' require a substructure of things and materials and actions; and *other* people may have rights and entitlements over these. No one has a right to something whose realisation requires certain uses of things and activities that other people have rights and entitlements over.[19]

So any theory of social and economic rights to carry weight has to undermine the Nozickian claim and the related claim that it is unjust to coerce people into paying tax to meet the alleged positive obligations to which social and economic rights entail.

Given that a good deal of this libertarian argument flows from the idea of personal freedom understood as negative liberty with the implication, as understood by the libertarian that one can have no rights or duties other than those to which one has expressly consented which essentially embodies the idea of self-ownership, it follows that if the reader is convinced by my more expansive account of freedom and autonomy then seeing, as for example Jan Narveson does, self-ownership as being part of what liberty means or as Steiner argues that rights including the right to self-ownership 'prescribe distributions of pure negative freedom' is too circumscribed a normative framework. If liberty also implies possession of, and access to, the generic goods of agency, then making liberty the foundation of politics will not lead one uniquely in the direction of the Nozickian view of rights and justice. These principles apply also to the generic positive goods of agency as well as to the negative ones.

If that is convincing, then the claim that there is no social pot that can legitimately provide resources for positive rights, because all aspects of such a putative fund will come with individual entitlements created by the process of production of these resources, looks less plausible since what is at the basis of this claim is an argument about self-ownership and appropriation, as the unique consequence of taking liberty is the fundamental principle of political philosophy. A broader conception of liberty can in fact free us from such a view.

NOTES

1. Coleman, J. (1998). 'Rethinking the Theory of Legal Rights', in his *Markets, Morals and the Law.* Oxford: Oxford University Press, p. 31.
2. Steiner, H. (1998). 'Working Rights', in M. Kramer, N. Simmonds, and H. Steiner. *A Debate over Rights.* Oxford: Oxford University Press.
3. Coleman, J., 'Rethinking the Theory of Legal Rights'.
4. Cohen, G. A. (1995). *Self Ownership, Freedom and Equality.* Cambridge: Cambridge University Press, chapter 2.
5. Fried, C. (1985). *Right and Wrong.* Cambridge, MA: Harvard University Press, p. 110.
6. Fried, C. *Right and Wrong,* p. 110.
7. Holmes, S. and Sunstein, C. (1999). *The Cost of Rights: Why Liberty Depends on Taxes.* New York: Norton.
8. Steiner, H., 'Working Rights'.
9. Barry, N. (1987). *On Classical Liberalism and Libertarianism.* New York: St Martin's Press.
10. Fried, C. *Right and Wrong.*
11. Narveson, J. (1973). *Morality and Utility.* Baltimore, MD: Johns Hopkins University Press, p. 235.
12. Holmes, S and Sunstein, *The Cost of Rights.*
13. Rothbard, M. (2002). *The Ethics of Liberty.* New York: New York University Press, p. 14.
14. Rothbard, M. *The Ethics of Liberty,* p. 7.
15. Barry, N., *On Classical Liberalism,* p. 176.
16. Gewirth, A. (1978). *Reason and Morality.* Chicago, IL: Chicago University Press.
17. Kant, I. (1974). *Groundwork to the Metaphysic of Morals,* trans. H. J. Paton. London: Hutchinson, p. 90.
18. Kant, I. (1974). *Groundwork to the Metaphysic of Morals,* p. 98.
19. Nozick, R. (1974). *Anarchy, State and Utopia.* Oxford: Blackwell, p. 238.

13

Concluding Reflections

It is now time to draw together the various threads and themes of the discussion carried out so far. It is a central contention of this book that, contrary to the neo-liberal's own perspective, there is in fact no categorical distinction to be drawn between social democracy and neo-liberalism and certainly not in terms of the rule of law. At the same time, there is in fact a clear distinction to be drawn between social democracy and a libertarian position. The neo-liberal accepts that there is a case for a basic form of welfare provision; the libertarian does not. This is the basis for the fact that the former cannot categorically be distinguished from social democracy, while the latter can. This is, of course, rejected by the neo-liberal. The neo-liberal claim is that there is a categorical distinction remaining because the basic form of welfare endorsed by the neo-liberal can be contrasted in terms of principle with a social justice driven conception of the welfare state sanctioned by social democracy. The neo-liberal welfare state is not inspired by social justice; it is limited in scope; it is not designed to change relative positions of individuals and groups within society; it embodies a view of negative liberty; it is compatible only with a set of negative rights; it does not seek the achievement of specific ends such as social justice or social solidarity and in this respect is nomocratic rather than telocratic; it operates with a modest level of bureaucracy; and it is not involved in the direct provision of welfare itself but is limited to a funding and a commissioning role. These features of the neo-liberal view of the welfare state, it is argued, both sharply distinguish it from the social democratic version and make it compatible with the rule of law. It is the thesis developed in this book that these claims cannot in fact be sustained. The conceptual structure of negative freedom, negative rights, and procedural rather than social justice cannot in fact be sustained and the institutional form of a welfare state justified in terms of these ideas would, in practice, be indistinguishable from one concerned with social justice. If the latter proves to be incompatible with the rule of law, then so will the former. As we have worked through the positive presentation of the neo-liberal case and subsequently the critical appraisal of concepts such as freedom, justice, and rights the main lines of the basis for the claim that there is no fundamental dividing line between neo-liberalism and social democracy should have emerged and the task of this chapter is to set out the basis of that case in a systematic and complete way.

Before moving on to that task, however, it is worthwhile at this juncture to say more about the rule of law which was invoked as a virtue of neo-liberalism and a basis for the critique of social democracy. As we saw in Chapters 1 and 2 for the neo-liberal the rule of law is a moral ideal. Neo-liberals such as Hayek are very critical of legal positivism on precisely this point. For the positivist, law is identified by its source, not its moral content; the law can be utilized to pursue a wide range of different social and political ends – some good and some evil. Some features of the rule of law such as its publicity, non-retrospective character, non-contradictoriness, etc. are, for the positivists, just efficiency conditions for the law, they are not part of its moral content or 'inner morality' to use Fuller's term. For the neo-liberal, on the other hand, the law is connected to the ideal of a free society, an abstract, deontological order characterized by negative liberty, procedural justice, and negative rights. It facilitates the maintenance of such an order, but because the order does not embody any substantive ends that order is nomocratic and not telocratic. The plausibility of this position depends crucially on two things. First on whether or not the neo-liberal conceptions of freedom, justice, and rights and closely linked concepts such as coercion, intention, foreseeability, collective obligations, etc. can be sustained; and, second, whether or not the form of welfare provision sanctioned by neo-liberals is in fact compatible with their own conception of the rule of law. It is the contention of this book that neo-liberalism fails both tests. The detailed claim here has been implicit in the critical analysis of both the concepts and institutions that has gone before. Utilizing the details of that critique the case will now be set out in a more interconnected way.

Obviously since the social, political, legal, and economic theory of neo-liberalism has the aim of giving content to the ideal of a free society and justifying that ideal in their conception of it, it is sensible to start with the issue of freedom since this is central to the whole argument. One important issue is the relation between the concept of freedom and that of agency. What is at stake here initially is what is it that makes the ascription of freedom intelligible? We do not regard sticks and stones as free although when they move their movements may be unimpeded when rolling down a hill or being blown by the wind. What is crucially lacking in such objects is the idea of agency. If we are to ascribe freedom to X in an intelligible way, then X must be an agent and, at least in some way, a centre of choice. To put the point another way the capacity for agency must be a necessary condition of the ascription of freedom and without it any such ascription is unintelligible. Therefore, in any account of liberty this capacity for agency must assume a central place. Indeed this much is obvious from one of the central texts of modern neo-liberal thought namely Ludwig von Mises' *Human Action*. At the centre of that book is an attempt to set out what human action means and what are its requirements. What Mises calls 'acting man' is at the centre of his analysis although we would today tend to use the language of agency and action. What is it that constitutes a human agent capable of acting in pursuit of ends, goals, values, and projects in the social environment in which an agent finds him or herself? In the view of Mises, this is not an empirical enquiry although it is one with overwhelming significance for how we understand human life and activity. In Mises' own terms the analysis of agency involves the establishment of synthetic a priori propositions – that is to say unpacking the necessary consequences of a foundational concept of agency which accounts for their a priori nature, while at the same time recognizing that these propositions will in fact be to the highest degree important in characterizing fundamental human capacities. Again, to modernize Mises' language we might say that he is engaged in conceptual analysis, in this case of the concepts of agency and action. Therefore, it does seem to be central to any philosophy which puts freedom at its centre that there must be some idea of agency and action and what both of these mean and what they require in order to be relevant to human experience even though these are conceptual claims and not generalizations from experience. The same assumptions are also present in Hayek, particularly, for example, his account of the limited and fragmentary forms of human knowledge which we considered earlier, but in Hayek the argument about the nature of agency is not as central as it is to Mises. It is also present in Buchanan's work although in a rather minimal kind of way. He presents the human agent wholly in terms of a centre of subjective choice combined with a rational maximizing set of motivational assumptions. It is also present in Nozick because his concept of rights rests upon the idea of the inviolability of the person which in turn turns upon his idea of the separateness of persons and the fact that each individual has a set of goals which give meaning to his or her life. From these sorts of considerations he draws out consequences for the nature of rights and of the side constraints which rights impose on the behaviour of others as well as the centrality of consent to his understanding of the role of law and politics. It is also explicitly present in the work of Rothbard – although he is a libertarian rather than a neo-liberal. Rothbard endorses natural law which, in turn, in his view, has to be based upon a quite detailed account of human nature and what, given that nature, matters most in human life. It is important to make this point that ideas of agency and action and indeed more broadly a conception of human nature within which agency and action play a central role is crucial for neo-liberalism. It would be easy to assume that such a conception would in fact pose major difficulties for the neo-liberal given the neo-liberal's claim (usually) to be subjectivists in ethics and to want to hold to rather minimalist conceptions in the light of that – a feature which is most marked, as we saw in the work of Buchanan. It has also been argued, for example, that from purely factual accounts of human nature it is not in fact possible to infer anything normative at all because of the is–ought or fact–value dichotomy. On this view, normative conclusions about politics and law cannot be deduced from an empirical and factual account of human nature. If we want to relate normative conclusions to accounts of human nature, then such accounts will themselves have to involve normative assumptions, for example, the claim that some needs are more important than others and that they have a greater claim for recognition on society or that some capabilities are more important than others. Such claims might well be the basic building blocks of a normative theory of law and politics but only because the claims about human nature have themselves become normative in content. This would then pose problems for the moral subjectivism of neo-liberal thinkers in that from such a subjectivist stance it would in fact be very difficult to provide a universalist normative conception of human nature. As we have seen a thinker like Buchanan takes this very seriously and that is why he does not want to go down this road beyond focusing on the person as a centre of subjective choice and a minimal account of rationality. It is also why, at least at the constitutional level, citizens have to agree to rules by unanimous consent because to do otherwise would be to elevate one set of convictions about the good above those of others. Unanimity is an uncontroversial decision procedure in the context of radical moral subjectivism. Other neo-liberal thinkers, particularly Hayek and Mises, are less direct in their insistence upon subjectivism but it is in fact central to their ideas about value and can also be seen in Hayek's critique of social justice – for example, his claim that we lack agreement on the criteria of social justice and that such disagreement is endemic and cannot be removed. Therefore, on this basis, neo-liberals cannot operate with strong or thick normative conceptions of human nature. They have to operate rather with thin and non-normative ideas or if they do operate with normative notions they are of a minimalist sort such as Buchanan's insistence on the person being understood as a centre of subjective choice or in the case of Nozick that persons are separate and that it is in the pursuit of personal ends that life is given a sense of meaning. In this respect Mises, Hayek, and Buchanan are rather different from Carl Menger whose work can be seen as being based upon a much more elaborated account of human nature and in particular of human needs and the goods that will satisfy them. Despite being one of the founding figures of neo-liberalism at least in this respect, Menger's work has a strong Aristotelian element to it.

So we can see why an idea of agency is at the centre of the work of neo-liberals because it is only by elaborating the concept of agency that their ascription of freedom to an individual can be intelligible, but equally we should expect that such a conception of agency will either be wholly non-normative or if it does involve normative elements they will be of a minimalist and claimed universalist sort.

Central to the requirements of agency and action for the neo-liberal is the doctrine of negative liberty and we have to ask whether this is enough and, we have questioned whether the neo-liberal's own account of negative liberty is strong enough to withstand criticism. It is easy enough to understand why neo-liberals endorse negative rather than positive liberty because it has certainly been argued that positive freedom logically implies some strong normative commitments – that is to say that it is only in pursuing certain sorts of goals that one is in fact free. Such a view could not be accommodated to the moral subjectivism of most of neo-liberal thought and in so far as an account of a free society included positive liberty, then it would mean moving the conception of a free society from a nomocratic to a telocratic one – that the society would only be free if it in fact realized the goods and goals of positive freedom.

We have seen however that the issues are not at all as simple as this. It was argued in Chapter 10 that coercion, once it goes beyond prevention and impossibility, becomes essentially normative and has to operate with some idea of basic goods so that any threat to such goods is coercive and, as we saw, Hayek, implicitly at least, accepts this. Given that negative liberty is identified as the absence of coercion, it would follow that even negative liberty would have a strong normative element built into it and that this would have to imply an appeal to a conception of certain shared goods and goals. In that sense, therefore, there could not be a categorical difference between negative and positive liberty in normative terms. Secondly, while neo-liberals such as Hayek might argue that neither the quantity nor the qualitative range of choices open to an individual is essential to understanding what liberty is, nevertheless such a view is implausible. It is of course easy to see why neo-liberals would take such a view because if a particular quantity of rules were made for freedom as opposed to unfreedom, or if a certain set of choices had greater moral significance than others in the determination of freedom rather than unfreedom, then this would cut across their moral subjectivism in that society would have to endorse either or both a quantity or quality view of freedom. It might well be possible to argue that neo-liberalism is compatible with a quantitative view of freedom in that it does not seem directly to involve moral norms in its identification. Nevertheless as I argued in Chapter 10 this is an implausible view and indeed produces deeply counter-intuitive results as the argument drawn from the work of Charles Taylor shows. Therefore, in these and in other respects it is not possible to argue that negative liberty is a demoralized concept of liberty and as such uniquely fitted to the subjectivist assumptions of neo-liberalism.

However, the issue at stake here goes much deeper than this and has to do with the neo-liberal account of agency in terms of negative liberty. The point here is that the neo-liberal neglects the extent to which agency depends on *needs* and *capabilities*. That is to say a person can only act as an agent or be an 'acting man' in Mises' terms if certain sorts of needs are satisfied and if an individual has certain sorts of capacities. If this turns out to be true, then there is, in fact, a whole dimension of agency missing from neo-liberal thought and yet, as I have argued, agency is a necessary condition of rendering the ascription of freedom to individuals intelligible. This point becomes clear if we go back to the point made in the two earlier chapters on liberty about freedom and ability or power. For the neo-liberal there is a categorical distinction between freedom and ability and, if there were not, then any link between freedom and ability would, as Hayek clearly argued, be used as a justification for the provision of resources to individuals to enable them to do what they are free to do. That is to say it would justify the collective provision of welfare goods in the interests of liberty. As we saw, neo-liberals reject this link. However, there are reasons for being dubious about this claim about the nature of the difference between freedom and ability. The reason being that a generalized ability to do *X* is a necessary condition for determining whether A is free or unfree to do *X*. Unless there is a generalizable ability to do *X*, the question of whether people are free or unfree to do what no one is able to do becomes meaningless. If there is such a link between freedom and generalized abilities, then there is a clear link between the idea of agency and powers or abilities and needs and capacities which underlie the possibility of achieving what is a generalizable ability.

Of course, the neo-liberal will argue that this involves a strong commitment to moral agreement about what are the significant generalizable abilities open to human beings, a form of moral agreement which in their view cannot be forthcoming. One can see why from their position of moral subjectivism they would take such a view. Nevertheless it is a mistaken view because the alternative position is *not* to argue that we should share a collective moral duty to meet all needs relating to the achievement of a particular kind of end, nor a moral duty to foster similar narrowly specialized capabilities. Rather what this alternative claims is that there are certain generic needs and certain generic capabilities which have to be in place before individuals can undertake any kind of action whatsoever. These are generic or universal goods which are the necessary conditions of action directed to any end whatever it might turn out to be. Such goods would include, for example, security, education, and health which are basic needs underlying the development of any sorts of capacity and within those forms of provision which would enhance peoples' generic capacities for attaining whatever turned out to be their purpose. Of course, this conception of agency includes negative liberty too. In order to be an agent one has to be free from various sorts of coercion, prevention, and interference and in that sense security is partly a matter of negative freedom. However, this negative freedom for reasons to do with the nature of coercion, as we have seen, is itself not to be regarded as morally neutral but does involve the recognition of certain basic goods of a generic sort, as Hayek himself implicitly acknowledges. So the position is that agency implies both negative liberty but, not of a demoralized sort; and positive freedom in terms of generic goods which are not necessary conditions of attaining a particular end but rather conditions of attaining any aim in human life. We need to have this complex view of freedom and agency if we are to have a convincing account of a free society. In a sense, as I have suggested, a lot of this is in any case implicit in Hayek not least in his recognition of the importance of the provision of basic welfare goods but for which he provides no morally convincing case of any sort.

It is, of course, still open for the neo-liberal to say that even if this agency-based view of freedom were to be accepted there is still a categorical difference between a welfare state which aims to meet basic needs and capacities, and a welfare state which seeks to achieve social justice. Thus, while the claimed distinction between neo-liberalism and social democracy in terms of freedom might collapse, this is not the case in respect of basic provision versus social justice. An additional argument here is that only basic provision rather than social justice is in fact compatible with the idea of the rule of law. These claims are, however, unconvincing for several reasons. The first has to do with what neo-liberals themselves see as the rather porous and open ended nature of needs. A need like health is capable of very considerable expansion particularly growing as a consequence of new technologies and the same is true, although perhaps less dramatically so, in respect of education and security whether security is understood as social security or the positive duty of government to protect people from threats of various sorts to their basic well-being. As we have seen in the years since 2001 security needs can expand depending on threats and indeed like health can expand in the light of technological advance. Given these ill-defined limits to what it is that is assumed to satisfy basic needs it is very difficult indeed to argue that issues of social or distributive justice do not arise in respect of meeting basic needs. Questions of fairness will arise in terms of the distribution of resources to meet various needs as will questions about responsibility, both in the sense of the responsibility of the state but also whether an individual has contributed to his or her own specific health needs, for example, through drinking or smoking. The only way of avoiding these distributive questions is to take the libertarian line and deny that there is any collective obligation to meet needs. If there is no welfare state, then issues about the role of the welfare state in respect of the rule of law do not arise. If however one accepts, as most neo-liberals – certainly Hayek and Acton do, that the state does have a duty to provide a level of welfare which will both meet basic needs and which will, as Hayek has argued, rise as national wealth increases, then it really is impossible to sustain the claim that there is a categorical distinction to be drawn between a residual welfare state and one which seeks to create greater social justice. If social justice and the rule of law are opposed to one another, then this argument applies equally to the neo-liberal version of the welfare state as much as it does to the more overtly social democratic version of the welfare state which seeks to achieve greater social justice.

This point is, in fact, underscored by another of the neo-liberal claims about the welfare state. Recall the endorsement of the public choice critique of bureaucratic behaviour. The idea here is that the welfare state set up in the interests of social justice will in fact spawn large scale bureaucracies which will embody undesirable features two of which are relevant to the present discussion. The first is that welfare bureaucrats as rational utility maximizers have an incentive to grow the size of their bureau and one way of doing this is to expand the scope of the particular aspect of welfare that they are charged with delivering. If this view is allied to the point about the porous nature of welfare needs, such as security, health, and education and the equally porous nature of the goods which satisfy those needs, then it can be seen that bureaucrats have a strong incentive to 'bid up' the area of welfare need with which they are concerned. So both types of welfare states are likely to expand since bureaucratic delivery is central to both. If both sorts of welfare state can expand under these pressures without any clear stopping point, then it is clear that there will be endemic distributive questions about the sharing of scarce resources to meet expanding needs. If distributive politics stand outside the rule of law, as neo-liberals maintain, then both types of welfare state – the residual and the social democratic one will equally fall outside the rule of law. As I have already said these issues can only be avoided if one rejects the idea of a collective responsibility in this sphere discharged by government – a position most neo-liberals as opposed to libertarians reject. The second element of the public choice critique which bears on the rule of law is that of discretion. The argument here is that the welfare state means entrenching discretionary bureaucratic power at the heart of government just because it is not possible to write rules of law which secure to individuals in a way that is compatible with the abstract and universal nature of law a bundle of goods to meet welfare needs. Any view of the positive duties of government against the background of scarce resources is going to have to have a large place for discretionary power which is contrary to the rule of law. However, it is again difficult to see that there is anything about the difference between the two models of welfare that enables the more residual neo-liberal model to escape from exactly the same difficulties on this point that the neo-liberal ascribes only to the social democratic version.

If these points have weight, then that weight is increased when we look at the other side of the generic goods of agency and action namely capacities and capabilities. Exactly the same points will be raised about these goods as can be raised about needs and the goods to meet needs. Indeed, it is at least arguable that the case of capabilities is even more complex than the case of needs. It may be true that in some sense basic needs are shared in more or less the same way across the population. It is their scope, rather than individual differences over needs, that creates issues about distributive fairness. Capabilities are, however, much more personal and crucially so. As Sen has persuasively argued, the capacity of A to transform good *Y* into something useful to him or her and B's capacity in relation to the same good is something quite differentiated and personal. The delivery of services in relation to capacities will then be more complex and will raise more difficult questions about fairness in distribution and the exercise of discretionary power than needs would.

Hence, there is a very strong case for saying that in so far as neo-liberals recognize, however implicitly, the basic or generic goods of agency and action on which they themselves place so much weight they cannot escape from issues to do with distributive justice and therefore their own position lays down a challenge as to how this recognition squares with the centrality of the rule of law. Of course it could be common ground between the neo-liberal and the social democrat that the rules governing the allocation of resources in relation to generic goods fulfil one requirement of the rule of law which as we saw in Chapter 1 is central to neo-liberalism, namely the fact that they are independent of specific ends. The whole point about generic goods is that they are goods necessary for agency and action whatever is the end which is held in view by any agent. Whatever the conception of the good of an agent and however he or she attempts to pursue that good through action, then that infrastructure of necessary goods has to be present. It is, however, one thing to point out that in this respect the emphasis on generic or necessary goods is compatible with the neo-liberal understanding of the rule of law, but in respect of the ways in which the recognition of necessary goods gives rise to questions of social justice this will not be so.

One further point might be made here which is relevant to the whole of the neo-liberal enterprise. Both neo-liberals and social democrats argue at present that while the state has a responsibility in respect of the funding of welfare that does not of itself mean that welfare has to be directly provided by the state. This is certainly the case mounted by Hayek and Buchanan. This point has overall relevance to the rule of law in the following ways. First of all it might be argued that while questions of distributive justice will arise in terms of fixing the funding of different branches of the welfare state, if the state contracts with other parties such as voluntary bodies, not-for-profit companies, or for that matter commercial companies, then the actual delivery of welfare is not being undertaken by state bureaucracies but by a whole myriad of organizations and that in various ways and in terms of the rule of law this is preferable to direct state provision. The first reason is that it breaks the monopoly of the state on provision. No doubt the state is the monopoly funder and commissioner of services but if the services are provided from a range of different sources, then this means that the state has no monopoly on the provision of basic goods. This is a powerful argument in that as Hayek argued in the spring in the oasis example a monopoly in a basic or indispensable good is coercive. In the context that we are now considering that monopoly in basic welfare goods which, as I have argued, to use Hayek's own phrase, constitute the generic 'data' of an individual's action, such a monopoly is potentially coercive. Since it is in large part the function of the rule of law to prevent coercion it follows that such monopoly power is incompatible with the rule of law. We do not, in recognizing this, however, have to follow the libertarian road of saying therefore there can be no collective responsibility for welfare because that would, for the reasons given, be incompatible with the rule of law but rather, as Hayek and Buchanan suggested, divide the funding function from that of providing. On the face of it, it does not matter in terms of the rule of law that funding is still a state monopoly and that there are many providers. It would also follow from this model that the behaviour of welfare administrators which expand the welfare state inexorably and which through the inevitable discretionary power they have makes welfare provision incompatible with the rule of law would also change. Under the proposed funder–provider split the administrator would be an employee of one of the contracting providers. These providers are in competition with one another for state funding. As such, the administrators are in a market or at least a quasi-market situation and subject to the disciplinary pressures of the market and the threat of bankruptcy if the state fails to renew the contract because of inefficiency. While discretion and judgement are still essential features of the provision and problematic from the rule of law standpoint at least the client or the consumer of the service can in principle escape some of the consequences of the operation of discretion which would apply in a monopoly service provider, in that the consumer could, in principle, exercise choice and move to another provider if he or she did not like the manner in which discretion was being applied in his or her case. This context of choice also mitigates but does not eliminate the effect of the arbitrariness of the discretionary judgements which necessarily have to be utilized. As we saw earlier some of this arbitrariness cannot be eliminated and is troublesome from a rule of law perspective but at least the customer can choose between alternative exercises of discretion if he or she has the option to choose one provider rather than another.

In principle then it would seem that such an approach can make the welfare state more compatible with the rule of law. It is also quite compatible with the idea of welfare rights defended in Chapter 12. A right of such a sort does not entail that the goods claimed under the right can only be collectively provided. For reasons that I gave they have to be collectively funded via the tax system but that does not of itself entail that they have to be collectively provided. Indeed, one possible mechanism for providing choice between providers would be instead of the state funding providers on a competitive basis, it would in fact just register permitted providers and give vouchers to citizens to utilize in the direct purchase of services between different competitive providers. This would probably increase the market disciplines even further on providers and the voucher would in a sense be a tangible version of a welfare right. Therefore, there is nothing at all incompatible between a rights-based approach to welfare and competition between providers. In addition, it might be claimed that such an approach would be more compatible with the idea of the rule of law. The reason for that would be that there would be a common value – funded equally by the state – and the rules governing such vouchers would have this universal and thus rule of law compatible element. Of course, the critic would argue that this neglects individual circumstances and the fact that one person in circumstances *X* would need less than a similar person in circumstances *X* + *Y*. This is no doubt true and it is doubtful whether a voucher system could become pervasive for that reason, but there might be a case for a core set of vouchers in different services while recognizing that this will not be capable of being made wholly comprehensive. As I said earlier this could even be seen as a way of embodying the idea of a welfare right as something over which the right holder had control. The other problematic effect of vouchers is whether or not the better off would be allowed to top up their vouchers and if they could, providers who depend for their income on consumers with vouchers would in fact be likely to prefer top-up vouchers compared with others. This is a long standing problem in respect of vouchers and the only thing to be said is that it is not unique to vouchers. At the moment in the United Kingdom the government is to change the rules in the state funded National Health Service to allow those who can afford it to buy private medication unavailable on the health service without losing their entitlements. This poses the same difficulties as top-up vouchers so there is nothing intrinsic to the idea of vouchers that makes them uniquely vulnerable to this criticism. It is also true that vouchers can be used in the interests of social justice to benefit the worst off by, for example, providing higher value vouchers for welfare goods, perhaps particularly education to those on the lowest incomes.[1] If vouchers could not be topped up but could be increased in value lower down the income scale they could be a way, long dreamed of by social democrats, to use welfare provision as a way of decreasing social inequality. However, the problem from the neo-liberal point of view is that both top-up vouchers and redistributive vouchers in fact move vouchers away from the idea of the rule of law. If a voucher had a common value which could not be altered, then in their operation they would meet the universality of the rule of law. Any move away from this would in fact compromise that advantage. This just shows the great difficulty in applying neo-liberal views about the rule of law to real life situations. Topping up vouchers seems to be presupposed by personal liberty to spend one's money as one sees fit and the redistributive voucher would see it as a device for social justice. Both of these strategies are incompatible with ideas about the rule of law promulgated by neo-liberal thinkers.

A further way in which neo-liberal thinkers believe that the funder–provider split enhances the rule of law is that it restricts the scope of public law. As we saw in Chapters 1 and 2, Hayek particularly is concerned about the increasing scope of public law which follows on from the increased role for the state. He wants to see this growth arrested and a resurgence of private law. In the sort of context that we are considering the contract between the funding body – the state and the provider – the voluntary body, the not-for-profit company, or the private company would be part of public law because one of the parties is the state, but the relationship between the consumer and the provider would be a matter of private law – if it is a matter of law at all. However, there have to be some doubts about this and doubts which, paradoxically enough from a neo-liberal perspective, might take public law much further into the realm of welfare provision than other arrangements but, because of this, might make welfare provision more compliant with the rule of (public) law. The reason for this in the United Kingdom is the Human Rights Act (HRA) which incorporates most the European Convention on Human Rights into UK law. The Human Rights Act applies to 'Public Authorities' which are defined in the Act as bodies carrying out public functions. So the issue arises as to whether a diverse group of welfare providers funded by the government (national or local) are in fact public authorities. If the state is contracting with other providers to supply welfare services there is at least a case for saying that those bodies are carrying out public functions for three reasons. First of all, such providers are being financed by public money to perform duties and provide services the nature and scope of which are prescribed by the state. Secondly, these functions provided by a range of providers may in most if not all cases be services for which there is a statutory basis. The state has a statutory duty to ensure services are provided and funded even though it does not directly provide them. If services are being provided in terms of statute, then it might be argued that the providers should be subject to the law applying to public authorities. Finally, it might be argued that prior to the establishment of the funder–provider distinction the services now provided by non-state actors would have been provided directly through the state and its agents and these would definitely have been public authorities. So does the fact that a range of providers are now contracting with government make any difference to their position as being public authorities or not? The position in the United Kingdom at the moment is that they are not and this has been established in some legal cases.[2] The Law Lords however have put their emphasis not so much on whether providers are in fact public authorities but rather on the nature of the contract between government whether national or local which are public authorities and providers who are not. Public Authorities are bound by the HRA and should ensure that their contracts with other parties respect convention rights. It is not, however, the duty of a provider to ensure that the contract reflects this; it is the duty of the contracting Public Authority. Having said this, the government has indicated that it might well legislate to bring providers of state funded statutory services within the purview of the Act.[3]

This is important in the context of neo-liberalism for the following reason. It has been central to thinkers like Hayek that the realm of public law should be limited and that it is a feature of a socialist or social democratic state that it will expand. This is linked to the very first chapter of this book where the idea of a telocratic state implied treating the law like the principles of an organization. Once the state is seen as an organization rather than a *catallaxy*, then the scope of public law becomes as broad as the purposes of the organization and in the case of the state its purposes embrace the whole of society. So on this view there is a good reason why all organizations which have a public function whether they are part of the state or not should be subject to public law. Therefore, in this sense despite the fact that Hayek is a proponent of the funder–provider split he would not want to see the provider brought within the purview of public law of which the HRA and convention rights would be a part. Many potential providers whether they be voluntary organizations, churches, social enterprise companies and the like are part of the fabric of civil society which in the neo-liberal view should be independent of the state and so long as they do not act coercively either towards individuals or other groups should be autonomous within a nomocratic order and not subject to public law requirements. On the other hand there is something of a paradox here. Hayek himself advocates the funder–provider split and, as we have seen, is convinced that the social democratic welfare state falls outside the scope of the rule of law. However, to treat providers as Public Authorities would bring them within the scope of the rule of law, in this case public law. In addition, because the HRA protects basic civil and political rights it would be hard to argue that such law was in fact telological. Rather it provides the framework within which individuals have the space to pursue their own ends and purposes. Hence, the HRA falls more clearly under a nomocratic form of law rather than a telocratic sort and in relation to providers of welfare brings them within the scope of what is one of the most basic forms of law namely human rights. Of course, it is pretty certain that Hayek and neo-liberals would regard this as a price that should not be paid because it is at the cost of compromising the autonomy of the providers. Nevertheless, given that Hayek (and indeed Buchanan) endorses the plurality of providers model, given that he does see welfare, though at a more basic level than the social democratic one, as a responsibility of the state, and given that he is concerned about the discretionary and arbitrary power of welfare bureaucrats, then to bring these quasi-public authority providers within the scope of a nomocratic Human Rights Act might be thought to be the most obvious way of reconciling his own welfare commitments to the idea of the rule of law. Although the examples that I have given are taken from the United Kingdom, the point would apply in a much more general way as to whether providers of services, although funded by the state, should fall under the public law provisions of whichever state adopted this policy.

I want now to move some of the legal and constitutional aspects of neo-liberal views about the role of government in relation to the economy. As we have seen, neo-liberals frequently argue that there should be constitutional rules which should constrain governments in relation to the economy. The role of government is to provide law as a public good and that law, in economic terms, should be nomocratic and concerned with contract and with property rights essentially. Markets are exchanges of property rights and thus clear laws about entitlements and titles to property are essential to the market order, and so is contract law just because again it is central to the market economy as a system of exchange. So long as these are effectively in place and prices are fixed by free exchange rather than being distorted by governmental interference, and so long as there is a clear recognition by those who exchange in markets that they are responsible for their own decisions and their consequences including bankruptcy, then there is no reason for government to intervene in markets. Government is about framework rather than outcome, and as long as the proper and limited framework of law is in place, the government should stay its hand. If problems arise in the market, then there ought to be market solutions to such problems. Attempts by government to provide solutions of its own is just as likely to lead to government failure as market failure but, as we saw earlier, by its very nature government failure is more pervasive since it covers the whole of society whereas market failure, it is held, is likely to be far more limited. As such government failure is likely to be much more difficult to correct. In addition, government intervention rather than market solution, creates moral hazard since it may well rescue individuals and firms from the consequences of their own actions when those consequences including bankruptcy are necessary for both discipline and rational choice in markets. Similar arguments also apply to regulation. On the neo-liberal view, if markets are working competitively, then there is little or no need for regulation. If there are problems, the solution lies in strengthening competitive markets not in greater regulation. Regulation is intrinsically goal directed when the thrust of a free society should be towards nomocratic arrangements, and as bureaucracies regulators are subject to the public choice critique including the criticism that they will be likely to 'go native' since if they are regulating complex markets for complex products they are very likely to have some kind of background or expertise in the fields which they are regulating.

There are several points to make about this critique of the role of government, the neo-liberal case for which was set out earlier in the book. It does seem that it is very difficult to see how the neo-liberal case for non-intervention can possibly apply in the case of something like the banking crisis of September 2008. It may well be that bankruptcy is an essential component of the learning mechanisms of the capitalist economy and that government intervention to prevent it may well distort those lessons and create moral hazard but it is very difficult to see how this can be true on the macro scale of the 2008 crisis. If the banks had been allowed to go bankrupt around the world it is very difficult to see that the outcome would have been other than catastrophic. Indeed, there were very few people advocating any such view by then despite the prevalence of neo-liberal views in banking circles. Market solutions may well be the best on a one off basis but when the crisis is systemic and market failure is pervasive it is difficult to see how there could be a response other than something like the one taken involving a central role for government. Indeed, there is a further argument which is that the crisis was partly due to the sub-prime mortgage selling in the United States, which, if it had been confined to one bank might have been rectified by some sort of exemplary bankruptcy, but the very liberalization of banking led to its spreading across the sector in that the securitization of these loans and the bundling up of them and selling them on to other banks were part of the consequences of liberalization. This problem was then exacerbated by two things both of which have to do with market price which the neo-liberal sees as fundamental. The first is that many of these so-called 'toxic assets' did not have anything like a normal market price emerging out of free exchange and once the housing market collapsed and mortgages which had been securitized had not been paid this problem became even worse since no one wished to buy these assets. So assets, the creation of which was a product of financial liberalization, paradoxically became detached from one of the central insights of neo-liberalism, namely the fundamental role of market price arising from free exchange. Outside of free exchange products and commodities do not have a value. This was central to the neo-liberal diagnosis of the calculation problem, under socialism and yet, in a sense, the toxic assets created from within a financially liberal regime has given rise to a capitalist calculation problem, namely the fact that banks have enormous sums of money bound up in assets for which there is not now a market price and for which there never was a market price in any normal sense of the word. So capitalism has created its own calculation problem! The other aspect of this issue is the role of rating agencies. In a sense rating agencies must signify for the neo-liberal some kind of failure of the liberal market and pricing through free exchange. Why would such agencies be needed if there was free exchange leading to transparent and publicly ascertainable prices? In addition, rating agencies are complicit in moral hazard in that they are routinely required to assess the value of assets and the firms that own them with their fee depending on the deal which has required the valuation in the first place going through. On the rational utility-maximizing view of human behaviour it is clear to see that this creates an intrinsic moral hazard which seems much more bound up with the enterprise than is the case of such motivation working in the public sector to which the public choice theorists have drawn attention. Again rating agencies, distant from market prices, and frequently working out (or conjecturing about) the value of assets using mathematical techniques rather than market price are a deeply paradoxical product of economic liberalism.

Of course, it has been argued that the central cause of the banking crisis was a failure of regulation particularly in relation to toxic assets but as we have seen already this would be a very difficult argument for the neo-liberal to deploy since it has been essential to modern neo-liberalism that regulation should be avoided at all costs and if it has to be imposed, then it should be very light touch indeed. We should rather rely on competition and prices which with the threat of bankruptcy will drive out bad practices – lending practices for example – rather than regulation. This, however, completely neglects the systemic nature of the problems – a systemic structure that has itself been developed as the result of liberalization, that is, the creation of new assets without normal market prices and their diffusion throughout the banking system. The neo-liberal alternatives to regulation only work on each case taken separately. It has no purchase on a systemic failure.

The other point to make about regulation is in relation to monopoly. Here we are back with the spring and the oasis example which I have cited several times in the book. Hayek himself regards a monopoly in an indispensable commodity – that is one satisfying a basic need – as potentially coercive if the price rises as the result of the monopolistic position. If a monopoly in a universal good may be coercive, then there is a case for regulation by the state since the creation of competition as an alternative to regulation is usually not possible. Given that it is the function of the law and behind the law the state to prevent coercion, then on impeccable neo-liberal grounds there is a case for the regulation of monopolies. That regulation, as Hayek himself makes clear, is not just to be concerned with price but might, for example, require monopolistic providers to deal with customers equally and impartially – for example not providing the service at differential prices or terms. This in some ways is a more stringent form of regulation than is sanctioned in extant social democratic models. Again this raises interesting questions about the sustainability of the neo-liberal view of the rule of law and nomocratic principles. If we just concentrate on the monopolistic case, which is the least controversial, the recognition of the case for regulations requires judgements to be made about the following: what is a need such that the monopoly provision of its satisfaction is potentially coercive? At what price does the threat of coercion implicit in the situation become explicit? Does this require some idea of a 'just' price independent of market price? And what are the implications if this price is to be enforced by the state? What role has the state in requiring monopoly providers to treat its customers equally and so forth? Isn't this as much of an extension of public law into the private sector of business as, for example, in welfare provision which was mentioned earlier in this chapter. All of these problems are raised for the neo-liberal theory of law in terms of the regulation of monopoly but it is not at all clear that the neo-liberal has a coherent answer from within his or her own account of the nature of law and the state.

In the final part of this chapter I want to go back to the set of issues linking market, state, and civil society and go back to the issue of trust which was a focus in Chapter 8. The issue is the extent to which market transactions depend on trust and indeed, more broadly, how far market institutions and practices require something similar to civic virtue in the civil sphere.[4] Assuming for the moment that they do, then there are profound questions to ask about whether markets can create and recreate these market virtues or whether markets presuppose a kind of well of social capital, of trust and virtue embedded elsewhere in civil society and on which it depends. And finally what if anything is the role of the state in facilitating the development of these virtues assuming that they are indeed needed? As we saw earlier there are a variety of responses to this issue to be found in neo-liberal theories but the most basic issue is how norms regulating collective behaviour in a voluntary way can emerge out of the pursuit of rational utility maximizing behaviour which is a fundamental assumption of neo-liberal thought. Part of the neo-liberal response is to stress that in a neo-liberal state these norms will in fact need to be quite thin and abstract. As we saw in Chapter 1 the neo-liberal ideal as far as possible, would be for a nomocratic order with limited government concerned with the framework of the market order and not with its results and which is not involved in other political projects such as the pursuit of social justice or social solidarity and creating a sense of political community. No doubt, from a neo-liberal perspective, these political forms do require quite rich conceptions of civic virtue and do engage a wide range of civic motivations. In the view of the neo-liberal many of these conceptions of civic virtue are opposed to the liberal ideals of freedom and autonomy and, indeed, have a much darker side than they have, for example, in their most positive presentation as we saw in Chapter 1, posing the threat of the political mobilization of the whole of society in pursuit of collective ideals like the *Volksgemeinschaft* or the creation of a classless society. For the liberal, however, the demands on civic virtue are strictly limited: it is to support the nomocratic framework of limited government and the market order. This support presumably involves having loyalty to it and having trust in it. So while the scope of civic virtue may in fact be more limited there is still a problem for the neo-liberal of explaining how rational economic man links these exercises of civic virtue to the rational pursuit of utility. If we take the example of the public choice critique of the idea of a public service ethic we can see how deep this problem is from this perspective. In that context, as we saw in Chapter 6, the neo-liberal case against the public service ethic rests on the fact that government bureaucrats are engaged in utility maximizing behaviour like everyone else and that it is sentimental and foolish to believe that a framework of public service ethic or ethos or an orientation to serving the common good can in fact arise from self-interested behaviour. Rather than relying on a sense of the public good we need to render bureaucracies more susceptible to market disciplines. If this is so in respect of public choice critiques of bureaucracy we cannot expect that there can be a straightforward answer to the question as to why a rational utility maximizer would in fact support the nomocratic order of the market and limited government.

There is, of course, a short answer to this but that answer seems rather unsatisfactory. The short answer is that each person as a utility maximizer has to recognize that the nomocratic order is in at least that individual's long term self-interest. Indeed the various bases neo-liberals used for justifying the nomocratic order that I set out in Chapter 2 show the following: (*a*) The nomocratic order enables us to deal with our fragmented knowledge as in Hayek's account; (*b*) The nomocratic order is justified in terms of moral subjectivism and unanimous decision making on Buchanan's account; (*c*) It is the best-known way for protecting basic rights in Nozick's view; (*d*) The free market order is true to our fundamental nature as in Rothbard; and (*e*) It meets the requirements of action and agency in a world of wholly subjective meanings on Mises' view. These justifications, which are, of course very different, provide the basis for explaining how rational self-interest can in fact lead to the emergence of collective norms – norms which can provide the fundamental basis for the positive laws of a neo-liberal order. Therefore, for example, laws against monopoly can be justified to someone whose rational self-interest lies in pursuing monopoly for his firm on the grounds that anti-monopoly is essential to the proper functioning of the market, a consideration which is in the long term self-interest of the particular individual. Therefore, on the neo-liberal view, contrary to the strictures of a thinker like Dahl, we do not have to appeal to a strong sense of civic virtue to explain how people will conform to anti-monopoly legislation. The justification can lie in the pursuit of rational self-interest.

There is, nevertheless, a serious problem left, namely that even on this rather thin view of the nature of the virtue required by the nomocratic state, the individual citizen of a nomocratic order still has to take a long and broad view of his or her utilities in order to engage that person's support for such an order. The individual may still regard it as being in his or her interest to pursue monopoly and may, taking an unlikely leaf out of Lord Keynes' book, reason that in the long run we are all dead. So why should utility be postponed and gratification deferred in pursuit of long term goals or, for that matter, the broader goals of the nomocratic order? There is still a problem about the justification of long run and broad constraints on the pursuit of utility.

So the question still remains as to how far a collective norm – even though a thin one about long term and broad constraints on utility maximization – can in fact be constructed using only the materials of rational self-interested behaviour without any other broader normative constraints. This issue has created a literature of its own and cannot be dealt with here in any way that would do justice to the ramifying complexities of game theory which is the tool largely used for exploring this question. However, let us take just one element for consideration just so that we can see that there is no simple answer to the question. I refer here to the work of the late Martin Hollis who explored these issues with his customary brilliance in his last book *Trust Within Reason*.[5] Hollis' example shows that there has to be some degree of, at least, tacit trust between people who recognize themselves and each other to be rational utility maximizers and who are engaged in a process directed towards a common end. If they do not possess this tacit degree of trust the pressure of their own utility maximizing propensities will mean that they will never arrive at their common end which would be mutually advantageous. The model is that A and B play a game in which there is a pile of coins on the table. Each may take one coin or two. When one coin is taken the turn passes to the other player. But as soon as either takes two coins the game stops and the remaining coins vanish. Therefore, if A is to start the game what is the rational utility maximizing thing for A to do? Assuming that there are six coins in the pile on the table, the best outcomes are for the players conjointly to get three coins each or for player A to take two coins in his penultimate move when he will end up with four and the other player two. It is not in the long interests of either player to take two at which point the game ends. However, given that both A and B are rational maximizers of utility and each knows the other to be so, then A will almost certainly take two as his first move and to close the game down because he does not know that B will not do the same in his or her first move after A. So without some sense of common trust they will not arrive at either their collective best outcome namely three each, nor will A or B, taken separately, reach what is their individual best outcome namely four for one and two for the other.

Hollis' conclusion from this example is that in fact in ordinary life people do create implicit agreements. That if A takes only one coin in his first move this is by way of a kind of tacit offer to B for her to do the same so that they can then proceed to play the game with the possibility of more optimum results either for them both or one getting more than the other, but the other will still be better off than the game finishing. But as Hollis' says this is a matter of reasonableness and not of rationality as defined either by the neo-liberal economist or the game theorist. On this basis then a degree of reasonableness and trust between people is essential even when they are pursuing rational utility maximizing goals. One can see how such trust might be presupposed in small scale interactions such as take place in a two person game but how does that work on a more macro context. How does trust which seems essential for good and rational outcomes actually get generated?

Leaving aside these complexities I want to explore some other aspects of loyalty to and trust in a nomocratic order utilizing less formal approaches. The first is the case of trust. In the light of the banking crisis of September 2008 and the subsequent credit crunch, which turns to a great extent on the lack of trust between banks, there could hardly be a more important aspect of what I have called civic virtue for a neo-liberal order. There is a good deal of sociological evidence to show that trust works best in two contexts: the first is the role of democracy; the second is the role of inequality. Studies suggest that trust is strongest in those societies which exhibit what might be called a high degree of democratic equality. This presupposes that there is scope for democratic decision making and also that there are not wide inequalities.[6] The reason why democratic equality seems to create a greater degree of trust is that in more stratified and less democratic societies those who are higher up the scale of inequality do not believe that they need the trust of those who are lower down the scale, while those who are lower down the scale think that their trust or lack of it is irrelevant to those better placed. As we have seen, however, the neo-liberal has rather limited views about both the scope of democracy and the scope of equality. The role of democracy has to be rather limited, on the neo-liberal view, by the basic constitutional order which constrains what otherwise might be seen as the demands of majoritarian politics and thus the scope for democracy as a sort of school for civic virtue and particularly trust is severely truncated. In limiting democracy in this way the neo-liberal may well also be limiting one of the factors that might otherwise be a source of greater trust in society. As far as greater social and economic inequality is concerned then, as we have seen, the neo-liberal rejects this as an illegitimate exercise in social justice. There is certainly no case on a neo-liberal basis for limiting social and economic inequality if this arises through the free operation of the market subject, at least in the case of Hayek, to the provision of a level of basic welfare. What matters to the worst off is whether their real income is increasing not whether there is a growing degree of inequality between the rich and the poor. The problem with this position in relation to trust, however, seems to be on the evidence that trust is connected with *inequality* not to whether everyone is getting better off against a background of growing inequality. If this evidence is cogent, then two things seem to follow. The first is that there is a case in terms of developing generalized trust in society to allow many more sorts of decisions than the neo-liberal would typically want to allow to be taken by democratic means rather than through market mechanisms. There is an obvious reason for the plausibility of this. In democratic contexts individuals are required to take some account of the interests of others and assess how their own preferences would have an impact on others. In market situations this is not so. This may well lead to outcomes that no one would have wanted if they had known the likely outcome. Just take a simple example: with deregulated systems there may be very few planning rules let us say about the building of supermarkets. It may well be that the opening of more supermarkets will lead to the closure of more and more independent shops. It may well be that those who use supermarkets still use local independent shops for small purchases which they have forgotten to buy at the supermarket and that the maintenance of these shops is in everyone's marginal interest. They will however be driven out of business by the unregulated growth of supermarkets. This overall outcome is not an issue that can be addressed directly by the market system or by the consumer as an individual expressing preferences in the market. It can however be addressed by a political process in which we at least look into the likely aggregate consequences of decisions. Free market defenders will argue that this is not necessary because if it subsequently turns out that there are unmet demands, then the market will adjust to change that. This is more difficult to do, however, if there has been a downward retail spiral in a neighbourhood with all sorts of small shops closing as the result of supermarket competition. Such neighbourhoods are notoriously difficult to resurrect. The point is relevant to trust in the sense that democracy and engagement in decisions of this sort may increase trust between people which we might call horizontal trust and it may well increase vertical trust between individuals and the state because it does mean that there are fora to address questions of concern which are just put off the agenda of a predominantly market society and which cannot be addressed within the market since as an individual there is no chance of being able to consume or express preferences in a strategic way. We can only make small decisions in markets but the aggregate effects may be large and we need democratic procedures to discuss the likely consequences of market changes. Otherwise, as Fred Hirsch argues, we shall fall victim to the 'tyranny of small decisions'[7] and be disabled from acting strategically.

The point about democracy and equality also enables the critic of neo-liberalism to respond to the claim that if trust and civic virtue depend upon inherited moral frameworks, as Karl Polanyi and others have argued, then there is in fact a recipe for total pessimism about the maintenance of a free society. These inherited moral frameworks, even assuming that they played the role that critics of markets argue that they did, are nevertheless being undermined all over the place and not just as the result of markets but by secularization, the growth of moral pluralism, ethnic, religious, and cultural diversity of national populations, and so forth. If the viability of markets depend on a constantly depleting stock of moral capital that we lack the means to shore up, then the outlook for the free market would seem bleak. If, however, both democracy and greater social equality are in fact creators of trust, then we need not be so pessimistic since it is perfectly possible to maintain a market order which does include space for the realization of such values. To create this space does no doubt involve some modification of the purity of a nomocratic order particularly in relation to social justice and equality, but as I have already argued in many respects the neo-liberal case against social justice does not stand up to scrutiny and in any case thinkers like Hayek have in fact conceded a good deal of their ground to their critics in allowing for a form of welfare provision which cannot in fact be categorically distinguished from one marked by a concern for social justice. It is worth pointing out again at this juncture a point made earlier, namely that Hayek himself clearly believes that a form of capitalism bereft of the idea of social justice will not in fact be able to secure a sense of its own legitimacy and one aspect of that which Hayek doesn't explicitly recognize is whether the neo-liberal order would be able to secure vertical trust from citizens or consumers without some commitment to greater social justice and social equality. The Hayekian answer to this is usually that as long as the neo-liberal order continues to create material prosperity, these moral issues about capitalism will not in fact arise. This is, however, very short sighted for two interrelated reasons. There can be no guarantee of unimpeded incremental growth without periods of recession when real incomes may fall and in these situations vertical trust in the system may well be eroded very quickly, particularly if the costs of that recession are allowed to fall where they do without the state in the interests of social justice trying to do something about it and secondly, as we have seen with the banking crisis, the recession may in fact be precipitated because of a loss of horizontal trust between key economic actors whether they be individuals or firms. So material prosperity cannot in fact be the ultimate guarantor of the popular legitimacy of the free market system. There has to be a source of trust and loyalty outside of that and neo-liberal thinkers have, I believe, to accept that the sources of trust and loyalty have to be found outside the market. That does not deny the point discussed in a preceding chapter that markets may create their own forms of trust via things like brands and franchises and that brand loyalty can be built up by firms meeting consumers' preferences at the level and at the standard that they want. This is, however, internal to the market order and we also have to consider basic trust and loyalty in and to that order and it is not at all clear that this can be created by markets themselves as opposed to being presupposed by markets. Democracy, social justice, and a broader conception of the rule of law are central to that but given their assumptions it is very difficult indeed for neo-liberals to make explicit space for such ideas within their nomocratic framework. However, as I have suggested throughout in what has in fact been a kind of immanent critique of neo-liberalism there are in fact ideas and principles within neo-liberalism which themselves push neo-liberalism in a much more social democratic direction. There is certainly a sharp divide between social democracy and radical forms of liberalism as defended by Nozick, but this is not at all the case with more central neo-liberal thinkers such as Hayek. It may be indeed that there is no stable doctrinal place on the spectrum of political positions for neo-liberalism. Most of that space is colonized by social democracy with the radical liberalism of Nozick marking a categorical difference at the outer edge.

NOTES

1. There are some very interesting policy related ideas on these themes to be found in Le Grand, J. (2007). *The Other Invisible Hand, Delivering Public Services Through Choice and Competition.* Princeton, NJ: Princeton University Press.
2. The important legal case here is to do with a challenge by residents of a care home run by a charity, the Leonard Cheshire Foundation. The Court of Appeal rejected the challenge but did emphasize the role of contract as a way of protecting rights. See [2002] EWCA Civ 366. Further discussion of the issues involved in this case can be found in the first report of the Joint Committee on Human Rights (JCHR) of the UK Parliament on The Meaning of Public Authority under the Human Rights Act, 7th Report, 2003–4 (HL paper/39; HC paper 382).
3. For the most up-to-date discussion see the most recent report of the JCHR on The Meaning of Public Authority under the Human Rights Act, 9th Report, 2006–7 (HL paper 77; HC paper 410). I should make it clear at this point that I was a signatory to this report and the previous one mentioned.
4. These views are found amongst social democrats and liberals. See Brittan, S. (1977). *The Economic Consequences of Democracy.* London: Temple Smith, p. 264; Habermas, J. (1976). *Legitimation Crisis.* London, Heinemann, pp. 36, 77.
5. Hollis, M. (1998). *Trust within Reason.* Cambridge: Cambridge University Press.
6. For the basis of these remarks see Uslaner, E. (2002). *The Moral Foundations of Trust.* Cambridge: Cambridge University Press. This book is very important to this debate and it assembles a great deal of empirical data.
7. Hirsch, F. (1977). *The Social Limits to Growth.* London: Routledge and Kegan Paul, pp. 40, 79, 106, and 168.

Bibliography

Acton, H. B. *The Morals of Markets*, ed. D. Gordon and J. Shearmur, Indianapolis, IN, The Liberty Fund, 1993.

Anscombe, G. E. M. *Intention*, Oxford, Blackwell, 1963.

Audier, S. *Le Colloque Lippman: Origines Du Néo Libéralisme*, Paris, Editions Le Bord De L'Eau, 2008.

Barnett, R. 'Fuller, Law and Anarchism', *The Libertarian Forum*, February 1976.

Barry, N. *On Classical Liberalism and Libertarianism*, New York, St Martin's Press, 1987.

Böhm Bawerk, E. *Kapital und Kapitalzins*, Vol. 1, Innsbruck, 1914.

Brittan, S. *The Economic Consequences of Democracy*, London, Temple Smith, 1977.

——— (1983). 'Hayek, Freedom and Interest Groups', in S. Brittan, *The Role and Limits of Government*, London, Temple Smith.

Buchanan, J. *The Demand and Supply of Public Goods*, Indianapolis, IN, The Liberty Fund, 1999.

——— *The Limits of Liberty*, Indianapolis, IN, The Liberty Fund, 2000.

——— and Brennan, G. *The Reason of Rules*, Indianapolis, IN, The Liberty Fund, 1999.

——— and Tullock, G. *The Calculus of Consent*, Ann Arbor, MI, University of Michigan, 1962.

Caldwell, B. *Hayek's Challenge: An Intellectual Biography of F. A. Hayek*, Chicago, IL, Chicago University Press, 2004.

Campagnolo, G. *Carl Menger entre Aristote et Hayek, Aux sources de l'économie moderne*, Paris, CNRS, 2008.

Carter, M. *T. H. Green and the Development of Ethical Socialism*, Exeter, Imprint Academic, 2003.

Cohen, G. A. *Self Ownership, Freedom and Equality*, Cambridge, Cambridge University Press, 1995.

Coleman, J. 'Rethinking the Theory of Legal Rights', in J. Coleman. (ed.), *Markets, Morals and the Law*, Oxford, the University Press, 1998.

Crosland, C. A. R. *The Future of Socialism*, London, J. Cape, 1956.

——— *Social Democracy in Europe*, London, Fabian Society, 1972.

——— *Socialism Now*, London, J. Cape, 1974.

Dahl, R. *Who Governs?* New Haven, CT, Yale University Press, 1961.

——— *Dilemmas of Pluralist Democracies*, New Haven, CT, Yale University Press, 1982.

Denord, F. *Néo Libéralisme: Version Française*, Paris, Editions Demopolis, 2007.

Durbin, E. *New Jerusalems, The Labour Party and the Economics of Democratic Socialism*, London, Routledge and Kegan Paul, 1985.

Dyson, K. *The State Tradition in Western Europe*, Oxford, Martin Robertson, 1980.

Ebenstein, A. *Hayek's Journey*, Basingstoke, Palgrave, 2003.

Engels, F. *Anti Dühring*, London, Lawrence & Wishart, 1962.

Findlay, J. N. 'Goedelian Sentences: A Non Numerical Approach', in J. N. Findlay, *Language, Mind and Value*, London, Allen & Unwin, 1962.

Fried, C. *Right and Wrong*, Cambridge, MA, Harvard University Press, 1985.

Friedman, D. *The Machinery of Freedom*, New Rochelle, NY, Arlington House, 1978.

Fukuyama, F. *Trust: The Social Virtues and the Creation of Prosperity*, New York, The Free Press, 1995.

Fuller, L. *The Morality of Law*, New Haven, CT, Yale University Press, 1962.
Gewirth, A. *Reason and Morality*, Chicago, IL, Chicago University Press, 1978.
——— *The Community of Rights*, Chicago, IL, Chicago University Press, 1996.
Gray, J. 'Classical Liberalism, Positional Goods and the Politicisation of Poverty', in A. Ellis and K. Kumar (eds.), *Dilemmas of Liberal Democracies*, London, Tavistock, 1983.
Gray, J. N. *Hayek on Liberty* (2nd edn), London, Routledge and Kegan Paul, 1998.
Green, T. H. 'Liberal Legislation and Freedom of Contract', in ed. L. Nettleship, *T. H. Green Collected Works*, 3 vols. London, Longmans, 1888.
Greenleaf, W. H. *The British Political Tradition, Vol. 1: The Rise of Collectivism*, London, Methuen, 1983.
Habermas, J. *Legitimation Crisis*, London, Heinemann, 1976.
Hampshire, S. N. *Feeling and Expression*, London, H. K. Lewis for University College London, 1960.
——— *Justice Is Conflict*, London, Duckworth, 1999.
Hare, R. M. *Freedom and Reason*, Oxford, The Clarendon Press, 1963.
Hayek, F. A. *The Road to Serfdom*, London, Routledge and Kegan Paul, 1944.
——— *The Sensory Order, An Enquiry into the Foundations of Theoretical Psychology*, London, Routledge and Kegan Paul, 1952.
——— *The Constitution of Liberty*, London, Routledge and Kegan Paul, 1960.
——— *Studies in Philosophy, Politics, and Economics*, London, Routledge and Kegan Paul, 1967.
——— *Law, Legislation and Liberty, Vol. 1: Rules and Order*, London, Routledge and Kegan Paul, 1973.
——— *Law, Legislation and Liberty, Vol. 2: The Mirage of Social Justice*, London, Routledge and Kegan Paul, 1976.
——— *New Studies in Philosophy, Politics, Economics and the History of Ideas*, London, Routledge and Kegan Paul, 1978.
——— *Law, Legislation and Liberty, Vol. 3: The Political Order of a Free People*, London, Routledge and Kegan Paul, 1979.
Hegel, G. W. F. *The Philosophy of Right*, trans. T. M. Knox, Oxford, The Clarendon Press, 1952.
Hirsch, F. *The Social Limits to Growth*, London, Routledge and Kegan Paul, 1977.
Hofstadter, D. R. *Goedel, Escher, Bach: An Eternal Golden Braid*, London, Penguin, 1980.
Hollis, M. *Trust within Reason*, Cambridge, Cambridge University Press, 1998.
Holmes, S. and Sunstein, C. *The Cost Of Rights: Why Liberty Depends on Taxes*, New York, Norton, 1999.
Hume, D. 'On the Independency of Parliament' in *Essays, Moral, Political and Literary*, Vol. 1, ed. T. H. Green and T. H. Grose, London, Longmans, 1875.
Joint Committee on Human Rights, The Meaning of Public Authority under the Human Rights Act, 7th Report, 2003–4. (HL paper 39; HC paper 382).
——— The Meaning of Public Authority under the Human Rights Act, 9th Report, 2006–7. (HL paper 77; HC paper 410).
Kant, I. *Groundwork to the Metaphysic of Morals*, trans. H. J. Paton, London, Hutchinson, 1974.
Kelsen, H. 'What Is Justice?', in H. Kelsen, *What Is Justice? Justice Law and Politics in the Mirror of Science*, California, Berkeley University Press, 1957.
Keynes, J. M. *The General Theory of Employment, Interest and Money*, London, Macmillan, 1973.
Klecatsky, H., Marcic, R., and Shambeck, H. *Die Wiener Rechtstheoretische Schule*, 2 Vols., Vienna, 1968.

Kornhauser W. *The Politics of Mass Society*, Glencoe, IL, The Free Press, 1959.
Kristol, I. 'When Virtue Loses All Her Loveliness', *The Public Interest*, No. 21, 1970.
Lawson, N. *The New Conservatism*, London, Centre for Policy Studies, 1980.
Le Grand, J. *The Strategy of Equality*, London, Allen Unwin, 1982.
——— *Motivation, Agency and Public Policy: Of Knights and Knaves, Pawns and Queens*, Oxford, Oxford University Press, 2003.
——— *The Other Invisible Hand, Delivering Public Services Through Choice and Competition*, Princeton, Princeton University Press, 2007.
Marshall, G., Swift, A., and Roberts, S. *Against the Odds: Social Class and Social Justice in Industrial Societies*, Oxford, The Clarendon Press, 1997.
Marx, K. 'Critique of the Gotha Program', in *Collected Works of Marx and Engels*, Vol. 24, London, Lawrence and Wishart, 1989.
Mead, L. *Beyond Entitlement: The Social Obligations of Citizenship*, New York, Free Press, 1986.
Meadowcroft, J. and Pennington, M. *Rescuing Social Capital from Social Democracy*, London, Institute of Economic Affairs, 2007.
Menger, C. *Investigations into the Method of the Social Sciences with Special Reference to Economics*, New York, New York University Press, 1985.
——— *The Principles of Economics*, Grove City, PA, Libertarian Press, 1994.
Middlemas, K. *Power, Competition and the State, Vol. 1: Britain in Search of Balance, 1940–61*, London, Macmillan, 1986.
Mises, L. Von. *Socialism*, Indianapolis, IN, The Liberty Fund, 1981.
——— *Epistemological Problems in Economics*, Indianapolis, IN, The Liberty Fund, 1990.
——— *Human Action*, New York, Foundation for Economic Education, 1996.
Murray, C. *In Pursuit of Happiness and Good Government*, New York, Simon and Schuster, 1988.
Nagel, T. 'Libertarianism without Foundations' in J. Paul (ed.), *Reading Nozick: Essays on Anarchy, State and Utopia*, Oxford, Blackwell, 1982.
Narveson, J. *Morality and Utililty*, Baltimore, MD, Johns Hopkins University Press, 1973.
Niskanen, W. *Bureaucracy and Representative Government*, Chicago, IL, Aldine-Atherton, 1971.
——— *Bureaucracy: Servant or Master?* London, Institute of Economic Affairs, 1973.
Norak, Michael et al. *The New Consensus on Family and Welfare: A Community of Self-Reliance*. Milwaukee, WI, American Enterprise Institute, 1987.
Nozick, R. *Anarchy, State and Utopia*, Oxford, Blackwell, 1974.
——— *Philosophical Explanations*, Cambridge, MA, Harvard University Press, 1981.
Oakeshott, M. J. *On Human Conduct*, Oxford, The Clarendon Press, 1975.
——— 'The Rule of Law', in M. J. Oakeshott, *On History*, Oxford, Blackwell, 1983.
——— 'Talking Politics', in M. J. Oakeshott, *Rationalism in Politics and Other Essays*, Indianapolis, IN, The Liberty Fund, 1991.
——— *Lectures in the History of Political Thought*, ed. T. Nardin and L. O'Sullivan, Exeter, Imprint Academic, 2006.
Olson, M. *The Rise and Decline of Nations, Economic Growth, Stagflation and Social Rigidities*, New Haven, CT, Yale University Press, 1982.
Parry, G. B. *Political Elites*, London, Allen & Unwin, 1969.
Plant, R. 'Democratic Socialism and Equality', in D. Leonard and D. Lipsey (eds.), *The Socialist Agenda, Crosland's Legacy*, London, J. Cape, 1981.
——— *Equality, Markets and the State*, London, Fabian Society, 1984.
——— *Modern Political Thought*, Oxford, Blackwell, 1991.
Polanyi, K. *The Great Transformation*, Boston, MA, Beacon Press, 1944.

Polanyi, M. *Personal Knowledge*, London, Routledge and Kegan Paul, 1958.

Puttnam, R. *Bowling Alone*, New York, Simon and Schuster, 2000.

Radbruch, G. *Rechtsphilosophie*, Stuttgart, Köhler Verlag, 1950.

Rawls, J. *A Theory of Justice*, Oxford, Oxford University Press, 1972.

Rodham, H. 'Children under the Law', *Harvard Educational Review*, 1973, 43(4): 487–514.

Rothbard, M. *The Ethics of Liberty*, New York, New York University Press, 2002.

Rowley, C. K. and Peacock, A. T. *Welfare Economics: A Liberal Restatement*, London, Martin Robertson, 1975.

Ryle, G. *The Concept of Mind*, London, Hutchinson, 1949.

Savigny, K. *Vom Beruf unserer zeit für Gesetzgebung und Rechtswissenschaft*, English trans. A. Hayward, London, Littlewood, 1831, reprinted by Ayer Co. North Stratford, New Hampshire.

Sen, A. 'Rights and Capabilities', in T. Honderich (ed.), *Morality and Objectivity*, London, Routledge and Kegan Paul, 1985.

——— *Development as Freedom*, Oxford, Oxford University Press, 1999.

Shearmur, J. *Hayek and After: Hayekian Liberalism as a Research Programme*, London, Routledge and Kegan Paul, 1996.

Smith, A. *An Inquiry into the Causes of the Wealth of Nations*, Indianapolis, IN, The Liberty Fund, 1998.

Steiner, H. 'Individual Liberty', *Proceedings of the Aristotelian Society*, 1974.

——— 'Working Rights', in M. Kramer, N. Simmonds, and H. Steiner, *A Debate over Rights*, Oxford, Oxford University Press, 1998.

Stockman, D. *The Triumph of Politics: The Crisis in American Government and How It Affects the World*, New York, Coronet, 1985.

Strawson, P. F. *Scepticism and Naturalism*, London, Routledge and Kegan Paul, 2008.

Sunstein, C. *Free Markets and Social Justice*, Oxford, Oxford University Press, 1997.

Taylor, C. 'What's Wrong with Negative Liberty?', in *Philosophical Papers, Vol. 2: Philosophy and Human Values*, Cambridge, Cambridge University Press, 1985.

Thibaut, A. F. J. *Über die Nothwendigkeit eines allgemeinen bürgerlichen Rechts für Deutschland*, Heidelberg, 1814.

Uslaner, E. *The Moral Foundations of Trust*, Cambridge, Cambridge University Press, 2002.

Walters, A. *Britain's Economic Renaissance, Margaret Thatcher's Economic Reforms 1979–84*, New York, Oxford University Press, 1986.

Weber, M. *Economy and Society*, Los Angeles, CA, University of California Press, 1978.

Whitman, J. Q. *The Legacy of Roman Law in the German Romantic Era: Historical Vision and Legal Change*, Princeton, NJ, Princeton University Press, 1990.

Williams, B.'The Idea of Equality', in P. Laslett and W. G. Runciman (eds.), *Philosophy, Politics and Society*, Series 2, Oxford, Blackwell, 1962.

Wolfe, A. *Natural Law Liberalism*, Cambridge, Cambridge University Press, 2006.

Index